Victorian Sages
and Cultural Discourse

Victorian Sages and Cultural Discourse

RENEGOTIATING GENDER AND POWER

EDITED BY

Thaïs E. Morgan

RUTGERS UNIVERSITY PRESS
New Brunswick and London

Library of Congress Cataloging-in-Publication Data

Victorian sages and cultural discourse : renegotiating gender and
  power / edited by Thaïs E. Morgan.
        p.   cm.
    Includes bibliographical references.
    ISBN 0–8135–1600–5 (cloth)   ISBN 0–8135–1601–3 (pbk.)
    1. English literature—19th century—History and criticism.
  2. Literature and society—Great Britian—History—19th century.
  3. Women and literature—Great Britian—History—19th century.
  4. Power (Social sciences) in literature.   5. Sex role in
  literature.   I. Morgan, Thaïs E.
  PR484.V53   1990
  820.9'32042'09034—dc20   90–30977
                                                         CIP

British Cataloging-in-Publication information available

Salamander ornament on title page and chapter openings
adapted from Frederick Sandys's *Medea* (1868).

Contents

Illustrations

Victorian Sages
and Cultural Discourse

Victorian Sage Discourse and the Feminine
An Introduction

THAÏS E. MORGAN

The creation of gender systems is a more reciprocal process than we
have sometimes believed.
>   ——Judith Newton, "Making and Remaking History:
>   Another Look at Patriarchy"

Whether written by a woman or by a man, a linguistic intervention
which ruptures accepted (acceptable) discursive practices reverts us
to the constitution of the social subject.
>   ——Nelly Furman, "The Politics of Language:
>   Beyond the Gender Principle?"

And your sons and your daughters shall prophesy.   ——Joel 2:28

The most signal impact of feminism on the humanities and the social sciences has been a problematization of sexual difference. Studies in anthropology, history, sociology, art, and literary criticism have disclosed,
according to Cynthia Fuchs Epstein, the "continuous work that must
be done in society to differentiate the sexes and to perpetuate inequality

between them."[1] Anatomical distinctions between the sexes, which have long provided the ground for male/female dichotomies such as aggression/nurture, culture/nature, public/private are being questioned and rethought. Researchers in various fields have come to use the term "gender" to designate differences between idealized types of masculinity and femininity that are more symbolic than biological. Gender, it is now widely agreed, is neither universally natural nor metaphysically essential but socially constructed. Speculating on the historical reasons for the increased "visibility" of the operations of the sex/gender system in the late twentieth century, Sandra Harding suggests that a gradual paradigm shift began with the social movements for equality in the 1960s.[2]

The essays collected here participate in this postmodern horizon through their focus on gender as crucial to the understanding of social, political, and aesthetic structures in nineteenth-century England. The essays also evince the heterogeneity characteristic of contemporary feminism, which deploys various critical theories to examine the representation of gender in written and visual texts. The contributors assess gender in Victorian discourse through a wide range of theoretical perspectives, including new historicism, reader reception, psychoanalysis, marxism, semiotics, and deconstruction. These critical methodologies are brought to bear upon one type of discourse—sage writing. Because of the commanding position it held within the Victorian hierarchy of genres, sage writing provides an exemplary site for analyzing the strategies used by both women and men in the establishment and contestation of cultural power during the 1800s.

What is sage writing and why is it important? Typically, sage writing has been treated as a specific genre within the field of Victorian studies. John Holloway in *The Victorian Sage* categorizes both the essay and the novel as sage writing, whereas George P. Landow in *Elegant Jeremiahs* defines sage writing as nonfiction prose that is typologically structured after the model of biblical prophecy.[3] As Landow implicitly recognizes, however, the intertextuality characteristic of sage writing, which moves around "within the context of biblical, oratorical, and satirical traditions," makes it a highly dynamic and heterogeneous kind of discourse.[4] One of the purposes of this collection is to explore the generic and interdisciplinary complexity of sage writing, which encompasses the essay (see Carol T. Christ on Carlyle, Paul Sawyer on Ruskin, and Linda H. Peterson on Martineau); the novel (see Janet L. Larson on Brontë, Mary Wilson Carpenter on Eliot, and Lori Hope Lefkovitz on Austen and Alcott); narrative and lyric poetry (see Linda M. Shires on Tennyson); drama (see Richard Dellamora on Wilde); the religious tract (see Antony H. Harrison on Rossetti); scientific and travel journals (see Susan Morgan on Darwin and female travel writers); the political manifesto (see Florence S. Boos on Morris); and the social prophecy (see George P. Landow on Nightingale).

Above all, Victorian sage writing is "discourse" in the sense of being a dialogue between a speaker—the sage—and a contemporaneous audience whose expectations about and reactions to the sage's words constitute what Mikhail Bakhtin has called "the verbal-ideological world."[5] As "a social phenomenon," sage discource of any genre is constantly "dialogized" by the "multiplicity of social voices" and ideological interests that comprise Victorian culture.[6] Although engaged in a dialectical process of persuasion, rebuttal, and promising, the sage always aims to establish her or his worldview as the right, true, and authoritative one. From a Bakhtinian perspective, then, Victorian sage writing, characterized by a mixture of genres, epitomizes the way in which "heteroglossia"—or competing affectional voices and ideological interests—enters written language, where differences are entertained but never completely resolved.[7]

In "Looking Forward: American Feminists, Victorian Sages," Elaine Showalter reflects on recent developments in feminism and Victorian studies.[8] Feminist scholars in the 1970s and 1980s carried out the crucial historical task of recovering women's presence during the nineteenth century. Recent feminist work in history has documented the complex trajectory of the nineteenth-century women's movement, in which women often worked together with men and looked to leading male reformers for the articulation of a social philosophy which included the ideal of sexual equality. As several of the essays show, the "Woman Question" dynamized sage discourse written by both women and men throughout the Victorian period.[9] Impelled by the socio-economic changes of the Industrial Revolution, fired by the egalitarian ideals of the French Revolution, and developed in tandem with middle-class Victorian liberalism, the "Woman Question" embraced a range of issues regarding a woman's place in the family, in religion, in education, in the professions, and regarding her status as a citizen. Since men themselves were affected by changes in women's lives, the "Woman Question" involved a gradual reconceptualization not only of femininity but also of masculinity.

As Florence S. Boos here argues in "An (Almost) Egalitarian Sage: William Morris and Nineteenth-Century Socialist-Feminism," Morris's practice of a socialist feminism presents an instructive case of renegotiating
gender and power. Male sage writers could go only so far toward supporting the women's cause within the predominantly masculinist verbal-ideological world of Victorian England. Thus, in poems, novels, and
manifestos, Morris frequently views women as equal to men in work and
in art, even encouraging a revolutionary androgyny: "women are sometimes 'heroic,' men sometimes . . . domestic . . . and both value the 'feminine' traits of a sense of beauty and kinship with the earth." Nevertheless,
as Barbara Taylor documents in *Eve and the New Jerusalem*, the relationship between socialism and feminism in Victorian England was not without conflict.[10] Sexual difference was often reinscribed within utopian and
socialist programs: "those aspects of women's existence which simply
could not be lived in the male mode" were largely ignored or erased in
favor of an emphasis upon class struggle as defined within a masculinist
political structure.[11] Morris's conservative insistence on a patriarchal family model notwithstanding, Boos maintains that he is "strikingly distinctive" among the canonical group of male Victorian sages—Carlyle,
Ruskin, Newman, Arnold, Pater—for the "sincerity of his insistence that
no legal or social coercion should constrain women's choices."

Besides feminist history, our understanding of Victorian culture has
been momentously changed by what Showalter elsewhere terms "gynocriticism" or "the study of women *as writers*," with special attention to
"styles, themes, genres, and structures of writing by women."[12] In the
1980s, the practice of gynocriticism has itself been changed by an increasing awareness of the roles that race and class play in cultural representations. This new awareness is reflected by Susan Morgan in her essay here
on "Victorian Women, Wisdom, and Southeast Asia," which explores the
parallels between Darwin's scientific journals and nineteenth-century Englishwomen's travel writing. Both male scientist and female traveler derive
the authority to pronounce "truth" as sages from their firsthand experiences of the biological or social world. At the same time, Morgan argues
that Victorian travel writing is distinctly gender-marked; as one nineteenth-century travel sage emphasizes in contrasting her own experiences
in Java with her husband's: "we looked upon them from an entirely differ-

ent standpoint." Yet Morgan cautions against privileging gender over all
other considerations, especially when reading Victorian travel writing: "At
least as important as gender and nationality is the actual country the book
is about."

Gynocriticism has also modified Victorian studies through its investigation of "the psychodynamics of female creativity," especially as it involves
the Victorian woman writer's relationship to male predecessors and contemporaries in the literary community.[13] Sandra M. Gilbert and Susan Gubar's *The Madwoman in the Attic* set the critical agenda of the "anxiety of
authorship" for many recent feminist studies. These studies focus on the
obstacles confronted by the woman writer under the Victorian sex-gender
hierarchy, which equates masculinity with power/knowledge and femininity with a docile innocence.[14] Feminists have paid close attention to the
ideological motivations not only of writers but also of readers. As Annette
Kolodny observes, because "interpretative strategies . . . are learned, historically determined, and thereby necessarily gender-inflected," we must be
aware not only of the contextual ways in which women and men read
during the 1800s but also of the ways in which we are reading as women
and men today.[15]

Working from such a diacritical stance, Janet L. Larson in "'Who Is
Speaking?': Charlotte Brontë's Voices of Prophecy" combines gynocriticism with Bakhtin's theory of discourse to analyze feminist strategies of
revisionism practiced by the early Victorian female sage. Hemmed in on all
sides by patriarchal models of sage writing—the biblical prophets and
their exegetes, the all-male visionary company of Romantic seers, and the
Victorian Men of Letters—Brontë dialogizes these intertexts by rewriting
them in the accents of a woman's voice and from a woman's point of view.
Interestingly, Brontë's revisionist tactics—such as countermanding the biblical injunction against female preachers by supplementing Moses's Pisgah
sight with a vision of her own—are similar to those employed by Elizabeth
Barrett Browning in *Aurora Leigh* (1859) when she appropriates the right
to prophesy by figuratively wresting the "clarion" from the male seer's lips
and pressing it on a "woman's lips" instead.[16]

As Landow establishes in his essay here, "Aggressive (Re)interpretations
of the Female Sage: Florence Nightingale's *Cassandra*," Victorian women
writers found in sage writing an avenue through which they could exercise

power in public. Sage discourse enabled women like Nightingale, Brontë, Barrett Browning, Christina Rossetti, and Anna Leonowens to break out of the confining Victorian idealization of the "feminine" as determined solely by domesticity (wifehood and motherhood), self-sacrifice for others, and moral emotions, and instead to enter the "masculine" world of socio-economic conflict, theological polemic, and sexual politics.[17] Nevertheless, entering the public arena of sage discourse and adopting a "masculine" tone of authority was not without its risks, especially for the woman writer. As Landow reminds us, Victorian women "were not supposed to speak in public, were not supposed to speak forth at all, and those that did . . . were savagely *spoken about*" by their male contemporaries. The fate of Barrett Browning's *Aurora Leigh* at the hands of Victorian reviewers illustrates this point: her feminist epic poem was widely disparaged as too "coarse" for a proper lady's writing, in other words, as too sexually frank on the topic of female desire and too politically explosive on the "Woman Question."[18]

The notion that the female Victorian sage was contradicting nature and breaching the bounds of femininity by addressing herself to the public on issues of public concern brings up a major issue that still troubles scholars in feminism and gender studies: Is there a correlation between sex-gender and language? In two well-known books, sociolinguists Robin Lakoff and Dale Spender have maintained that women are socialized to speak and to think in a register of language that is demonstrably different from the one in which men are trained, and that, consequently, language habits reinforce the subordinate socio-economic position of women, or "woman's place."[19] The female Victorian sage continually must confront the "inherent contradiction in being a woman speaker (who speaks to men)."[20] Moreover, to the extent that the female sage is aware of the opposition between devalued "feminine" language and authoritative "masculine" language in nineteenth-century British culture, her very act of writing signifies an intentionally revolutionary gesture. As Spender remarks, "women cannot have equal access to discourse and at the same time leave the rules for male access to discourse undisturbed."[21]

Ensuring that the privilege of establishing power/knowledge through discourse remained in the hands of Men of Letters is the main function of the canon of Victorian sage writers constructed by male critics, according to Carol T. Christ in her study here, entitled "'The Hero as Man of Letters': Masculinity and Victorian Nonfiction Prose." Reconsidering literary history and criticism from the mid-1800s through the early 1900s from a feminist perspective, Christ demonstrates how the relation between gender and genre has crucially shaped our understanding of sage discourse. Instigated by Thomas Carlyle's widely read essay, "The Hero as Man of Letters" (1841), a "strenuously masculine ideal" of authoritative discourse became attached to the sage. One hundred years later, this ideal, which binds masculinity to religious and cultural truths spoken by the sage, is still operating normatively in Holloway's influential *The Victorian Sage*. With Carlyle as the inspired leader of an all-male band that includes John Henry Cardinal Newman, Benjamin Disraeli, Matthew Arnold, Thomas Hardy, and the odd woman out, George Eliot, Holloway claims that the writers in this canon share the same "outlook on life," thereby eliding differences of class and gender entirely.[22] In short, Christ's feminist archaeology of the canon of Victorian sage writing reveals it to be an exemplary case of what Michel Foucault has called a "fellowship of discourse," that is, a hegemonic group that controls the production of discourse in a given society by formulating and enforcing "rules of *exclusion*" for who can speak to whom, when, and on which topics.[23]

Yet Victorian women writers were far from helpless vis-à-vis the reigning patriarchal model of sage discourse. We should not be too quick to assume their absolute subordination to "man-made language." What Martha Vicinus has termed the "paradox of power and marginality" that characterizes the position of Victorian women is exemplified by the way in which female sage writers manipulate the rhetorical convention of self-deprecation.[24] As Landow explains in his essay here and in *Elegant Jeremiahs*, a skillful balancing of aggressiveness and deference is a generic trademark of sage writing.[25] For example, a main source of Arnold's persuasiveness is his calculated shifting between a severe criticism of the audience and an admission of his own weaknesses. This rhetoric operates throughout *Culture and Anarchy* (1867), in which Arnold 'humbly suggests' that the Victorian middle-class is ridden with provincial prejudices and is in great need of the "sweetness and light" that he, as cultural sage, is beneficently offering.[26] By contrast, due to the Victorian stereotyping of the feminine in terms of 'natural' acquiescence rather than aggressiveness, discursive conditions are different for the female sage at the outset. Maneuvering within this cultural framework, Victorian women writers deploy the rhetoric of self-deprecation as a means of insisting on their proper femininity while actually criticizing their contemporaries as aggressively as the male sages do. Thus, in *Cassandra* (1852), Nightingale presents herself as a modest, "womanly" woman who has been forced to speak out by the intolerable social injustices she sees around her. Moreover, as a parable of the female prophet whose truths go unheeded because she is a woman, *Cassandra* at once conveys the female sage's awareness of her second-class status in the realm of public discourse and an ironic rejection of that status. Such a delicate balancing of gender and power is observable in sage writing by Brontë, Rossetti, women travelers, and Barrett Browning as well, all of whom prove that: "Even discourse that is seemingly deferential can have aggressive consequences—veiled by the submissiveness of the style."[27]

Still, the rhetoric of self-deprecation can ultimately work against the female sage precisely because it participates in the devalorization of women's speech and of the kind of knowledge associated with the domestic sphere. One possible way out of this dilemma is for the female sage to address her insights to an audience comprised only of women, that is, to a female subculture in which her insights will be understood and appreciated. In a recent article, Jane Marcus considers the textual inscription of a "private self" addressed only to the female reader as a strategy adopted by women writing in the public sphere. Through a "*collaboration*" that entails a "reproduction of women's culture as conversation" between female writer and reader, claims Marcus, the patriarchal presuppositions of language are bypassed and even subverted.[28]

Addressing her revisionist readings of the Bible exclusively to an all-female audience is the tactic employed by Rossetti in her religious tracts, according to Antony H. Harrison in his study here, "Christina Rossetti and the Sage Discourse of Feminist High Anglicanism." On the one hand, by speaking forth as a woman to women Rossetti establishes an empowering stance: her reinterpretation of Christ in terms of the feminine in divinity effectively displaces the "strenuously masculine ideal" promoted by Carlyle and the "muscular Christianity" promoted by Charles Kingsley. On the other hand, by addressing a constituency of the already disempowered, and by choosing to convey many of her feminist views through minor, non-canonical genres, Rossetti risks remarginalizing the feminine. As Harrison suggests, by confining herself to an all-female community, Rossetti implicitly reconfirms the Victorian ideology of separate spheres and may at least partly undermine her own authority as a sage writer.

Of late, the theory that language is essentially linked to the sex-gender of the speaker, and hence that speech and writing can be identified as exclusively "masculine" or "feminine," has come under fire from feminist scholars working in many fields. In sociology, after surveying the experimental evidence, Epstein refutes Carol Gilligan's theory of women's "different voice" and concludes: "Men and women do not have *one* trait such as timidity or aggression; they have many."[29] Similarly, reviewing the main directions in feminism from the 1970s to the present, Toril Moi declares that "the pursuit of sex difference in language is not only a theoretical impossibility, but a political error."[30] To maintain the historically exclusive opposition between two sex-gender types—male/masculine versus female/feminine—is to "impose an arbitrary closure on the differential field of meaning" and to preempt any possibility of thinking in terms of a "third sex" or thinking ourselves out of the binary opposition of sexual differences altogether.[31]

Interestingly, a feminist skepticism toward gendered language dates back to the nineteenth century, as Linda H. Peterson shows in her essay here, "Harriet Martineau: Masculine Discourse, Female Sage." Rejecting the ideology of "the feminine sphere" in language as well as in intellectual and social space, Martineau tries to "make it possible for women to write as sages by demonstrating their competence in masculine rhetoric" through her own mastery of classical disciplines, including mathematics and political economy. Language, insists Martineau, is a neutral, universal mode of communication available to both women and men. Moreover, in disputing the notion of women's inferiority that pervades the Christian tradition, Martineau departs from the sacred models characteristic of Victorian sage writing in her work, replacing these with Comtean positivism as the main ground for her authority as a sage.[32] However, as Peterson admits, Martineau's efforts to counteract the gender hierarchy encoded in nineteenth-century cultural discourse are finally only partially successful. Indeed, Martineau's difficulties with adapting patriarchal intellectual models to her own needs parallel the difficulties that postmodern feminist scholars are experiencing when they seek to position themselves in relation to male-authored, masculinist theories. Thus, in an analysis of "The Philosophical Bases of Feminist Literary Criticisms," Ellen Messer-Davidow states that the greatest challenge now facing feminists is to negotiate a position between the center and the margins of cultural discourse: "It is a crucial problem because we find ourselves awkwardly situated; we are . . . *of* the disciplines in using their methods and correcting their knowledge, but we are *outside* them" as well.[33]

Particularly keen debate has arisen around the problem of gender-bias in theoretical models in the area of psychoanalysis: Can the Freudian-Lacanian model of subjectivity, desire, and power serve the goals of a postmodern feminism? According to Jane Gallop, the encounter between the fathers of psychoanalysis and their feminist daughters "can bring each to its most radical potential."[34] In her essay here entitled "The Trouble with Romola" Mary Wilson Carpenter uses a reader-response approach in tandem with psychoanalysis to illuminate the triangulation of desire among the writer, the reader, and the text which is constructed by Eliot's novel, *Romola* (1862–1863). Challenging the mainstream psychoanalytic theory that language and other functions of the symbolic order must always be paternal, Carpenter argues that the linguistic development and hence the empowerment of Eliot's sage heroine depend primarily upon the daughter's relationship to her "maternal imago." As a result, Carpenter concludes, Romola is "an anti-Oedipus": the violence against men in the novel signifies a displacement of "the daughter's desire to 'kill' the father who distances her from her mother." In this way, Carpenter shifts our attention from the masculinist framework of the Oedipal complex toward the feminist ground of the mother-daughter bond. Furthermore, Carpenter's essay on Eliot suggests a new direction for gynocriticism: an inquiry into the functioning of the maternal imago within the female literary tradition that would complement the emphasis on the conflict between the woman writer and her paternal precursors as outlined in *The Madwoman in the Attic.*

One of the main purposes of this collection is to demonstrate the ineluctable historical connection between Victorian constructions of femininity and masculinity. What Carpenter terms the "maternal imago" powerfully transforms representations of gender not only in sage writing by women but also in that by men. In his essay here entitled "Ruskin and the Matri-archal Logos" Paul Sawyer shows how this famous Victorian sage began by strategically positioning himself "amidst a huge network of women" in order to secure middle-class wives' continued service to patriarchy and ended by becoming obsessed with the vast possibilities of feminine power. Drawing on poststructuralist marxism, Sawyer argues that "there is no such thing in the Victorian period as a Woman Question that is not also a question about bourgeois hegemony." He demonstrates how Ruskin's aes-theticization of the feminine through idealized images of girls and women makes a central contribution to middle-class male hegemony. In *Of Queen's Gardens* (1865), his best-known work, Ruskin offers the Victo-rian woman an ideological bribe. In exchange for her self-sacrifice and domestic service to husband, father, brother, and son, he promises to make her queen for a day: the Victorian woman may exercise a "queenly power" or influence in the family if she agrees to stay home and to carry neither her grievances nor her desires into the public sphere. Ironically, however, Ruskin is eventually both seduced and terrified by his own vi-sions of the feminine. In *The Queen of the Air* (1869), an amalgam of the Hellenic icon of wisdom, Athena, and of her Hebraic counterpart, Sophia, generates a figurehead for the patriarchal state that also facilitates the re-turn of the repressed feminine within Ruskin himself. Finally, then, the strain between the hegemonic feminine and the revolutionary feminine rep-resented by the Athena-Medusa figure conveys Ruskin's ambivalent male response to the increasing feminization of Victorian culture; his sage dis-course both supports and resists it.[35]

The centrality of the feminine in renegotiating power in Victorian cul-ture is further attested to by the popularity of paintings representing women endowed with supernatural powers of body and mind. Susan P. Casteras analyzes a range of works by both male and female painters which focus on this motif in her study here, "*Malleus Malificarum* or The Witches' Hammer: Victorian Visions of Female Sages and Sorceresses." Ruskin's ideal of woman as custodian of hearth and heart is reversed by such paintings as Dante Gabriel Rossetti's *Lady Lilith* (1868) and Evelyn Pickering de Morgan's *Medea* (1889). Whether drawn from classical myth, biblical stories, or Arthurian legend, the sorceresses depicted in Victorian art stand for the increasing empowerment of women from the 1860s on-ward. In John W. Waterhouse's *The Magic Circle* (1886), a female sage wields a magic wand which symbolizes the traditional view of woman's special intimacy with the secrets of Nature but which also introduces a vision of modern woman's access to male technology. Like many other renditions of the sorceress by male artists, Waterhouse's displays a fearful fascination with the female body and mind as potently Other.

In *Woman and the Demon*, Nina Auerbach calls for a reconsideration of the significance of the numerous icons of the feminine produced by Victorian culture: "Until recently feminist criticism has deprecated [the] interaction between myths of womanhood, literature, and history, seeing in social mythology only a male mystification dehumanizing women."[36] Casteras's study of sorceresses responds to this reorientation of feminist criticism toward an appreciation of the various ways in which an acknowledgement of the independence of feminine desire overlaps with the attempt to contain it in nineteenth-century cultural discourses.[37] That the (en)gendering of power in the feminine was carried out through male-authored as well as through female-authored sage discourse is one of the most important insights offered by the contributors in this collection.

Given his influential position as poet laureate from 1850 to 1892, Alfred Lord Tennyson's double valorization and repression of the feminine may be taken, along with Ruskin's similar textualizations, as representative of the importance of gender in Victorian male sage discourse. Describing Tennyson's career as a series of "evasions and compromises," Linda M. Shires uses semiotics and deconstruction from a feminist perspective to grasp the complex inscriptions of the feminine in his work in her essay here, entitled "Rereading Tennyson's Gender Politics." Although critics have linked Tennyson's poetry with the presumably feminine traits of emotionality, imaginative withdrawal, and passivity, Shires is careful not to assume that the author's frequent depiction of the feminine (as in "The Lady of Shalott" [1832]) amounts to proof of his feminism. Instead, Shires argues that the feminization of male characters and voices in Tennyson's poetry is a subterfuge necessitated by mid-Victorian sexual politics. All too aware of the taboo against "the love that dare not speak its name" in Victorian culture, and anxious for canonical status, Tennyson appropriates the feminine not in order to favor women's power but rather to consolidate "hegemonic masculinity, while concurrently opening up" a discursive space for homoeroticism.[38] To this end, Tennyson positions himself both inside and outside the norms of heterosexist, masculinist discourse in texts

such as *The Princess* (1848). Boldly interrogating sexual difference
through the motif of crossdressing in this poem, Tennyson also conser-
vatively reasserts the subordinate status of women by making Princess Ida
relinquish her ambitions for education in order to perform the traditional
roles of wife and mother. Likewise, although a homoerotic community is
envisioned through the brotherhood of the Round Table in *Idylls of the
King* (1859–1888), Tennyson stops short of fully endorsing this alternative, focusing attention instead on the heterosexual battles of power and
desire between Merlin and Vivien, Arthur and Guinevere.

The studies of male Victorian sage writers included in this collection do
not aim, however, merely to indict the men themselves or patriarchy in
general. "The mistake of many feminists," observes Messer-Davidow, "is
to accept the categorization [of opposite sexes] and to adjust the formulaic
attributions within it by reassigning traits to male and female, valorizing
female and devaluing male."[39] Victorian women, too, actively participated
in drawing the lines between the public and the private spheres, and in
identifying femininity with domesticity and a refusal of power. More specifically, not only were the female Victorian sages unable wholly to evade
or to transform the "verbal-ideological world" in which they lived—the
world of bourgeois masculine hegemony—but in some contexts they may
not have even wanted to do so. In "Making—and Remaking—History:
Another Look at 'Patriarchy,'" Judith Newton emphasizes that "feminine
values—nurturance and feeling—are not automatically antagonistic to the
status quo."[40] Rather, Newton maintains, the "ideology of the woman's
sphere . . . helped to forge a class compact" between middle-class men and
women that overrode any loyalties among women themselves.[41] Along
these lines, in *Intellectual Women and Victorian Patriarchy*, Deirdre David
examines the simultaneous cooperation with and challenge to hegemonic
values that characterizes works by Martineau, Barrett Browning, and
Eliot.[42] The political ambiguities of female sage discourse notwithstanding,
David urges us "not to assume in dispiriting fashion that *all* is neatly subject to patriarchy."[43]

The way in which sage writing by Victorian women both reinforces and
resists heterosexist, masculinist norms is analyzed by Lori Hope Lefkovitz
in her study here, entitled "Her Father's Eyes, Staff, and Support: The Sage
Author as Phallic Sister in Nineteenth-Century Fiction." Considering
novels by Austen, Eliot, and Alcott, Lefkovitz finds a recurrent pairing of

an ideally "feminine" sister with a deviantly "masculine" sister, the former portrayed as docile and marriageable, the latter as intellectually aggressive and "wise." According to Lefkovitz, the male-identified or "phallic" heroine is celebrated by each female sage author as a fantasy version of herself—a Victorian woman who dares to speak forth and to challenge nineteenth-century norms of femininity. An equally strong feminist message in each female Bildungsroman is conveyed by the eventual reconciliation of the opposed sisters who learn to appreciate one another's special talents. By this means, Austen, Eliot, and Alcott promote the power of bonding between women: the most important marriage in each story "occurs between the sisters themselves," thereby confirming the value of women's communities as an alternative to patriarchy.

On the other hand, these female sage narratives reinscribe many of the hegemonic norms they set out to contest. A pattern of recuperating the phallic sister for patriarchy informs each novel: the transgressive daughter is eventually re-enclosed within the middle-class social economy represented by the conventional marriage plot in Austin, Eliot, and Alcott. Presumably, the "phallic" sister feels compensated for her loss of independence by "the fantasy of a women's community" based on friendship and domestic values which is put into place by the end of each novel. Yet Eliot leaves the reader in some doubt about this trade-off in *Middlemarch* (1871–1872): Is Dorothea's contented home life worth giving up the opportunity to realize the heroic feminine ideal of a Saint Theresa? Furthermore, in view of sisterhood's equivocal role in mediating the conflict between "phallic" self-assertion and True Womanhood, these novels raise the question of the hegemonic function of sisterhood itself. In *Woman to Woman* Tess Cosslett argues that if "female friendship is the point where the female community asserts its claims and values," it is also a major social mechanism for persuading a woman with "unfeminine" ambitions to accept the traditionally "feminine" trajectory of marriage and motherhood.[44]

As several of these collected essays indicate, one of the most striking socio-cultural developments during the mid- to late Victorian period is the emergence of a new gender type within the category of the feminine itself: the so-called masculine woman. Clearly, the idea of empowering women by endowing them with traditionally masculine traits, such as aggression, intellect, and large physical size or strength, appealed to Austen, Eliot, and Alcott. The figure of the masculine woman also appears in Brontë's *Villette* (1853), which features a cross-dressing heroine, Lucy Snowe, and the alternately maternal and sadistic schoolmistress, Madame Beck.[45] Admirably ambitious and a potential role model for women though she is, the "phallic" woman personified by Madame Beck is finally judged by Lucy to be a dangerous aberration. Because she allows her desire for personal power to displace her loyalty to other women, Madame Beck seems to transgress against femininity itself and thus to represent women's inability to handle authority without falling into the excesses of which Brontë's sage heroine in *Jane Eyre* (1847) accuses the men in Victorian society. Brontë's ambivalence toward women's power contrasts with Martineau's confident vision of women's great achievements once they are admitted into masculine preserves of power/knowledge. For Martineau, the woman who seeks to think and to write as masterfully as do men signifies a positive stage in the progress of history rather than a betrayal of femininity.

Documenting the "steady proliferation of discourses concerned with sex" during the 1800s, Foucault has theorized that the increasing recognition of "peripheral sexualities"—lesbianism and homosexuality—toward the end of the century had the doublt effect of enabling women and men to admit alternative gender identities while also facilitating a suppression of these sexual "perversions" through mechanisms of discourse such as the law and public scandal.[46] Like all cultural representations, then, the figure of the masculine woman in the nineteenth century was invested with a range of ideological interests. Whereas she is a liberating construct for Eliot and Martineau, the "phallic" woman stands for the triumph of masculine bourgeois hegemony in Ruskin's Athena and for fear of feminine desire in Tennyson's Vivien.

The multivalence of femininity as a subject position in Victorian cultural discourse is epitomized by the doubly gendered, cross-dressed figure of Oscar Wilde's eponymous heroine Salomé—a masculine woman both figuratively (a woman who aggressively uses her power to pursue her desire) and literally (a man in drag and/or a hermaphrodite).[47] That Wilde's daring refiguration of the feminine through the masculine, and the masculine through the feminine, served as a model for both homosexual and lesbian writers and artists at the end of the Victorian period and into the era of High Modernism is a crucial point made by Richard Dellamora in his essay here, entitled "Traversing the Feminine in Oscar Wilde's *Salomé*." On the one hand, the spectacle of Salomé's fatal attraction to St. John the Baptist enacts a "prophylactic mockery of the anxieties that explicit female desire for a male provoked" within the community of homosexual men that made up part of Wilde's audience. In its linking of the feminine with ideal beauty and violence, *Salomé* (1892–1893) directly addresses the fin-de-siècle avant-garde, which was itself largely made up of homoerotically inclined men. On the other hand, *Salomé* could also be taken up by New Women, feminists, and the lesbian community "to assert female power." Negatively stereotyped as ugly and deviant, these different groups of nonconformist women found common ground in the triumph of feminine desire and power represented by Salomé.[48] As Dellamora explains, Aubrey Beardsley's illustrations for Wilde's play privilege neither feminine nor masculine eroticism but invite both at once. The well-known depiction of Salomé and St. John entitled *The Climax* (1894) can thus be read as alluding to either male or female pleasure, according to the viewing subject's desires.

In *Sexchanges*, Gilbert and Gubar document the diverse strategies invented by male and female modernist writers in their attempts to undo the traditional sex-gender hierarchy. According to Gilbert and Gubar, lesbian modernists such as Willa Cather and Renée Vivien would have had to look to turn-of-the-century male sexologists Havelock Ellis and Edward Carpenter for precedents for their work.[49] Yet as several essays in this collection demonstrate, the gender-crossing that is widely assumed to be a hallmark of early twentieth-century literature was already an important part of Victorian sage discourse. Indeed, the foregrounding of the feminine by male and female sages alike testifies to the rise of "*gynesis*," or the "putting into discourse of 'woman'" and the "valorization of the feminine" which Alice Jardine has identified as the defining "condition of modernity."[50] Thus, Tennyson is a man writing as a woman in poems like "Mariana"; Morris envisions a general feminization of society in the utopian future; Ruskin locates the origin of power in a matriarchal logos; and Wilde invites us to contemplate the sinister wisdom of a woman who is a man who is a woman.

In several ways, then, our study of Victorian sage discourse takes part in one of the controversies of contemporary critical discourse: the place of men in feminism. Skeptical as to the motives of male critics who are entering feminism, Showalter draws a parallel between the late 1800s and the late 1900s: "Is male feminism a form of critical cross-dressing, a fashion risk . . . that is both radical chic and power play?"[51] As the "(almost) egalitarian" world projected by Morris and the homoerotically-invested masculine woman constructed by Wilde show, the motives for gynesis among the Victorian male sages were decidedly mixed—partly a "power play" and partly an incipiently feminist practice. By contrast, the motif of cross-dressing was used by female sages as a liberating and even revolutionary gesture, a way of transcending the confining limits of the Victorian ideal of domestic femininity. Moreover, in contrast to Showalter's pessimism, the implicit argument of this collection is that, in Teresa de Lauretis's words, a "feminist frame of reference . . . cannot be either 'man' or 'woman.'"[52] Instead, the following essays on Victorian sage discourse aim toward a better understanding of the "continuous work that must be done in society to differentiate the sexes," a symbolic work whose pivot is the relation between power and gender, and whose historical subjects are both women and men.[53]

A word to the reader about the organization of this book: rather than adhering to a strictly chronological line, the thirteen essays are arranged dialogically, in order to suggest points of ideological convergence as well as divergence among female and male sage writers as they confront the central issues of gender and power in Victorian culture. Christ's study of the canon of Victorian sage writing opens the book by way of providing an overall historical context and a feminist framework. Landow's essay on Nightingale provides another angle on canon and gender politics, and also reviews the main rhetorical conventions of sage discourse. Shires's essay on Tennyson pursues the question of gender politics through the complex investments at work in the poet laureate's representations of the feminine. These three essays may thus be read together as an introduction to the major issues that are considered from various other theoretical perspectives in the rest of the book.

The second grouping of essays focuses on the revisionist attempts of female Victorian sages to transform the patriarchal values underpinning the Bible and the typological tradition of prophetic writing. Larson examines Brontë's feminist intertextualization of biblical and Victorian sage discourses authored by men. Harrison traces the relationship between High Anglicanism and feminism in sage writing by Rossetti. Carpenter brings out the tension between maternal and paternal imagos in Eliot's reworking of the religious tradition.

At the center of Victorian culture and at the center of this collection is the visualization of power in the feminine. Sawyer discusses how Ruskin's idealized icons of women at once reflect a conservative masculinist ideology and release repressed feminine energies. Casteras shows us the great diversity of inscriptions of feminine wisdom and power in Victorian painting.

The next three essays consider the turn of sage discourse away from biblical models toward secular philosophies in response to the increasingly egalitarian, protofeminist impulses within Victorian society. Peterson's essay on Martineau looks at the connections between gender, language, and cultural authority. Boos weighs Morris's contributions as a male feminist committed to the socialist movement. Susan Morgan draws attention to the political importance of the fact that female travel writers based in Southeast Asia used the conventions of sage discourse to highlight women's suffering under social injustices throughout the world.

The two essays that conclude the book foreground gender-crossing in Victorian sage discourse as an important site for cultural change. Lefkovitz and Dellamora provide complementary studies on the emergence of the masculine woman in female- and male-authored texts, respectively. On a closing note, Dellamora suggests connections between representations of gender and power in Victorian and modernist literature.

As the reader will find, all thirteen essays in this collection engage contemporary critical theories and controversies in their study of the power of gender and the gender of power in Victorian sage discourse.

"The Hero as Man of Letters"
Masculinity and Victorian Nonfiction Prose

CAROL T. CHRIST

When John Holloway published *The Victorian Sage* in 1953, he used the term "sage" as if its application to the writers he treats—Carlyle, Disraeli, Eliot, Newman, Arnold, and Hardy—was obvious. From the evidence of the reviews of Holloway's book, it appears that scholars in the early fifties found his designation apt, whatever criticisms they offered of the method or substance of his analysis. Although a number of the reviewers questioned the book's grouping of novelists with writers of nonfiction prose, none questioned its use of the term sage for the Victorian prose writer. Yet the modern consensus about the term obscures the complex history both of the classification of prose writing and of the profession of letters in the nineteenth and twentieth centuries. And, at every point, this history is inflected in striking ways by gender.

In the fifth lecture of *On Heroes and Hero Worship*, "The Hero as Man of Letters," Thomas Carlyle provides the definitive statement of the Victorian conception of the writer as prophet or priest. Following Fichte's argument in *Ueber das Wesen des Gelehrten*, he writes:

Men of Letters are a perpetual Priesthood, from age to age, teaching all Men that a God is still present in their life; that all 'Appearance,' whatsoever we see in the world, is but as a vesture for the 'Divine Idea of the World,' for 'that which lies at the bottom of Appearance.' In the true Literary Man there is thus ever, acknowledged or not by the world, a sacredness: he is the light of the world; the world's Priest;—guiding it, like a sacred Pillar of Fire, in its dark pilgrimage through the waste of Time.[1]

Carlyle's discussion of the man of letters does not designate any particular genre, and his three examples—Johnson, Rousseau, and Burns—create a sense of the generic plurality of the endeavor. Thus, Carlyle's hero as man of letters was not specifically a writer of nonfiction prose. He was, however, emphatically, a man. Carlyle's greatest praise for Johnson, Rousseau, and Burns is to call them all "Genuine Men" (177–178). In order to make the writer heroic, Carlyle constructs a strenuously masculine ideal. The essay virtually rings with the repetition of the word *man*, a man who must push his way through a world that is "an inorganic chaos," a "Pandora's Box of miseries" (170).

In this world of heroic masculinity, women have almost no place. Carlyle devotes only one sentence of his lecture to women, where they function as the basest example of the influence of books, the influence which thereby proves his point: "Do not Books still accomplish *miracles* as *Runes* were fabled to do? They persuade men. Not the wretchedest circulating-library novel, which foolish girls thumb and con in remote villages, but will help to regulate the actual practical weddings and households of these foolish girls" (160). In Carlyle's construction, the novel is the province of these foolish girls; its feminization provides the only exception to his heroic masculinization of the world of letters. Thus, "The Hero as Man of Letters"—the paradigmatic Victorian text which establishes the ideal of the writer as prophet, priest, or sage—defines that role as exclusively male.

Carlyle also defines the man of letters as a specifically modern phenomenon. The hero as man of letters, he writes, "is altogether a product of these new ages" (154). What makes the man of letters modern for Carlyle is his writing for money:

Never, till about a hundred years ago, was there seen any figure of a Great Soul living apart in that anomalous manner; endeavouring to speak-forth the inspiration that was in him by Printed Books, and find place and subsistence by what the world would please to give him for doing that. Much had been sold and bought, and left to make its own bargain in the marketplace; but the inspired wisdom of a Heroic Soul never till then, in that naked manner. (154)

In characterizing the man of letters as someone who sells his writing in a marketplace economy to make a living, Carlyle anticipates the modern histories that have been written of the nineteenth-century profession of letters. The first thirty years of the nineteenth century saw a massive expansion of the periodical press, with 155 new magazines started in London alone. The growth in the publication of magazines accelerated until the 1860s, with the initiation of 170 new periodicals in London, after which there was a rapid decline.[2] The expansion of the periodical market gave rise to a new class of writers, whom the Victorians called men of letters. Both John Gross in *The Rise and Fall of the Man of Letters* and T. W. Heyck in *The Transformation of Intellectual Life in Victorian England* analyze this new professional class.[3] In the term men of letters, the Victorians included a very wide variety of writers: poets, novelists, journalists, biographers, historians, social critics, philosophers, and political economists. What these writers had in common was that they wrote books, or articles in periodicals, offered for sale to the public in a market system. According to Heyck, men of letters were usually not connected to the universities; they were not interested in the production of new knowledge, but rather in the exposition and diffusion of various interpretations of experience to a general public. They tended to be generalists, who wrote in many different fields.[4]

They also tended to be men. Of the 11,560 authors indexed in the *Wellesley Index to Victorian Periodicals*, about 13 percent are women, but many of them are recorded as having written merely a letter to the editor or a single article. Only eleven women in the entire index have more than fifty entries to their name, and four of them are novelists.[5] The eleven are: Agnes Mary Clerke (1842–1907), historian of astronomy and miscellaneous writer (109 entries); Frances Power Cobbe (1822–1904), miscellaneous writer (104 entries); Marie Louise de la Ramée [Ouida] (1839–1908), novelist (62 entries); Lady Elizabeth Eastlake (1809–1893), art historian (51 entries); Catherine Grace Gore (1799–1861), novelist (93 entries); Eliza Lynn Linton (1822–1898), novelist (97 entries); Hannah

Lawrance (1795–1875), miscellaneous writer (65 entries); Margaret Oliphant (1828–1897), novelist and historical writer (252 entries); Violet Paget [Vernon Lee] (1856–1935), critic (68 entries); Lady Anne Isabella Ritchie (1837–1919), novelist and essayist (56 entries); Ellen Wood (1814–1887), novelist (84 entries). By way of comparison, thirteen male writers, none of whom are novelists, have more than fifty entries to their names under the letter *A* alone. Entries for prominent male nonfiction prose writers also outnumber those for comparable women. The *Index* lists twenty-two entries for George Eliot; forty-four for Harriet Martineau; seventy for Matthew Arnold; and forty-eight for Carlyle. These figures suggest that women who earned their living by their pens in Victorian England rarely did so by writing nonfiction prose for the leading periodicals, the principal venue for so-called "sage writing."

Women, of course, did write novels in great numbers. A lively debate flourished in the periodical press, reaching its peak in the 1850s, about "lady novelists," in which the novel was frequently represented as a feminized genre.[6] It was this debate to which Eliot contributed with her essay, "Silly Novels by Lady Novelists," published in 1856. In an 1852 essay for *The Westminster Review*, George Henry Lewes explains the conjunction between women writers and the domain of the novel:

> Of all departments of literature, Fiction is the one to which, by nature and by circumstance, women are best adapted. Exceptional women will of course be found competent to the highest success in other departments; but speaking generally, novels are their forte. The domestic experiences which form the bulk of women's knowledge find an appropriate form in novels; while the very nature of fiction calls for that predominance of Sentiment which we have already attributed to the feminine mind. Love is the staple of fiction. . . . The joys and sorrows of affection, the incidents of domestic life, the aspirations and fluctuations of emotional life, assume typical forms in the novel.[7]

Because the novel took as its principal subject domestic experience and the emotional life implicit within it, the Victorians often represented it as a particularly appropriate domain for the woman writer. Her knowledge and experience qualified her to portray its characteristic subjects.

As the century progressed, poetry too was increasingly seen as a feminized genre, although less by the presence of poetesses than by the promi-
nence of subjects and attitudes that were seen as feminine, or even
effeminate. In his book *The Poetry of the Period* (1870), whose title referred to Eliza Lynn Linton's critical portrait of the new woman, "The Girl
of the Period," Albert Austin, who was to succeed Tennyson as poet laureate, asserts that "in these [times], as far as the faculty of the imagination
and the objects on which it is exerted are concerned, we have, as novelists
and poets, only women or men with womanly deficiencies, steeped in the
feminine temper of the times."[8] He goes on to criticize Tennyson and
Swinburne at length for what he calls their feminine muse, which has made
poetry "the mere handmaid of [women's] own limited interests, suscep-
tibilities, and yearnings."[9] Like Austin, a number of other reviewers criticize the aesthetic poets of the second half of the century for their
effeminacy. In his infamous attack, "The Fleshly School of Poetry," for
example, Robert Buchanan observes of Dante Gabriel Rossetti's sonnet,
"Nuptial Sleep," that its theme is "neither poetic, nor manly."[10]

Nonfiction prose seems to have been the one literary genre that the
Victorians did not represent as subject to feminization, perhaps because of
the sociology of authorship described above. But to speak of nonfiction
prose as a single category is something of a misnomer, in that the Victorians did not treat it as a distinct genre. If, until the 1860s, the Victorians
applied the term "man of letters" to the professional writer, they did not
mean by the term someone who applied himself principally to the writing
of nonfiction prose. Burns, Scott, Tennyson, and Thackeray, as well as
Carlyle, Mill, or Ruskin would have been seen as men of letters.[11] In the
last thirty years of the nineteenth century, however, a different disciplinary
sense had developed. According to Heyck, by the end of the century, the
following disciplines had emerged: philology, sociology, anthropology,
economics, political science, and psychology. History changed from a form
of literature to an academic discipline with standards of investigation that
its practitioners claimed were scientific. Similar claims were made for literary study.[12] Thus, for the most part the disciplinary divisions that currently
structure the university had been established.

Histories of Victorian literature written in the last thirty years of the
century reflect this disciplinary division; none treats nonfiction prose as a
single genre. Margaret Oliphant and F. R. Oliphant's *The Victorian Age of*

English Literature (1892) treats history, biography, science, philosophy, writing on art, and the essay as distinct kinds of writing, to which separate chapters are devoted. Clement Shorter's *Victorian Literature: Sixty Years of Books and Bookmen* (1897) has chapters on poets, novelists, historians, and critics. Hugh Walker's *The Age of Tennyson* (1904) contains chapters entitled "The Historians and the Biographers," "Theology and Philosophy," "Science," and "Criticism, Scholarship, and Miscellaneous Prose." Walker organizes his subsequent book, *Literature of the Victorian Era* (1913), into the following major divisions: Speculative Thought, which includes theology, philosophy, and science; Poetry; Fiction; and Et Cetera, a category in which he places chapters on history and biography, literature and aesthetic Criticism, and miscellaneous prose. In his "concentric table" of Victorian men of letters, Laurie Magnus, in *English Literature in the Nineteenth Century* (1909), has columns devoted to fiction, theology, philosophy, history, criticism, poetry, and humor. In his *History of Nineteenth-Century Literature* (1919), George Saintsbury treats history, philosophy and theology, "Later Journalism and Criticism in Art and Letters," and "Scholarship and Science" in separate chapters.[13]

These histories of nineteenth-century literature do not treat their various categories as species of nonfiction prose; history, philosophy, science, and criticism (which includes writing on art and literature) are all headings parallel to fiction and poetry. Furthermore, these histories never associate the nonfiction prose writers that twentieth-century literary historians tend to see as a group: Macaulay, Carlyle, Mill, Newman, Ruskin, Arnold, Huxley, Pater. Macaulay and Carlyle are treated as historians, although Carlyle often receives a chapter to himself; Mill as a philosopher; Newman as a theologian; Arnold, Ruskin, and Pater as critics; Huxley as a scientist. Although the Victorians had a rather large discourse on the subject of prose style, which often associated these writers together, this discourse also included the novel.[14] W. C. Brownell's book, *Victorian Prose Masters* (1901), for example, includes chapters on Thackeray, Eliot, Meredith, Arnold, Ruskin, and Carlyle.[15] As such, nineteenth-century literary historians employ a very different organization of prose discourse than our current one.

In all of this writing about prose, with Eliot's presence in Brownell's book a single exception, women writers scarcely appear, except when the subject is specifically the novel. On the rare occasions when they do appear, they are praised as translators. Walker says of Martineau that "she is most memorable, not as an original thinker, but as a translator and expounder."[16] Margaret Oliphant has the following to say about the essayist and translator Sarah Austin (1793–1867): "Sarah Austin held an individual position in literature, such as at that time was held to be especially befitting to a woman. She did not pretend to be an original woman, notwithstanding some able articles in the *Edinburgh Review*, chiefly on foreign subjects, but she was a translator of singular ability and success."[17] Both Walker's and Oliphant's remarks suggest that a woman, "notwithstanding some able articles" that she may have penned, could not lay claim to the discursive space occupied by the man of letters. Women were seen as suited not to the *act* of original thought but to the *art* of translation. (One cannot help recalling that Eliot began her literary career as a translator.) It was thus difficult for women writers to assume the role of the sage, with its claims to broad learning, original thought, and spiritual authority.[18]

The discursive space that women could claim was that of the novel, and, to a much slighter extent, poetry. Nineteenth-century literary histories do represent women writers' achievements in these two spheres. Whereas they tend to treat women poets in a separate section, they often represent women novelists as dominating the genre. Walker writes, for example:

> The powers so long unnaturally pent up at last had their vent, and women more and more plied the pen until, in the sphere of fiction, they came to rival in quality as well as in volume the work of men. Of no other form of literature can as much be said. There is no English poetess whom any responsible critic would rank with Keats and Shelley, to say nothing of Shakespeare and Milton; but in the delineation of character Miss Austen has been pronounced the inferior only of Shakespeare, and Edmond Scherer regarded George Eliot as the greatest of English novelists.[19]

Not all literary historians, however, were as pleased with the prospect of women's domination of the novel. In his *Studies in Early Victorian Literature* (1895), Frederic Harrison laments what he sees as an age of "ladies' novels":

It is the lady-like age: and so it is the age of ladies' novels. Women have it all their own way in romance. They carry off all the prizes, just as girl students do in the studios of Paris. . . .

Men, revolting from this polite and monotonous world, are trying desparate expedients. . . . Mr. Stevenson was driven to playing Robinson Crusoe in the Pacific, and Mr. Rudyard Kipling once seemed bent on dying in a tussle with Fuzzy-Wuzzy in the Soudan. But it is no gooo. A dirty savage is no longer a Romantic being.[20]

The concern that Harrison voices about the feminization of the novel has important implications for the valence of nonfiction prose. He considers the greatest achievement of the Victorians to be the literature of sociology, with its revelation of social laws; and their greatest writer to be Carlyle—he "was a pure and true 'man of letters,' looking at things and speaking to men."[21]

In "Modern Prose Style" (1876), Saintsbury laments the effect not of feminization but of democratization on literature.[22] He associates democratization with the novel and with newspapers. Only what he calls "criticism," whose masters he feels are Ruskin and Arnold, maintains his preferred standard of prose style. Thus Saintsbury, like Harrison, makes a species of nonfiction prose an important locus of social value. While neither conceives of nonfiction prose as a single discursive category, both do classify authors now identified with "sage writing" according to a standard of social and aesthetic achievement that is lacking in the novel. Although only Harrison is interested in associating gender with the terms of the opposition, the potential for such a gendered contrast is clearly there. Within the way in which the Victorians began to privilege nonfiction prose, sage discourse could become a heroic masculine bulwark set up against a democratized and feminized novel. In his 1924 essay, "English Prose in the Nineteenth Century," John Middleton Murray develops the opposition between nonfiction prose and the novel in just this way.[23] He argues that the history of prose is a struggle of the novelist against the rhetorical tradition of the historian and the orator, and relates the novel both to the rise of democracy and of the woman reader. Murray's sympathies are with the novel, but he nonetheless incorporates the valence that nonfiction Victorian prose had taken on by the beginning of the twentieth century.

Despite the nineteenth-century opposition between nonfiction prose and the novel, literary histories did not begin to treat nonfiction prose as a single category until the 1930s. At that point, two major anthologies of nonfiction prose were published: Craig and Thomas's *English Prose of the Nineteenth Century* (1929) and Harrold and Templeman's *English Prose of the Victorian Era* (1938). Both books reflect the entry of Victorian nonfiction prose into the college curriculum. Harrold and Templeman are conscious of the new market for their anthology as well as of the newness of their venture: "The study of the great Victorians has grown so rapidly in recent years, as has the critical and scholarly approach to their best work, that it has seemed to the editors an opportune moment for the presentation of the best Victorian 'non-fiction' prose within the covers of one volume, so that the reader may gain in one continuous sweep a vivid and accurate picture of that prose."[24] The apostrophes around the term 'nonfiction' suggest a certain self-consciousness about the novelty of the designation. Craig and Thomas also consider the prose they have collected to be so different in its purposes from what a contemporary audience would expect that it demands explanation. They take pains to describe what seems to them a difference in the Victorian understanding of the function of literature. Literature for the Victorians, they assert, is not a fine art: "They desire to instruct and inspire the great mass of their fellow-men. . . . They seek to improve the world in which they live, to make men wiser and better."[25] Victorian literature, Craig and Thomas conclude, is concerned with "spiritual regeneration."[26]

Thus, the abandonment of disciplinary distinctions among Victorian prose writers as a move to absorb them into the category of Victorian nonfiction prose, and the sense of the prose writer's mission as that of prophet or sage seems to become embedded in academic discourse in the 1930's. As Emile Legouis writes, in 1934: "The prophetic spirit of the great Romantics still survived; but it had passed from the poets to the prose writers. The guides to whom men turned when uncertain of their path were, apart from the scholars proper and the philosophers, such thinkers as Carlyle or Ruskin, and later, for a more limited public, Matthew Arnold."[27] Such a development reflects the intellectual culture of the time—the emergence of academic specializations and an increasing distance from the Victorians, allowing them to become objects of study.

But what is particularly interesting about the representation of Victorian prose in the thirties and forties is the sense of heroic masculinity with which writers often identify it. In their introduction, Harrold and Templeman write: "In the confusion of nineteenth-century transition—in religion, business, government, and scientific outlook—men sought for a way to preserve their identity, to remain personalities rather than to become economic or political or material victims of the machine civilization which threatened to enslave them."[28] The conclusion to these introductory remarks rings with even more heroic energy:

> In those years we see the age at its height—confident, earnest, laborious, practical, moral. Those years were filled with a sustained effort and a devouring earnestness which are the qualities needed to produce work worthy to be remembered. Perhaps even more memorable than their actual work, or their ideas and aspirations, is the fact of their powerful individuality. Their age was one which produced men of strong character, integrity, and conviction, as exemplified in Sir Robert Peel, Thomas Arnold, Herbert Spencer, Lord Shaftesbury, John Bright, the Duke of Wellington. Victorian individuality is reflected in the variety of its prose: in the tortured and dynamic utterances of Carlyle; in the fine, flexible, intellectual prose of Newman; in the passionate though lucid eloquence of Ruskin; in the 'sinuous, easy, unpolemical' prose of Matthew Arnold; in the subtle, low-voiced, delicate rhythms of Pater. The work of these men is a splendid literary expression of their age, of its amazing energy and variety, and of its hopes, despairs, and ideals.[29]

In *Victorian England: Portrait of an Age*, G. M. Young makes a similar characterization of the mid-Victorians, by way of contrast to the end of the century: "But, fundamentally, what failed in the late Victorian age, and its flash Edwardian epilogue, was the Victorian public, once so alert, masculine, and responsible."[30]

The sense of historical crisis that characterized the 1930s as well as the growth of a morally committed criticism in the Arnoldian tradition on the part of F. R. Leavis and his followers must have had an effect upon this new heroic construction of the Victorian prose writer. In *Human Dignity and the Great Victorians* (1946), Bernard Schilling makes an explicit comparison between the contemporary historical crisis and that of the nineteenth century. After quoting a passage from Thomas Mann's *The Coming Victory of Democracy*, he writes: "This same union of knowledge and hope is found in the work of seven men whose age faced a threat to human dignity even as our own has been menaced by the total state."[31] The seven men were Coleridge, Southey, Carlyle, Kingsley, Arnold, Ruskin, and William Morris. Schilling portrays them as great spiritual leaders who defended human dignity and oneness in the face of a society that considered men as things, as means to an end. When Victorian nonfiction prose enters the academic canon, it comes clothed in a garb of heroic masculinity akin to Carlyle's. Now, however, the hero as man of letters is located in the specific domain of nonfiction prose. Using elements already present in the Victorian representation of the writer, although not exclusively associated with nonfiction writers, nonfiction prose takes on a certain gendered valence in a contemporary social crisis perceived as similar to the threat to human individuality and dignity experienced by Carlyle.

Thus, when Holloway published *The Victorian Sage* in 1953, he was aestheticizing a group of writers that had been reclaimed by critics in the previous decades as moral authorities. The reviews of his book indicate the estimation in which Victorian nonfiction prose was held. On the one hand, some reviewers greeted Holloway's study of style as an approach that freed the reader from an appreciation of the Victorian sage based merely on the content of his teaching. Here, for example, is Henry Gifford writing in *The Review of English Studies*:

> The teachings of the major Victorian prophets or sages, when reduced to summary form, are bafflingly simple. In their own days, they were living blossoms that captivated, but who, fingering these crushed, faded petals, can convince himself that it was really so? To careless eyes the revelations of Carlyle or Arnold seem portentously trite. . . . Mr. Holloway examines the activity of the Victorian sage and is able to bring back the original bloom of their thought.[32]

And here is S. C. Burchett, writing in *The Yale Review*: "Among many of our other misconceptions about the nineteenth century is a belief that we must detach significant "messages" from the voluminous writings of the various sages and prophets who jostled each other on every London street. . . . In an excellent and perceptive book, "The Victorian Sage," John Holloway takes pains to correct this puerile approach."[33] On the other hand, A. Dwight Culler initiated a long debate in *The Victorian Newsletter* by criticizing Holloway for his formalistic approach to Victorian prose writers: "If we read Arnold today, it is not to see how he can adopt a bland and persuasive manner but because he and his contemporaries did some hard thinking about problems which lie at the roots of modern thought. And we want to know what the answers were and whether they were true—not whether they were rhetorically effective."[34]

The debate that followed Culler's review of Holloway's book articulated two opposing attitudes toward the reading of Victorian nonfiction prose: one of aesthetic appreciation of the writer's rhetorical art, the other of sympathetic engagement with his responses to historical problems seen as similar to the critic's own. These two attitudes have shaped the criticism of Victorian prose following the publication of Holloway's book. Neither, of its very nature, focuses much attention upon the place of sage writing within the field of Victorian discourse or upon gender.

Yet gender inflects nonfiction prose and its place within that field of discourse in important ways. Given the increasing presence of women, both as writers and as readers, in the nineteenth-century literary marketplace, many Victorian images of the writer emphasize gender. There were "lady novelists," "feminine poets," and "men of letters." As the term men of letters suggests, this class of writers was predominantly male. Moreover, the prose that these men of letters wrote acquired the added valence of heroic masculinity. The Victorians' own conception of the social and spiritual crisis that they were experiencing, the success of the lady novelists, and the pressure of democratization all contributed to a heroizing of the male writer's role. Sage writing came to be seen as a strenuously masculine endeavor. When Victorian nonfiction prose entered the academic canon as a category in the 1930s, a similar sense of historical crisis and of the moral and social responsibility of the writer reinforced the heroic masculine image of the Victorian sage. Many feminist critics have called attention to the fascinating interplay between gender and genre in literary history. In the sexual politics implicit within the representation of

Victorian genres, nonfiction prose has played a conservative role, not only in the nineteenth century but also in subsequent literary historical analysis. Sage writing served as the locus for an image of masculine heroism in a literary marketplace in which the identity of the writer was quickly changing and in a social world where the center no longer seemed to hold.

Aggressive (Re)interpretations of the Female Sage
Florence Nightingale's Cassandra

GEORGE P. LANDOW

Were there any female Victorian sages? Were there any women who wrote the kind of aggressive prose created by Thomas Carlyle and John Ruskin, a prose modeled on that of Jeremiah and Daniel? Florence Nightingale offers an interesting test case. Certainly, her *Cassandra* (1852) makes use of many techniques that characterize the writings of the Victorian sage in England and America, and in doing so it raises interesting questions about the relation, particularly during the nineteenth century, of gender and genre.

Like the writings of the Victorian sages and the Old Testament prophets from whom they derived many of their strategies, *Cassandra* positions the sage's voice outside society and in opposition to the audience. In other words, unlike the wisdom speaker or Augustan satirist, both of whom speak and write as if they confidently embody their culture's accepted wisdom, the sage aggressively stands apart from others. One reason for this strategy involves the prophetic claim that whereas the speaker has continued to follow the laws of God and nature, his listeners have not. The speaker's aggressive positioning of himself in opposition to his listeners and readers, then, plays a part in his claim to higher moral vision.

Like Old Testament prophets, Victorian sages chiefly concerned themselves with the present and not the future. As a modern authority on the Old Testament has stated this opposition, Jeremiah and other prophets were essentially *forthspeakers* about present events rather than *forespeakers* (or predictors) of future ones.[1] Both prophetic writings and sage writings, therefore, exist as records of public voices speaking forth on contemporary issues of interest to all in society. These public voices have almost always been male, and both Old Testament and Victorian prophecy have been essentially male genres with strong patriarchal associations. The question arises: What accommodations does a woman have to make to employ—and appropriate—sage writing?

Before examining Nightingale's modifications of this historically male genre, I propose to set forth a working definition of sage writing and then look at several ways in which *Cassandra* fulfills it. Then I shall suggest that Nightingale employs the sage's characteristic acts of interpretation and reinterpretation to extend the form and take possession of it as a female sage. Finally, I shall suggest some reasons why more Victorian women did not employ sage writing, which, despite its origins, seems so obviously suited to feminist as to other controversial concerns.

Sage writing is a form of postromantic nonfictional prose characterized by a congeries of techniques borrowed, usually quite self-consciously, from Old Testament prophecy, particularly as it was understood in the nineteenth century.[2] I should point out here at the beginning of our examination of Nightingale's relation to the male tradition of sage writing that I distinguish this literary form from two others that share a few of its techniques: wisdom writing, an essentially noncontentious genre that purports to record a culture's received wisdom, and the novel, a narrative genre, some instances of which create credibility for a wisdom-speaking narrator.[3] The writings of Ralph Waldo Emerson and many British Victorian essayists exemplify the wisdom tradition in discursive prose, and the novels of George Eliot exemplify its appearance in fiction.

In contrast to these other two genres, sage writing, which is an essentially hermeneutic form, takes a far more aggressive attitude towards the audience and its beliefs, something possible in part because of biblical precedent. Carlyle, who essentially invents sage writing, and the other sages all employ a four-part prophetic structure that derives from the Old Testament.

In the first part of this structure, the sage points to some sign of the times, which is often a general condition, such as the joblessness of English workers (in Carlyle's *Chartism*), or an apparently trivial phenomenon, such as the design of a pub railing (Ruskin's "Traffic") or advertisements for London hatters (Carlyle's *Past and Present*). *Cassandra's* third paragraph states the general issue in the form of a question: "Why have women passion, intellect, moral activity . . . and a place in society where no one of the three can be exercised?" (25).[4]

In the second part of the pattern, the sage interprets the indicated phenomenon as a symptom of a falling away from the paths of God and nature. *Cassandra*, for instance, describes the way women, when denied the opportunity to exercise their natural passion, intellect, and moral ability, live in dreamworlds of erotic reverie and erotic renunciation. Nightingale then concludes with the standard prophetic denunciation of the audience's abandonment of the ways of God and nature: "But the laws of God for moral well-being are not thus to be obeyed" (27).

Third, the sage warns his contemporaries of coming disaster if they pursue their present course. In *Cassandra* this part of the pattern is least apparent but appears in Nightingale's portrayal of a continuing state of death-in-life when she describes British women of the middle and upper classes living useless lives "wearied out" and with "the springs of will broken" (37).

Finally, the sage offers the audience a vision of future bliss if it returns to the ways it has forgotten, or else the sage calls stirringly for that change in the language of visionary awakening. Thus, near the close of *Cassandra*, Nightingale makes the characteristic call—"Awake, ye women, awake . . . all ye that sleep, awake!"—after which she offers the consolatory and inspirational promise, however qualified, of a better future when she tells her reader, "the time is come when women must do something more than the 'domestic hearth'" (52).

This quadripartite structure combines with a set of other techniques. As we have already observed, in addition to employing this kind of structure, the sages again follow the Old Testament prophets by self-consciously setting themselves in opposition to contemporary society, especially to its rulers or priests, and thus speak from off-center or in a deliberately eccentric manner. Furthermore, sage writing employs grotesque analogies and various forms of redefinition and satiric definition of key terms.

Episodic (or discontinuous) structure further characterizes sage writing, and this quality in turn relates to its aggressive confrontations with the audience. Sage writing is a high-risk form: like few other genres and modes, it attacks the audience, and in so doing it risks alienating it. One reason for sage writing's episodic or discontinuous structure lies in its risk-taking. Since attacking the audience and its beliefs demands that the audience make a leap of faith, thereby shifting its emotional and intellectual allegiances, the sage will not always succeed. Therefore, a form that permits repeated separate attempts at moving the audience has a greater chance of succeeding than does a more tightly unified one.

Arguing from unpopular positions, the sage employs all his techniques to transfer the allegiance of his audience from popular or received opinions to him. All the sage's techniques serve to create an ideal speaker who makes unusual and even controversial points, but who, in the end, turns out to be more believable and more worthy of trust than those who represent conventional wisdom. The final argument of all sage writing, in other words, is what Aristotle and rhetoricians after him termed *ethos*, or the appeal to credibility. *The Rhetoric* (1356a) explains three modes of argumentation: *logos*, the appeal to logic or reason that includes use of evidence, statistics, appeals to authority, and the like; *pathos*, the appeal to emotions; and *ethos*, or the appeal to the speaker's credibility. As Aristotle points out, in matters like politics where no preponderance of clearcut evidence exists, the appeal to credibility carries the day.[5]

The sage's definitions provide one way of establishing credibility. Like Carlyle, Thoreau, Ruskin, and Arnold, Nightingale commandeers the discourse at crucial points by taking control of key words and phrases, as when she explains that "true marriage—that noble union, by which a man and a woman become together the one perfect being—probably does not exist at present on earth" (44). By defining a commonly accepted, important word (she would probably claim that for most women "marriage" was unfortunately their most important one), Nightingale both controls the direction of the argument and proves the sage's often implicit point, that the audience, which has been corrupted by those in authority, has fallen away from the true meaning of things and needs the restorative help of the sage.

The sage uses definition as a means of convincing his audience that he deserves its attention despite the oddness or unpopularity of his views. The sage's claims to understand words better than others do contains an implicit argument for moral and spiritual superiority, since he suggests that the true meaning of words has been lost in a corrupt society, and that only he can restore language to its authenticity and truth. By redefining key words in his discourse, the sage obviously seizes control of it and asserts his claim to provide a truth necessary to the well-being of the audience.

The sage's satiric definitions, which Nightingale also uses, have the additional effect of providing a convenient means of attacking society while continuing to establish the sage's own credibility. Thus, Nightingale satirically redefines those ideals given to women by patriarchal Victorian society when they are taught to "idealize 'the sacred hearth.' Sacred it is indeed. Sacred from the touch of their sons almost as soon as they are out of the touch of childhood—from its dulness and its tyrannous trifling *these* recoil. Sacred from the grasp of their daughter' affections, upon which it has so light a hold that they seize the first opportunity of marriage, *their* only chance of emancipation." (52). Again, as in more straightforward definition, this satirical form has the effect of undermining the opposing ideas that enslave the audience. Furthermore, as with her definition of "true marriage," Nightingale, like the male sages, also combines definitions of key terms with a commonplace opposition between true and false that derives, ultimately, from Samuel Wilberforce's immensely popular *Practical Christianity* (1819).[6] Like Ruskin, Carlyle, and Thoreau, she mocks those who follow the forms of religion without the spirit: "People talk about imitating Christ, and imitate Him in the little trifling formal things, such as washing the feet, saying his prayer, and so on; but if any one attempts the real imitation of Him, there are no bounds to the outcry with which the presumption of that person is condemned" (54). Definition here combines with an assertion that the speaker has finer moral and spiritual faculties than those she opposes, for part of the sage's strategy, which Nightingale here adopts, involves building her own credibility.

Another result of such aggressive uses of definition is to point out that religion itself, which one expects to be a source of inspiration and spirituality, has become corrupt. Pointing out that "insanity, sensuality, and monstrous fraud have constantly assumed to be 'the Christ,'" Nightingale argues that such "blasphemy" is not "very dangerous to the cause of true religion in general, any more than forgery is very dangerous to commerce in general. It is the universal dishonesty in religion, as in trade, which is really dangerous" (53n). Her assertions position the sage outside and against her audience. As Nightingale points out, in the present state of affairs, "religious men are and must be heretics now—for we must not pray, except in a 'form' of words, made beforehand—or think of God but with a prearranged idea" (45). Nightingale, in other words, creates herself in the presence of the reader as one who thinks with authentic, rather than with "prearranged," ideas. As *Cassandra* continues, she reveals that these authentic, radically new ideas include a female reconception of the deity.

Another version of this emphasis upon authentic faith appears when Nightingale claims with satiric bite that "dinner is the great sacred ceremony of this day, the great sacrament" (30). Like Ruskin in "Traffic" (1869), she implies that whatever her contemporaries might claim to be their religion, they in fact worship something very earthly. Ruskin argues that despite his contemporaries' energetic professions of Christianity on Sunday, they actually devote sixth-sevenths of their time to working in the service of their true religion—the service of Mammon, or the Goddess-of-Getting-on.[7] Nightingale similarly implies that her contemporaries in fact worship an idol—Society and social success. Much of *Cassandra* argues that this idol worship requires just as cruel human sacrifice as did Nebuchadnezzar's Babylon and as does Ruskin's Manchester, Bradford, and London: "Look at the poor lives which we lead. It is a wonder that we are so good as we are, not that we are so bad (30). . . . See how society fritters away the intellects of those committed to her charge! (33). . . . What wonder if, wearied out, sick at heart with hope deferred, the springs of will broken, not seeing clearly *where* her duty lies, she abandons intellect. . . ? . . . This system dooms some minds to incurable infancy, others to silent misery" (37).

Nightingale uses other techniques of the sage, including a characteristic organization of argument and structure by means of grotesque emblems and analogies. Her grotesques, like those of Carlyle, Thoreau, and Ruskin, take two basic forms. The first is the kind found in contemporary reality, such as the child murders cited by Carlyle and Arnold, the public railing in Ruskin's *The Crown of Wild Olive*, and the "happy unconscious" (25) state of Victorian women in Nightingale.

The second form of the grotesque, which the sage creates out of whole cloth, appears as an elaborate analogy or fable, such as that of the enchanted glass dome that imprisons English workers in Carlyle, Britannia of the Market (or the Goddess-of-Getting-on) in Ruskin, and the chained statue in Nightingale. She argues with fine bitter wit by means of a set piece that draws upon a range of conceits, including those of love poetry that put women on a pedestal. Whatever may be woman's potential, "now she is like the Archangel Michael as he stands upon Saint Angelo at Rome. She has an immense provision of wings, which seem as if they would bear her over earth and heaven; but when she tries to use them, she is petrified into stone, her feet are grown into the earth, chained to the bronze pedestal" (50).

A second use of such a satirical grotesque occurs earlier when Nightingale mentions that the modern British woman, trained to do nothing, is "like the Chinese woman, who could not make use of her feet, if she were brought into European life" (42). The symbolical grotesque receives much of its power from the way it combines a fresh perception about social reality with a perverse mixture of states and conditions that appear appropriate to that reality. Nightingale's uses of this form of polemical analogy derive their power specifically from the fact that they reveal the unnatural ways in which societies distort and contort women's nature, thus rendering the natural unnatural.

In addition to thus employing the sage's grotesques, Nightingale uses other thematized techniques, or literary techniques that merge so completely with themes that separating them becomes difficult. For example, like the male sages, she attacks the present by comparing it to the past, and like them, she criticizes the present in part because it has no heroes to emulate and makes no use of contemporary capacity for heroism (36). Then, having attacked the present, she points towards the future—thereby creating a literary structure that alternates satire with visionary promise.

Nightingale's main points also recall those of the Victorian sages. Like them, she reminds the members of her audience that they have abandoned the ways of God and nature, and like them, she points out how a corrupt, unnatural language and culture reinforce each other's worst tendencies, thereby creating a downward spiral toward inevitable disaster. One of her main themes, whatever the ostensible subject, always turns out to be the loss of health and happiness—the death, in short, of the pleasures of mind and imagination that make us, finally, fully human. "To have no food for our heads, no food for our hearts, no food for our activity, is that nothing?" (41). This sounds like Ruskin on the way factory owners starve the minds and spirits of English workers, but it is Nightingale.

All these similarities between *Cassandra* and the writings of the Victorian sages raise interesting and fundamental questions about the nature of genre in general and that of sage writing in particular. Although traditions of biblical hermeneutics, classical rhetoric, neoclassical satire, Romantic vision, and the English sermon all contribute to the formation of sage writing, this genre derives primarily from Old Testament prophecy, and that source produces problems for the modern reader of such prose. Without the close acquaintance with the Bible and its interpretative tradition that the Victorians had, we miss many allusive gestures toward scripture that not only provide so much of Victorian imagery, even in works of patent nonbelievers like Swinburne, but also serve as genre signals that tell us how to read.

One message this genre conveys immediately, whether or not one recognizes its roots in Jeremiah and Isaiah, is that it concerns matters of public, not private, interest. Although the sages frequently draw upon private experience, their speech is essentially public. I might point out that sage writing, like the Victorian novel, is paradigmatically Victorian just because it makes objective, public, political use of subjective, personal, private thought and experience.[8] In keeping with the sage's purpose, all the genre's techniques contribute toward creating an idealized public self and public voice.

But Victorian women were not supposed to have public voices, were not supposed to speak in public, were not supposed to speak forth at all, and those that did, like Dickens's Mrs. Jellyby, were savagely *spoken about*, since if a woman spoke forth and entered the public sphere, she obviously had abandoned domestic duties with the seemingly inevitable result that those closest to her suffered. "Suffer and be still," or speak out and make those nearest and dearest suffer. As Nightingale explains or complains (and *Cassandra* is largely about women's right to complain), we do not "see a woman making a *study* of what she does. Married women can not; for a man would think, if his wife undertook any great work with the intention of carrying it out, —of making anything but a sham of it— that she would 'suckle his fools' and 'chronicle his small beer' less well for it,—that he would not have so good a dinner—that she would destroy, as it is called, his domestic life" (44).

Nonetheless, women did speak out. In fact, they did so to such an extent that the rule that women should have no public voice was frequently honored as much in the breech as in the observance, though often at great cost to the women themselves. Women, for example, may not have been *supposed* to comment on public issues or to make statements about men's actions and writings, but they did, publishing anonymously in intellectual periodicals, such as *The Westminster Review*, in which all authorship, male and female, was cloaked or hidden.[9] Similarly, they published novels anonymously and pseudonymously, and they published widely in forms, such as poetry, devotional works, and children's literature, through which (even more than novels), they could speak and even gain a reputation. But to speak thus publicly, women writers had to make accommodations that ranged from choosing less prestigious literary forms to disguising—that is, denying—the fact of their female identity.

Sage writing, however, presented an even more fundamentally difficult problem for Victorian women because it derived so importantly from one particular emphasis of Old Testament prophecy, the speaker's interpretations. The sage, like the prophet, presents himself as an interpreter, an exegete of the real, for he begins by pointing to some contemporary phenomenon, which he then reads for the members of his audience, thereby revealing some truth or warning that they need in order to survive. In both Old Testament prophecy and sage writing, these acts of interpretation depend heavily on the techniques of biblical interpretation—typology, allegory, and apocalyptics—that women were not supposed to apply or to which they were not supposed to have access. As Linda H. Peterson has shown, such prohibitions created major difficulties for women autobiographers since both nineteenth-century spiritual and secular autobiography borrowed structuring patterns from scripture.[10] In the first place, almost all the relevant rolemodels were male, and in the second, the application of these biblical figures to one's own life required interpreting the Bible, something women were not supposed to do any more than they were supposed to preach—a rule made especially clear by the Methodist prohibition against female preachers that brought the sect into conformity with all other Christian denominations. Women did, however, write autobiography, poetry (Rossetti's "Easter Sunday"), and fiction (Brontë's *Jane Eyre*) that seized male exegetical prerogatives, but to do so they often made accommodations.[11] As Peterson, Mary W. Carpenter, and Janet L. Larson have shown, during the Victorian years female authors increasingly created their own, often subversive, readings of scripture.[12]

What subversive or female readings, then, did Nightingale make in order to write and speak the interpretations of a female sage? She denies societal restrictions on female interpretation by making such interpretations in the first place, and she makes them specifically those of the female sage by aggressively reinterpreting the commonplaces of male-centered biblical and classical interpretation. I must emphasize the importance of Nightingale's reinterpretations of male-centered tradition. In historical terms, *Cassandra* marks the point at which the historian of British prose no longer writes "the sage, he" but must write "the sage, she *or* he." With *Cassandra*, sage writing becomes a genre that is no longer gender-determined. The prophetic tradition had always been fundamentally aggressive—and fundamentally patriarchal. By writing as a female sage, Nightingale in one stroke makes the sage's aggressiveness no longer the sole property of men.

The female sage's aggressive style of reinterpretation appears in the first words of *Cassandra* that the reader encounters—Nightingale's title and the epigraphs that follow. Her title, *Cassandra*, alludes to the figure from the Trojan wars who sees all but is not believed—an embodiment of the fate of the woman who tries to speak forth and save others. The title, which becomes an image of what Nightingale, as female sage, fears she is or may become, simultaneously places her in opposition to her audience and, in the manner of the male sages, curries favor with that audience by a kind of implicit self-deprecation.

In thus entitling her work, Nightingale also aligns herself with a mythic figure who blends the Old Testament prophet and a Victorian woman's version of the experience of privileged but suffering isolation. Cassandra, we recall, had access to divine knowledge of the future but bore the curse that no one would believe her in the present. In Greek myth, she received both her prophetic gift and its associated punishment from Apollo, and both gift and punishment involve her status as a woman and relations of sexual power: Apollo gave her the seer's vision of the future in order to obtain her sexual favors, and he then punished her when she refused to grant them. From a conventional male perspective, her actions can be seen

either as a dishonest breaking of her word or else as a blasphemous betrayal of the divine; from a female point of view, on the other hand, her
actions may appear as a doomed attempt to obtain independent vision and
see truth for herself. Nightingale has chosen a female image that bears a
heavy freight of mythical allusion, and in so doing she has found something in ancient texts that speaks directly to the experience of women in
the power of men. Cassandra's combination of prophetic vision, alienation, and ambiguity well embodies the position of the woman who seeks to
be a Victorian sage. It also exemplifies the female sage's mode of taking a
social phenomenon, treating it as a text, offering a nonconventional reading, and then using this unexpected intonation to enhance her credibility.

Similarly, Nightingale's reinterpretation of commonplace texts, images,
and narratives, all of which we encounter in the way she uses the figure of
Cassandra, exemplifies characteristically female intonations of sage writing. This reinterpretation of cultural commonplaces, which provides an
obvious and effective means of communicating a woman's perspective,
permeates British women's poetry, fiction, and nonfiction during the nineteenth century.

This Principle of Reinterpretation appears early in *Cassandra*, for not
only the title but also the epigraph embodies it. Whereas the title proposes
woman's subversive view of Greek myth, the epigraph does the same for
the Bible. Like a sermon or a religious tract—in part the models for *Cassandra*—Nightingale's tract takes as its point of departure a passage from
scripture, the mention of John the Baptist that appears in three of the
Gospels: "The voice of one crying in the crowd, 'Prepare ye the way of
the Lord.'" In Matthew 3:3, Mark 1:2, and Luke 3:4, the voice cries "in
the wilderness," not "in the crowd," and Nightingale's careful use of quotation marks emphasizes that she expects her audience both to recognize
the original source and her deviation from it. Once again, she has co-opted
a male text, taking it out of its usual context (and understanding) and
placing it in another. She uses biblical allusion to accomplish two things:
first, to claim for herself the position of a female John the Baptist preparing the way for a female Christ, and, second, to reinterpret that martyred
seer as a person isolated within the crowd rather than by a spatial removal
from it. In other words, Nightingale has doubly feminized the commonplace figure to make it fit better with her own experience. By claiming a

role analogous to that of John the Baptist, she shows that there is apparently no limit to the outrageousness (as judged by conventional standards) of her rewriting of tradition and of the discourse that presents it. In reinterpreting John the Baptist's isolation, however, she makes a different point—that the sensitive woman always exists alone in the crowd.

Having implicitly claimed the prophet's isolation in her title and epigraph, Nightingale immediately emphasizes it in her opening sentence, in which she states that "One often comes to be thus wandering alone in the bitterness of life without" (25). Such a lonely one, she explains, "longs to replunge into the happy unconscious sleep of the rest of the race! they slumber in one another's arms—they are not yet awake" (25). Like the male Victorian sages and their Old Testament models, Nightingale claims, by such portrayal of herself as a sage-speaker, greater spiritual and moral knowledge than that possessed by her contemporaries.

Nightingale's most powerful act of reinterpretation comes at the climax of *Cassandra* when she cites one of Christ's parables from the Gospels:

> Christ was saying something to the people one day, which interested Him very much, and interested them very much; and Mary and his brothers came in the middle of it, and wanted to interrupt him, and take Him home to dinner, very likely—(how natural that story is! Does it not speak more home than any historic evidence of the Gospel's reality?), and He, instead of being angry with their interruptions of Him in such an important work for some trifling thing, answers, "Who is my mother? and who are my brethren? Whosoever shall do the will of my Father which is in heaven, the same is my brother and sister and mother." But if *we* were to say that, we should be accused of "destroying the family tie," of diminishing the obligation of the home duties. (54)

In her citation of Matthew 14:48, Nightingale aggressively shows that as a woman, she feels free to interpret the scriptures, choosing those passages that she wishes to ground her argument. In fact, having again just made her distinction between true and false religion, she emphasizes the difference between true and false "talk" about religion in order to prepare for her radically literal reading of the Gospels. Nightingale, who is in the process of arguing that women should not be entirely enslaved by family considerations, urges upon her listeners a particularly subversive form of *imitatio cristi*.

The question arises: why did not more Victorian women write as sages? Since women readily adopted and then adapted other literary forms, including that of the devotional tract and novel as well as the poem and autobiography, one might expect that many of them would have appropriated this male form as well. At least four factors seem to have prevented more Victorian women writers from employing sage writing. First of all, it is a public form that places extraordinary emphasis upon creating a public self in an age when women were not supposed to have public selves. Second, the genre derives from a patriarchal form that emphasized the speaker's original acts of interpretation, and in the nineteenth century women were conventionally barred from making such interpretations. Third, sage writing, however radically subversive, nonetheless retained its association with a religion that confined women. Finally, the emphasis upon eccentricity and the irrational that characterizes sage writing may well have proved repugnant to many women who were anxious to appear rational and logical.

Having already discussed the first two factors, I must emphasize why some women shied away from this genre because of its associations with religion. Whereas some female believers might have hesitated to work in a form in which women almost automatically risked committing blasphemy, others avoided it, one may guess, precisely because using it would suggest too much commitment to Christianity. As Frank M. Turner has pointed out, writers like Frances Power Cobb, Olive Schreiner, and George Eliot abandoned Christianity in large part because of its associations with home, family, and women's role.[13] Male authors like Carlyle, Ruskin, Arnold, and Thoreau, none of whom had orthodox Christian beliefs, could easily use the form because they found support in its patriarchal origins, from which they adopted a range of literary devices. For women, who experienced Christianity as a means of their oppression, however, the religious origins of the form had become repugnant. Few were able to do what Nightingale did when she used the sage form to argue for a female Christ and a woman's right to speak out—to use the sage's devices to attack the religion that had engendered these devices.

A more fundamental reason that few women adopted sage writing for feminist and other topics lies, I suspect, in the potentially irrational nature of the form itself. Sage writing not only demands that authors foreground themselves by a range of aggressively individualistic techniques, all of which contribute to their ethos, but it also radically challenges conventional wisdom and conventional notions of rationality. As a result, those who write as sages frequently risk being accused of irrationality, inability to reason logically, and even insanity. Carlyle, Ruskin, and others encountered such charges. Since women and members of ethnic or racial minorities are often marginalized by claims that they are less rational than those in power, they are highly unlikely to employ a literary form that patently courts charges of irrationality. Mary Wollstonecraft and W.E.B. DuBois, for example, both strive to demonstrate that, even when judged by conventional standards, they are more rational than those whom they argue against. In contrast, Ruskin, who rejects the premises of classical economics, and Thoreau, who rejects the premises of democracy, explicitly refuse to think in conventional terms that are accepted as defining the rational. Those who belong to already marginalized groups cannot risk being considered irrational, since they may find it—or believe they may find it—doubly difficult to convince the audience that reason in fact lies with them.

Rereading Tennyson's Gender Politics

LINDA M. SHIRES

Readings and Rereadings

Aubrey de Vere, the Victorian essayist and poet, once told a friend that there existed in London only one person for whom he would keep late hours. "A lady?" the friend inquired. "Certainly" replied de Vere, "if, as old Coleridge said, every true Poet is inclusively woman, but not the worse man on that account—Alfred Tennyson."[1] Gender has remained a major issue in discussions of Tennyson. In 1948, for instance, Lionel Stevenson isolated the symbol of the 'High-Born Maiden' not only as central to Tennyson's early work, but also as his anima, the female aspect of his soul, working itself out in phases of his art.[2] An argument for the androgyny of the poetic imagination is one way to account for the presence of the feminine in a male Victorian sage, but it remains ahistorical and cannot address the more interesting questions which even the title of this volume stimulates: What is the feminine in language? What is the position of the feminine in canonical Victorian male sage discourse? Such theoretical issues are inextricably bound up with political ones, including the complicated relationship of Tennyson both to the gender ideologies of his time and to the critical ideologies of our time—in other words, to gender politics and to (re)reading (gender) politics.

A certain paradox emerges when one reviews commentary on Tennyson, a paradox built, in part, on his early recognition as a major poetic voice and, by the end of his life, as a spokesman for the age.[3] In other words, he was indubitably a Sage, even if not included in John Holloway's 1953 analysis of the rhetoric and philosophy of six great Victorians who appealed to their audience by more than reason and logic.[4] Yet as a male aesthete who started his career by insisting on the autonomy of art, Tennyson also courted his own feminization. The earliest remarks on Tennyson and gender occur in nineteenth-century debates about Aestheticism, a movement requiring that art serve as a retreat from commerce, much as the middle-class domestic space appears (somewhat misleadingly) to be firmly divorced from the struggles of a capitalist ethos.[5] This nineteenth-century linking of privacy, lyricism, and the feminine resulted from various cultural negotiations (assertions, negations, relegations) at institutional sites such as the church, the home, and the marketplace, not merely in literary discourse. This multiply-based ideology established both a view of the poet and a role for the poet which proved distinctively different from those current, say, even in 1818–1819 when Shelley published *The Revolt of Islam* and "The Mask of Anarchy." The poet's progressive refusal of political interventions reinforced a situation that proved healthy for the Victorian bourgeois cultural economy, with its reduced use value for art, a situation which remains largely unchanged in the West today.

The historical positioning of Tennyson, then, critically affects our understanding of how he was read in the previous century, and how we are to read and to assess him now. He is the last great poet laureate, great in the sense that he was the most loved and publicly revered poet writing in English by the 1850s, if not before. In accepting the laureateship, he undertook a socially central role and honor at a time when poetry was losing its social function. It becomes clear from his *Letters* that while Tennyson disliked being assigned topics about which to write, he tried his best to perform the required tasks. One may, in fact, read his poetic career as a progressive but also qualified and deeply ambivalent attempt, strongly influenced by certain negative critical reviews and by the laureateship, to move further away from aestheticism and charges of idiosyncrasy towards more regularized prosody and more public, and thus more manly or active, concerns.[6]

Following on this historical paradox, which insists that a "feminine" poetry still have some "masculine" public role, Tennyson has usually been critiqued in four major ways. All four, intentionally or not, relegate him to the margins while allowing or promoting his centrality. The first and second kinds of critique determine that he is too feminine. He is assessed in terms that criticize his "effeminate" voice—he writes too much about domestic desire and features the female too much, and thus does not work in the service of patriarchy.[7] Or he is assessed in terms that laud his feminine sensitivity and poetry of "exquisite sensations" in order to support his status as a visionary; thus, while removing him from the cultural center, this praise still carves out a central and manly role for him.[8] The third and fourth kinds of critique determine that he is too masculine. One view emphasizes his strong patriarchal voice—which contains or exchanges women in the service of male homosocial bonds, and thus works quite clearly in the service of an oppressive hegemony.[9] The other view praises his manliness, but finds him supporting the wrong ends of hegemony, as when he seems to promote the Crimean War at the end of *Maud*.[10]

Taken together, these responses demonstrate that Tennyson—his career and poetic discourse—provides a vexed but fascinating ideological site of contestation for literary critics from 1827 to our own day. The alternatives seem to be four: (1) Tennyson should be less feminine and the fact that he is not is worrisome; (2) Tennyson should be more masculine but he doesn't have to be, because there is virtue in his feminine sensibility; (3) he is too masculine because of his oppressive treatment of women; (4) his masculinity serves the wrong ends. One might be forced to the conclusion that Tennyson is best loved when most unmanned. But what does that mean?

The first of these alternatives demonstrates a particularly rigid notion of gender division that was perpetrated during the Victorian period in order to regulate the triangulated relation of the feminine, the domestic, and the poetic. Concurrently, urban growth, industrial development, class movement and revolt, colonialism, and female education and its relation to female independence continued to destabilize power relations and to cause havoc for those seeking to maintain control.[11] The second alternative dubiously claims (from a line of retreat) that poetry is not really divorced from public issues, even though it is spoken from a realm apart—it just seems less powerful. The third alternative, though rightly acknowledging men's oppression of women, still cannot take fair account of Tennyson's own vexed relation to the patriarchy, particularly to male aggression, nor can it imagine asymmetrical gender systems.[12] The fourth alternative is so sure of its own hegemonic manliness and its vision of what the truly "poetical" should do that it is unable to understand the poetry it critiques.

The last remark implies that there is a better way to read Tennyson, even as earlier I have suggested that some ways of reading gender politics are more powerful than others. Let me acknowledge that rereading such a "central" figure as Tennyson, who remains unread by most people in our culture today, and writing him as a figure of ideological contest for the intellectual elite as part of its own gender/power/knowledge struggles, makes me keenly attuned to just how marginal we literary critics have all become. Nevertheless, I proceed and do so from certain assumptions about culture, texts, and subjectivity. I cannot agree that Tennyson's "project" is "holding together the contradictions of male homosocial and heterosexual desire . . . in order to parlay sublimated knowledge into social control."[13] My problem here is one of emphasis. Any writer, or career, or text is a site of struggle for ideological control, so that I cannot speak assuredly at all about Tennyson's projects or aims. Holding together the contradictions may be the project of a realist reader, trained to read conventionally by following a hierarchy of discourses towards a closure which discloses the "truth" of the text.[14] Smoothing out contradictions may well be the project of Victorian hegemony. But while Tennyson himself remains within ideology, his relationship to "coherence," as well as to the hegemony, may be fraught indeed.

The ways in which Tennyson's texts subvert gender ideology are more important. Ideological contradictions are obvious in the verse itself. In turn, his readers over generations have intervened to restate, revise, and disfigure his "project," whatever it was. I assume that if there ever was a single "project," such as typology as a last stand against the doom of history, it did not remain static and uncompromised, even at its most ideal. Finally, his contradictory cultural positions as poet and as male poet laureate are very much connected, albeit without direct and predictable lines, to his other contradictory social positions. His class positioning, for example, as a son of a disinherited landholder, marks him as belonging in family origin to one class but in present circumstances to another. His sexual positioning, as an erotic friend of Hallam and an erotic mate of Emily Sellwood Tennyson, marks him as homosexual but also as heterosexual. Therefore, I interpret his works and his career as both reproducing and contesting ideologies in a field of multiple and varied discursive relations.

This essay will take soundings in Tennyson's poetry in order to discover the changing status and use of the feminine. By the feminine I mean several things: the construction of the female subject; the cultural construction of femininity, which is attributed not only to women but also to men; and a gendered strategy of poetic form and language which questions and resists hegemonic control. Such resistance may itself be articulated in various ways: lyric outbursts which puncture linear narratives; the depiction of abnormal states of consciousness and of unconsciousness which call reality into question; the emphasis of sound and rhythm over sense; and the primacy of signifier over signified. Thus section 2 of this essay investigates Tennyson's appropriation of the female voice and body in his early lyrics and reads the gender mixings of *The Princess* (1848) as paradigmatic of his handling of the feminine, the masculine, and sexuality.

Section 3 explores *In Memoriam* (1850) as a poem of unfulfilled desire, and as Tennyson's poetic achievement which most compellingly puts the subject on trial, thus destabilizing culturally fixed gender roles. Its accommodation to linearity and to hegemonic notions of masculinity is far more vexed than that of *The Princess*. In this regard, *In Memoriam* is closer to *Maud*. For, in his major elegy, Tennyson engages in feminine writing by splintering the logic of opposition into a play of differences.

Section 4 turns to a richly symbolic scene from "Merlin and Vivien" (completed in 1856 and referred to as "Merlin," privately published as "Nimuë" in 1857, and finally as "Vivien" in the 1859 *Idylls of the King*). Here Tennyson locates "knowledge" in gender, places "wisdom" beyond gender categories, and reluctantly endorses the power of sexual difference and heterosexual desire, while mocking his very acknowledgment. I do not argue that Tennyson is a feminist, for he most certainly is not; however, his treatment of subjectivity and his archaeology of masculinity necessarily expose important gaps in the cultural hegemony he also represents so magisterially.

Appropriating the Female and the Feminine

The prevalence of female subjects in Tennyson's verse is not incidental. From his fascination with preserving marital fidelity in *The Devil and the Lady* at the age of fourteen, to the early lyrics where he draws portraits of women or impersonates them, to his treatment of debates on female education in *The Princess* (1848), to the juxtaposition afforded by the four idylls "Vivien," "Guinevere," "Enid," and "Elaine" (published alone in 1859), Tennyson finds in the female both a source and a subject for his art.

Like the Romantics, Tennyson appropriates women in order to suggest a connection between femininity and the imagination. In the 1830s his own poetic persona alters from that of a male youth standing on a mountain seeing a vision (a junior version of the pose of "The Ancient Sage") to that of a maiden isolated either in a building or in nature by a stream (see "Claribel," "Mariana," and "The Lady of Shalott"). A. Dwight Culler argues that Tennyson's new symbol for the poet emerges in three types of poem: that of interior landscape or garden of the mind; that of nature; and that of the lady.[15] I want to suggest not only that these three types are inextricably interwined, but also that the appropriation of the female in Tennyson's early poems serves as more than just an aspect or representation of the poet-figure. The female represents the undersense of poetry itself, melody and pure sound, and even unconsciousness.

Tennyson's early handling of the nineteenth-century connection between lyricism, privacy, and the feminine consists of linking the female to more than poetic imagination, for he also associates her with eternal, cosmic process. Culler is surely right that many of the lady poems are no more than a kind of poetic finger exercise, as if the young poet had "simply taken the varying moods of the feminine soul as an analogue of the kind of beauty he was attempting to produce."[16] At one end of the spectrum—pure sound and meter with little sense—is a short poem recently printed for the first time by Christopher Ricks in the appendix of his revised edition of Tennyson's *Poems*. The first of two similar stanzas runs:

> Juliana, Julietta,
> Juliana, Juliet,

> Let me walk with Juliana,
>   Let me talk with Julietta,
> Arm-in-arm with Juliana,
>   Hand-in-hand with Juliet. (1833–1834)[17]

Just the rehearsal of these female names, full of vowels and with slight variations, affords great pleasure and seems to stand in for whatever sort of intimacy "Hand-in-hand" suggests but does not scrutinize. Other early poems type women in light of specific attributes. So we find the fierceness of a "Kate" who will not find a mate; or the sudden, flaming passion which marks and markets a Madeline; or the reknowned chastity of an Isabel, and so on. Yet exercises in prosody and mood such as the Juliet poem, and portraits similar to these, proved a fertile training ground for Tennyson's connection of female figures, such as Mariana, with liminal times of dusk or dawn, extreme states of consciousness, and terminal situations. Herbert F. Tucker, Jr. has written more eloquently than any other critic about Tennyson's evocation of emotional atmospheres, of the verbal and nonverbal music that rings subtle changes on moods such as melancholy or hopelessness, or on states of being such as mystic passivity or even naked aggression. Characteristically, Tennysonian waves of sound blend into an urgent, finally unutterable but powerful inevitability.[18] These tidal melodies do not progress in a linear fashion; rather, they whelm the ear, they double back on each other. Often the poet singles out the watery deep as a figure for this primal rhythm or pulse of time and timelessness—in such poems as "Ulysses," "Crossing the Bar," or "The Holy Grail." Yet Tennyson always persists in conveying this compelling undersong in as vague a manner as possible, fastening it to no precise physical shape, person, or thing.

The same regressiveness that leads Tennyson to render the unconsciousness of a Kraken's "uninvaded sleep" or of a grasshopper who remains blissfully immune to human "sorrow" or "tears" also informs his appropriation of the female figures so prominent in the early poems.[19] The budding Laureate's Orianas, Claribels, and Marianas dramatize his eagerness to lose self-consciousness, the burden of intellect he always regards as painful. His playful variations of Juliana, Julietta, Juliet are much like the onomatopoeic hootings of the owl, the too-whits and too-whoos, which were seized upon by his early reviewers as evidence of his immaturity and effeminacy. Tennyson's lyric sweep leads him in "The Dying Swan" to create pools "flooded over with eddying song" (42), in which he tries to obliterate his own consciousness and, at the same time, to drown his readers in sounds that are mellifluous, Lethean, and feminine.

Although Wordsworth and Keats, at corresponding stages of their poetic development, were similarly eager to evoke a state of being in which unconsciousness is associated with nature and femininity, they inevitably introduced complications which Tennyson is not yet prepared to dramatize. The boy who lingers in the "virgin scene" in Wordworth's "Nutting" soon ceases his harmless play and systematically proceeds to mutilate, with "merciless ravage," the "shady nook" and bower which give up their "quiet being."[20] At first, the play in Keats's "Sleep and Poetry" seems desexualized: the speaker, after all, promises just to "touch" the shoulders of the nymphs he seeks in "shady places" and to make them shrink with a toothless "bite/As hard as lips can make it."[21] The eroticism involved in such games is unmistakeable, but it is presented as a mere prolegomenon for a "nobler life" that the speaker can no longer find in the thoughtless pleasures which once he derived from Leigh Hunt's palaces of art.[22]

Still, the shadowy life that envelops Mariana and the Lady of Shalott can no more be maintained than the Keatsian pleasures at first created for—and then withdrawn from—the aesthetic "she" who inhabits "The Palace of Art." For Tennyson also projects onto women like Mariana and the Lady of Shalott the self-consciousness he is so eager to avoid: they live in a world of contingency after all. The look that implicates the Lady and draws her into a sexually charged world or the morbid sensitivity to detail occasioned by Mariana's desire for the "he" beyond her moat are Tennyson's acknowledgments that these figures, like the Kraken, cannot remain intact forever. Having appropriated their sex and/or voice, he can offset the impinging world of consciousness and temporal progression only by nullifying them. Once again, he arrests them, but this time in a state of death, desired by Mariana and granted to the Lady of Shalott, who is now equated with a dying swan.

Tennyson appropriates women, erasing their subjectivities into refrains of sound, in order more fully to explore a primal level of consciousness. For he considers their be-moated and walled-in lives to be highly desirable compared to a male world of action. In this connection, I am reminded of his polite but Bartleby-like refusals to attend many functions away from

Farringford or Aldworth: "It is not pleasant to say no"; "With all thanks to all, I must absolutely decline"; "I am a shy beast and like to keep in my burrow."[23] Tennyson is drawn to withdrawal. Indeed, because of the cultural gendering of poetry as feminine and its progressively marginal position, he cannot afford, as Frank Lentricchia says of another belated poet Wallace Stevens, totally to repudiate the feminine, or he would be even more self-divided.[24]

Tennyson's early poetic engagement with the female also previews his later insistence that men should be more feminine. Sinfield proposes that Tennyson in his mature work is offering an alternative program for his brutally efficient, materialistic society.[25] This is most obvious in "Locksley Hall" and *Maud* with the contempt for Mammon, and in the idealized Arthur, the feminized King of *Idylls*.[26] Tennyson's strategy of moving closer to femininity also gains him distance from a masculinity and a sexuality he associates with violence, self-consciousness, and a fall into the corrupting capabilities of language. Whether such a "kinder, gentler" program for the individual and for culture, *pace* George Bush, offers a real alternative to brutal commodification and imperialism, or whether it merely puts a human face on exploitation and warmongering, is not always clear. Most likely, feminization solidifies hegemonic masculinity, while concurrently opening up a space for other definitions of masculinity and of femininity that, in a cultural moment of anxiety about gender and power, are judged by the hegemony as alternately permissable and expendable.

For all his interest in a state of being he seems to consider elementally mysterious, Tennyson is deeply ambivalent towards a blending of his identity with the female. Recall the withering immortality of Tithonus which results from "mixing" with Eos (607). Perhaps Tennyson subliminally senses that he confirms his aggressive masculinity all the more when he struggles to evade it.[27] *The Princess* provides a powerful example of Tennyson's use of the female and of feminization. It reinstitutes a binary opposition of sexual difference both in its frame narrative and in the closure of the "story," and flirts with androgyny after feminizing its hero and masculinizing its heroine. Still, *The Princess* is critically important for its ideological contradictions, and for its multiplicity and compromises, rather than for its reassertion of heterosexual marriage as the most viable option for a man and a woman as a life's work.[28] In other words, radical gender constructions do remain in play, exceeding the stability of a hermeneutic closure, which attempts to suppress differences.[29]

The Princess offers a paradigm for the contradictions in gender ideology which Tennyson inadvertently exposes and for the compromises he is forced to make in his treatment of the feminine. By grafting together the contemporary Woman Question with a struggle for governing power between the landed aristocracy and the bourgeoisie, the poem exposes class conflict and even the questionable status of Victorian literary discourse, but it foregrounds gender conflict. The ideological ground on which this text rests is the slash of sexual difference, or m/f. The "true" male, that is, he who is kingly material, is coded as heterosexual and military, while the "true" female, that is, she who deserves the name of princess, is coded as sweet and maternal. Yet not only is sexual difference destabilized by male crossdressing, female independence, and a vision of androgyny, but also the very codes of the military and the maternal remain sites of struggle and irresolution.

Drawing a semiotic square of sexual differences with social values attached for The Princess reveals that the masculine male (Gama, whose masculinity is marked by his desire for war, or Arac the fighter) is in opposition to the feminine female (Psyche, whose femininity is marked by her motherhood). Further, each of them is countered by an opposite: the feminine and unaggressive male Hilarion (whose "mixed" status is marked by his epileptic seizures which cast him into a state of feminine unconsciousness, a symbolic castration), and the masculine and independent females led by Ida (whose own "mixed" status is marked by her founding of a college and her mastery of male discourses such as philosophy). If the poem was successful in papering over differences and sorting out such mixtures into homogeneous sexualities and social roles, Ida would become a Psyche, and Hilarion would become a Gama. This does not occur. Despite a traditional closure that strips Ida of her independence and recuperates her into a heterosexual marriage with Hilarion, her maternity is qualified and he is no military conqueror. In fact, as others have pointed out, he wins her not by his military prowess, but by his need for nurture, as she remakes her college into a hospital for the wounded. She becomes a mother-surrogate, but gives up the child to its rightful mother, Psyche, and mothers her future husband instead. The male thus remains childlike, while the female remains in a position of emotional control, but is stripped of her intellectual pretentions and is redomesticated.

Because of Tennyson's strong and necessary ideological investment in the feminine ideal, neither the aggressive male nor the aggressive female are endorsed, yet they are also left unpunished. Gama, Arac, and Blanche fade out of the poem, even as philosophy and other master discourses seem to disappear along with the college soon after the Princess miraculously becomes a "woman," as "her falser self slipt from her like a robe" (146-147). Although a vision of heterosexual union takes over the poem, the alternatives remain visible in the compromises the poem effects.

In spite of the fact that the narrator has collected seven collegemates' contributions into one narrative, has bound "the scattered scheme," (Conclusion 8), and has closed off the play of desire by a repeated desexualization of Ida—from intellectual to mother-surrogate for her husband—unsettling questions remain. As Eagleton notes, it is unclear, given the compromise offered, how the kingdom will continue to function with a still powerful mother-figure who is childless and with a husband who gains his manhood by Ida's assumption of wifehood, rather than by an entrance into the public sphere of action and battle.[30] While the poem appears to close down any problems of a marriage between a desexualized but powerful wife and a feminized husband, the critique of gender roles and the disturbance of power/knowledge relations continues to disrupt the text. The force required to marry this couple is so great, in fact, that the text evades it by offering miracles of the unconscious: the mystic trances of the Prince suddenly end and the "womanliness" of Ida is revealed as having been merely in hiding all along. The strain of this compromise is finally too much for the poem to bear, which is precisely what makes it so fascinating and so much of an index of Tennyson's whole career.

Formally, *The Princess* is a narrative interspersed with songs set within another narrative frame. It presents a mythic story constructed in medley fashion by seven college undergraduates who are on holiday. The female auditors contribute too, by singing lyrics concerning the child figure, love, and domestic life, "to give us breathing-space" (Prologue 235), as the narrator candidly and unabashedly remarks. The ideological strain in the poem can be measured further by the lack of integration between these embedded songs, engendered female, and the narrative(s) proper, engendered male. The embedded lyrics delay the narrative while heightening the temporal drama. Moreover, while the seven male voices are gathered together into a unified whole by the narrator, they are also undifferentiated by speech patterns or interests, thus causing Eagleton to comment on the real lack of any "dialectic of discourses" or "interplay" in the poem. There is no sense, he argues, in which one voice is contradicted or interrogated by another; rather, the narrative is inexorably centered.[31] Yet, the very notion of binding sheaves interrogates the authority of the male voice. More important, as in *Maud*, the "coherent" identity and "autonomy" of male narrative is fragmented by female lyric. The content of the lyrics may well be in accord with the thrust of the poem towards domesticating the female's desire—Tennyson added the lyrics two years later and remarked that the "child is the link through the parts, as shown in the Songs, which are the best interpreters of the poem."[32] However, again as in *Maud*, a digressive lyric energy still plays against and subverts the unfolding of the narrative. And the songs themselves are not always as "clear" as Tennyson retrospectively makes them out to be. "Now Sleeps the Crimson Petal," harbors, without resolving, the same gender mixing that the inner and outer frames also negotiate.[33] Thus the poem, while accommodating and attempting to smooth over internal contradictions, cannot erase traces of ideological conflict at the site of gender. The gender differences and mixings that erupt in *The Princess* may serve the interests of the hegemonic, but at the same time they subversively resist the stable logic of opposition by which Victorian culture defined itself.

"I Take the Pressure of His Hand"

In Memoriam (1850) repeats one of the major moves of *The Princess* by opening up a series of gender positions and at the same time offering a mythic narrative of growth towards a mature, socialized, masculinity.[34] It attempts to contain, in other words, the transgressive nature of its own desire. Possibly because *The Princess* is more tightly constructed, the compromised conclusion on which it depends does attempt a resolution, although by evading many of the problems raised by the poem, this conclusion can act as only one more irresolution. The closure of *In Memoriam*—the displacement of feminine desire and homosocial eroticism onto heterosexual desire and marriage—proves even less satisfactory. Indeed, one would have to say that this ending is tacked on, an assertion not hard to make about many of the verses, lines, and 133 sections of the poem. In spite of the ordering of holidays and seasons which clearly structures the poem, *In Memoriam* strongly resists sequence. Tennyson's explanation of his arbitrary composing process, the sticking of poems into any blank spaces he noticed over seventeen years, appears to bear some truth.[35] This resistance means that the poem itself is almost arbitrary, not in its doubt as a prelude to faith, but in the exchangeability of its lines and its gender roles.

A more positive way to articulate the same point is, perhaps, to count *In Memoriam* as one of the greatest poems of desire in the English language. Desire by definition goes unfulfilled; it is merely an endless progression of signifiers. Desire traces the curve and depth of a negativity, erasing itself as it moves, but leaves a residue of its having been. Unlike religious faith which moves to believe in and joyfully to accept that which is measureless, desire attempts to take measure of that which is measureless. One can understand the interrelationship between desire and faith, but one can also read *In Memoriam* differently than does T. S. Eliot, so that faith finally rests on the residue of a desire that has been lived and has repeatedly articulated itself. It is significant that among Tennyson's suppressions from the manuscript is his phrase subsuming religious belief in human desire: "Yet art thou oft as God to me."[36] In the poem desire which is stronger than faith traces the curve of Arthur Hallam's absent hand, the breadth of his coffined body, the timbre of his voice departed. And it relies on a particular rhyme pattern and rhetoric to perform that tracing.

Tennyson's circling mode of desire in this his longest elegy, often relying on paradox, can be remarkably similar in its lack of logic to the parody Swinburne made of Tennyson's "The Higher Pantheism" entitled "The Higher Pantheism in a Nutshell." Furthermore, the rhyming scheme (*abba*) is especially suited, as Ricks points out, to turning round rather than going forward.[37] Added to Tennyson's doubts and disclaimers within and outside of the poem, the advance and retreat of the elegy means that the desire expressed is finally more persuasive than the narrative transformation of Hallam into God or the final notes of optimism in the Epilogue. Celebrating the marriage and the future progeny of Cecilia, Alfred's sister, and Edmund Lushington, the Epilogue replaces the epithalamium Tennyson might have written for Hallam and his sister Emily. More pointedly, it translates homosocial desire into heterosexual marriage.

The nature of desire in the elegy is homoerotic, if not homosexual, though labelling it as such is less important than realizing its power and subversive potential.[38] Whether Hallam and Tennyson ever shared a bed is not irrelevant, but it is unable to be known. On 14 December 1833, Robert Monteith, a college friend of Hallam and Tennyson's, who understood the tenor of their relationship, wrote his condolence letter to Tennyson and offered "common friendship." He imagined that the "sorrow of all others combined cannot be supposed equal to that of you and your family. . . . and all wish as I do, for still stricter friendship with you, if it might be (which is all but impossible) that together we might help to fill up the gap."[39] Monteith's "mights" suggest that he harbors serious doubt that anything, much less a stronger bond with him, could fill for Tennyson the gap which Hallam has vacated. His whole letter is marked by a hesitant generosity both anxious that it will not be accepted and that it will be taken the wrong way.

This letter is one more equivocal, semierotic document in the writings about Hallam and *In Memoriam* that any critic must read and interpret in making a decision about the nature of desire in the poem. The text itself, as has been repeatedly noted, is often unclear. For instance, one of the most important motifs is the unsaid—that there remains something that cannot be spoken: "There is more than I can see,/and what I see I leave unsaid" (74). Yet the text names Hallam as "my prime passion in the grave" (85) and speaks of love undying in "the shape of him I loved, and love/for ever" (103), thus pointing to a love relationship that goes beyond what can be called "common" friendship. At some points, it seems that Tennyson, in his revisions, attempts to write out intense(r) desire but stops short: "Stoop soul and touch me: wed me: hear/The wish too strong for words to name" is replaced by the even more erotic "Descend, and touch, and enter" (93). Any rethinkings or anxieties that Tennyson harbored, however, were doubled or trebled in his son. Hallam Lord Tennyson, writing his *Memoir* in the 1890s, took extra pains that the relationship between his father and Arthur Hallam should not be misconstrued as homosexual. Yet the disturbing aspect of this love relation is just what the poem itself takes up and socializes away. The speaker seeks to overcome his feminine desire and feminine sorrow, as Benjamin Jowett pointed out, because it is not manly to dwell on them.[40]

The difficulty and the challenge of representing a male/male relationship in the mid-Victorian period is highlighted most forcefully in the poem by gender slippage. The first two stanzas of Section 13 may serve as a prime example of the contradictions of homosocial desire:

> Tears of the widower, when he sees
>   A late-lost form that sleep reveals,
>   And moves his doubtful arms, and feels
> Her place is empty, fall like these;
> Which weep a loss for ever new,
>   A void where heart on heart reposed
> And where warm hands have prest and closed,
>   Silence, till I be silent too. (1-8)

At different moments in the text, the speaker dons the roles of brother, lover, maiden, child, husband, and wife to Hallam. In its bold resistance to sequence, and in its playful variety of roles for the speaker and for the object of desire, Hallam, *In Memoriam* acts as a forerunner to avant-garde works written by men and women which more fully exploit the semiotic possibilities of language.[41] Tennyson's text does, however, take a major step in destabilizing a coherent subjectivity, in dissolving the bar between signifier and signified, and in charting the course of desire against symbolic regulation, before closing these down through a narrative of maturity which is equated with assuming one's proper gender role as a man.

The feminine must be excluded, by ideological necessity, for the male to be properly masculinized. To this end, the speaker calls on Time and Sorrow (as wife) to school him against private fantasies about an erotic relationship with the dead in the service of a greater compensation and a stronger bond (117 and 59). He renounces the female personification of knowledge, which submits "all things to desire," in favor of "Wisdom," the higher hand which must help her know her place (114). Finally, the image of the hand, which has accrued more and more erotic meaning during the poem, is translated from the hand of a lover to the hand of God. Claiming that his new love is vaster and not exclusive of the earlier love, the speaker derides his own childishness and embraces the Other as a "father" who is near: "And out of darkness came the hands/That reach through nature, moulding men" (124). From this narrative of male maturity, the speaker moves with ease to comment on his sorrows as "echoes out of weaker times" (Epilogue 10) and to acknowledge his friend Edmund Lushington as a worthy spouse for Cecilia Tennyson. In addition, the Epilogue suggests that Tennyson himself is now worthy—worthy as a kind of father of the bride to give away a woman in marriage instead of adopting the role of maiden himself.

In Memoriam, like the long poems preceding and following it, *The Princess* and *Maud*, features the feminized male only to remasculinize him. The poem constructs a bulwark of an epilogue to prevent the speaker's further mixing with the dead in an erotic ecstasy of sorrow and grief. In gender terms, it doubly excludes the feminine. First, the Epilogue refuses to allow the male any further connection with the feminine, except in unions with women which are socially sanctioned. Heterosexual marriage will support rather than disturb gender distinctions that must be held in place. Second, the Epilogue rewrites fluid desire into a more acceptable and manly kinship, replacing the uncommon with the common. But the traces of homoerotic desire and the male adoptions of feminine roles are far more powerful than this closure.

"Lost to life and use and name and fame"

In his sixth *Idyll*, "Merlin and Vivien," Tennyson offers us a richly symbolic scene.[42] He presents a conflict of knowledge and control between the male seer Merlin and the seductive damsel Vivien over a powerful wisdom book passed down from one man to another. In the complicated relationship between Merlin and Vivien, Tennyson exposes most clearly the binary opposition which structures his entire corpus: accepting the cultural approval of sexual difference and heterosexuality versus proposing a dissolution of such an opposition. He makes this dissolution part of male poetic wisdom. This wisdom, as I have argued, is marginalized and feminized by culture, and yet the poet conceives of it as also transcending gender. Tennyson repeatedly struggles to explore both sides and somehow to accommodate them to each other. In this scene, however, the text mocks its own endorsements, as Tennyson recognizes the impossibility of either a final accommodation or a single solution.

If *In Memoriam* closes with what feels like a phony narrative of marriage, *Idylls of the King*, its looking-glass image, ends its first idyll, "The Coming of Arthur," with just such a "closure," the marriage of Arthur and Guinevere, which is then burst open. In this poetic sequence, Tennyson earnestly returns to the issue of desire, specifically the double and deadly threats of female desire, and desire for the female. It is probably significant that he started writing about the seduction of Merlin in 1854 and broke off to work instead, morning and evening, on *Maud* which opens memorably with a landscape, a symbolic vision of the female as womb and tomb, where the father's corpse lies crushed: "The red-ribbed ledges drip with a silent horror of blood,/And Echo there, whatever is asked her, answers 'Death'" (519). Tennyson's deep ambivalence about female power is here registered most graphically, but it is no less strong in *Idylls*.

Like the Princess, Vivien wishes to acquire knowledge and, like the Prince, she uses her seductive powers to attain her goal. Coyly prompted by her flattery, Merlin actually reveals to Vivien some history behind his book of magic. The first owner, he recounts, was a "glassy-headed hairless" (618) hermit-sage who rejected all earthly things and chose to live alone in a "great wild on grass" (619), so that he might focus more purely on studying the text. This unnamed seer, possessed of secrets and powers unknown to other men, was dragged off to the local king who found a phallic use for him. Interestingly enough, the King needed help with gender politics and not party politics. He demanded a charm to control his unsubmissive wife, which the old seer wove, making her invisible to all men except her husband and her husband visible only to her. Having provided this charm, the old man returned to live off grass in the wild.

Eventually, Merlin inherits the book of charms, which he describes as "writ in a language that has long gone by" (672). While Vivien continues to ask him to share his knowledge as a pledge of faith to her, indeed threatening that even if he locks the book within a chest within a chest, she will "strike upon a sudden means/To dig, pick, open, find and read the charm" (657-658), he resists. A woman, he claims, cannot read this book with "every margin scribbled, crost, and cramm'd/With comment, densest condensation, hard/To mind and eye" (675-676). Even if Vivien could master it, Merlin confides, she would use it wrongly, to destroy Arthur's brotherhood out of spite, instead of employing it rationally and logically as a man would.

Barred from the book's secrets, Vivien continues to beg and cajole, drawing on all her wily seductive powers to lure the Sage into releasing the charm. Finally, moved by her barrage of compliments and sexual overtures, and giving up his quest to keep wisdom pure, Merlin yields, "overtalked and overworn" (963). No sooner does he reveal the greatest secret, however, than Vivien turns it against him, robbing him of "life and use and name and fame" (968). Merlin lies in the hollow oak, obsolete, and as if dead.

This crisis of control over the text is also a crisis of gender. For power over the magical word, the charm of poetry and prophecy, is not only a battle of the sexes but also a conflict about self-consciousness enacted through sexual division and cultural constructions of gender difference. In this sense, the scene between Merlin and Vivien enacts Tennyson's poetic struggle and reiterates his subject matter by joining together themes of bardic authority, a male's desire to avoid the foulness of sexual difference, a strong desire for death, and yet a sexuality that cannot be avoided.

In this idyll Merlin is old and depressed. Though he has attempted to build a world in which sexual difference can be sidetracked—where desire ceases and unquestioned fidelity stays fixed—he has failed. Merlin resembles King Arthur in this respect, but he is far more sexual than the king who, lured by Vivien's seductive wiles, characteristically "had gazed upon her blankly and gone by" (159). Confronted both by his own strong sexual arousal and the impossibility of his earlier endeavor, Merlin cannot afford to be so disdainful or so unconscious. He realizes that escaping sexuality in the service of an ideal brotherhood proves absolutely impossible. Not only will woman intervene, but man will also seek her out or at least welcome her. The male sage now confronts the heterosexuality which Tennyson has played with, evaded, impersonated, reversed, elided, and crossdressed in many other poems. Merlin's response is to withdraw. Searching for the kind of isolation his predecessor had embraced, living off

grass in the wild beyond gender politics and humanity, Merlin flees Arthur's court by boat. He seeks to be a Lady of Shalott, immured in four
towers, devoted only to art, and invisible to the world. So, instead of sailing to Camelot as she did, he sails away from Camelot, but he still meets
sexuality and death. For Vivien is with him in the boat; the sexuality that
taints Camelot has stuck to him. He is not like the "glassy-headed" old
man who, unlike all other men, did not covet the king's wife, but he is
more like a Lancelot than he thought.

Merlin pays the price for his heterosexual desire by becoming an enclosed, death-like object. Ricks reminds us that such a living death, "imprisoned forever, conscious but paralyzed," haunted Tennyson.[43] Yet,
paradoxically, Merlin also gets what he wants. He gains transcendence, a
removal from the world of generation and gender binaries. The disappearance of Merlin, presaging the disappearance of Arthur, points to the
end of the pure male bonding symbolized by the ideal of the Round Table.
Yet the idyll also registers nostalgia for past male bonding. It still worships
the feminine male and the dissolution of sexual difference. It at once
chooses the threat of heterosexuality, and chooses the dissolution of gender and fidelity to an earlier ideal. Finally, it mocks itself for both choices.
The last lines of the idyll articulate the price of sexual choice:

> Then crying 'I have made his glory mine,'
> And shrieking out 'O fool!' the harlot leapt
> Adown the forest, and the thicket closed
> Behind her, and the forest echoed 'fool.' (969-972)

In the first instance, Vivien calls Merlin "fool," but the echo spoken by a
power larger than either of them, repeating her name for Merlin, names
her "fool" as well. In one of Tennyson's most marvelous evasions, all gender and power positions are equally taken and forsaken.

As consciously as *In Memoriam*, this idyll examines the hollow founda-
tions and measureless reach of desire. When Vivien hugs Merlin close,
appealing to his protectiveness in her apparent fear of a lightning bolt that
"furrows" a nearby oak, she "Nor yet forgot her practice in her fright"
(945). The idyll is unclear about where practice begins and true emotion
ends, or to what degree they may be intermingled. So too, the idyll questions, without resolving, what is natural design (imposed by the gods), and

what is not (where free will and preference begin); what is artifice and what real feeling; what is lust and what love; what is masculine and what feminine. The idyll answers only that eschewing desire inevitably places one in an unhuman realm that can be as deadening as a Tithonus-like giving over to desire.

The use of the female figure and the instability of the feminine and the masculine in Tennyson's work illustrate a disturbance in gender roles that would only increase as the nineteenth century wore on. His particular evasions and compromises, however, become all the more important in light of his social role as laureate, a role that, once given, becomes retrospectively difficult to divorce from an entire career of influence on other writers and on the nineteenth-century reading public. The kind of influence that his writings had in subverting orthodoxies about gender or in reconfirming them all the more cannot be measured. It seems incontrovertible that Tennyson's texts served multiple and varied political ends, even as they do inside and outside of the academy today.

"Who Is Speaking?"
Charlotte Brontë's Voices of Prophecy

JANET L. LARSON

It is not surprising that apocalyptic and prophetic texts should long have
held engendering power for Charlotte Brontë's sense of herself as an "author." From her youth upward in deeply biblical Yorkshire, the mode of
the classical prophets, with whom Brontë seems to have felt a 'natural'
affinity, was even more deeply embedded in her religious training, reading,
and experience than the language of domestic Christian piety, in which she
often falters to speak. From the Haworth pulpit Reverend Patrick Brontë
liked to preach on eschatology and the signs of the times. In the family
parlor hung the lurid and fantastical panoramas by John Martin which
made the Bible a heroic universe for the Byronic imaginations of the young
Brontës. In the nursery, apocalyptic visions of total destruction and re-
creation authorized the terrible genii to annihilate the wicked and to bring
fictive worlds to life.[1] Prophetic denunciation of such "terrible wickedness"
also fired Charlotte's editorializing voice in the juvenilia and inspired her
own book of prophecy foretelling Angria's downfall (*A Leaf from an Unopened Volume*, 1834).[2] Most of all, the visionary aspect of prophecy
compelled her early creative work. The well-known passage on imagination in the Roe Head Journal recalls the language with which God called
the prophet Elijah: "if the illustration be not profane, as God was not in
the wind nor the fire nor the earthquake so neither is my heart in the task,

the theme or the exercise. It is the still small voice alone that comes to me at eventide," calling her to the ecstasy of creative vision.[3]

While Anglican teaching mystified the patriarchal nature of the texts Brontë loved, and helped to postpone the moment of demystification, the privilege and familiarity of the Bible gave her access to scriptural "myths of power" as she explored her writing gifts.[4] Yet for all her immersion in the prophetic sublime, Brontë's uses of its various discourses typically manifest a "basic conflict between her attachment to her subject and her critical conscience."[5] Throughout her life, even as she worked within the prophetic tradition she resisted it for a complex of reasons: as the skeptical reader of ominous portents and "frenzied fanaticism" in her aunt's "mad Methodist Magazines"; as the child trained to obey Duty before Imagination; as the female visionary taught to distrust her visions; as the social prophet reluctant to bear her most radical messages; as a conscientious objector to apocalyptic violence; as the novelist wary of "court[ing] charges of irrationality" and determined to write about the real world of women and men she knew.[6]

For the young Brontë, using and resisting male prophetic traditions were not yet consciously gendered acts. From the evidence we have, it was not until the period of her study in Brussels (1842–1843) that the gender contradictions in her emulations of prophets were forced closer to exposure. Creative "imitations" of a wide range of male literary models prescribed by her master, the Belgian school exercises empowered new forms of expression by challenging Brontë to find her own voice as "a word that [was] more than [her]self."[7] This founding gesture of the public discourse of the Victorian sage is also deeply embedded in the biblical tradition, for the *prophētēs*, however individualized his voice, is one-who-speaks-for-another. Significantly, in writing her *devoirs* on genius and vocation, Brontë reflected indirectly (and anxiously) on her own calling as a writer by engaging with a tradition of prophetic-heroic types, from biblical times into the nineteenth century, such as Mahomet and Peter the Hermit (and Napoleon), who uprooted and transplanted whole nations as Moses and Joshua did.[8] Brontë worked at a time when biblical scholarship, influenced by the new source criticism as well as by modern ideas of spirituality, was replacing the longstanding Protestant view of the prophet as the obedient interpreter of Mosaic law with a newly discovered prophetic type, independent and creative, the "brilliant religious personality, standing close to

God."⁹ Such reinterpretations of Scripture released this figure of male genius from his ancient historical context and Yahwistic religion for use not
only by Romantic poets and Victorian social critics eager to discard Mosaic Covenant and Jewish messianism, like Carlyle and Dickens, but also
by female reformers and preachers who were working out a tradition in
which to place their own public work.¹⁰ All of the prophetic figures Brontë
celebrates in the Belgian essays fit the Romantic-charismatic model her
feminist contemporaries preferred; nonetheless, the tradition of which and
in which she writes leads back to a past when messengers of God were
male and other. Tellingly double-voiced, digressive, and circuitous, these
ambitious essays register Brontë's uneasy consciousness that identifying
with such emissaries of God and figures of the artist was bold presumption
for a woman of her time and place.

Brontë's *devoir* entitled "The Vision and Death of Moses on Mt. Nebo"
(27 July 1842) is the most important instance of these contradictions, for
the Pisgah sight would be repeatedly reworked in her mature fiction as the
biblical *locus classicus* of the ambitious woman's anxiety of authorship. In
this essay, Brontë moves swiftly beyond the figure of Moses as historian
and lawbearer to the prophetic poet: "After Moses the lawgiver and leader
had spoken, Moses the prophet and elect of God took up the word, and
ordinary language no longer sufficing him to express the thoughts with
which his soul was moved, he launched forth into the figurative language
of poetry, that beautiful biblical poetry which borrows its fire from the
Eastern sun and its inspiration from God himself."¹¹ But before launching
into this poetry, Brontë swerves from her enraptured narrative of Moses
climbing Mt. Nebo to answer the Victorian rationalist's doubts about miracles in the Bible, and to defend the faithful reader's belief in its literal
truth (368–370). Implicitly defending her own enraptured writing that follows as the product of "Faith," Brontë tellingly encodes this interruption
as apologetics, cast into the form of an allegory of rival female "guide[s]"
for man's Bible-reading. Skeptical Reason asks "useless questions . . . because she feels herself incapable of comprehending the mysteries of Revelation" and "pride encumbers her wings"; but "Happily Faith comes to
man's aid, an angel with a humble look but a lofty flight, a seraph, who
soars . . . to the very throne of the Eternal" and "raises her lamp" to
illuminate the page (369–370).

When the narrative resumes, the reader learns that Moses has been climbing all the while: he now "has gained the summit" that Brontë's excursus has also enabled her to scale and "has lost sight of the crowd" (370), as this writer must lose sight of her detractors and doubts.[12] Now she can encompass the godlike in Moses with her deeper knowledge of the prophet's rapture, known only to herself, and tell what God had barred the dying prophet from communicating. Now she paints the Promised Land in the colors of Martin's sublime, plumbs the prophet's soul as his spiritual psychologist, and typologically connects him with Isaiah and Simeon as she reveals the sweep of sacred and human history to the coming of the Messiah, like the Archangel Michael showing it all to Adam from the highest point of Paradise (while Eve sleeps). If Brontë's extension of the Pisgah sight is more poetically detailed than the interpretations of Victorian typologists, unlike Henry Melvill's popular christological version Brontë's does not include Calvary:[13] in the climax, Moses's revelation discloses "between the stars and the earth, the figure of a woman, holding in her arms a child" (374).

In "The Death of Moses" Brontë chose an apt subject for an expansive stage when she glimpsed the promise in herself, yet her essay betrays anxieties about the costs and ironies of the Pisgah sight for a female Moses in the nineteenth century.[14] Before she can soar to the height from which to foresee the promised prospect—and display her exegetical powers over not only Deuteronomy 34 but the whole sweep of biblical narrative—she figures herself as a humble angel with a "lamp" (as though Cassandra *could* masquerade as Florence Nightingale), "lean[ing] over the volume" (370) like the Angel in the House radiating spiritual light. Brontë's treatment of her chosen subject—a male genius traditionally understood as a historian, lawgiver, and seer—also manifests tensions that recur in her later writing between the woman's lyrical vision and realistic historical plot under the sign of patriarchal law. Making history visionary, as Brontë does in this Pisgah sight, is one way to evade the problematic androcentrism of the biblical past, including misogynist aspects of Mosaic law elided here. Misogyny reenters Brontë's discourse nonetheless through the female figures for evil that she incorporates from the sacred text, such as Jezebel, the infamous queen who cut off the prophets (372). At the same time, Brontë's subjectively rendered details and dramatic emphasis intimate the female writer's reluctant identification with the fallen "virgin of Zion" (372) and her distrust of her own propensity to "idolatry," a term she associates with worship of the male and with creative writing as transgression. ("Again [Israel] brings banishment upon herself and again she shakes off the yoke of slavery and returns bruised and exhausted to the banks of her cherished Jordan" [372].) Given these guilty identifications, Brontë needs all the more to tell Israel's whole story of "her" rescue and to place the female component of divine salvation foremost—especially in a historical world which, she does recall, did not "coun[t] the women and children" (368). In contrast to the climactic Marian figure, the male prophet is presented by the voice of "Faithful Interpretation" as a sacrificial "victim" on the smoking mountain (368), as though she knows or foreknows "the bitter regrets of the man condemned to die at the moment when life offers him most charms" (372). As the visionary, Brontë brings forth land, seed, and futures, like the word of the Lord in Deuteronomy 34:4; as the biblical historian and enforcer of law, in her last terse paragraph she cuts the prophet off (374).

In "The Death of Napoleon" (May 1843), a discursive *devoir* composed amid the distresses of Brontë's second stay in Brussels, she writes as a prophet in exile more aware of the limits of male genius and the painful anomaly of the woman writer's position. This awareness she presents aslant through her story of the exiled hero condemned to solitude for presuming to bring forth a world.[15] This account is framed by a long excursus pondering both the nature of genius and the presumption of the writer who attempts to estimate its worldly powers (274). At the close, Brontë casts her prophecy—of how posterity will view this hero—into an ironic biblical figure: "Like Jonah's vine, Napoleon's glory grew in the space of a night, and in a night it withered" (280; cf. Jonah 4:6–11). Merely conventional here, the allusion will become radically transformed in the context of *Villette*'s theme of female vocation. When the young Lucy Snowe launches forth into the world urgently questioning, "Whence did I come? Whither should go? What should I do?" Snowe as wizened narrator calls up Jonah's flowering gourd as a prophetic emblem of her "soul," anticipating the rapid rise and fall of her expectations in a patriarchal world where "feminine soul" is destiny without a future tense.[16] And by recalling this very reluctant prophet, Lucy offers early on in her autobiography a masked sign of the ambivalent and skeptical kind of prophecy to which she has been called by just such life experiences.

Brussels gave Brontë a "season of mental culture."[17] But continued writing in the Belgian manner was unlikely to be published in Victorian England, where a middle-class woman's appointed work outside the home, as Master Heger insisted, was not preaching or Bible interpretation but quite another kind of teaching which Brontë knew was not her vocation. In 1844–1845, her prophetic impulse rose up in a newly tortured form as a *crie de coeur* in the wilderness of Haworth. In the most desperate passages of her letters to Heger, biblical allusion becomes a veiled means of prophetic attack on the faithlessness of her master, who had encouraged her talents but urged her to abandon her own creative writing before abandoning her.[18] There is nothing religious about Brontë's epistolary prophetic mode: the "other" on whose behalf she speaks in these biblical allusions is her own alienated self muted by the master's silence. This emergent personal voice helped to generate the female persona whose causes Brontë would defend in her mature works.[19] Here, in the revelations of the Actual that Carlyle preached, Brontë as a woman at last found a crucial impetus for her prophetic message, if not her ideal nor yet a public form in which to speak.

By the time her long apprenticeship in prophetic discourse bore fruit in her mature fiction, Brontë came to manifest a troubled awareness of the gender politics she had to contend with as a Victorian woman writer. She was still attracted to the Romantic male ethos of the artist as God—and wrote as a female prophet in Carlyle's train, if not as his uncritical follower.[20] Yet increasingly she understood what it meant for her calling that the dominant culture did not entrust its established pulpits in the church or the press to women. Males are "the chosen"; a woman's appointment requires her subjection to male mediators of her relationships with the divine, Holy Scripture, and culture in a line of vertical descent. Brontë knew the subordinationist argument well, but she also had been nourished on the Protestant tradition which had taught her to "read, mark, learn, and inwardly digest" the Scriptures (cf. *Villette* 382). These exercises of "the right of private judgment," emotional response, and conscientious application engaged her mature critical powers of interpretation.[21] To read Scripture in the line of the Reformers was virtually to become a latter-day prophet, in Luther's older sense of the word, by finding in the Bible grounds of protest against the institutionalized infidelities of the present. To make Scripture her own by thoroughly digesting and retelling it, rather than passively "receiv[ing] Revelation" (*Villette* 381) or reproducing its

visions in the enraptured discourse of desire, was for Brontë a necessary
step toward opposing the patriarchal ideology that would deny critical
powers and hermeneutical skills even to womanhood eulogized as "divine." To discover the "internally persuasive" word of the Word, as distinguished from its mere recitation, was also for Brontë a way to confirm the
desire to write as a divine call.[22] Eventually these discoveries empowered a
kind of prophecy that demanded her analytical and literary talents—and
that drew upon her capacity for communing with a divine force sometimes
addressed in her mature works as "other than God" the Father (*Villette*
208).[23]

The far reach of Brontë's prophetic protofeminist hermeneutics is
glimpsed in the notorious chapter of *Shirley*, "Which the Genteel Reader is
Recommended to Skip, Low Persons being Here Introduced." Here, Shirley Keeldar's imagination engenders an originary figure of female power
and a living tradition: "The first woman's breast that heaved with life on
this world yielded the daring which could contend with Omnipotence: the
strength which could bear a thousand years of bondage,—the vitality
which could feed that vulture death through uncounted ages,—the unex-
hausted life and uncorrupted excellence, sisters to immortality, which, after millenniums of crimes, struggles, and woes, could conceive and bring
forth a Messiah" (315). As in "The Death of Moses," the syntax of Shirley's Pisgah sight generates a Messiah in a woman's arms; but here "he" is
embedded in the rhetoric of female messianism that proclaims the triumph,
despite countless *viae dolorsae*, of woman as life-force. Shirley's communion with her Titaness then empowers further heretic interpretations of
Scripture when she and Caroline Helstone tangle with a Bible-quoting misogynist (321–324). Reinflecting the central questions that Higher Criticism
was asking—who is speaking and with what authority in this Book?—
they expose the sexual politics of man's reading of scriptural texts, ridi-
cule the vanity of androcentric Bible-worship, and offer feminist counter-
readings of St. Paul that anticipate the radical revisionism of *The Woman's
Bible*.[24]

In *Jane Eyre* and even more in *Villette*, like Elizabeth Cady Stanton's
commentators Brontë demystifies androcentric uses of Scripture to expose
the false prophets of middle-class male supremacy, idolatrists who create a
god in their own image and practice injustice in "His" name; she protests

the stunting of women's growth by bad theodicy and otherwordly preaching; and she inscribes into her books connections between institutionalized injustice, cultural faithlessness, and patriarchy's grounding Logos. Brontë's progressive attitudes nonetheless remain in tension with her more traditional views, for she both revered the heroes and male authority figures who influenced her and needed to evade, revise, or oppose their models. Her early Victorian ambivalence takes its most creative form in the dialogism of her mature works, although biblical allusions (among other features of the texts) can also simply inscribe contradictions. The gender-neutral language of her childhood creed must have also disguised from her some of the tensions between the masculinist and the protofeminist impulses in her uses of Scripture.

Not surprisingly then, Brontë as the *prophētēs* speaks with more than one voice, and for more than one "other." Drawing upon the rhetoric, narrative, and poetry of biblical prophecy, her prophetic discourse takes at least three distinctive forms: the sermons of the preaching prophet; the call narratives of the prophetic storyteller and sage; and the rapt utterances of the lyric seer. None of Brontë's prophetic modes is quite stable: in different instances the sermonic, the narrative, and the lyric can be found at shifting locations on the boundary between masculine and feminine discourse, serve various ends, and exhibit differing degrees of authorial self-awareness. Appearing conjointly within single works, articulated with other voices as well, Brontë's discourses of prophecy carry forward implicit dialogues on the nature and power of authoritative speech. As a reader following the intratextual dynamics of these voices, which provoke and respond to one another in her major works, one is compelled to ask, as Bakhtin put the question, "Who is speaking?"[25] Further, to read these discordant prophetic modes whenever they appear to be displacing, ignoring, or covering for one another requires a hermeneutics of suspicion that has its roots in Brontë's own skepticism toward contemporary religious language, a defining disposition of the Victorian sage. Examining the full interarticulation of prophetic (and other) voices in Brontë's novels lies well outside the scope of this essay. Here I want to define further some of the forms that sermonic and narrative prophecy take in *Jane Eyre* and, more briefly, in *Villette*: novels in which Brontë wrote the Victorian sage tradition through the woman's "book of life."

When Brontë's female protagonists speak as sermonic prophets, they preach in a well-established line of male descent. This line Brontë strives to author herself, as it were ex post facto, by rewriting male precursors so that their influence can flow only through her interpretation. Whether with superior demonstrations of prophetic ethos, more powerful figuration, re-accentuated content, or mimetic subversion, she attempts to master in the pulpit what Matthew Arnold in "Haworth Churchyard" called her "mas-ter's accent." These efforts nonetheless constitute a set of female-gendered practices which can be charted on a continuum from imitation to rejection. In any given sermon, further, these differing practices are likely to be con-joined. Even the comparatively simple subgenre of pulpit discourse, so of-ten deplored and dismissed by critics, can be tellingly double-voiced in Brontë, especially when the accent is on the prophetic.[26]

The preface to the second edition of *Jane Eyre* (dated 21 December 1847) demonstrates some of the problems with Brontë's imitation of male sermonic prophets and inscribes the competitive pressures she felt. In her introductory paragraphs the newly established author, signing herself "Currer Bell," "curries favor with [the] audience" by a more explicit "self-deprecation" than her male sage counterparts practiced.[27] She then abruptly seizes control of the discourse with a diatribe against her critics ("I turn to another class").[28] Throughout the preface, she presents herself as a faithful follower of the male prophets she names, but it soon becomes clear that she invokes them in order to master them through allusion and trope. In the dedicatory conclusion, Brontë anoints Thackeray as the fore-most continuer of the biblical-prophetic tradition (he "flashes the levin-brand of his denunciation" against "the great ones of society"), and hails him in Carlylese as her own Master—"the very master of that working corps who would restore to rectitude the warped system of things" (36). While she claims no direct descent herself from the "son of Imlah" (36), to anoint Thackeray in the line of the ironic prophet Micaiah is to assume an equal if not superior position. This is one object of "allud[ing]" to him, as she reveals in her concluding tribute, which tropes the master in a figure of distinctly female power: "Why have I alluded to this man? . . . because I think no commentator on his writings has yet found . . . the terms that rightly characterize his talent. . . . His wit is bright, his humour attractive, but both bear the same relation to his serious genius that the mere lambent sheet-lightning playing under the edge of the summer-cloud does to the electric death-spark hid in its womb" (36).

If Brontë seems to borrow Thackeray's authority for her own expression of righteous indignation, such authorization is hardly needed, for demonstrations of her prophetic ethos entirely surround reference to this master. In the middle paragraphs, where she defends *Jane Eyre* from attacks on its impious "tendency," she sharply "remind[s]" her critics of "certain simple truths" and hammers home "certain obvious distinctions" (35) in a series of unqualified assertions and binary oppositions in the familiar pulpit manner of the Victorian sage. In this discourse, Brontë situates herself as an "obscure [literary] aspirant" firmly within the male sage tradition, in which the marginal critic typically unveils the real spiritual marginality of his readers from his own location at the center of Reality, while his command of words sets right their "warped system of things."[29] What makes this tactic especially shocking in a Victorian woman's hands is the semantic aggressiveness with which Brontë "seize[s] control" of her culture's religious discourse.[30] She then piles up bodies in the last paragraphs (with allusions to "charnal relics," "bloody death," and a "fatal Ramoth-Gilead") before unleashing the final "death-spark" in the womb (36). These three hubristic rhetorical climaxes completely overturn the threefold avowal of authorial humility with which she had begun. Framed by these antithetically parallel expressions of ethos, the preface reveals its fundamental structure of absolute prophetic reversal.

Fired by an evangelical zeal to use her God-given talents well, Brontë confessed it "a part of my religion to defend this gift [of imagination] and to profit by its possession."[31] The extreme religious language she employs to defend *Jane Eyre* would seem to be an appropriate mode, intensified by justifiable anger, in which to launch a defense of God's gifts and uncompromised truthtelling even if it was offensive. The all-but-explicit claim of divine authority in this preface did offend: as the *Christian Remembrancer* reviewer objected, "our authoress is Micaiah, and her generation Ahab; and the Ramoth Gilead, which is to be the reward of disregarding her denunciations, is looked forward to with at least as much of unction as of sorrow."[32] While Brontë insisted that Thackeray did not "delight to exterminate,"[33] a dubious revenge motive does infuse her sermon, where "doubters" of her book become unbelievers in the Book—persecutors of

Christian writers who do not know the difference between "whitewashed walls" and "clean shrines" (35–36), as Jesus did, because they do not know Him. As she widens this reply to "the timorous or carping few" (35) into judgment on her generation, she commands Jahweh's punitive powers to damn them all with unseemly delight, revelling in the conquering power of her own words. In this preface, what Brontë's zeal for truth and justice tellingly produces is a masculinist polemics of prophecy, in which militant biblical rhetoric authorizes the notion that absolute male power can express the divine will.[34] Enlisting *these* powers in *Jane Eyre*'s defense, she reauthorizes the male dominance that the novel more creatively resists.

Brontë's attempt to master this kind of male prophecy also manifests a broader problem in some Victorian male sage writing: the evasion of personal feeling by assuming a stylized public voice in order to address the largest questions of the age. The contemporary sages whom Brontë imitates incur considerable psychological cost whenever their striving to "overcome the personal" becomes self-repressive and drives them toward "views of life either drearily or vindictively stoical, or imperialistic and nakedly seeking dominance."[35] The Victorian female prophet might justify her "speaking for Another" as a form of self-renunciation appropriate to her sex. But as Brontë's "temper rises to the transcendental pitch," in the words of the *Christian Remembrancer*,[36] she conflates personal indignation with divine anger. In so doing she acts the "total stranger" (as she finally signs herself, 36) to the nuanced truths of the intimate "autobiography" that she has so recently written: a story that establishes, not evades, the self as Jane learns deftly to master male texts and interpretations with self-respect and womanly discernment.

A more subtle female prophet than the preacher of the preface, Jane is at her most skillful in the rhetorical climax of her autobiography. In its closing paragraphs, Jane invokes the favorite texts of her namesake St. John Rivers in order to show, as Carolyn Williams argues, how successfully she has generated her vocation in life against both the lofty language of his missionary calling, which would subordinate women to the male cleric's vocation; and against the coercive language of his calling her to Christian service, a rhetoric of male desire for dominance disguised as God's will which she has managed narrowly to resist.[37] In this overtly valedictory ending, Jane alludes to a future reward for this warrior-priest (477); but through the precise wording and placement of her religious allusions, she covertly looks backward at her own text, encoding her recollections of how this "exacting" and "ambitious" man (477), "inexorable as death" (391), had intimidated her with hellfire, while failing to understand God's mercy and lacking Christ's peace in himself (378).[38] St. John had cast the call for Jane's conversion into Revelation's patrilineal language of promise: "He that overcometh shall inherit all things; and I will be his God, and he shall be My son" (442; cf. Rev. 21:7). Using St. John's own epistolary texts to bear witness against him, and taking command of his discourse in order to right his wrong order of things, Jane implies that this self-appointed son and heir, this "high master-spirit," is unlikely to "inherit all things" from a God he casts to the end in his own image (477). Dutifully following the biblical custom that the woman who would prophesy must be covered, Jane veils herself in pious language as she unveils this male species of idolatry and self-delusion. Asserting her superior spiritual discernment as she closes her own revelations, she deftly writes St. John's creed of male mediation and the privilege of apocalyptic marriage out of her book of life.[39] Thus, in a higher spirit of mastery, Jane perfects the revenge that Brontë in the preface more nakedly desires. And Jane does so with greater success, for she incorporates into her deceptive praise of St. John a critique of the masculinist prophet's coerciveness that Brontë can forget.

Longstanding readings of this conclusion as nonironic have responded to ambiguities surely also present here, deriving from Brontë's confessed ambivalence toward pious language and the problematic attraction she long felt for St. John the Seer.[40] Yet it is toward this more skeptical interpretation of its ending that the whole of *Jane Eyre* moves: Jane progresses from victimage by men's books and by prooftexts drawn from "the best book in the world" to her own use of it against the official forces that would thwart the formation of the female self.[41] In one such episode, Jane portrays her child-self dwelling on the inscription over the door of Lowood Institution: "Let your light so shine before men that they may see your good works, and glorify your Father which is in Heaven" (81). In the Anglican liturgy, Matthew 5:16 is read after the sermon and during the collection of alms for the poor. Defamiliarized in its novelistic context, this passage becomes Jane's own sermon, as eloquent in its irony at the expense of Lowood's benefactors as in its defense of the orphan poor. As little Jane puzzles to connect this sentence, with its prominent male terminology, to the meaning of the hard world "institution," and as she tries to follow the religious logic of these inspiring words inscribing this unhappy place, she is distracted by Helen Burns's cough behind her. This concrete answer to her riddle fitly comes from the most dutiful of Bible readers, whose Scripture helps her to pass time and to pass away with calm courage and without inconvenient complaint. The founders of this school for female submission have converted the spirit of Jesus' words into the letter of charitable works. Refusing this interpretation, Jane converts the Matthew gospel text into a prophetic word of warning and instruction that preserves its compassionate content. Unlike Helen's own "pulpit eloquence," Jane's word is this-worldly and sweeping.[42] Without sermonic flourishes, and embedding her message in lived experience, she exposes the conjunction of male power, a privileged social class, and a Logos emptied of compassion to produce the institutions of patriarchy which oppress "others"—women and children here—to death.

This passage from the novel is a long way from the preaching of the preface, although both are fuelled by Brontë's personal indignation at injustice. Through the writing of *Jane Eyre*, Brontë developed an alternative form of prophetic discourse that was more effective for her purposes than imitations of the masculine sermonic—a form capacious enough to include the righteous outburst and such tactics of the Victorian polemical sage as the satirical grotesque.[43] If establishing ethos is the preeminent rhetorical purpose of male sage writing, which persuades through an experiential discourse, the challenge for the Victorian Cassandra is to establish public credibility for the voice of female experience publicly "known" primarily as innocence and silence.[44] Brontë answered this challenge by inventing a gendered form of sage writing that was more acceptable for a woman in the literary marketplace than the polemical essay, and that constituted its own defense of the female voice. This new genre, the sage narrative, incorporates broad criticism of patriarchal culture within the heroine's own extended story of her quest for her calling.

As a cultural junction of private and public voices, the Victorian novel offered a dialogical form, narrative time, and social space in which the female prophet, joining spheres her culture tried to separate, could explore the gender dynamics of the tension between these voices for women. The prophetic novelist also could exploit the novel's history of hybridization and, like the biblical prophets, use "all manner of forms in which to clothe

[her] message."[45] Among available forms, Brontë's female sage narratives most prominently unite Puritan spiritual autobiography, which tells of the individual's response to God's call, with Romantic writing about the development of self and the unfolding of the artist's consciousness: a generic merger Barry V. Qualls has traced in Brontë's work from *Sartor Resartus*.[46] But Brontë reinflects the conventions of these genres within the structure of a new kind of female narrative that merges the social and the romantic quest. In this story the heroine seeks to define a life-vocation that integrates critical observation of her culture with personal fulfillment in work and in love. For such a heroine, the call comes and is answered, as in Carlyle, "here or Nowhere," but the route of her journey lies through a Mammon-worshipping patriarchy whose practices and ideological self-justifications she judges, like the biblical prophets, for betraying fundamental religious and moral values. The hybrid result is an intimate but more than personal novel of education that also educates the reading public on contemporary issues. Among the topics brought into play in Brontë's novels through plot, characterization, and allusion are female education and work, the politics of the marriage market as well as the literary marketplace, class privilege, commercial materialism, industrial conflict, war and revolution, racial ideology, British mercantilism and colonialism, religious hypocrisy, ecclesiastical politics, sectarianism, Papal aggression, biblical interpretation, religious doubt and theodicy. Dispersed among a number of these areas is an issue fundamental to the enterprise, the delegitimation of the woman's public voice. Challenging conventional constraints, the plot of Brontë's fictive autobiographies that is everywhere implied (sometimes alluded to self-consciously) is the genesis of female authorship and of the narrator's newly forth-speaking word.

While *Jane Eyre* is not a full-fledged sage narrative in this sense, like *Villette*, Jane's passion united with her "vocation" for making "inquiries" (145) unquestionably transgress the boundaries of what Brontë feared was a "mere domestic novel."[47] In *Jane Eyre* she transforms some of her debts to the life-writing of *Sartor Resartus* and to Carlyle's "this-worldly ethic" of Natural Supernaturalism by recontextualizing the master's paradigm as the story of a woman's "writing from the margins and coming into speech."[48] Defying Carlyle's dismissal of the novel and of female testimony as vehicles of truth, *Jane Eyre*'s paradigmatic plot requires novelistic scope to work out the heroine's repeated "nays" to the Juggernaut of the male social universe—to apologists for patriarchy who challenge her to articu-late self-definition—before any heartfelt "yea" can be pronounced. Through these maneuvers of fictive autobiography, by which plot creates ethos and "the personal" produces an educative cultural text, the narrator shows how she became the whole person her creator believed one must be in order to claim authority as a spokesperson for others: Jane Eyre at least as a part-time prophet in the "Quaker dress" of the dissenter and a canny critic of male prophecy.

In so defamiliarizing the Victorian sage paradigm, Brontë could make the religious unorthodoxy of its wisdom peculiarly offensive, for reviewers' rebukes of her "coarseness" were aimed at her attitudes toward religion as well as toward sexuality and gender.[49] For example, Jane gives the Chris-tian construct of the valiant woman perfected by suffering an ironic read-ing by calling the Thornfield schoolroom a "very pleasant refuge in time of trouble" (195) before rejecting this "sanctum" (both the room and the sacred convention) as no "asylum" for her (196). This reading insists that the pious model of womanly (and "plebeian") resignation, rather than Jane's unorthodox biblical allusion, is "blasphemy"—against nature, the locus of Jane's supernatural (204). Typically, such sagelike Brontëan expo-sures of empty formula do not call readers to return to "the truth" so much as immerse them in new facts about women's experience and new "oracles of nature," for which both the old religious language and revi-sionary male sage discourse are inadequate media of understanding.

It is tempting to speculate that one clue to Brontë's leap forward into gendered prophetic writing is to be found in the reworking of Revelation that gives *Jane Eyre* its masterful writerly ending, for this first of Jane's favorite Bible books (65) had long been one of Brontë's most important authorizing texts.[50] Her earlier imitations of male apocalyptic writing are typified by the 1832 poem "St. John in the Island of Patmos," in which the speaker identifies in a gender-neutral way with the prophet and draws comfort from his transcendence of exile through his grand-scale visions of holy warfare and beatitude.[51] By 1847, with Jane as narrator, Brontë is reading Revelation through the lens of gender, which shows her a different St. John, an island of narcissism and a fatal model women must resist if they value their lives in this world. Reading, marking, learning, inwardly digesting, and retelling this familiar text, she has discovered the Book of

Revelation within, not as the refuge of dreams but as an internally persuasive word giving birth to a new consciousness and unforeseen possibilities of reinterpretation (which will emerge most boldly in the apocalyptic passages of *Villette*). This generating biblical text becomes regenerative for Brontë as an adult author and prophet when it is construed through a female hermeneutic of skepticism and faithful resistance.

In a discussion of how Jane Eyre presents her development out of orphanhood, Carolyn Williams has described the psychodynamics of "internalization and differentiation" that lie behind such processes of reconstrual. Jane as autobiographer "produces figurative representations of the primary, gendered others from whom the self derives and in relation to whom the self defines itself," introducing them *in order that* they may in some sense be contradicted, so that the narrating 'I' can distinguish herself from them" and discover who she is.[52] For Brontë biblical texts also serve as fixed points from which she and her narrating protagonists swerve in order to define their difference. *Jane Eyre,* for example, employs a pattern of biblical allusions to Genesis-Exodus that revises hereditary subordinationist and liberationist texts to produce a new mythos of male-female relationships that also materializes the (redefined) Promised Land the heroine sights. In passages of *Shirley* and *Villette*, deviating from conventional readings of sacred texts courts heresy, while in the ending of *Jane Eyre* and elsewhere such deviations can serve Brontë's moral aesthetic, just as ironic twists on revered religious formulas empower the rhetoric of the biblical prophets. In her satiric revisions, typically Brontë preserves the binarism of prophetic and apocalyptic discourse, often specifying the opposing term with scriptural types—St. John Rivers as an evangelical antichrist, Reverend Brocklehurst as a Pharisee, John Graham Bretton as an Old Testament patriarch. For these and other reasons, Brontë cannot afford to reject the sacred canon, wrestle exclusively with its discourse, or write *Jane Eyre*'s closure as though it were the unmediated Word.

A more radical counter-patriarchal consciousness develops as *Villette*'s heroine tries to read women's lives through Scripture texts. The hermeneutic process reverses: as Lucy Snowe learns, when seen through the interpreting medium of female experience, this Word of Another must be reread or swerved from, the spirit of its roles altered or defied. In an audacious expansion of Jane's textual mastery, Lucy writes a complete woman's bible (following a general sequence of allusions from Genesis to Revelation) from the standpoint of the critical feminine as an outlaw position in culture. The story of her journey through patriarchy is simultaneously a combat narrative of encounters with male religious texts, struggles that take place (far more than in *Jane Eyre*) on the plane of figure and allusion. Notably, it is through such repeated writerly acts of resistance that Lucy regenerates here prophetic vocation and produces its "heretic" logos (146). Not surprisingly, some of these resistant acts skeptically revisit themes from Brontë's Brussels *devoirs*. An internal dialogue in volume 2 serves as a prophetic sign of how the meaning of the Bible's patriarchal paradigm can leak away as a woman's "way of sorrows" bleeds into Lucy's discourse: "My mind . . . made for itself some imperious rules, prohibiting under deadly penalties all weak retrospect of happiness past; commanding a patient journeying through the wilderness of the present, enjoining a reliance on faith—a watching of the cloud and pillar which subdue while they guide, and awe while they illumine—hushing the impulse to fond idolatry, checking the longing outlook for a far-off promised land whose rivers are, perhaps, never to be reached save in dying dreams, whose sweet pastures are to be viewed but from the desolate and sepulchral summit of a Nebo" (209). If Lucy momentarily has found on this dreary summit woman's place, she soon rallies to picture the dramatic overthrow of female types by a new warrior-prophet and visionary who displaces the dying dreamer on Nebo. The actress Lucy names Vashti confronts conventional womanhood with "the magian power or prophet-virtue gifting that slight rod of Moses [which] could, at one waft, release and re-mingle a sea spell-parted, whelming the heavy host with the down-rush of overthrown sea ramparts" (235). If to Victorian eyes this fiery actress is "a spirit out of Tophet," she provokes Lucy's prophecy of a female messiah: "may not an equal efflux of sacred essence descend one day from above?" (235), she asks. Decades hence the *Woman's Bible* commentators would embrace Vashti, the Persian queen in the Book of Esther who defied the king's commands, as a Moses-like ancestress of their work to release women from patriarchal bondage. If Brontë's "Vashti" inspires Lucy Snowe's antipatriarchal prophecy, however, the *kairos* of this liberating female figure has not yet arrived in young Lucy's story, nor even quite yet in the adult narrator's *récit*. The storyteller's allusive crossdressing of the great prophet is notably strained, obscuring the bold comparison of Vashti to Moses in a crabbed figure; and in the plot this paradigm of liberation goes up in actual smoke. Its conflagration remains in the text as a cautionary prophetic sign of Lucy's fear even of gazing too long on her "sight," for she has learned that for one woman alone to revolt against the fathers' story is to court exile and martyrdom.

Brontë's female sage novel is a latter-day expansion of the biblical call narrative, usually a brief account told to justify the prophet's unprecedented opposition to the majority's practices and institutions. In the Book of Jeremiah such a narrative expansion takes place as the suffering prophet's story becomes everyone's in the last days before the destruction of Jerusalem and the Babylonian exile. Despite Jeremiah's conventional misogynist language, the distinctive, inwardly persuasive note of the "Weeping Prophet" comes from his identification with women's suffering—especially with his ancestress Rachel, the paradigmatic Mother in Israel who "refused to be comforted" for her lost children (Jer. 31:15; cf. *Villette* 398). Giving a fuller biographical picture than usual of a new type of prophet, the scribe Baruch shows how Jeremiah's whole life, which summed up the desolation of Judah, became his prophecy—an embodied sign for the nation, whose desperate condition could be seen "through the medium of the prophet's soul and its suffering."[53] With Jeremiah's life as sign (to Christian readers, a type of Christ), Israel discovered that "there was more to being a prophet than mere speaking."[54]

Brontë's writing underwent a profound transformation when she moved beyond the playfully verbal prophetic mode of the juvenilia and creative imitations of male discourse in the *devoirs*, to find her calling as a woman in Jeremiah's dark vale. *Villette* is the novel that most fully witnesses to this transformation—and to the difference between "mere speaking" and living the prophecy. As an expanded narrative of vocation, *Villette* fills the Jeremiah model with new, problematic content that preserves the notion of the suffering prophet as public sign. Brontë conveys her message about patriarchal culture's fallen condition by presenting the female *via dolorosa* as an instructive paradigm through the voice of Lucy Snowe, a heretic prophet whose sufferings at once embody, provoke, and inhibit her testimony—and whose very inhibitions contribute to her public signification of "woman's condition." Despite concealments and hesitations, Lucy can construct her life story as a prophetic sign because she is both an undercover prophet in her world and her own scribe. In her vocational plot, she develops the analytical vision to link her own story with those of Paulina, Miss Marchmont, Madame Beck, and other female figures she includes or calls to mind through allusion. Beginning her narrative by telling several of these "other" stories is a veiled early sign of the public vocation the adult Lucy has found, and it establishes the wider political context in which her own *via dolorosa* is to be read. The indirect style in which she has learned to deliver subversive truths also testifies to the powerful unseen presence of patriarchal culture deforming and decentering female speech. With Lucy's heretic narrative, Brontë produced the most extravagant example of the "symbolical grotesque" in all Victorian sage writing.[55]

Lucy's narrative records her gradual awakening to a more conscious, articulate, and actively courageous life. But as a reluctant prophet who resists living and telling her own story, she witnesses throughout to the need for relief from the new suffering of her raised consciousness. One suspect form this consolation takes is her periodic ascent to the pulpit as the sermonic prophet. At such moments, her mode abruptly shifts from the fluid experiential medium of the narrator's speech—which induces the reader to enter the fiction of interarticulated, contesting social voices that constitute "Lucy Snowe"—to the sermon that abandons the nuanced self, objectifies its audience, and disguises its subject. In the peculiar suspended time of these didactic discourses, the preacher aspires to "stan[d] above the social and historical flux" of female narrative, abandoning her role as a novelistic "exegete of the real."[56] But in these passages the speaker's "very refusal to enter into dialogue is itself both dialogic and dialogizing."[57] As with Jane Eyre's prophetic editorial leader on women's rights followed by Bertha Mason's laugh (141), these interpolated sermons are at once formed "in an atmosphere of the already spoken" (or the muted) *and* "determined by that which has not yet been said but which is needed and in fact anticipated by the answering word," determined by forces present in the culturally located narrative that continues when the sermon is done.[58] Lucy's jeremiad against Rome in Chapter 36, for example—which seems necessary, among other things, to exorcise Roman Catholicism as an obstacle in the romance plot—is invaded by personal issues of love and vocation that precede and follow it. This intratextual dialogue (of the novel with itself) is complicated by the intertextual dialogue Brontë's writing engages at this point—with, at the least, Carlyle and John Henry Newman, whose influential lectures on the "Certain Difficulties Felt by Anglicans" she attended in 1850. The gender contradictions evident in the sermonic Lucy's language register not only her identity confusions but also the female author's unease with her unlawful occupation of a Victorian pulpit, one Carlyle too had mounted in 1850 in his *Latter-Day Pamphlet* "Jesuitism." Just as the staunchly Protestant Brontë's diatribes suggest her guilty fascination with Rome, so Lucy's sermonic voice draws attention, in spite of itself, to the woman who is speaking from under the preaching-prophet's cloak. To the skeptical reader who asks, "Who is speaking?" Lucy's discourse further discloses the public meaning of her rhetoric for the problem of female authority and the need for this male disguise. Ironically, for the reader who experiences these stylistic jolts and contradictions in the text, the separation of sermonic from narrative discourse is itself a sign of the secret alliances between the preacher's personal project and his/her public voice.

Raising issues of preacherly ethos, such passages implicitly call into question the claims of the Victorian sage to objective truth and truth for all: does he speak for "Another" and for others, or merely for a dimension of "the personal" (like St. John Rivers) that he does not recognize? At the same time, in their specified contexts of the woman's *via dolorosa*, Lucy's sermons can also be disturbing revelations of what the Victorian spiritual crisis means for the feminine sensibility that registers fluid interconnections between the subjective and the cultural, while patriarchal thinking and sage writing would insist on their difference. Lucy interrogates a host of religious and philosophic types in the Great Tradition whom she imagines would lecture her roundly—the "religious reader," the "moralist," the "stern sage," the "stoic," the "cynic," and the "epicure"—but none of them is "circumstanced like me" (140–141). Not one answers her needs amid the uncertainties of this life, which extend well beyond the sex-gender system but for Lucy are experienced inescapably within it. For this marginal woman the leading philosophico-religious questions, which she frames differently from her fellow sages, cannot be separated from the social politics of her condition.[59] "What was I doing here alone in great London? What should I do on the morrow? What prospects had I in life? What friends had I on earth?" she asks, before reaching the standard questions of spiritual autobiography: "Whence did I come? Whither should I go? What should I do?" (39). With experience rather than revelation as Lucy's primary measure of truth in her quest, the critical *vie d'une femme* she writes roots up more than it can build or plant in this Actual.

In a sense she did not intend, Virginia Woolf was right that Charlotte Brontë is not read "for a philosophic view of life"—nor for any alternative mythos such as Carlyle and Stanton called for near the beginning and the end of the period.[60] For Brontë can also write as a reluctant antisage, signifying not only that received formulas are empty but also that the search for definitive wisdom may be a delusive quest, morally presumptuous, and injurious to the psyche. Written from the viewpoint of the skeptical feminine, *Villette*'s exegesis of the real conveys, with considerable subtlety, why the emancipation of the female voice *and* the Victorian prophet's objects of desire are "not yet." With more nuanced understanding than is found in some writings of her male sage contemporaries, Brontë sees and foresees the multidimensionality of her culture's crisis—its interlocking problems of gender, money and class conflict, religion, hermeneutics, epistemology, ideology, social formation, and more—as these bear upon the feminine soul.[61] Indeed, her last and most densely written novel documents the impossibility of the wholesale spiritual renovation for which her contemporaries called, so long as patriarchy continued to flourish at home and abroad. Of this impossibility, the woman's *via dolorosa* is Brontë's prophetic sign.

Christina Rossetti and
the Sage Discourse of
Feminist High Anglicanism

ANTONY H. HARRISON

[W]hile knowledge runs apace, ignorance keeps ahead of knowledge:
and all which the deepest students know proves to themselves, yet
more convincingly than to others, that much more exists which still
they know not. As saints in relation to spiritual wisdom, so sages in
relation to intellectual wisdom, eating they yet hunger and drinking
they yet thirst.

It may never indeed in this world be [God's] pleasure to grant us
previsions of seers and forecastings of prophets: but He will assuredly vouchsafe us so much foresight and illumination as should suf-
fice to keep us on the watch with loins girded and lamps burning; not
with hearts meanwhile failing us.

——Christina Rossetti, *Seek and Find*

Three months before she died of cancer, Christina Rossetti wrote to her
close friend Frederick Shields in order to bid "good-bye for this life" and
request his "prayers for a poor sinful woman who has dared to speak to
others and is herself what God knows her to be."[1] Ironically, by the date
of this letter (5 September 1894) Rossetti had a reputation in both England

and America as a saintly, reclusive writer of highly wrought and effective poems (both secular and devotional) as well as six widely read books of religious commentary. In all of these works she "dared to speak to others" in a characteristically humble, but nonetheless firmly sagacious, indeed often prophetic, voice. Commentators toward the end of the century commonly acknowledge the power of Rossetti's work which for them is inseparable from her religious piety. "She is an inspired prophetess or priestess," according to one reviewer.[2] For another, she is a "poet and saint" who "lived a life of sacrifice . . . [and] unreluctantly endured the pains of her spirituality."[3] One eulogy acknowledges that "her language was always that of Christian assurance and of simple . . . faith in her Saviour . . . . [H]er life was one of transcendent humility."[4] After the turn of the century, we are told that Rossetti "needed not to pray, for her life was an unbroken communion with God."[5]

Rossetti's reputation as a devout "prophetess" and saintly woman, along with consistently strong reviews of her work (especially her devotional poems and prose), attracted a remarkable audience, as other commentators late in her career indicate. A long essay in *Harper's* for May 1888 insists that "Christina Rossetti's deeply spiritual poems are known even more widely than those of her more famous brother."[6] Two years earlier William Sharp had acknowledged that "the youngest of the Rossetti family has, as a poet, a much wider reputation and a much larger circle of readers than even her brother Gabriel, for in England, and much more markedly in America, the name of Christina Rossetti is known intimately where perhaps that of the author of the *House of Life* is but a name and nothing more."[7] Reviewing Mackenzie Bell's biography of Rossetti in 1898, a writer for *The Nation* noted that her income rapidly increased during the last years of her life "less because of a growing appreciation of her poetry than because of her manuals of piety" which "secured her an extensive following."[8] And a writer for *The Dial* remarked that Rossetti's "devotional books . . . have both found and deserved a large and appreciative audience."[9] Such observations appear to confirm a widespread agreement among the Victorian reading public that "[T]here is no higher form [of Christianity] than that of a highly educated, devout English woman."[10]

As these commentaries also suggest, Rossetti's work is most often patently didactic. In that respect it resembles the sage discourse of Carlyle, Ruskin, and even Arnold at times, but the language she speaks, the stances she most often adopts, and her intended audience are uniquely "feminine" (according to Victorian stereotypes) and otherworldly. These latter traits afford Rossetti a perspective on the values and behavior of her contemporaries that is unavailable to male writers of the era and enable her to launch a quietly comprehensive attack on the entire network of patriarchal values which even the most stringent social critics of her day normally accept without question. Surprisingly, and it may seem, paradoxically, Rossetti is able to accomplish this goal by positioning herself as a devout adherent of High Anglican religious doctrine and, ostensibly, as an advocate of the more widespread Victorian ideology of "woman's sphere." By embracing religious values with a uniquely radical fervor, however, Rossetti's work undercuts the domestic ideology of middle and upper-class Victorians, and functions to subvert both the patriarchal values that governed Victorian England and their extension in industrial capitalism.

Historically, criticism of Rossetti has properly emphasized her renunciatory mindset. *Vanitas mundi* is her most frequent theme, and no work better illustrates her employment of it than the sonnet "The World" (1854):

> By day she wooes me, soft, exceeding fair:
>   But all night as the moon so changeth she;
>   Loathsome and foul with hideous leprosy
> And subtle serpents gliding in her hair.
> By day she wooes me to the outer air,
>   Ripe fruits, sweet flowers, and full satiety:
>   But thro' the night, a beast she grins at me,
> A very monster void of love and prayer.
> By day she stands a lie; by night she stands
>   In all the naked horror of the truth
> With pushing horns and clawed and clutching hands.
> Is this a friend indeed; that I should sell
>   My soul to her, give her my life and youth,
> Till my feet, cloven too, take hold on hell?[11]

Rossetti's use of image patterns from religious and classical sources here is striking, as is her craftsmanship. But the fact that Rossetti personifies as a duplicitous woman the world she repudiates is of even greater interest because her procedure in this poem is typical of her poetry as well as of her prose works. Rossetti appropriates traditional antifeminist (that is, Medusan) iconography in order to highlight its patriarchal origins by conflating the image of the "foul" seductress with her male counterpart from Christian tradition, Satan. The speaker employs these representational traditions of "the world" not only to expose the materialism, hedonism, and false amatory ideologies that they serve, but also to renounce the degraded constructions of woman's nature and her accepted roles that these ideologies depend upon and perpetuate. Clearly, the wholly fallen, "loathsome and foul," world that is disparaged includes the stereotypes that have been associated with duplicity and corruption ever since the myths of Medusa and Eve were generated within patriarchal cultures.

Much of Rossetti's poetry and, more significantly, all of her devotional writings are designed for a female audience and exploit an array of assumptions about women's social and moral roles that were fundamental to the Victorian ideology of the "woman's sphere." This domestic ideology insisted that a middle-class woman, as a leisured Angel in the House, occupy herself by ministering to the moral and spiritual needs of her husband and children while undertaking tasks (embroidering, arranging flowers, playing music) that were largely ornamental. Retaining her spiritual purity by transcending, or at least remaining oblivious to, all worldly—that is economic, political, or in any sense utilitarian—concerns was essential to the Victorian woman's success as a spiritual minister. Joan Burstyn has explained usefully a rationale for the inculcation of this stereotype and the assumptions on which it was based:

> [According] to this ideal, women played a crucial part in providing stability for men who were torn by doubts and faced by insoluble problems. Few people were prepared to confront social, economic and intellectual changes in society by changing their own terms of thought, which was what the psychological crisis of the age called for; most Victorians turned, instead, to an intensification of personal relationships and an exaggerated adherence to domestic virtues. Religious writers, in their exaggeration of domestic virtues, described women as saviours of society. Men might be assailed by religious scepticism, but women never.[12]

Rossetti's work consistently engages this ideology in its clear connections with the material seductions of the world, and insists, in effect, that both be renounced. In the work of less radical writers, commentaries like Rossetti's would appear merely to reinforce middle-class Victorian ideals of the woman's sphere. But, as I will demonstrate, the stance that she takes regarding worldly renunciation is far more militant than that of most of her contemporaries, and ultimately undercuts the material assumptions upon which the stereotypical roles of middle-class women were based.

One aim of the domestic ideology in Victorian England was to compensate for the almost complete usurpation by men of economic activities (such as spinning, sewing, and other domestic labors) previously undertaken by women of all classes. These activities had provided women with social status and a degree of economic independence unavailable to them in Victorian England. Judith Lowder Newton has examined how "the ideology of woman's sphere . . . served the interests of industrial capitalism by insuring the continuing domination of middle-class women by middle-class men and, through its mitigation of the harshness of economic transition, by insuring the continuing domination of male bourgeoisie in relation to working-class men and women as a whole." The domestic ideology assured women "that they *did* have work, power, and status" in the world after all.[13] Through her insistent advocacy of worldly renunciation, Rossetti implicitly repudiates the fundamental economic and political values of industrial capitalism and thus subverts the ideology of the "woman's sphere" which operated in the service of those values.

Rossetti's most fervent monitions are associated, in the predictably orthodox manner of "The World," with the figure of Satan. In *Time Flies* (1885), for instance, she decries the fact that, "over and over again we are influenced and constrained by the hollow momentary world we behold . . . while utterly obtuse as regards the substantial eternal world no less present around us though disregarded."[14] At one point, she compares this "hollow momentary world" to a funnel-shaped spider's web: "it exhibits beauty, ingenuity, intricacy. Imagine it in the early morning jewelled with dewdrops, and each of these at sunny moments a spark of light or a section of rainbow. Woven, too, as no man could weave it, fine and flexible, frail and tenacious. Yet are its beauties of brilliancy and colour no real part of it. The dew evaporates, the tints and sparkle vanish, the tenacity remains, and at the bottom of all lurks a spider" (82) . The spider is, of course, Satan who, according to Rossetti's theological literalism, owns this world: "it must be perilously difficult to set up one's tent amid Satan's own surroundings and continue in no way the worse for that neighborhood. The world and the flesh flaunt themselves in very uncompromising forms in the devil's own territory. And all the power and the glory of them set in array before a man whose work forces him to face and sift them day and night, may well make such an one tremble" (267). In the event,

> Earth is half spent and rotting at the core,
> Here hollow death's-heads mock us with a grin,
> Here heartiest laughter leaves us tired and sore.
> Men heap up pleasures and enlarge desire,
> Outlive desire, and famished evermore
> Consume themselves within the undying fire. (116)

In order to assist readers in avoiding such a fate, Rossetti typically presents them with parables. In the approximately two thousand pages of devotional commentary she published between 1874 and 1892, Rossetti instructively discusses an extraordinary range of topics from the perspective of a fervent adherent of the High Anglican devotionalist doctrine.[15] These include such matters as what and how to read; the probability of Christian election; the possibilities for self-perfection through the imitation of Christ; prospects for immortality; varieties of love; the necessity of patience, obedience, and humility; the maintenance of moral purity, or the controversy over virginity; the need for empathy and charity; the problems of knowing truth in a fallen world; the achievement of harmony with the divine will; the necessity of faith; the inevitability of suffering; the multitude of temptations in the world (especially the problem of vanity); and the constitution of true happiness. Rossetti usually approaches such issues through an analysis of religious texts, the lives of saints, or personal experiences rendered figuratively. Because Rossetti clearly anticipated a female audience for her devotional works, the treatment of all these subjects bears ultimately on her perception of the prescribed roles for Victorian women.

Early in *Seek and Find* (1879) Rossetti makes explicit her intent to address a variety of issues derived from the Benedicte primarily in connection with "the feminine lot."[16] Here, as elsewhere throughout her devotional prose, Rossetti insists upon the spiritual superiority of women by compar-

ing expectations of their behavior with the example of Christ. More com-
plexly, however, she is able to reconcile herself to women's subordination
to men in worldly affairs only by looking forward to an eventual equality
of the sexes in heaven.

> In many points the feminine lot copies very closely the voluntarily
> assumed position of our Lord and Pattern. Woman must obey: and
> Christ "learned obedience" (Gen. 3. 16; Heb. 5. 8). She must be
> fruitful, but in sorrow: and He, symbolised by a corn of wheat, had
> not brought forth much fruit except He had died (Gen. 3. 16; St.
> John 12. 24). She by natural constitution is adapted not to assert
> herself, but to be subordinate: and He came not to be ministered
> unto but to minister; He was among His own "as he that serveth" (1
> St. Peter 3. 7; 1 Tim. 2. 2, 12; St. Mark 10. 45; St. Luke 22. 27). Her
> office is to be man's helpmeet: and concerning Christ God saith, "I
> have laid help upon One that is mighty" (Gen. 2. 18, 21, 22; Ps. 89.
> 19). And well may she glory, inasmuch as one of the tenderest of
> divine promises takes (so to say) the feminine form: "As one whom
> his mother comforteth, so will I comfort you" (Is. 66. 13)
> In the case of the twofold Law of Love, we are taught to call one
> Commandment "first and great," yet to esteem the second as "like
> unto it" (St. Matt. 22. 37–39). The man is the head of the woman,
> the woman the glory of the man (1 Cor. 11. 3, 7). . . . But if our
> [pride] will after all not be stayed, or at any rate not be allayed (for
> stayed [it] must be) by the limit of God's ordinance governing our
> sex, one final consolation yet remains to careful and troubled hearts:
> in Christ there is neither male nor female, for we are all one (Gal. 3.
> 28). (30–32)

Clearly Rossetti herself has a "careful and troubled" heart when considering these vexed matters. I quote this lengthy passage in full because its
rhetorical strategies mark a conflict within the patriarchal religious doctrine to which Rossetti subscribes. Repeatedly in her poetry, her prose
works, and her letters, she wrestles with the glaring contradiction between
her culture's insistence upon the inferior social status of women and their
spiritual exaltation. She obediently and humbly claims to accept the illogic
of this contradiction. But, as in this passage, her ultimate subordination of

power relations in this world to expectations for the afterlife subverts the domestic ideology that her exegetical discourse would appear to serve. The final purpose of her prose works is to insure that women, deemed "last" in the affairs of this world, will be "first" in heaven, and thereby to inspire each of her female readers to give "all diligence to make her own personal calling and election sure" (224). Rossetti's general procedure is to translate "symbols, parables, analogies, inferences" into "words of the wise which are as goads" (223). Her aim is that, as a result of such efforts as her own, "we" women "shall demean ourselves charitably, decorously according to our station; we shall reflect honour on those from whom we derive honour; out of the abundance of our heart our mouth will speak wisdom; kindness will govern our tongue, and justice our enactments;—thus shall it be with us even now, and much more in the supreme day of rising up, the Day of Resurrection" (223).

This passage and many of her poems—from "Goblin Market," "A Triad," and "Maude Clare" to "The Lowest Room," "The Prince's Progress," and "Monna Innominata"—adapt the discourse of gender-marked power struggles to the language and formulae of religious doctrine. That is, within the conventional language of such passages that clearly accepts the patriarchally ordained position of women, a deliberate subtext of resistance to cultural determinations operates. Such a strategy appears again in *Time Flies* in the entry for March 23: "In common parlance Strong and Weak are merely relative terms: thus the 'strong' of one sentence will be the 'weak' of another. We behold the strong appointed to help the weak: Angels who 'excel in strength,' men. And equally the weak the strong: woman 'the weaker vessel,' man. This, though it should not inflate any, may fairly buoy us all up" (57). Ultimately, Rossetti believed in the potential of all women to be "elect," as the title of her volume published in 1881, *Called to Be Saints*, indicates. In *The Face of the Deep* (1892) she explains, "now the saints are they who know not their names, however they name each other. Thus *Patience* will not discern herself, but will identify a neighbour as *Charity*, who in turn will recognize not herself, but mild Patience; and they both shall know some fellow Christian, as *Hope* or *Prudence* or *Faith*; and every one of these shall be sure of the others, only not of herself." [17]

Very often in Rossetti's work, as in the passages I have cited, the rhetoric of orthodoxy and acquiescence gradually becomes a rhetoric of resistance. This writing is "a mode of social strategy" and "a form of struggle"—as Newton has described certain Victorian novels—directed to a specific literary and religious subculture in Victorian England that, by extension and projection, assumes a degree of solidarity and sisterhood.[18] Elaine Showalter was the first to discuss this "feminist" phenomenon in connection with the literature of Victorian England, emphasizing that "it is important to understand the female subculture not only as . . . a set of opinions, prejudices, tastes, and values prescribed for a subordinate group to perpetuate its subordination—but also as a thriving and positive entity."[19] Rossetti's position illustrates Nancy Cott's view that "women's group consciousness [is] a subculture uniquely divided against itself by ties to the dominant culture. While the ties to the dominant culture are the informing and restricting ones, they provoke within the subculture certain strengths as well as weaknesses, enduring values as well as accommodations."[20] In assaulting her dominant culture's primary social and material value systems through a critique based in the religious beliefs that traditionally complemented and served those systems, Rossetti deploys subversive strategies of extraordinary power and complexity.

In order fully to understand the operations of these strategies, it is crucial to explore the particular sociohistorical contexts of her work. Rossetti's adherence to Victorian High Anglicanism, as a culturally specific and unique system of religious values, actually reinforced the femininist subversiveness of her writing.

As is evident from even the most cursory reading of Rossetti's poetry and devotional prose, her work finds its primary inspiration in her High Anglican religious beliefs. Her agnostic brother W. M. Rossetti described her as "an Anglo-Catholic, and, among Anglo-Catholics, a Puritan."[21] In this century, Raymond Chapman has successfully argued a case "for seeing Christina Rossetti as directly and fully a product of the Oxford Movement," and he insists that she is "the true inheritor of the Tractarian devotional mode in poetry."[22] More recently, George B. Tennyson and others have extended Chapman's argument, and the history of Rossetti's involvement with High Anglican churches and church figures has been documented thoroughly by her biographers.[23] In 1843, at the impressionable age of twelve, Rossetti began regular attendance at Christ Church, Albany Street, "noted at the time for the incendiary sermons of the Reverend William Dodsworth, one of the chief preachers of the Oxford Movement, a man closely associated with both [John Henry] Newman and [Edward] Pusey."[24] As Lona Mosk Packer notes, citing an article from the *Edinburgh Review*, this church was becoming "a principal centre of High Church religionism in the metropolis."[25] Rossetti's early religious education in this environment and her lifelong involvement with major figures from the later days of High Anglicanism profoundly influenced her particular appropriations of a system of religious beliefs that pervaded every aspect of her existence. Rossetti's most recent biographer, Georgina Battiscombe, insists that "for [Rossetti] this form of religion came to be, quite simply and without question, the most important thing in her life."[26]

Readers of Rossetti's works today tend to forget the extent to which Anglo-Catholicism was perceived in mid-century as a radical movement. As Packer explains, "this exhilarating . . . Tractarian Renascence" was "an avant-garde movement accepted alike by the Regent's Park worthies and the Albany Street literati."[27] Rossetti's involvement with the institutional extensions of this movement continued and deepened throughout her life. All but one of her books of devotional prose were published by the Society for Promoting Christian Knowledge, a press with close ties to Anglo-Catholicism.

More significantly, Rossetti developed important connections with the High Anglican movement to resurrect sisterhoods, conventual institutions that many Victorians found threatening because they undercut the roles and functions widely accepted for middle-class women. One Anglican convent opened about 1850 a few doors from Christ Church:

> founded and directed by Dr. Pusey, who chose the Albany Street church as the scene of a novel experiment, . . . the religious community of women caused amazement and consternation even in a parish as radical as [William] Dodsworth's. 'The special vocation of a Sister,' wrote Pusey's biographer, 'the character involved and the claims of such a character, were altogether unknown. . . . That young ladies [of good families] should shrink from society, and entertain thoughts of a vow of celibacy in the face of an eligible marriage was almost inconceivable.'[28]

In 1874, Rossetti's sister Maria, to whom she was extremely close, joined the All Saints' Sisterhood in Margaret Street. Yet already two decades earlier Rossetti had been composing poems, such as "Three Nuns" and "The Convent Threshold," that clearly reflect her fascination with these new institutions that liberated women from the temptations of "the world," especially the world of the Victorian marriage market (attacked parodically in "Goblin Market") and the domestic ideology of which they were a crucial component.

In her sonnet "A Triad" Rossetti concisely exposes the unsatisfactory vocational alternatives for Victorian women.

> Three sang of love together; one with lips
>   Crimson, with cheeks and bosom in a glow,
> Flushed to the yellow hair and finger tips;
>   And one there sang who soft and smooth as snow
>   Bloomed like a tinted hyacinth at a show;
> And one was blue with famine after love,
>   Who like a harpstring snapped rang harsh and low
> The burden of what those were singing of.
> One shamed herself in love; one temperately
>   Grew gross in soulless love, a sluggish wife;
> One famished died for love. Thus two of three
>   Took death for love and won him after strife;
>   All on the threshold, yet all short of life. (Crump 1: 29).

For Rossetti, becoming a bride of Christ was the only vital alternative to the stereotypical roles of prostitute, wife, and lovelorn spinster, and it is one she advocates repeatedly in her poems and devotional works, sometimes with extraordinary passion. Renunciation of the world, with all its misguided social institutions and material temptations, is the unique route to self-fulfillment, as is made clear in "A Better Resurrection":

> My life is like a faded leaf,
>   My harvest dwindled to a husk;
> Truly my life is void and brief
>   And tedious in the barren dusk;
> My life is like a frozen thing,
>   No bud nor greenness can I see:
> Yet rise it shall—the sap of Spring;
>   O Jesus, rise in me.

My life is like a broken bowl,
    A broken bowl that cannot hold
One drop of water for my soul
    Or cordial in the searching cold;
Cast in the fire the perished thing,
    Melt and remould it, till it be
A royal cup for Him my King:
    O Jesus, drink of me. (Crump 1: 68)

Rossetti herself never joined a sisterhood, in part because of a compulsion to exercise whatever influence she could through her writings in order to expose and to subvert the system of cultural values that denied genuine fulfillment for women. She did so by advocating strict, devotional alternatives.[29] (Unexpectedly, at one point in *Time Flies* she wryly interjects, "But Bishops should write for me, not I for Bishops!" [123]). Rossetti did, nonetheless, become an associate at one of the many Anglican Church-related homes founded at mid-century for the redemption of prostitutes, working regularly at St. Mary Magdalene's on Highgate Hill until her health broke down in the late 1860s. As Martha Vicinus has observed, the "reform of fallen women" was one of the three major tasks undertaken by the Anglican sisterhood.[30] Rossetti's involvement in it had visible effects on her many poems about fallen women (including "Goblin Market," "The Convent Threshold," and "An Apple-Gathering") as well as on her devotional prose works.

Rossetti's intimate connections with the newly developing Anglican sisterhoods, although she remained outside their conventual restrictions, gave her a unique position from which freely to present a critique of her society. These institutions, conservative as they might appear in the late twentieth century, were, in fact, radically liberating for the women who became involved with them. As an extension of the Oxford Movement, the convents "played an important initial role in the emancipation of women in England," presenting "a wide variety of opportunities to women in the fields of teaching, nursing, social work, and community organization."[31] Vicinus has traced the origins, development, and social influence of the Anglican sisterhoods, emphasizing the extent to which they empowered Victorian women: the "sisters carved out an area of expertise and power within their male-dominated churches. . . . [They] were clearly in the vanguard of women's single-sex organizations, in both their organizational autonomy and their insistence upon women's right to a separate religious life."³² Vicinus also remarks upon the varieties of freedom offered to Victorian women through the sisterhoods, which were among "the most important women's communities in the nineteenth century":

> They were among the first to insist upon a woman's right to choose celibacy, to live communally, and to do meaningful work. They demanded and received great loyalty from their members and were in turn deeply supportive of each other . . . [T]he orders maintained a very high standard of religious life, proving convincingly that women could lead women, live together, and work for the greater good of the church, the people, and God.³³

One sister's commentary suggests the radicalism of the Anglican sisterhood movement: "It was a wonderful thing at that period to be young among young comrades. . . . It was an era of religion and faith, and at the same time of intellectual challenge. We read, discussed, debated and experimented and felt that all life lay before us to be changed and moulded by our vision and desire."³⁴

Rossetti could not have been unaware of the potentially liberating effects of Anglican sisterhoods upon Victorian women, and of the fact that these sisterhoods were perceived by many to be disturbingly subversive of dominant patriarchal ideologies, including that of the woman's sphere. John Shelton Reed has recently discussed the public controversy that swirled around the sisterhoods. He explains that "there was widespread uneasiness about the development of sisterhoods" because they clearly presented an "affront to Victorian family values." For instance, "Prebendary Gresley of Lichfield, a sober Tractarian . . . gave the anglo-catholic view when he remarked matter-of-factly that 'Home and comfort have been too long the idols of Englishmen, a settlement and establishment in life the *summum bonum* of Englishwomen. It is a great point to have it admitted that there may be something nobler and more desirable than these acknowledged blessings."³⁵ Earlier, Florence Nightingale, a heroine of Rossetti's early adulthood, had described the Victorian domestic ideology derisively as a "Fetich": "'Family'—the idol they have made of it. It is a kind of Fetichism. . . . They acknowledge no God, for all they say to the contrary, but this Fetich."[36] Sisterhoods strongly threatened this idol. Conventual life "took women out of their homes. It gave important work and sometimes great responsibility. It replaced their ties to fathers, husbands, and brothers by loyalties to church and sisterhood. It demonstrated that there were callings for women of the upper and middle classes other than those of wife, daughter, and 'charitable spinster,'" offering "an alternative to a life of idleness or drudgery—exotic, but safely exotic, and cloaked in the respectability of religion."[37]

But as Reed has demonstrated, the sisterhood was only one of many Anglo-Catholic innovations that threatened the social and economic values of the Victorian patriarchy. The revival of auricular confession and the establishment of "free and open seating" in the churches (as opposed to private family pews), among other Anglo-Catholic alterations of church ritual, were also seen as powerfully subversive, especially because these changes were strongly supported by women who, as most observers agreed, were drawn to Anglo-Catholicism in disproportionate numbers. One commentator complained that "The Ritual movement is a lay movement . . . but it is more than that; it is a female movement. . . . The Ritualistic clergyman is led, or rather misled, by a few ladies."[38] In fact, the religious movement to which Rossetti fervently committed herself and the audience to whom she directed her devotional prose commentaries and poems must finally be seen as feminist:

> By its sometimes studied disregard for conventional standards of manliness and by its revaluation of celibacy, the movement issued a series of subtle but continual challenges to received patriarchal values. That these challenges were heard and understood by the movement's male opponents is evident in their denigration of women's part in the movement, and in the alarm and contempt evoked in them by the movement's 'effeminacy.'[39]

As I have already remarked, the quality of Rossetti's own devotionalist feminism is complicated and often disguised by her ostensible subscription to orthodox notions of male supremacy, especially in her prose writings. (Her poems, however, are full of male villains.) But a number of passages from her devotional books, letters, and unpublished remarks expose a radically femininist bent. Rossetti's insistence that women patiently endure

this life in expectation of the life to come upholds the dogmas of the patriarchy, but only in anticipation of the ultimate dissolution of these dogmas
in that afterlife which is a "flowering land of love" where men and women
will be "happy equals" ("Monna Innominata," Crump 2: 89). Typical is
Rossetti's modulation (in a discussion of St. Hilary) from an acceptance of
an "unknown" wife's subordinate position in matters of worldly reputation to an insistence on her ultimate equality with her spouse: "now of St.
Hilary's wife I read nothing further, beyond such a hint of her career as is
involved in that of her husband. Wherefore of her I am free to think of as
one 'unknown and yet well known'; on earth of less dignified name than
her husband. . . . in Paradise it may well be of equal account" *Time Flies*,
11–12).

Rossetti's discussions of marriage and of the marital relations between
the sexes are, in her devotional works, most often cautiously critical. Her
poems almost never broach the topic, except to renounce the prospects of
marital union, to depict betrayed or disappointed love, or to celebrate the
prospect of marital union with Christ in the afterlife. (In the preface to
"Monna Innominata" she goes so far as to suggest that Elizabeth Barrett
Browning would have written better sonnets had she been "unhappy,
rather than happy in love" [Crump 2: 86].) Because worldly marriages for
Rossetti most often require that women "grow gross in soulless love," she
often implicitly disdains the institution. In one passage from *Letter and
Spirit* she obediently acknowledges that "A wife's paramount duty is indeed to her husband, superseding all other human obligations."[40] But she
immediately proceeds to subvert the patriarchal ideology underlying that
dogma: "yet to assume this duty, free-will has first stepped in with its
liability to err; in this connexion woman has to reap as she has sown, be
the crop what it may: while in the filial relation all is safe and flawless, for
all is of Divine ordaining" (43).

When discussing prospects for immortality in particular, or moral virtue
and purity in general, Rossetti frequently recurs to Christ's commandments regarding marriage:

Change and vicissitude are confined to this life and this world: once
safe in the next world the saved are safe for ever and ever. So our
Lord deigned to effect to teach us all, when answering certain
Saducees, He said: "The children of this world marry, and are given

> in marriage: but they which shall be accounted worthy to obtain that
> world, and the resurrection from the dead, neither marry, nor are
> given in marriage: neither can they die any more: for they are equal
> unto the angels. . . ." And further we gather hence by implication
> that not all shall "obtain . . . the resurrection from the dead." (*Face
> of the Deep*, 100)

The clear implication here is that the unmarried are more likely to be
saved than those who succumb to this worldly institution. Earlier in *The
Face of the Deep*, when discussing how "the precarious purity of mortal
life shall become the indefectible purity of the immortal" (93), Rossetti
compares the individual who succumbs to the world's temptations to trod-
den snow which turns to mud. By contrast, those who remain pure are like
"snow on mountain summits" that "endures alone": "Even so chaste virgins choose solitude for a bower" (93). Such implicit attacks upon marriage in Rossetti's work must finally be seen discursively to reify the
subversion of patriarchal social values—especially the "Fetich" of the
family and its extension in the ideology of the "woman's sphere"—a
revolt that took on institutional form in the revival of the Anglican sisterhoods.

Because Rossetti strategically positions herself on the margins of "the
world" in her prose works, focusing her commentaries on preparing for
the afterlife, she rarely presents cultural critiques that do not take on cir-
cumspect, parabolic forms. In her secular poems, however, especially the
dozens that expose patriarchal amatory ideologies that victimize women,
she is more outspoken; but even many of these works (including "Goblin
Market," "The Prince's Progress," and "Dream-Love") are allegorical.[41]
Occasionally, Rossetti's letters also demonstrate the feminist directions of
her thought quite explicitly. One in particular, written to the widely published suffragist Augusta Webster, reveals Rossetti's view of sexual roles as
artificial "barriers" that are exclusively this-worldly in their provenance.
Rossetti is apparently responding to a request from Webster that she support the suffragist movement. "You express yourself with such cordial
openness that I feel encouraged to endeavour also after self-expression,"
Rossetti explains candidly, as she begins a discussion of the appointed

roles of the sexes that modulates into a speculation on their power relations.[42] I quote the rest of this extraordinary letter in full:

> Does it not appear as if the Bible was based upon an understood
> unalterable distinction between men and women, their position, du-
> ties, privileges? Not arrogating to myself but most earnestly desiring
> to attain to the character of a humble orthodox Xian, so it does
> appear to me; not merely under the Old but also under the New
> Dispensation. The fact of the Priesthood being exclusively man's,
> leaves me in no doubt that the highest functions are not *in this world*
> open to both sexes: and if not all, then a selection must be made and
> a line drawn somewhere.—On the other hand if female rights are
> sure to be overborne for lack of female voting influence, then I con-
> fess I feel disposed to shoot ahead of my instructresses, and to assert
> that female *M.P.'s* are only right and reasonable. Also I take excep-
> tions at the exclusion of married women from the suffrage,—for who
> so apt as Mothers—all previous arguments allowed for the mo-
> ment—to protect the interests of themselves and of their offspring? I
> do think if anything ever does sweep away the barrier of sex, and
> make the female not a giantess or a heroine but at once and full
> grown a hero and giant, it is that mighty maternal love which makes
> little birds and little beasts as well as little women matches for very
> big adversaries.[43]

Rossetti begins with an unquestioning acceptance of the dogmas of patriarchal orthodoxy. But her fear—irrepressible in this letter as in so many of
her poems—that men cannot be expected, finally, to protect "female
rights" inspires her to take a line that is, even at the end of the century,
distinctly radical.

That radical line emerges in part from Rossetti's customary exaltation
of motherhood, her significantly *partial* acceptance of the ideology of the
"woman's sphere." (Most often in her work, Rossetti elides any discussion
of husbands and marriage as a necessary institutional prelude to the production of children.) But her radicalism also results from a literal acceptance of a basic premise of the domestic ideology: that men are inevitably
seduced and sullied by involvement with "the world." Although Rossetti

acknowledges that women are men's helpmates (the "weaker vessels" appointed to assist "the strong"), it becomes clear in this letter and throughout her secular poetry that "goblin" men will prove difficult, if not impossible, to redeem, participating as they do in the "loathsome and foul" world controlled by Satan.[44] Hence, the most consistently positive relationships among characters in Rossetti's poems are between mothers and daughters or between sisters. These relationships reinforce a spirit of subcultural solidarity that, ultimately, can deal with "the world" only by wholly renouncing it.[45]

Thus, Rossetti's sage discourse always advocates renunciation and resistance. Addressing a female audience whose values, like her own, had been molded primarily by patriarchal religious, amatory, and domestic ideologies, she consistently appropriates elements of those ideologies in order to expose their inability to fulfill the spiritual, moral, and even intellectual needs of Victorian women. In response to the misguided values of "the world," she urges the acceptance of alternative, radically devotionalist values whose origins are avowedly patriarchal but whose otherworldly goal for adherents is an eventual assumption into a genderless, egalitarian utopia—Paradise.

Despite the unwavering strength of her faith and the consistency of her vision of the fallen world, Rossetti was characteristically humble and cautious, especially in her prose works, when she assumed the authoritative role of sage that her reformist ambitions demanded of her. In *The Face of the Deep*, her last work, she comes to final terms with the spiritual dangers and ideological difficulties facing any Victorian woman who engaged in sage discourse. As usual, however, a prospectively feminist self-confidence emerges in the very act of self-effacement:

> Far be it from me to think to unfold mysteries or interpret prophecies. But I trust that to gaze in whatever ignorance on what God reveals, is so far to do His will. If ignorance breed humility, it will not debar from wisdom. If ignorance betake itself to prayer, it will lay hold on grace. . . . [A]t least I . . . may deepen awe, and stir up desire by a contemplation of things inevitable, momentous, transcendent. (146)

The Trouble with Romola

MARY WILSON CARPENTER

For many women readers the trouble with George Eliot's novel *Romola* is Romola herself. For Mathilde Blinde, writing in 1904, "the effect produced by the high-souled Romola is not unlike that of an antique statue, at once splendidly beautiful and imposingly cold."[1] For Anne Fremantle, writing in 1933, George Eliot had imposed on her heroine "a priggishness of outlook and narrowness of mind which could belong only to a Victorian prude."[2] For Carole Robinson, writing in 1962, the sole convincing "truth" of the novel is "Romola's confusion, isolation, and despair."[3] For Sandra M. Gilbert and Susan Gubar, writing in 1979, Romola is one more of the figures George Eliot uses to analyze "female enthrallment, born of women's complete dependence on men for self-definition and self-esteem."[4] And for Margaret Homans, writing in 1986, Romola is the submissive bearer of the (male) word.[5]

I should add that male readers are not more positive about Romola, but tend simply to find her less "interesting" than her clever, egotistical husband, Tito. Women readers, however, are often troubled by their lack of sympathy with Romola: they become extensively analytic about what is *wrong* with her. That this should be so concerning the novel which U. C. Knoepflmacher marked as the beginning of George Eliot's move into narrative forms that "sought to stimulate sympathy for 'the historical life of man'" suggests a problem centered in the conjunction of gender and discourse.[6] Knoepflmacher's formulation points to the possible location of women readers' "trouble" with Romola in women writers' trouble with a discourse intended to be public—specifically, a discourse intended to articulate a wisdom common to all mankind.[7] As Mary Jacobus argues, the problem central to feminist literary criticism is "the nature of women's access to culture and their entry into literary discourse."[8] If women's access to discourse necessarily involves their "submission to phallocentricity, to the masculine and the symbolic," then the woman writer's text can be "properly" or sympathetically read only by subjects constituted as male—and only if the writer's submission is complete and unresisting.[9]

In Felicia Bonaparte's and my own decoding of the elaborately symbolic structure of *Romola*, George Eliot planned a narrative project that maps out an epic history of Western civilization and a prophetic interpretation of Christianity.[10] This reading positions George Eliot as a phallic speaker, manipulating a hermeneutic tradition that had long been jealously guarded as an exclusively male sanctum. Despite, or perhaps even because of, her revisionary feminist apocalyptics and her inclusion of a female protagonist of mythic proportions, George Eliot appears to write as a man, submitting to the yoke of phallocentricity in order to wield the power of the Mosaic rod. Such a reading suggests that our difficulty with Romola inheres in our construction of her as Woman, our pre-Oedipal (M)Other, a passive, silent madonna-figure whom we know all too well and cannot find interesting.

Yet it is men readers who find Romola merely uninteresting, tending to skip over her and dissect other reasons for the novel's "failure."[11] If we are to understand why Romola troubles us, we must revise our reading of women as reading subjects, particularly our dutiful Lacanian reading of the Mother as constructed in the pre-Oedipal (pre-linguistic) register. We must ask what it means for a woman reader/writer to "identify" with a mythic female figure. Here I wish to underline specifically the monovocal Oedipal ideology of Freudian and post-Freudian literary psychoanalytic theory. What if the trouble with post-Freudian psychoanalysis is precisely that it chooses to suppress the multiplicity in Freud's text? Kaja Silverman reminds us that all of Freud's examples of the fantasies that organize psychic life derive from the Oedipus complex, and that this appears to restrict the list rather severely. But if, she notes, we grasp "the possible permutations of each fantasy," the list becomes "rich and varied."[12]

Silverman's development of Freud's brief reference to the "negative Oedipal complex" produces a revisionary feminist theory of the daughter's desire for the mother in which that desire is initiated by symbolic castration, or the entry into language. The mother is not constructed wholly in the pre-Oedipal order but is integrally bound up with the daughter's access to language and the symbolic order. In this context we may read George Eliot's construction of Romola as a pivotal point for negotiating those fantasies of the maternal voice that constitute an authorial subject of a particular kind—that is, the daughter of the mother. But I suggest we need to go still further afield and exploit non-Lacanian psychoanalytic theory in order to escape the restrictions of the feminine in Lacanian theory and to facilitate our reading of "the mother's daughter" in the text. Such recourse may help explain how George Eliot's relation to the mother troubles the novel, and why it interferes not only with her attempt to speak as a prophet but with our ability to feel sympathy with Romola.

George Eliot and the "woman clothed with the sun"

In what seems an unusual narrative detail, Romola's hair is presented before Romola herself. Nello remarks to Tito that "Our old Bardo de' Bardi is so blind that he can see no more of his daughter than, as he says, a glimmering of something bright when she comes very near him: doubtless her golden hair, which, as Messer Luigi Pulci says of his Meridiana's, '*raggia come stella per sereno*.'"[13] Romola's hair is much more than simply gold: it is the "light" that penetrates the old scholar's darkness, and as the narrator presents it, it is also the "light" by which the reader sees Bardo's ancient library (Fig. 1).[14]

> The only spot of bright colour in the room was made by the hair of a tall maiden of seventeen or eighteen, who was standing before a carved *leggio*, or reading-desk, such as is often seen in the choirs of Italian churches. The hair was of a reddish gold colour, enriched by an unbroken small ripple, such as may be seen in the sunset clouds on grandest autumnal evenings. It was confined by a black fillet

1. Frederick Leighton, *The Blind Scholar and His Daughter*, from *Romola*, *Cornhill Magazine* (July 1862).

above her small ears, from which it rippled forward again, and made a natural veil for her neck above her square-cut gown of black *rascia*, or serge. (93)

This stellar hair over which the narrator lingers with such pleasure is the first signal of Romola's link to the apocalyptic "woman clothed with the sun, and the moon beneath her feet, and upon her head a crown of twelve stars" (Rev. 12: 1). Romola's hair makes her a creature of light— and the object of a fetishistic perception. This perception is compounded in a later description of Romola on the day of her betrothal: "It was not long before Romola entered, all white and gold, more than ever like a tall lily. Her white silk garment was bound by a golden girdle, which fell with large tassels; and above that the rippling gold of her hair, surmounted by the white mist of her long veil, which was fastened to her brow by a band of pears, the gift of Bernardo del Nero, and was now parted off her face so that it all floated backward" (258). The "white mist" of the long veil and the floating movement of her hair multiply the fetishistic elements already introduced.[15]

The fetishization of Romola's hair is a crucial detail in the reading of what Silverman terms a "female authorial subject" as constructed by a negative Oedipus complex. The significant distinction between Silverman's exposition of the negative Oedipus complex and Lacan's interpretation of symbolic castration is that in the former feminine desire is not repressed in language but constituted in it. The woman writer's construction of a fetish signals her simultaneous recognition and denial of the mother's "difference." It figures, as for the male subject, her recognition that the mother both has and lacks the phallus. But this perception, in classic Freudian and post-Freudian theory, is not possible for a woman because there can be no "difference" between the mother and daughter. It is precisely here, however, that we see the male-privileging slippage in the Lacanian use of the term phallus. If, as Lacan insisted, the phallus has nothing to do with the penis, signifying only the mother's desire and the child's recognition that it is not that desire, then the daughter's desire to be the mother's desire may be disrupted by something other than a *paternal* signifier.[16] Or as Jane Gallop puts it, "this Oedipal intrusion of the man is but a late form, a repetition of an otherness already there in the early mother."[17]

The detail of the fetish in the woman writer's text, then, constructs both desire for and identification with the mother: it postulates a subjectivity both non-phallic and symbolic. As Naomi Schor has suggested, it constitutes a paradigm of undecidability and bisexuality; of the woman writer's refusal to give up either her femininity or her feminism; of both her continuity with the mother and her difference from her.[18] This psychoanalytic reading begins to suggest the heterogeneous potential that the apocalyptic "woman clothed with the sun," her head crowned with stars, may have offered to a nineteenth-century woman writer and reader.[19]

To explore this heterogeneous potential, we must ask what it means for a reader to "identify" with an ideal image in a text. This question, I think, is more profitably addressed in the context of "self psychology," which theorizes the parallel development of narcissistic and object-relations structures, rather than in the Lacanian system of pre-Oedipal and Oedipal (imaginary and symbolic) orders. In his formulation of the "idealizing transference" Heinz Kohut is concerned primarily with a narcissistic pathology, or a blockage in the development of the "self" structure. In order to protect itself against an early, traumatic loss, the child's psyche internalizes an idealized parental imago and thereafter strives to maintain continuity with it, forever seeking external representations of it. The therapist mirrors this idealized parental imago, enabling the patient to merge with it and, ultimately, to transmute it into an idealized superego, where it supports a sense of the self as "firm" and "coherent." Because the trauma that precipitated the parental imago is assumed to have been a very early event, Kohut notes that its psychoanalytic formulation is "difficult and fraught with danger, since the reliability of our empathy . . . declines the more dissimilar the observed is to the observer." Kohut also emphasizes, however, that an early or archaic experience does not vanish with cognitive maturation. Rather, the psyche tends to "telescope" earlier events with later, analogous ones, thus rendering prelinguistic events accessible to interpretation.[20]

Kohut's theory here suggests its limitations as well as its potential for women readers, or for any readers marginalized by the constructions of dominance. In the reading and then the writing of the "woman clothed with the sun," we may postulate an idealizing transference of the maternal imago in the text of *Romola*—that is, that the "woman clothed with the sun" mobilized George Eliot's (Mary Anne Evans's) archaic maternal imago and the narcissistic rage associated with its construction. But if we are to read these prehistoric events through their "telescoping" with later, "historic" events, everything depends on how we as readers put things together—that is, on how we narrativize. In other words, what troubles women readers about Romola's functioning in the narrative—what seems to this group of readers most disturbing and yet most interesting—may be most revelatory.[21]

Thus the fetishization of Romola's hair becomes a starting point for a reading of the multiple ways in which Romola's functioning in the narrative is disturbingly contradictory. Although women—and especially feminist—critics have emphasized Romola's passivity, she actually oscillates between passivity and activity, submission and rebellion, much as Jane Eyre does.[22] At first, the narrative seems to emphasize Romola's "simplicity" (145) and her "noble womanhood" (145), descriptive comments that imply passivity and even vacuity or emptiness. In her presence Tito feels "something like the worship paid of old to a great nature-goddess, who was not all-knowing, but whose life and power were something deeper and more primordial than knowledge" (145). Yet the narrator tells us that Romola's simplicity results partially from her ignorance "concerning the world outside her father's books" (104), and she herself later not only recognizes that she had been "very foolish and ignorant in her girlish time" but also that she had been "inwardly very rebellious" (308).

Just before Tito reveals that he has sold her father's library, Romola makes the telling discovery that she liked "being shaken and deafened" by the bells, feeling like a "Bacchante possessed by a divine rage" (305). Once he has told her his news, she faces him with "a flash of fierceness in her scorn and anger," a scorn that "scorched" him (355). She remains implacably opposed to Tito after this, making plans to run away from him and to seek out a learned woman from whom she hopes to learn how to support herself (393). But Romola is "arrested" in this design by the voice of Savonarola, and sent back to Florence to devote herself to her fellow citizens and keep her marriage bond intact. Here she moves again into a period of passivity: "she had submitted her mind to . . . [Savonarola's] and had entered into communion with the Church" (464). As the narrator explains, her submission answers an unfilled need. Yet when her trust in Savonarola is breached, she angrily confronts him and then resolves to set out once more, leaving everything she knows behind her.

There seems little doubt, then, that Romola is not solely passive. She

swings between submission and revolt, a pattern that Nancy Chodorow has theorized as typical of the daughter's ambivalent relation to the mother.[23] Similarly, while critics have often read the references in *Romola* to "the Madonna" as indicating George Eliot's identification of her heroine with the saintly, passive figure of the Virgin Mary, the association of Romola with the apocalyptic "woman clothed with the sun" produces a very different, and more complex, reading of her. Nineteenth-century Protestant exegetes saw the "woman clothed with the sun" as a figure exemplifying the activity, change and even violent revolt of the Protestant Reformation (Fig. 2).[24] At the same time, Catholic interpretations identified the "woman clothed with the sun" *as* the Virgin Mary and valorized her as a figure of self-negating sacrifice. Protestant interpretations therefore con-

2. Westall and Martin, *The Woman Clothed with the Sun,* from Hobart Caunter, *Pictorial Illustrations of the Old and New Testaments by Westall and Martin* (London, 1838). "And there appeared a great wonder in heaven; a woman clothed with the sun, and the moon under her feet, and upon her head a crown of twelve stars: and she being with child cried, travailing in birth, and pained to be delivered. And there appeared another wonder in heaven; and behold a great red dragon, having seven heads and ten horns, and seven crowns upon his heads" [Rev. 12.1–3]. "The reader may observe," says Dr. Dodd, in this representation, "with M. Daubuz, that the sun may signify Christ, the moon the Holy Ghost, and the twelve stars the twelve Apostles; or he may understand it with Mr. Mede, of the Church shining round about, by the faith of Christ the Sun of Righteousness; treading under foot the rudiments of the world, whether Jewish shadows or Gentile superstitions, and glorious with the ensigns of the apostolical offspring; or he may consider with Mr. Waple, that the apostolical doctrine is the chief ornament, crown and glory of the Church. Of the woman being with child," Dr. Dodd further observes, "it is an easy figure to consider the Church as a mother, and the converts to truth and righteousness, the true worshippers of God, as her children." The red dragon is a well known symbol of Satan. Red was the distinguishing colour of the Roman emperors, consuls, and generals. His seven heads allude to the seven hills upon which Rome was built, and the seven forms of government which successively prevailed there. His ten horns typify the ten kingdoms into which the Roman empire was divided; "and the seven crowns upon his heads" denote that at this time the imperial power was in Rome, "the high city, seated on seven hills, which presides over the whole world," as Propertius describes it. For a full exposition of this remarkable prophecy, see Bishop Newton and Lowman.

structed an image of woman as protester, rebel, and initiator of new values—figure of a radical change in the political order—even as Catholic interpretations promoted the opposite (Fig. 3).[25]

The "woman clothed with the sun" might well serve as a focal point for the mobilization of the woman writer's idealized maternal imago—an imago experienced both as continuity or fusion, and as the anger or protest of division from the mother. Romola's oscillation between passivity and rebellion, and the tendency of women readers to ignore or deny it, points to the construction of a narcissistic split in Romola's character. She is neither the "daughter," or Mary Anne Evans, nor the "mother," or Mrs. Evans, but *both*: she stands in for the ambivalence of the daughter's relation to the mother, now passively merged with her, now actively rebelling against her.[26] Romola's relation to Tessa doubles this split, for one character functions as a childless "mother," and the other as a childish mother, or a mother who is nevertheless a child. Both construct the daughter's fantasies—the mother who has no other child, the child who is a mother like her mother. *Adam Bede* exhibits a very similar configuration in Hetty Sorrell and Dinah Morris—the child-mother and the childless "mother" whose identities and histories merge at a number of points in the narrative.

But in *Romola* a significant change takes place in the positioning of Romola between the beginning and end of the narrative. This change reflects not only George Eliot's trouble with another woman writer's reading of the "woman clothed with the sun," but also our trouble with certain functions performed by the maternal voice. Silverman points out that the functions of the maternal voice in the early years are actually those of the symbolic order: the mother functions as language teacher, expositor, and storyteller.[27] But in order to establish the discursive potency of the child (the emerging subject), however, the mother's voice must be stripped of all claim to verbal authority and is therefore typically relegated to meaningless sound, babble, nonsense or to silence in narrative. Cultural subjectivity constructs a fantasy of the maternal voice as "sonorous envelope" that may appear either as an utopian bliss and plenitude or as a dystopian "uterine night" of silence and entrapment.[28] This fantasy displaces the maternal voice as symbolic function. If we compare *Romola* to *Aurora Leigh*, we see that George Eliot reverses this typical narrativization by restoring symbolic function to the mother's voice.

3. Tintoretto, *Michael Fights the Dragon*, from Clifton Harby Levy, ed., *The Bible in Art: Twenty Centuries of Famous Bible Paintings* (New York, c. 1936).

It hardly seems necessary to suggest that Elizabeth Barrett Browning's story of a female prophetic figure with shining gold hair probably also alludes to the apocalyptic "woman clothed with the sun." At the end of the narrative, the now blind male protagonist exhorts Aurora, "my morning-star," to "shine out for two."[29] She then begins to name the foundation stones of the visionary city in The Book of Revelation. In her 1857 review of this novel-in-verse for the *Westminster Review*, George Eliot objected to this ending, partly because she regarded it as derivative of *Jane Eyre*, but also because "the lavish mutilation of heroes' bodies, which has become the habit of novelists, . . . weakens instead of strengthening tragic effect.[30] I shall return to her objection to the "mutilation of heroes' bodies," but for the moment I wish to focus on her revision of Aurora's conclusionary function as a female visionary or seer.

Like Aurora, Romola "shines out," providing "light" and acting as "seer" for a blind male figure. However, Romola appears as "light" for a blind male at the beginning of the narrative, a reversal which suggests the identification of light with a prelinguistic or early function. Romola's light is initially associated with sunset—the last light in the old world of scholarship, a light that Bardo only partially sees. Figured as light rather than as words, Romola is thus positioned in a primarily prelinguistic function at the beginning of the story. Although she reads for her father and has been instructed in Latin and Greek, this education has given her a knowledge only of men's books, a condition the narrator equates with ignorance. She seems to lack words, or a mind of her own. Yet instead of remaining in this quintessentially Lacanian feminine position, she moves through increasingly violent, rebellious encounters with the male "word" until the pivotal moment of "drifting away," after which she reemerges as both nurturing and naming madonna—a female figure who combines the symbolic with imaginary functions. Her final position in the narrative is not that of visionary or seer but rather that of "language teacher, expositor, and storyteller" to Tessa's son Lillo. It may thus be argued that George Eliot's narrative works to reconstitute the *symbolic* functions of the maternal voice, emancipating that voice from its consignment to a prelinguistic, specular realm.

Undoubtedly the most disturbing aspect of that narrative movement from "shining out" to speaking out is the moment when Romola "drifts away" (586) and awakens to find herself in a plague village. For Carole

Robinson, this scene is "absurd"; for Gillian Beer, it is "almost wholly unsatisfactory."[31] George Eliot defended this part of the narrative as having preceded her writing of the novel, being "by deliberate forecast adopted as romantic and symbolical elements."[32] I would suggest, first, that the story of the "woman clothed with the sun" functions as a focus for the mobilization of an idealizing transference in this episode, serving as a "mirror" for the writer's archaic maternal imago; and second, that it constructs the "authorial subject" as a subject of a narcissistic trauma relating both to the daughter's trouble with the mother and to her rage against an intervening father-figure.

In the Revelation story, of the "woman clothed with the sun" a woman brings forth a "man child" who is to rule all the nations and who is "caught up" to God (Rev. 12:5) The woman then flees into the wilderness, where a "place" is prepared for her. There is "war in heaven," and the devil or dragon is cast out of heaven and returns to the earth to persecute the woman. At this point the narrative seems both to split and to repeat itself, for the woman is carried away on eagle wings into the wilderness, "into her place," but we are also told that the dragon (now a "serpent") casts out a flood to carry her away. The earth, however, opens "her" mouth and swallows up the flood, thus coming to the aid of the woman. The dragon is "wroth" and goes to make war with the "remnants of her seed."[33]

In this narrative the woman may be read both as a mother, for she has a child, and as a daughter, for the maternal earth rescues her. Indeed, the narrative repeatedly returns the woman to her place, as if this were its desire: The woman flees to the wilderness, where her place is prepared for her; she flies to it on eagle wings; and she floats to it on a flood. But in each case, she returns to her place on the earth, a configuration we may read as the daughter's desire for union with the idealized archaic imago of the mother. In *Romola*, elements from this Revelation story of the "woman clothed with the sun" are reconstructed as both dystopian and as utopian fantasies of the maternal voice. The dystopian fantasy, however, is not one of entrapment; rather, it is one of expulsion and loss. Moreover, it is succeeded by a fantasy of a blissful recovery of and enclosure within the maternal voice—an enclosure from which Romola is wakened by the cry of a child.

Like the "woman clothed with the sun," Romola is carried away on a flood of "waters" (589) and eventually comes to what the narrative calls a "green land" (640). But let us attend to the details of that journey. She drifts out in a boat under a sky where "the stars were disclosing themselves like a palpitating life over the wide heavens" (590). The soft night air breathes on her as she glides over the water and watches "the deepening quiet of the sky" (590). The "silence" of this scene constructs the maternal voice as a "sonorous envelope": we "hear" the sounds of "palpitating life," breathing night air, and "deepening quiet."

But the passage also develops a sense of Romola's devastating loss. "Memories hung upon her like the weight of broken wings that could never be lifted—memories of human sympathy which even in its pains leaves a thirst that the Great Mother has no milk to still" (590). Though carried on the waters, Romola does not fly away on eagle wings like the "woman clothed with the sun." Rather, she is crushed by the weight of memories—memories of a "human sympathy" now lost, of a "thirst" for which there is no milk. Romola feels orphaned. She cannot read any "message of love for her in that far-off symbolic writing of the heavens, and with a great sob she wished that she might be gliding into death" (590).

Romola has been cut off from the "chief relation of her life" (586)—a phrase that suggests something much more global and all-encompassing than the status of her long-term, growing alienation from Tito. As she drifts off to sleep, she feels herself "touching the hands of the beloved dead beside her, and trying to wake them" (590). In this moment, Romola seems to reach back toward archaic memories such as those we had earlier been told she had inherited—"memories of a dead mother, of a lost brother, of a blind father's happier time" (105). As if to mark the profound significance of this moment, the narrative now forms a hiatus in Romola's story. The next six chapters cut in with the stories of Tito and of Baldassare, and ultimately with the "killing-off" of these figures of father and son. When the narrative returns to Romola, it discovers her in a moment of utopian peace and contentment. Her eyes open to "one of those scenes which were and still are repeated again and again like a sweet rhythm" as the "delicious sun-rays" fall on her and thrill "her gently like a caress" (640). She experiences a "Lethe" in which the "exquisiteness of subtle indefinite sensation creates a bliss which is without memory and without desire" (640). She is roused from this experience of plenitude, significantly, by the cry of a child. In this scene that George Eliot called "romantic and symbolical," Romola recovers the child in herself.

Reconstructing first some archaic experience of loss and expulsion as she drifts away, Romola appears to reencounter that blissful moment of complete envelopment by the "sweet rhyhm" and indescribable sensation of the maternal voice. When awakened by the cry of a child, she proceeds to both nurture and name the child. Although the villagers superstitiously believe her to be a vision of the Virgin Mary, Romola tells them that she "came over the sea," and promptly takes charge of burying the dead and caring for the living, speaking "in a tone of encouraging authority" to the local priest (648). The little child to whom she has offered milk is a Jew, one of those expelled from the homeland by the Inquisition. Before she leaves, Romola has seen to the baptism of the child and its renaming with a Christian name. The child, whose race and color both identify it as alien outsider, has thus been incorporated into Romola's world: though still the "queer little black Benedetto" (649), it has been "adopted," brought into the family. After she has set this village of the dead to rights and put the baby back where it belongs, Romola returns to Florence, where she takes up residence with Tessa and her children and Monna Brigida. Her final act is to instruct Lillo on the history, the meaning, and the value of men's lives.

What is it about this story that troubles women readers? Let me suggest first that the story is a new one. Unlike the familiar Oedipus myth that constitutes us as reading subjects, we do not know the Protestant interpretation of the "woman clothed with the sun" as a myth that constructs human desire, let alone female desire. Like Romola at the beginning of her story, we are relatively illiterate in stories of female desire, and we find them hard to read.[34] But a second element in Romola's story also contributes to its difficulty: its relation to a deeply painful, early trauma in the writer's life. Turning for a moment to the author "outside" the text, we may note those events in Mary Anne Evans's history which bring a particularly telling significance to Romola's story. Although it is known that the little Mary Anne Evans was banished at five years of age to a boarding school where she suffered "night terrors," the reason for this expulsion from the family is less certain. Haight tells us that "Mrs. Evans had not been well" following the death of her twin sons, born when Mary Ann was about sixteen months old.[35] What is meant by the state of not being well is unknown, but depression seems likely. Whatever the cause, the outcome was the sending away of a five-year-old daughter who never thereafter, so far as can be determined, developed much of a relation to her mother. Mrs. Evans was alive until Mary Anne was sixteen years old, when she died an agonizing death (perhaps from cancer), yet there are almost no references to her in all of George Eliot's many volumes of letters.[36]

In Romola's story, George Eliot constructs a "negative Oedipal conplex," or a daughter's desire for and identification with her mother, a movement pursued through an idealizing transference in which the apocalyptic "woman clothed with the sun" acts as a mirroring agent for the mobilization of the archaic maternal image. At the nodal moment of Romola's story, we find an episode that articulates the devastating loss of the maternal voice—a loss brought about through Romola's rejection of Tito and Savonarola, the father-figures in her world. Do we read here the telescoping of a symbolic or historicized event with a presymbolic event—that is, a telescoping of the writer's rage against the father who carted her away to school, thus acting as an agent in the separation from her mother, with a much earlier sense of a division from and traumatic loss of her mother at the time of the twins' death? A seemingly extraneous detail in the text supports the possible accuracy of this interpretation: as Monna Brigida excuses her indulgence of Tessa's children, she says that Romola must "give up" to her a little in this because "I had twins, only they died as soon as they were born" (659).[37]

Freud suggested that, instead of adoration, there could be "jealousy and hostility" toward the parent of the opposite sex in a "negative Oedipal complex."[38] What we see in *Romola* is rather more than jealousy and hostility. The narrative constructs ambivalence toward Romola, but it develops a carefully calculated, sadistic rage toward Tito and Savonarola. This is not an Oedipal story: it is an anti-Oedipus. It constructs the daughter's desire to "kill" the father who has distanced her from her mother and suggests that the narcissistic rage produced by the loss of the mother is displaced onto him. The only "happy" end to this story is the death of the father, or the killing off of the historicized paternal figure, while the idealized maternal imago is reconstituted as a feminine superego, as a recovery of the maternal voice as storyteller, interpreter, and teacher.

George Eliot and the Trauma of
Language

There is a marked contrast between Romola's recurrent passivity, which has troubled so many women readers, and the consistently active violence which the narrative directs toward male characters. Women readers have only recently begun to note this violence. Sadoff points out that while George Eliot "scourges Romola and so a figure for herself for daring to have her own desires," she "purges fathers and brothers from the narrative" altogether, and that Tito enacts "all the narrative's unjustified desires voluntarily to abandon fathers."[39] Beer comments that the "extraordinary violence" with which images of the father are treated suggests a "psychodrama" which has to do with the author's own need.[40] Despite her objection to the "lavish mutilation of heroes' bodies" in *Jane Eyre* and *Aurora Leigh*, George Eliot's own narrative proceeds to subject one male character after another to a painful death. The narrative makes Savonarola in particular the object of a torturous investigation analogous to the Inquisition represented in its account of history.

This narrative sadism, I would argue, is part of the novel's program to work out a trauma constructed in language itself. The repeated motif of forgetting—and remembering—in the narrative constructs language as both the site of loss and the means by which that loss is "recognized," identified as one thing because it is not something else. But it is not the absence of the mother that seems necessary to narrative subjectivity in *Romola*: it is the violent "killing-off" or expulsion of the father(s). It is as if "language"—meaning all the various languages of men—is exposed as conspiring in a male plot to absent or to silence the mother, whose voice the narrative must nevertheless recover. A narrative program to rid itself of fathers is therefore in place from the beginning.

Tito, for example, may be the locus of "unjustified desires" to abandon fathers, but he is himself always slated for destruction. Even before he marries Romola, the narrative voice informs us that "he had sold himself to evil" although "the poison could only work by degrees" (170). Narrative loathing for him has already been revealed in a decidedly jealous assessment of the "gentle, beseeching admiration" of his glance which, we are told, "is perhaps the only atonement a man can make for being too handsome" (106). The "voice" of the daughter in love with the mother and hostile to her chief rival, the father, surely makes itself heard here.

The fact that Romola's father Bardo is introduced as a *blind* male scholar suggests George Eliot's inability to resist the most notable of the mutilations to which she objected, although she places her blind hero at the beginning of the narrative rather than at the end. Romola's brother Dino also dies a rather ghastly death early in the narrative. Her godfather Bernardo del Nero is hanged late in the narrative. Tito's foster father Baldassare undergoes various kinds of physical and mental suffering, and finally dies in the dead embrace of the son whom he has just strangled. The narrative subjects Savonarola, however, to its most sadistic operations.

Although Savonarola seems to exert a strange power over Romola from the time of their first encounter at the bedside of the dying Dino, the narrative consistently objectifies him, almost italicizing, as it were, his difference and separateness from her. Romola is "called" by Savonarola just as Maggie Tulliver is "called" by Thomas à Kempis in *The Mill on the Floss*, but the difference in the narrative construction of these two male "voices" is instructive. Maggie's encounter takes place through the process of reading, and the "text" of Kempis is indistinguishable from Maggie's own "text": his "voice" penetrates hers, mingles with it on the page. Significantly, the chapter is titled "A Voice from the Past," and its self-renunciatory ethic merges with Maggie as if constructing some archaic, inner voice of her own.[41] By contrast, Savonarola is an "arresting" voice that *halts* Romola on her way to find a "learned woman" (428). Though she reacts to his voice almost as if she cannot distinguish it from her own feelings, the narrative definitively situates Savonarola "outside" Romola, separate from her. The narrative dispassionately observes his "penetration" of Romola, noting that he "arrests" her on her way to another goal.

This narrative objectification of Savonarola, at first subtle, becomes more overt. While Romola makes her rounds as "visible Madonna" (459), the narrative carefully explains what it is about Savonarola that has such a hold on her: "She thought little about dogmas, and shrank from reflecting closely on the Frate's prophecies of the immediate scourge and closely-following regeneration," but she "submitted her mind to his and entered into communion with the Church because in this way she had found an immediate satisfaction for moral needs" (464). Her trust in Savonarola made up a large part of the "strength" she needed. Should that trust be removed, there would be nothing to keep her from falling.

The desire to tell the story of the father-hero Savonarola turns out to be the desire to tell the story of the daughter's fatal disillusionment in the father. In effect, the narrative defends Romola for failing to see through him in the beginning. At the same time, it increasingly exposes Savonarola, probing more and more into his innermost feelings, rendering him the object of a precise analysis: "But at this moment such feelings were nullified by that hard struggle which made half the tragedy of his life—the struggle of a mind possessed by a never-silent hunger after purity and simplicity, yet caught in a tangle of egoistic demands, false ideas, and difficult outward conditions" (576). The narrative moves into the prophet's very cell and even "under this particular white tunic," revealing the hopes and fears concealed in the man facing the Inquisition and probable martyrdom (610). Savonarola is "mastered" with an excess of historical and psychological detail, as the narrative voice moves freely in and out of its historical object's time, as in the comment that Tito could see but not read "an address in the Frate's own minute and exquisite hand-writing, still to be seen covering the margins of his Bibles" (618). Here the narrative voice seems almost to assume a posture of grandiosity, a fantasy of omnipotent control over its extensively historicized, masculine object.

The excess of historical detail in *Romola* functions as part of George Eliot's narrative program to "lavishly mutilate heroes' bodies." Though she refrains from actually describing the particular methods of torture used on Savonarola, the "horrible implements" (668) are everywhere implied, and the agonizing stages of his confessions and retractions are recounted in detail. George Eliot has often been accused of being "uneasy" with the mountainous historical detail of this novel, of producing a text that "smells of the lamp." But perhaps it is actually her readers who are uneasy with it—uneasy in particular with the desire it enables her to construct. The lavish descriptions of crowd scenes, the elaborate and unamused paintings of street-play, "fooling," pageants and carnivals, all position the narrator as "master" of history, master of men and, finally, master of memory.

But the marshaling of masses of remembered detail is inherently self-defeating, for these piles of data only circulate around the desired remembrance; they do not produce it. In this context it may be useful to invoke the concept of "hypermnesia," or the overabundance of memory. Nineteenth-century French medical studies concluded that with such over abundance, memory could become an agent of disorder, overwhelming the present. This superabundance of remembered detail represented the opposite extreme of amnesia, particularly the "amnesia of signs," in which it was assumed that the subject had lost the power to translate "sentiments and ideas" into "expressions," and hence the power to order the past.[42] In *Romola* a recurrent motif of forgetting, of difficulty in remembering counters the pervasive excess of remembered detail. While the narrative overwhelms us with historical detail, Tito is repeatedly troubled by a "face in the crowd" whose identity nags at him but cannot be precisely named. Baldassare is afflicted with the loss of his scholarly memory, a more devastating "amnesia of signs" which turns the languages he once knew into meaningless black marks on the page. We may consider both the "hypermnesia" of the text and its instances of an "amnesia of signs" as symptomatic of a trauma in the authorial present—a trauma which can be constructed only by "forgetting" the known symbolic orders.

Tito's first glimpse of an unknown face in a crowd puzzles him: there is some faint suggestion in it which he cannot identify (135). Later he finds himself preoccupied by whatever it is about the face that cannot by identified. The friar "had some irrecoverable association for him . . . where in all his travels could he remember encountering that face before? Folly! such vague memories hang about the mind like cobwebs" (144). Ultimately, when the face is identified as that of Romola's brother Dino, we learn that the "irrecoverable association" is with Bardo, Dino's father and the man who wishes to become another foster father to Tito.

But the incident takes on new significance when we compare it with the highly similar incident in *Aurora Leigh* in which Aurora, walking through the streets in Paris, suddenly sees a face she both recognizes and does not recognize. The face seems to intrude explosively into her thoughts:

> WHAT FACE IS THAT?
> What a face, what a look, what a likeness! Full on mine
> The sudden blow of it came down, till all
> My blood swam, my eyes dazzled . . . [43]

As Dolores Rosenblum astutely demonstrates, the face not only recalls the identity of Marian Erle, whom Aurora believes to be dead, but the dead face of the mother. Aurora must come to terms with this mirror image both of herself and of the other woman before she can assume the identity of female poet-prophet and speak as female subject.[44] Tito's undecipherable "face" is an interesting rewriting of this episode: where the face in *Aurora Leigh* constructs the mirroring face of the mother and the daughter's imperative to "identify" it as both self and other, the face in *Romola* is the face of the father and constructs the desire to kill the father (Baldassare) and the father's mirror-ego or son (Tito).

When Tito unexpectedly recognizes his foster father, we are told that the face "came not simply as the face of the escaped prisoner, but as a face with which he had been familiar long years before" (330). Like the "sudden blow" of the face seen by Aurora Leigh, everything seems "all compressed into a second" for Tito, "the sight of Baldassare looking at him, the sensation shooting through him like a fiery arrow" (331). But Baldassare experiences an almost identical sense of familiarity compounded by strangeness when he looks at his own face in a barber's mirror. At first afraid that Tito might really not have known him at the time when he pretended not to recognize his foster father, saying only *"Some madman, surely,"* Baldassare feels a "painful shock" (283, George Eliot's italics). But on scrutinizing his face in the barber's mirror he feels that Tito would have known him had he "searched for him with the expectation of finding him changed, as men search for the beloved among the bodies cast up by the waters. There was something different in his glance, but it was a difference that should only have made the recognition of him the more startling" (334).

Tito is himself, of course, among those "bodies cast up by the waters" when he first surfaces in the narrative as a shipwreck survivor. Similarly, it is as a body cast up by the waters that Baldassare will find him again—and carry out his desire to kill. Baldassare's very action of examining his face in a mirror repeats Tito's similar examination after his first arrival in Florence. The son's face thus "mirrors" the father's as the father's does the son's in moments of mutual recognition and desire, desire for murder. But the narrative goes on to further expand this mirroring between father and son into a "mirror" of remembering and forgetting. After examining his face in the barber's mirror, Baldassare stops by a pool because he wishes to contemplate the image of himself more slowly than he had dared to do in the presence of the barber. The pool's still surface mirrors "the vague aching of an unremembered past within him—when he seemed to sit in dark loneliness, visited by whispers which died out mockingly as he strained his ear after them, and by forms that seemed to approach him and float away" (335). At such moments, he realizes, there must be a "blank confusion in his face, as of a man suddenly smitten with blindness" (335).

Unlike Bardo, Baldassare's "blindness" is to languages, specifically to the languages of men and men's scholarship. His condition is that of an "amnesia of signs," the sudden loss of the ability to read the scholarly languages, the "rare knowledge," "close thoughts," and "various speech" (335) that had once been a part of him. "Was it utterly and for ever gone from him, like the waters from an urn lost in the wide ocean? Or, was it still within him, imprisoned by some obstruction that might one day break asunder?" (335). But in this forgetting of language, Baldassare remembers his one desire. When the waters cast up a man's body (Tito) at his feet, his only concern is that Tito *must* see him and know him—know his father as his killer. The narrative tells us that Tito does know him, but does not know whether it is in life or death that he perceives "the face of the hideous past hanging over him for ever" (638). Baldassare strangles his son, then dies in an ecstasy of revenge, locked in a mortal embrace with him. Even this is not enough for the narrative, which breaks in on the grisly murder scene with the information that, "Not long after those two bodies were lying in the grass, Savonarola was being tortured, and crying out in his agony, 'I will confess!'" (639).

Confession, it seems, is only possible if "language" is forgotten and some unknown face from the "hideous past" can be named. Baldassare's partial amnesia, like Tito's sense of memories hanging on like cobwebs, constructs an archaic desire, split from conscious subjectivity and seemingly "forgotten." This symptomatic amnesia is linked to the narrative's pervasive cynicism toward men's use of languages, particularly toward the scholarly translation of languages such as Latin, Greek, and French which functions to reproduce male egotism and misogyny. Bardo's humiliating consignment of his daughter to a "lower category" of Nature is the product of his translation from the Latin, and before that, he gloatingly comments, of his translation from an earlier Greek (101). In the chapter titled

"A Learned Squabble," the narrative "spells out" the misogynistic terms in which male scholars dispute grammatical minutiae. Tito, who is recognized as a scholar because of his fluency in several languages, exploits this knowledge solely for his own aggrandizement. In his last act of scholarly translation, he appears to interpret the Latin proclamation for the people, but the meaning of the words remains inaccessible to the crowd, and the proclamation becomes one more instance in which the ecclesiastical establishment manipulates "prophecy"—a speaking in tongues—for its own power. In the very beginning of the narrative, Nello the barber points out that words, like signs, may have more than one meaning, but the narrative demonstrates that the "knowledge" of languages constitutes power over meaning, for it is the scholar's privilege to define meaning. It is not accidental, I think, that this text repeatedly confronts the reader with Baldassare's experience of the "amnesia of signs": phrases in non-English languages are frequently incorporated *without translation*.[45] The reader is placed in much the same position as Tessa, who is fooled into thinking that Tito has married her by the "thieves' Latin" (205) used by the conjuror.

Such male-defined meanings in language must be forgotten if the daughter's desire is to be "remembered" and put into words. Not only the father (as agent of the separation from the mother) but also the language of the father must be "killed off" if the daughter is to reconstruct the maternal voice. George Eliot's "lavish mutilation of heroes' bodies" is here put in service to the daughter's "confession" of desire for the mother, and finally of her identification with the mother. Or we may assume, at least, that this is why the narrative interrupts Romola's "drifting away" with the killing-off of father and son and with the prophet's tortured cry, "I confess!," before refinding Romola in the bosom of a green land, wakened by the cry of a child.

In the epilogue, Romola completes her movement from "shining out" to speaking out: the last words in the narrative are hers. She appears in a stable position, recast as maternal instructor, interpreter, and narrator. Both the violence and the ecstasy of her history seem to have been quieted. We could say that she now speaks in the still, small voice that came after the earthquake and the fire, or we could say with equal validity that she speaks in the voice of the good mother.

Yet there remains something troubling about her. Is it because, simply, she is *too* serene? Romola's face is marked by placidity now, the narrator tells us, because she had known her worst sorrows while her "life was new" (673). I listen in vain for the accents of energy found in George Eliot's "Killed Tito in great excitement!"[46] Perhaps we must read Romola's last words as the final fetishistic detail in the narrative—the final construction of "difference" between herself and her authorial "daughter," herself and her maternal creator. If there is to be a difference between this maternal voice and that of the "writer" in the text, then perhaps this female prophetic protagonist must take up the position of quietness, of stability, of a kind of passivity, so that her author may take that of energy, initiative, and activity. Perhaps the trouble with Romola is not that she has been silenced, but that we who have been trained to listen to the unitary voice of the (male) prophet know that we have heard more than one (maternal) voice in this text—and we are troubled by *that* difference.

Ruskin and the Matriarchal Logos

PAUL SAWYER

To define Victorian nonfiction prose as a discourse is almost invariably to
think of it as masculine discourse—at least so long as we accept the customary description of the sages as a group of secular prophets. At the very
beginning of the Judeo-Christian tradition, the Hebrew prophets marked
all sacred human speech as masculine by virtue of their roles as oracles of
a patriarchal deity, a gender distinction repeated through the centuries by
male clergy who have preached the law. In general, the figure of the Victorian sage as a prophet underscores the notion of discursive authority itself
as patriarchal—which was perhaps the chief reason for the figure in the
first place. Attempts to define sage writing as a prose genre have been valid
and useful.[1] Yet the gender-marking of the notion of a prophet, if unex-
amined, subtly influences our sense of who really counts among Victorian
nonfiction prose writers, of who belongs to that visionary company and
who begets them. Most studies of the sages, for example, name Carlyle as
prime progenitor, the virtual inventor of Victorian nonfiction prose, but
since few Victorians tried to write in Carlylese, Carlyle's "invention" must
be rather the prophetic stance itself, a pose or assertion that required the
support of personal temperament. In this context, Carlyle's toughness, his
rages, his hints of silent suffering, his exaggerated manliness in general,
made lively theater for his reading audience.

Carlyle's radical suppression of the feminine, in both his works and his personality, was anomalous in the group of Victorian sages that he supposedly fathered. Such disparate figures as Mill, Newman, Arnold, Ruskin, and Pater, if they share anything at all, share an interest in the power of the aesthetic sensibility to uplift and ennoble, to soften, refine, humanize, and harmonize—the power of what Arnold called the Hellenic as opposed to the Hebraic. All of them were in some way apostles of culture. In terms of gender this label is mildly paradoxical, since the notion of cultivation and refinement, like the notion of gentility, was associated with the feminine sphere of the domestic as opposed to the masculine sphere of economic competition. Arnold's famous description of Newman ("Who could resist the charm of that spiritual apparition . . . rising into the pulpit, and then, in the most entrancing of voices, breaking the silence with words and thoughts which were a religious music—subtle, sweet, mournful?") defined an androgynous charisma more appealing to a mid-century audience than the Carlylean warrior-hero—a charisma powerful precisely in its mingling of feminine sweetness and masculine authority.[2] Arnold's Newman is an Angel in the house of God.

Of all the sages, John Ruskin—the product of both a sternly "masculine" Evangelicalism and an affluent, "feminized" childhood—most fully embodied the complex interplay of gender and writerly authority in Victorian times and the cultural tensions this interplay symbolized. His first published book, the opening volume of *Modern Painters* (1843), presents an extended portrait of a male deity, who is most awesome when He displays his power and most powerful when He reveals His wrath. Twenty years later, Ruskin delivered his honey-tongued defense of the subjection of women in "Of Queens' Gardens"—the most widely-read of his works in his lifetime (and perhaps again today, though for opposite reasons). Yet, in these same years, he positioned himself amid a wide network of women, ranging from distant correspondents to enraptured disciples: aristocratic patronesses, philanthropists, artists, drawing pupils, elderly neighbors, enraptured readers, and of course schoolchildren. In 1868 he wrote the gendered reverse of *Modern Painters*, *The Queen of the Air*, an extended portrait of a female deity who, as the Logos, inspires her creatures with the breath of life and sustains them with her presence.

Gracious yet autocratic, utopian and reactionary, patron of women and advocate of their suppression, Ruskin attracts or repels readers today in equal measure. His chief interest for intellectual history resides not in any single one of his positions but in the degree to which he internalized the conflicts of his culture, including the Victorian male's ambivalence toward female authority. In what follows, I consider the figure of the Ruskinian woman and her distinctive power: the moral force he called "wisdom." My texts will be some books of the 1860s—*The Ethics of the Dust, Sesame and Lilies,* and *The Queen of the Air*—which touch on the most scandalous of Ruskin's interests, his obsession with girls and their pedagogy. I want to show why this obsession, however eccentric or aberrant, nevertheless expressed an essential feature of the Victorian construction of womanhood, specifically, the tendency to view the pure maiden as a symbol of social order itself. When he sings the praises of girls, housewives, and the goddess Athena, Ruskin slips on the mantle of Carlylean prophet, embodying in his gentler manner a social ideal based not on masculine force of will but upon feminine sweetness and light—the ideal, in short, of a hegemonic order. I will argue, ultimately, that there is no such thing in the Victorian period as a Woman Question that is not also a question about bourgeois hegemony.

In 1858 Ruskin met Margaret Bell, headmistress of a girls' academy in Cheshire, and in the following decade he paid sixteen visits to the school as an unofficial benefactor and resident man of letters. Winnington Hall is a spacious sixteenth-century manor house twenty-two miles south of Manchester, with an excellent view of rural Cheshire; Bell leased it in 1851, knowing that an aristocratic residence would attract the daughters of the local gentry, the clergy, and the Manchester "Cottentots" (as the owners of the house called them).[3] Though she was the daughter of a Methodist clergyman, Bell had imbibed the Broad Church opinions and progressive pedagogy of F. D. Maurice and his associate, Alexander Scott of Manchester. (On his first visit, Ruskin saw four portraits on the drawing room wall: Maurice, Samuel Wllberforce, Archbishop Hare, and himself.) Female education in England had usually been a matter of rote learning, often administered by overworked and underpaid governesses in a cramped environment, resulting in a superficial smattering of facts and a few elegant "accomplishments." In his influential lectures on female education, Maurice banished frivolous pursuits and rote learning, proposing instead serious subjects and an emphasis on experience, self-expression, and respect for individual differences. Girls were to be made aware of themselves as "spiritual creatures" and of the divine presence in all things, so that education would not be simply subservient to commerce or politics.[4] Winnington put these precepts into practice. In addition to the serious subjects—mathematics, natural history, reading—the girls drew, sang, and danced. Above all, they kept healthy through athletics: they played cricket, bowled hoops, and swung ten or fifteen feet off a high bank in a rope swing.

Ruskin's descriptions, characteristically, convert Winnington into a paradise of girls: "the drawing room is a huge octagon . . . like the tower of a castle (hung . . . with large and beautiful Turner & Raphael engravings)—& with a baronial fireplace,—and in the evening, brightly lighted, with a group of girls scattered round it, it is a quite beautiful scene in its way."[5] The choral parts of the Sunday service remind him of Rome; the light and shade of the table cloth and the girls' dresses at dinner of a Venetian painting—"a 'marriage in Cana' or some such thing."[6] These words are from Ruskin's letters to his father, and no doubt he saw in Winnington Hall the image of a gentlemanly ideal—the kind of estate his father, a wine-merchant, showed him as a boy when on visits to wealthy clients. He would also have seen an image of his own suburban education, except that at Winnington he was part playmate, part tutor and always in charge: he conducted the girls' drawing lessons and supervised their Bible readings, while Bell, who worshiped him, moved in the background as a facilitator.

But if Ruskin was vicariously recapturing his own childhood at Winnington, he was also rewriting it, for this charmed place was free of the faults of his own upbringing: its harsh rigidities, its seclusion, its neglect of physical culture. And of course the Winnington world was free from the faults of adulthood. He wrote to Bell, "You can't conceive how few people I know with whom I can be myself . . . . My Father & Mother themselves, much as they love me—have no sympathy with what I am trying to do . . . sometimes I get very sulky—so that it really *is* no wonder that the feeling of being made a pet of as I was—at Winnington, made me wonderfully happy."[7]

The book based on the Winnington visits is one of Ruskin's most eccentric, yet it conveys precisely the cultural significance of Bell's pedagogy. *The Ethics of the Dust* (1865) is a set of feminized Socratic dialogues featuring an amiable, "ageless" Lecturer and a group of adoring girls with names like Lily, Florrie, and Iris. The children clamor to learn the elements of mineralogy, and the Lecturer manages to incite their wonder and curiosity, partly by showing them crystals and precious stones, partly by telling them miniature creation myths that are also moral allegories. At one point, he has the children dance quadrilles so that they can visualize the molecular structure of crystals. When at last they grasp the analogy between themselves and crystals—that they are themselves "vital" or organic structures, the crowning link in the chain of being that begins with crystals—the book's lesson has been achieved and its religious meaning revealed: "You may at least earnestly believe, that the presence of the spirit which culminates in your own life, shows itself in dawning, wherever the dust of the earth begins to assume any orderly and lovely state."[8]

The Ethics of the Dust is a child's view of romantic nature philosophy, but even more, it is an allegory of romantic pedagogy. By grasping that they are the very subject they are studying, the girls do not memorize precepts, they internalize a sense of "Life." The quadrille, strictly ordered but seemingly free, like a work of art, is the emblem of Ruskin's (and Bell's) pedagogy, and of the beautiful, perfectly-bred child who is its end product. Subject and object are one, since Life, the force pervading organic structures, is the objective manifestation of an instinctive will to good. Puritanism had depended on an ethics of earnestness that required breaking the child's will and forging a conscience stern enough to do battle with temptation; the new liberalism constructed a pedagogy requiring the gentle training of instincts, now represented (somewhat inconsistently) as both natural and regulated. A similar argument appears in Ruskin's essay on fairy tales (1866), which advocates the reading of tales that will awaken a child's love and reverence for the created world rather than the teaching of didactic tracts that will threaten and stifle her. Imagination replaces conscience, and romantic vitalism replaces Christian dogma. In effect, this idealized pedagogy constituted a new religion for Ruskin, succeeding to the collapse of his biblical faith and requiring as the central figure of its mythology a young girl—a suburban version of the romantic doctrine of innocence. Moreover, as Ruskin makes clear, internalizing a sensibility controls a child more efficiently than inculcating maxims; if anything, the "natural" purity of Ruskinian liberalism imposes a more stringent discipline than the old: "A child should not need to choose between right and wrong. It should not be capable of wrong; it should not conceive of wrong. Obedient, as bark to helm, not by sudden strain of effort, but in the freedom of its bright course of constant life."[9] No child, of course, can live up to such a standard. Presumably, the after effect of such a failure would be a perpetual nostalgia of the sort that Ruskin experienced at Winnington.

What are the implications of this myth of innocent childhood for adult relationships? *Sesame and Lilies* (1864), the collection containing his most famous lecture, was Ruskin's most popular book. Its burden is that gentility carefully nurtured and internalized is the first principle of social cohesion. "Of Queens' Gardens" (like its masculine companion piece, "Of Kings' Treasuries") was delivered in December 1864 at Manchester to the very "Cottontots" and their wives who might have sent their daughters to Bell's school. This now-classic (and, for some, classically repulsive) statement of the ideology of separate spheres uses a sweet tone and a stock of pseudochivalric images, presenting to the mind both a sermon and a sentimental genre painting.[10] The "true place and power" of women, Ruskin says, are not inferior to those of men but different: the man encounters "all peril and trial" in his "rough work in the world," whereas the home is "the place of Peace; the shelter, not only from all injury, but from all terror, doubt, and division."[11] Women are not excluded from all political power: for example as Ruskin argues, the Circassians had been driven recently from their homeland, yet this could not have happened had English ladies cared about it and wept over it. Nor are women excluded from all knowledge: they ought to learn just enough to sympathize with their husbands' pursuits. Within their spheres, women must be the moral guide of men and "incapable of error . . . instinctively, infallibly wise—wise, not for self-development, but for self-renunciation: wise, not that she may set herself above her husband, but that she may never fall from his side; wise, not with the narrowness of insolent and loveless pride, but with the passionate gentleness of an infinitely variable, because infinitely applicable, modesty of service—the true changefulness of women." It turns out that the woman's sphere is not only the home and garden per se but that greater "home" and "garden," the English nation, bound together in a spirit of benevolence and wisdom. Over that nation the virtuous wife is the true "Queen."

The wifely children of *The Ethics of the Dust* and the childish wife of "Of Queens' Gardens" share a predominant feature: the paradoxical combination (caught in the queen metaphor) of submissiveness and economic power. As Plato's philosopher starts his spiritual ascent with the contemplation of physical beauty, so Ruskin's bourgeois children begin their spiritual ascent with the right acquisition of clothing, books, and healthy looks. The very rhetoric that circumscribes the bourgeois wife in her activities and subordinates her to her husband serves to elevate the bourgeoisie, legitimizing its rule by prescribing a moral education in which the feminine virtue of sensibility (which Ruskin calls wisdom) is paramount.

Feminist critics have provided major insights into this linkage of bourgeois hegemony with the doctrine of separate spheres. Nancy Armstrong, for example, has suggested that women's writing—conduct books and novels in particular—created the bourgeois domestic woman, a refined, cultured subject who was a necessary prerequisite to the triumph of the bourgeoisie as a class: "such writing provided people from diverse social groups with a basis for imagining economic interests in common. Thus it was the new domestic woman rather than her counterpart, the new economic man, who first encroached upon aristocratic culture and seized authority from it." According to Armstrong, the new domestic woman could become the ideal wife for men in different walks of life, and she was able to compete with the aristocratic woman because her virtues were inherent elements of character, not surface shows.[12] If this analysis is correct, the Ruskinian woman is a close descendant of the late eighteenth-century domestic woman, belonging to a now-dominant bourgeoisie that seeks to legitimize its claims. In a similar vein, Catherine Gallagher has argued that the ideal Victorian housewife contained the moral contradictions of capitalism by acting as a subordinate helpmate to her husband. She occupied a region—the home and family—that represented the antithesis of capitalist society while imitating its structure:

> If the family were to function as a normative model of industrial society, it had to be both hierarchical and harmonious. It had to be uncontaminated by the competitive spirit of the as yet unregenerated society. In short, it had to be a protected enclave where women and children gave voluntary and loving submission to a benign patriarch. . . . if the family itself were divided by a consciousness of separate and antagonistic interests, it could not serve as a model for countering the competitive ethos in the sphere of production and commerce.[13]

In Ruskin's books, the girl-woman is the emblem of an organic society because she exemplifies sympathy, the first virtue binding that society together; yet in submitting herself to her husband she exemplifies obedience, the other virtue binding that society together. In "Of Queens' Gardens" Ruskin suppresses the possibility of separate and conflicting interests by means of a metaphor: the housewife "rules" the nation that is also her home.

Ruskin's career as a domestic ideologue is ironic, but the irony lies more in his audience than in himself. His own wife's elopement and the ensuing annulment formed the prime topic of society talk in 1854, yet by the end of the century *Sesame and Lilies* had sold 160,000 copies, in addition to countless separate issues of "Of Queens' Gardens." Ruskin's difference from his countrymen seems to have been the literalness by which he defined a wife as child, servant, and spirit of perfection. A marriage founded on such definitions resulted in scandal, but a lecture founded on them sold well. For the same reasons, his desperate love for Rose LaTouche—a child some thirty years his junior—carries the logic of separate spheres to its extreme. He seems to have craved Rose narcissistically, as an innocent child-other who would satisfy both his need to be indulged and his need to dominate. I have argued elsewhere that by marrying Rose (or any child-wife), Ruskin could use the doctrine of separate spheres to "marry" two inner contradictions: the split between the independent, aggressive adult and the perfectly obedient son; and guilt over a life of leisure built on the backs of those who toiled and starved.[14] Ruskin's contradictions mirror those in the culture as a whole. The industrial middle classes could reconcile the conflict between capitalist greed and Christian charity by dividing competitiveness and piety between the two sexes. In Ruskin's construction, Rose becomes on the one hand the obedient child and on the other the savior of suffering humanity. He himself becomes the sufferer at the end of "Of Queens' Gardens": "Oh—you queens—you queens! among the hills and happy greenwood of this land of yours, shall the foxes have holes, and the birds of the air have nests, and in your cities, shall the stones cry out against you, that they are the only pillow where the Son of Man can lay His head?"[15] Thus, although Ruskin's "queen" is an abstraction, she is visually concrete and so becomes, as Rose, the sign of male desire. She also becomes a figure for the social order as a whole.

In his recent, important study, *The Ideology of the Aesthetic*, Terry

Eagleton offers a historical explanation for the rise of figures like Ruskin's queen. This book ambitiously links notions of the aesthetic in Western thought with the rise of an autonomous bourgeois subject and a social order governed by hegemonic persuasion rather than by autocratic coercion. Eagleton's complex argument appears most concisely in his remarks on Rousseau:

> The ultimate binding force of the bourgeois social order, in contrast to the coercive apparatus of absolutism, will be habits, pieties, sentiments and affections. And this is equivalent to saying that power in such an order has become *aestheticized*. It is at one with the body's spontaneous impulses, entwined with sensibility and the affections, lived out in unreflective custom. . . . To dissolve the law to custom, to sheer unthinking habit, is to identify it with the human subject's own pleasurable well-being, so that to transgress that law would signify a deep self-violation. The new subject, which bestows on itself self-referentially a law at one with its immediate experience, finding its freedom in its necessity, is modelled on the aesthetic artefact.[16]

Just as an aesthetic artefact is an autonomous system of self-regulating, harmonious interrelationships, so the new bourgeois subject, obeying what seems to be the law of one's own nature, functions as part of what seems to be a harmoniously self-regulated whole. To explore another feature of this ideology, Eagleton turns to Burke's gendered distinction between the sublime (masculine) and the beautiful (feminine). If the sublime is felt to be coercive, then the beautiful—the thing one loves but does not fear or respect—is hegemonic: "The Law is male, but hegemony is a woman. . . . The woman, the aesthetic and political hegemony are now in effect synonymous." It is important to note, though, that if beauty must be included "within the sublimity of the masculine law, in order to soften its rigours," the reverse is not true: "Beauty is necessary for power, but does not itself contain it; authority has need of the very feminine it places beyond its bounds."[17]

Eagleton's reading of Burke most obviously resembles the bourgeois gentleman of sentimental fiction, with his characteristic blend of sweetness and strength—strength humanized by a feminine sensibility and sensibility emboldened by a masculine power to govern and direct. In Victorian times this union of traits reinforced the doctrine of separate spheres by negating the contradiction between Christian ethics (the female part) and competitive capitalist practice (the male part); it also ensured that actual governance, however well-counseled by female "wisdom," remained in the hands of men. In more general terms, the ideology of the aesthetic provides a powerful means of rethinking what has elsewhere been called, in relation to nineteenth-century England and America, the "feminization of culture." Conversely, the notion of a feminized culture suggests that the ideology of the aesthetic is also an ideology of the feminine—that since bourgeois hegemony intimately involves the subordination of bourgeois (and other) women, the aesthetic philosophers that support that system will be patriarchal as well.

The career of Ruskin—the major Victorian aesthetic theorist—offers evidence for this broader claim. I have argued that Ruskin's increasing interest in young women and their education was not merely a personal eccentricity but a logical extension of his thinking about art and society. By describing the natural and social order in powerfully sensuous terms, he feminized beauty at the very time that he was aestheticizing women through a similar technique of sensuous description. By the 1860s, his writings about women's place in society developed the figure of the pure woman as a symbolic expression of hegemonic control. In *The Ethics of the Dust* the girls are patterns of hegemonic subjectivity, introjecting the Law as a principle of spontaneous consensus; in "Of Queens' Gardens," wives are simultaneously hegemonic subjects and symbols of hegemony as a whole—they rule, one might say, in a Pickwickian sense. As I have suggested, Ruskin uses the half-disguised narrative of his own erotic desire to lend enormous affective power to hegemonic persuasion. But the opposite of hegemonic control—anarchy, insurrection, the resort to tyranny—is similarly feminized. The Ruskinian woman seems capable of radically unsettling the balance of forces she supposedly also contains. Might she in fact represent the very site at which those forces are generated?

By settling on the girl as an emblem of purity, Ruskin seems almost to acknowledge the impossibility of his vision of social unity. In one of the lessons of *The Ethics of the Dust*, the girls mistake a piece of gold for an ugly brown stone; in another, he allegorizes capitalist society as a dangerous valley where serpents sing in the trees; in a third, he tells the tales of "male" crystals that do fearful battle against evil in the "after life"; in yet another, the girls pretend he has dozed at the fire and lost track of time. Like the Red King in *Through the Looking-Glass*, Ruskin is sleeping through the dream he has created, a child-world of memory in which neither greed nor struggle nor suffering nor death can yet be thought. But that child-world will end and the unthinkable will become thinkable when the children reach maturity. For the moment, they are but "little housewives," whom Ruskin endows with the names of deities and compares playfully with dragons. The girl is the creature who has the seed of her own opposite almost ripe within her—that is to say, the breakdown of social control.

Three years after this book Ruskin published his fullest portrait of female power, *The Queen of the Air*. First delivered as a set of lectures on Greek mythology, it sets forth the cosmology of Winnington in Greek terms for Christian (or post-Christian) adults. But if the "little housewives" are figuratively goddesses, Ruskin's goddess-queen is only figuratively a housewife: her "home" is all of nature, and the contradictions willfully denied in the figure of the child reappear as the several natures of a manichean deity. Ruskin's Athena blends certain Greek myths and the idea of a universal generative goddess with the Old Testament figure of Wisdom, said to be God's helpmate at the Creation. Ruskin's concluding hymn to her is a Universal Prayer to a kind of *natura naturans* which is also the objectivized form of moral virtue inscribed in the physical order. But in her other manifestation, Athena is not a maiden but a war-goddess; as the mark of an old victory, she bears the emblem of the gorgon on her sleeve, and in the frantic third lecture, Ruskin's vision of her is direful and apocalyptic: "her wrath is of irresistible tempest: once roused it is blind and deaf—rabies—madness of anger—darkness of the Dies Irae . . . Wisdom never forgives."[18]

Wisdom is Ruskin's name for what Eagleton calls the "ideology of the aesthetic," the introjection of the social law experienced as spontaneous consensus. In *The Queen of the Air*, Ruskin now inscribes a hegemonic order in the cosmos itself, which is governed by an indwelling feminine divinity combining sweetness and strength. That divinity is lovely and graceful, the object of devotion and affection, with some sign upon her of the strength of Law—a Law having obvious relations to the Victorian woman's domestic responsibility for supervision, ordering, and surveillance, but whose ultimate sanction, though hidden, is nevertheless absolute. For Ruskin the mark of that sanction is the gorgon head, emblem of the woman's presumed castration and, therefore, in Athena, the emblem of her castrating power, her power to condemn, to cast off, to darken, never to forgive.[19] In contemplating the extremities of that power, Ruskin's text becomes disturbed and disjointed.[20]

What does it means for a Victorian patriarch to have written a book that freely revises the deity of the Judeo-Christian tradition, envisioning the Logos as present, full, and female?[21] The answer is an acute paradox. *The Queen of the Air*, the one text which of all writings by Victorian men seems most pervaded by an apprehension of female power may also be read as a full-scale allegory of the patriarchal social order, an order that maintains its control (in times of relative calm) by appeals to the feminine virtues and to feminine images of domestic harmony. Literary representations of strong women no doubt could have had a utopian, transforming power, inspiring their women readers and opening up subversive possibilities. As a mythological abstraction, however, Ruskin's goddess-queen, like his queenly housewives, inhabits the looking-glass world of hegemonic ideology—an ideal region that reflects in reverse the power relationships maintained by the sexes in the actual social world in order to perpetuate them. In that mirror of the bourgeois order, women rule and guide and uplift: it is a "kinder, gentler nation" there.[22]

This is not to argue that Ruskin's political thought is merely an elaborate mystification of the status quo—that is untrue. What was generally at stake for the men known as Victorian sages was less the status quo than the question of who should control the necessary changes. For Ruskin, Arnold, and many others, the regulators should be men of culture and sensibility (and perhaps also, on application, women) who could perceive the "ideal": the dynamic and flexible harmony of a system of unequals, where each unequal developed to the limits of her or his capability. Because this system lacks the possibility of internal conflict, it should not be disrupted, for example, by feminist or trade union agitators. It should also not be disrupted by an unregulated industrial system, the usual metaphor for which in sage writing was the machine, but which was also seen as the active producer of filth and disorder.

Probably all representations of female power produced by these writers are bivalent, confirming patriarchal hegemony but also making new roles for women thinkable: in this sense, one might say that the "feminine" contests or subverts patriarchy. But we must also remember that Victorian patriarchal culture used the "feminine" to legitimize itself from the start. Obviously, femininity so conceived was a very different matter from granting actual rights to actual women: the Victorian ideology of womanhood became a polemical weapon not only against working class aspirations but also against the woman's movement itself. For these reasons, I have preferred not to speak of the "feminine" as something that acts on its own to subvert or to contest. Ultimately, texts have no invariant political meaning divorced from the history of their social interpretations. Only when women are able to demonstrate their power concretely and to speak in their own voices can the lives of both women and men be understood in their true relations to the hegemonic structures that seek to define them. And only then can we give adequate readings of the books written about them.

Malleus Malificarum or The Witches' Hammer: *Victorian Visions of Female Sages and Sorceresses*

SUSAN P. CASTERAS

That Victorian art was engulfed by images of femininity is no longer a revelation, and the darker side of womankind—the prostitute, the fallen woman, and the femme fatale—has also begun to be scrutinized iconologically alongside the more predictable icons of unsullied virginity and domestic virtue.[1] What has not yet received much close attention in this feminine pantheon is the representation of the female seer and sage in the fine arts.[2] The Victorian painted image of the female with uncommon creative or intellectual ability was a decided outsider and anomaly, in some ways analogous to the rarity of female genius in contemporary literature and psychological treatises. As shall be shown, the woman endowed with superior creativity typically found a visual equivalent in the witch or sorceress, whose supernatural powers permitted her to exercise her half-human, half-demonical or monstrous inspiration, autonomy, and degeneracy. In some ways, as an emblem of extraordinary creative achievement—even though in the context of the black arts—this often irrational, strident female seer and sage and her very existence on canvas ironically served to underscore the imagination, independence, and knowledge denied to real women. Moreover, she arguably personified a Romanticized notion of mad genius, nature gone awry in creating a wild and aberrant female, and many viewers probably deemed her both pathological and frightening.

How did such atypical images of women interact with or cancel out the images of their tamer "sisters" and challenge the feminine norm? When and why were figures of the female seer and sage most popular? To what extent did these images expand upon dominant gender roles and identity? Did these images dehumanize, masculinize, or feminize the practitioners of the black arts? Was the alien nature of the witch and the sorceress part of the attraction for viewers? What characteristics did these personages possess which were otherwise taboo, unspoken or feared in mortal women?

The negative connotations of women as supernatural monsters, and especially as witches and brides of the devil, have been analyzed in the past decade in terms of Romanesque and Gothic sculpture, as well as in the context of mostly fifteenth- and sixteenth-century prints and paintings.[3] The *Malleus Malificarum*, a late fifteenth-century encyclopedia of demonology, ironically became a standard "bible" of information and misinformation on witches and witchcraft through the nineteenth century. It promulgated the view that these "daughters of evil" were Satan's concubines whose insatiable sexual appetites were an inherent part of their depravity.[4] The witch and the sorceress—both of whom had sold their souls to the devil—functioned as embodiments of evil, or as diabolic agents or accomplices. As such, they established a misogynistic norm of behavior for women that was largely defined by the prevailing patriarchal culture of writers, theologians, and painters. Representing female anomaly and inversion, they served as spectacles for erotic consumption by men (both artists and spectators) as well as manifestations of masculine fears, desires, and fantasies. While these female figures attained a kind of divine status through their necromancy, in Victorian art they were generally distinctive from personifications of goddesses, which ranged from the patient, subservient women who supported men—notably Hera/Juno and Demeter/Ceres—to models of autonomy—like Artemis/Diana and Athena/Minerva. Nonetheless, in some ways the psychological attributes of the sorceress allied her with the latter camp of independent femininity, reinforcing her nonhuman status by a clear disjunction with nineteenth-century standards of propriety: her daring deeds and "masculinized" traits of strength, resourcefulness, and aggressiveness would have utterly doomed her in Victorian drawing rooms.

Compared with the earthbound, parlorbound bourgeois Victorian lady, the seer, the sage, and the witch refigured the boundless psychic powers

and energies of women in prehistory and mythology, counteracting the
normative signification of femininity in nineteenth-century genre painting
with their inscrutable potency and exhilarating liberation. Like the countless vignettes of solitary, pretty women with flowers or other accoutre-
ments which were produced in vast numbers by Victorian artists, the
portrayals of aberrant or exceptional, even extraterrestrial, women were
made to be looked at—if not stared at—and subjected to a male gaze that
would both judge and ultimately offer either acceptance or approbation.
By contrast, women viewers had the opportunity to behold and to evaluate
the forbidden freedom and the empowerment of goddesses and enchantresses through such images, instead of identifying with constricting Victo-
rian-style attire and rooms full of knicknacks or lush gardens full of
blossoms. Little was forbidden to the witch and her sisters, for they transcended mortal law. Unfettered by temporal imperatives, or even by the
Victorian lady's corset and yards of heavy dress material, sorceresses acted
according to their own dictates and wore bewitched garments that generated an energy of their own.

Painted images or personifications of feminine wisdom are rare in the
Victorian period, although examples of maternal wisdom in the context of
genre painting—such as the good or wise mother—were quite common.
Given the penchant for depicting otherworldly females in the last quarter
of the century, there are surprisingly few Victorian paintings of female
divinities such as Athena as the goddess of wisdom, the counselor, and
peacemaker (aside, for example, from personifications of Britannia as an
armed maiden.[5] (Athena, generally considered to be the patroness of
women's work as well as a mistress of weaving and spinnning, also possessed magical powers of transfiguring herself, as when she tricked Odys-
seus.) Occasionally the poetesses of antiquity such as Lesbia or Sappho
qualified as subjects, notably in Lawrence Alma-Tadema's *Sappho* (Wal-
ters Art Gallery), or his *Catullus at Lesbia's* (ex-Funt collection) of 1865
and *At Lesbia's* (ex-Funt collection) of 1870. In both of the latter works,
however, Lesbia is depicted as an enthroned odalisque, looking more like a
coy Victorian woman on a chaise longue than a poetic genius or an embodiment of feminine sagacity.

Victorian painting also includes sporadic images of ancient priestesses,
again in Lawrence Alma-Tadema's oeuvre, among them *A Priestess of
Apollo* (Tate Gallery) circa 1888. Here a young priestess both holds and

wears sacramental objects and vestments and is shown in the act of singing or calling others to prayer. Some priestesses were vestal virgins, and many were taught by patriarchal authorities to sing magical songs or incantations that had a hypnotic effect on listeners. In some cases the magical, bewitching sound of their songs allegedly caused them to serve as organs or conduits of the spirits, and they supposedly swayed, glowed, and sometimes gained the ability to transform objects. Near Alma-Tadema's priestess of Apollo stands a large vessel, perhaps emblematic of her purity, and in the right background is a glimpse of an altarlike area. Significantly, she wears a leopard skin; this implied kinship with animals—suggesting a tendency to bestial behavior or secret powers of transformation—is a common trait among depictions of sorceresses as well.

While there are few surviving personifications of positive feminine knowledge in Victorian painting, many images produced from the 1860s until the turn of the century delved into the negative side of female sapientia or wisdom, namely, witchcraft. One of the most important pictorial prototypes is found in the work of Dante Gabriel Rossetti. Beginning with early works like the 1849 watercolor entitled *The Laboratory* (Birmingham City Museum and Art Gallery), Rossetti frequently dealt with subjects concerning the heinous deeds and necromantic potential of women. In this watercolor a dangerous female has been jilted, and, amid a litter of books, flasks, and chemicals, she turns to alchemy in order to achieve revenge. Similarly, in Rossetti's 1860 *Lucretia Borgia* (Tate Gallery), the female protagonist poisons her own husband. This notion of the black arts was also addressed by Rossetti in his poem "Sister Helen," in which a jealous, rejected woman practices voodoo by melting a waxen surrogate of her faithless lover in order to cause his death. The macabre theme surfaced as well in illustrations by other Pre-Raphaelites, Elizabeth Siddal and Edward Burne-Jones.[6]

The heady mixture of woman's sexual allure, malignant beauty, and powerful magic recurred in other forms as well, notably in various Rossetti compositions dominated by dressing tables, balconies, and enclosed boudoirs. An excellent example is his *Lady Lilith* of 1868 (Fig. 1; Delaware Art Museum), which evokes, along with his own accompanying poem, the figure of Adam's first wife, as "the witch he loved before the gift of Eve." Like many femmes fatales, she has "enchanted" or "strangling" golden hair that ensnares and "draws men to watch the bright web she can

1. Dante Gabriel Rossetti, *Lady Lilith*. 1868. Oil on canvas, 37 ½ × 32″. Delaware Art Museum.

weave."[7] This inert yet voluptuous "spider woman" in her luxurious bower seemed to F. G. Stephens, an original member of the Pre-Raphaelite Brotherhood, to have a modern witch's face and a cold soul: "she has passion without love, and languour without satiety—energy without heart, and beauty without tenderness or sympathy for others."[8] Rossetti's poem "Eden Bower" describes Lilith as taking on the serpent's shape in order to ruin Adam and Eve, making her one of many *belle dame sans merci* types who become Victorian snake-women.

Although she is also a cruel temptress Lady Lilith functions in part as a witch enacting rituals not of beauty, but rather of entrapment and possibly even self-transformation. Hers is less a dressing table than a horrific, Gothic altar of power, and while the emblems of femininity—mirror, flowers, brush—are present, the witch Lilith flouts fixed feminine meanings and is instead quite aggressive, menacing, and virile. Her toilette and her actions are thus subversive, and, combined with emblems of male power, create a weirdly androgynous and unfixed effect. Lilith appears to be a passive beauty, yet in her mirror she can behold the aggressive, invisible, monstrous side of her personality. Rossetti has defused the danger of his temptress and of the boudoir by embedding it in a traditional context—but the otherness of the claustrophobic chamber and its altar to the black arts (including votive candles and a censer) becomes particularly evident when compared with subsequent examples of witchcraft.[9]

A related scene of a femme fatale's incipient crime and evil in Burne-Jones's *Sidonia von Bork, 1560,* a watercolor of 1860 (Fig. 2; Tate Gallery), takes its inspiration from a tale by a Swiss author whose works Rossetti and Burne-Jones both knew in translation.[10] As an old woman, Sidonia was burned as a witch, but Burne-Jones instead presents viewers with a beautiful young temptress, another blonde with serpentine hair and a malevolent expression. Yet she carries evil within her and, like a latter-day daughter of Lilith, she seems to have made a pact with the devil or to have become a sort of she-devil. Like Nimue or Vivien in subsequent examples, she too casts a glance over one shoulder, as if to assess the impact of her sorcery and criminal activities. The snakelike chain or weblike pattern of her dress and hairnet underscore her entrapment of male victims; these are her "death garments—white with black stripes" like a spider's web.[11] (In fact, a tiny spider crawls across the signed scroll at bottom right.) She too will use necromancy for amorous purposes and can inflict pain as well as pleasure on her victim. As John Christian has remarked, the appeal of this archetypal image of the femme fatale, based on "combined themes of beauty, evil, and magic, together with a wealth of descriptive detail, proved irresistible to a collective imagination centred on the cult of the 'stunner' and profoundly influenced by notions of the supernatural."[12]

The celebrated magician Medea—known for killing her two children by

2. Edward Burne-Jones, *Sidonia von Bork, 1560.* 1860. Watercolor with body-color, 13 × 6 ³/₄″. Tate Gallery, London/Art Resource, New York.

Jason (and also for mutilating her brother Absyrtus and destroying her rival)—was one of the most popular choices for signifying feminine sorcery. In the early 1860s, William Morris offered a retelling of her tale, and the subject of one event in his poem—when Medea gathers "mystic herbs" at midnight so that she can cast a spell to bind Jason to her—is depicted by Valentine Cameron Prinsep in *Medea the Sorceress* (Fig. 3; South London Art Gallery) of 1888. Medea appears in the natural world, using her knife to cut and dig up mushrooms, herbs, and other plants, thus illustrating Morris's lines: "within her caught-up gown/Much herbs she had, and on her head a crown/Of dank night-flowering grasses, known to few"[13] She performs these acts covertly in the dark, perhaps at midnight, the classic bewitching hour for magic. Like other sorceresses, Medea defines her acts in terms of nature and herself, not mortal law. The snake coiled on a nearby tree is not only reminiscent of the tree of knowledge, but also of the Satanic connotations of Eve's transgressions. Curled in a kneeling pose, Medea is associated with reptilian or snakelike creatures. In his essay "The Queen of the Air" John Ruskin equates snakes with sensuality and with tainted Christianity, and indeed Medea is an obvious example of an anti-Christian, inverted morality.

A somewhat different approach to Medea is found in Evelyn Pickering de Morgan's *Medea* (Fig. 4; Williamson Art Gallery, Wirral Borough Council) of 1889, a picture which was accompanied by the following quotation: "Day by day/She saw the happy time fade fast away/And as she fell from out that happiness/Again she grew to be the Sorceress/Worker of fearful things, as once she was." Instead of representing Medea as a homicidal mother who murdered her offspring as part of her mad revenge against Jason, De Morgan depicts Medea as a sorceress, a "worker of fearful things" holding a possibly fatal potion in a vial. Nature is not her infernal laboratory; rather, Medea practices her magic in a combined interior/exterior setting that resembles a temple. The steps at left function as a quasi-altar of black magic—with two winged females (harpies or sirens) that stand atop the railings and hold out incense or ointment bowls. At the base of the harpies is a statuette of a lion, symbolic of masculine strength. Amid the marbled and barrel-vaulted splendor, Medea stands resolute and calm, not cruel but seemingly immobilized by the realization of what she has become. Is she contemplating the destruction of Glauce, of her children, or of Aegeus (whom she married and later plotted to poison)? De

3. Valentine Cameron Prinsep, *Medea the Sorceress*. 1888. Oil on canvas, 56 × 44″. South London Art Gallery.

4. Evelyn Pickering de Morgan, *Medea*. 1889. Oil on canvas, 59 × 35 ⁷/₈″. Williamson Art Gallery, Wirral Borough Council, England.

Morgan also painted *The Love Potion* (The De Morgan Foundation, Battersea House) in 1903—complete with a golden-robed witch endowed with the power to mutilate, paralyze, or destroy men. While an ominous black cat rests at her feet, she mixes a secret potion at her altar; nearby are treatises and handbooks on witchcraft. One of these books is labelled "Paracelsus," a reference to the sixteenth-century German (the subject of Robert Browning's 1835 poem of the same name) who travelled widely and practiced black magic, alchemy, and astrology. In the distance on a terrace stands the object of her malevolent revenge and magic: a pair of lovers.

Like Rossetti's Lilith, William Holman Hunt's Lady of Shalott, although not a sorceress, was a seminal image which influenced the iconography of female necromancy, in late examples such as de Morgan's *Love Potion* as well as in Frederick Sandys's experiments in the 1850s and 1860s. Hunt's illustration of *The Lady of Shalott* for the 1857 Moxon edition of Tennyson's poems (Fig. 5; later reinterpreted in an 1894 oil painting, now at the Wadworth Athenaeum) signalled the onset of a steady stream of portrayals (by William Maw Egley, J. W. Waterhouse, and many others) of this Arthurian heroine and artist figure imprisoned in her workspace.[14] Although she is not described as a witch by Tennyson, she nonetheless has characteristics that qualify her as one. Spellbound, she has seen the future, as in a crystal ball, and is literally caught in a skein of fate, a tangled web that captures her; her bewitched hair, magical as well as ensnaring, makes her a kind of femme fatale as well. In the altarlike mirror at which she stands like a priestess or sorceress, a visage of Lancelot materializes, and this empowers her magic. The sacred vow she has made in fact has placed her under a sort of spell which has created her bondage to her art as well as to her love. Her vision and spell are failed and flawed, however, and at the end of the poem she laments her seclusion and the prison of romantic rejection that her art has helped to create. As Debra Mancoff has aptly noted, the ultimate failure of the Arthurian revival in the Victorian era is perhaps encapsulated in this picture of the doomed Lady, "who rises slowly, bound in a spell, as she is forced out in a world in which she could not survive."[15]

Indeed, it was the Arthurian legend itself which, beyond the realm of classical mythology and literature, contributed the major enchantresses in English lore and fueled the imagination of Victorian artists. The most

5. William Holman Hunt, *The Lady of Shalott*. Engraving, 3 ¹/₄ × 3 ¹/₄″ plate size. Engraved for the 1857 Moxon edition of Tennyson's *Poems*. Private collection.

prominent figures to emerge from this filtering of Arthurian legend with Celtic and Druidic mythology were Morgan le Fay and Vivien, Nimue/ Nyneve, and the Lady of the Lake, a group arguably identifiable with one mythic female (capable of both malicious and benevolent deeds).[16] Both Thomas Malory's fifteenth-century *Morte d'Arthur* and Tennyson's *Idylls of the King* were popular and well-known among Victorian audiences. A central and recurring enchantress figure in contemporary literature and art was Morgan le Fay, the cruel half-sister of Arthur; when Arthur presented her with the scabbard to his sacred sword Excalibur, she forged it and gave away the real one. Duplicitous and fierce, she was, like Lady Guinevere, one of the key personalities in Victorian fantasies of the Arthurian saga.

Sandys, whose fixation on female necromancers is evinced in works such as *The Queen of the Serpents*, produced one of the most famous images of this legendary sorceress in *Morgan le Fay* of 1862–1863 (Fig. 6; Birmingham City Museum and Art Galleries). Sequestered within a claustrophobic chamber of strange objects, like a Lady of Shalott locked in her tower and gone mad, the figure has Pre-Raphaelite wiry hair and an extraordinarily fierce expression. An incarnation of evil, she has a contorted, inhuman face which, so very different from the calm, composed masks of most Victorian images of ladies or goddesses, aligns her more with the primeval female or with the madwoman. In fact, even in this crowded workshop she seems to move violently and to be on the verge of becoming a whirling dervish. Wild and uncontrollable, she is possessed by magic, like a frenzied shaman; her floating hair, open mouth, and unblinking stare suggest that she is in the act of asserting her great power by casting a spell, conjuring up new worlds.

Surrounded by alchemical vessels and books, Sandys's Morgan le Fay is, again like the imprisoned Tennysonian Lady, in a heightened state of frustrated creativity and intensity (even hysteria, or female madness). But in this case and that of other images of sorceresses, the madness liberates the woman from the constraints of masculine-defined normalcy. In some ways, Morgan le Fay and other sorceresses are less mad, in effect, than paradoxically wise. She and her "sisters" are not merely possessed by the irrational and overwhelmed by the quasi-orgasmic rapture of magical visions; they also have the capacity for self-fulfillment through their power over their own states of being as well as the destinies of others. Their "hysteria" is therefore empowering.

In Sandys's depiction, Morgan le Fay's movements and her language or chants are supernaturally charged. Moreover, like the Lady, she too inhabits a suffocating artist's space, in this case one with a malevolent atmosphere. Her world is animated by fascinating symbols and talismans. She wears rich furs that ally her with animal world and, like Tennyson's Vivien, wears other strange and luxurious garments. The skirt of Morgan le

6. Frederick Sandys, *Morgan le Fay*. 1862–1863. Oil on panel. 17 ¹/₂ × 24 ³/₄″. Birmingham City Museum and Art Galleries.

Fay's robe is embroidered with serpent motifs and necromantic symbols. Animalism and animals appear everywhere (perhaps invoking the feminine unconscious or anima): fierce, sinister creatures on the backdrop, and a strange lionlike incense carrier or lamp that may evoke masculine or "leonine" strength. In fin-de-siècle art, some homoerotized witches are shown with cats' paws or in half-bestial states that suggest miscegenation with animals as well as their relation to man-eating, sphinxes, and chimeras.[17] Sandys's priestess of black magic also wears a leopard skin, causing one to wonder whether she (like Leda or Pasiphae) mated with animals or simply inherited their rage or appetite.[18] There is also a possible allusion to Artemis, the virginal goddess of the hunt who wore a panther skin. Morgan le Fay's exotic garb and its atavistic associations may also refer to her predatory qualities and to her capacity to turn men into animals at a whim. Her own attire contrasts with the cursed robe she is conjuring up for her brother, for on the loom in the background she has been weaving a garment that will burst into flames as soon as he dons it. Jealous, passionate, and somewhat out of control, she exhibits another frequent attribute of witches—weaving—which makes these females even more spiderlike as they enchant and ensnare men.

Two other works by Sandys also contribute to this genre. One that predated *Morgan le Fay* was his illustration of *Rosamund, Queen of the Lombards* (Fig. 7; private collection) for a poem in *Once a Week* in 1861. Rosamund, as a captive of her father's killer, Lord Cunimond, was ordered by Cunimond to drink "the good wine from thy master's cup/made of thy father's head"; raising "the skull-cup to her lips," and "smiling, she touched it, bubbling fresh/Like the broth of a wizard's charm—That night she caught him in her mesh, And slew him, gorged with wine and flesh."[19] Rosamund turns the evil of her captor upon him instead and in vengeance kills him; his body is seen on a bed in the background left. A belle dame sans merci and a femme fatale, Sandys's Rosamund belongs to the legion of witches or female wizards, surrounded as she is by necromantic objects. In addition to the fiery tripod, there are tiny vials and secret documents which mingle curiously on the prie-dieu with either a Bible or prayer book. Moreover, the upside-down "cup" of her father's skull is placed next to a crucifix, reminiscent of emblems of the devil as an anti-Christ in shrouded, upside-down crosses. Like Medea (whom she resembles), Rosamund practices solitary but potent magic; similarly, her tresses seem bewitched and

7. Frederick Sandys, *Rosamund, Queen of the Lombards*. Engraving, 5 × 4″ plate size. Engraved by Swain for *Once a Week*, 5 (30 Nov. 1861): 591. Private collection.

her garments seem to twist around her as a sign of her agitated state. Perhaps Hunt was influenced by this image when he painted *Isabella and the Pot of Basil* (Delaware Art Museum) in 1867, in which the heroine—in her melancholy madness and sorrow—has withdrawn from the world and worships at a gruesome shrine where her lover's head, hidden in a pot of basil, becomes an object of veneration.

In *Vivien* of 1863 (Fig. 8; Manchester City Art Gallery), Sandys utilizes a decidedly Rossettian format to enshrine the beautiful Tennysonian sorceress. A gypsy in appearance like Morgan le Fay, she is surrounded by peacock feathers (symbolic of vanity) and other emblematic objects such as a sensuous rose and the apple of Eve's seduction and fall. Over her shoulders is a golden mantle that looks like an enchanted wizard's robe. Moreover, Vivien looks away from the viewer and instead focuses on a special flower she has learned about through necromancy, here a poisonous daphne (which ironically had connotations of purity in the language of the flowers) and also a red rose of passion.[20] Tennyson's Vivien has a reptilian nature: lissome and glittering, she clings like a snake when seducing the wizard Merlin. In a dramatic reversal of power, Vivien wins from Merlin the secret spell for imprisoning a victim inside a tree, and then turns this charm upon him. Her debilitating and emasculating effect upon Merlin was even noted by Ruskin, who said that, "broadside ballads would do *me* not the least harm, while Tennyson's 'Vivien' would do me much."[21] However, in Sandys's image Vivien is no longer sinuous or creeping on the ground; rather, she has become erect and dominant in order to reverse roles and to force men into subjugation.

Another balcony-bound woman who barely seems restrained by her environment is Sandys' *Medea* (Fig. 9; Birmingham City Museum and Art Galleries), completed in 1868 and also rejected that year for the Royal Academy walls. (It was published the next year as a frontispiece for a poem of the same name by Col. A. B. Richardson.) Time and past events are compressed in the friezelike background, where at left a ship alludes to Jason, Medea's lover, and at right refers to his quest of the golden fleece. But there are tribulations to come, as one can predict by looking at the figure's serpentine hair, bracelet, and bizarre earrings. Like Vivien, she is embowered or held in check by a wall behind and in front of her, in this case with cryptic Egyptian motifs in the backdrop.[22] Her transcendent state, and her powers of transmuting persons or things from one state to another, are implied in various ways. She holds a strange vessel, from which is pouring a magical draught, whose very shape seems to be in the act of changing. There is also a curious part-animal, somewhat phallic blue carving at left, and a lizard or chameleon decoration on the fire brazier which reinforce Medea's reptilian traits. These objects, along with the inclusion of a strange furry object and a frog at right, suggest the

8. Frederick Sandys, *Vivien*. 1863. Oil on canvas, 25 × 20 ¹/₂″. Manchester City Art Gallery.

sorceress's ability to transform nature; these very things may actually be human victims imprisoned by her black magic. The bestial symbolism may also allude to Medea's regressive, primordial attributes. Moreover, what appears to be the skein of fate—akin to the web that binds the Lady of Shalott—intersects here with the poison berries and with the pages inscribed with esoteric symbols and coded language. But the most startling

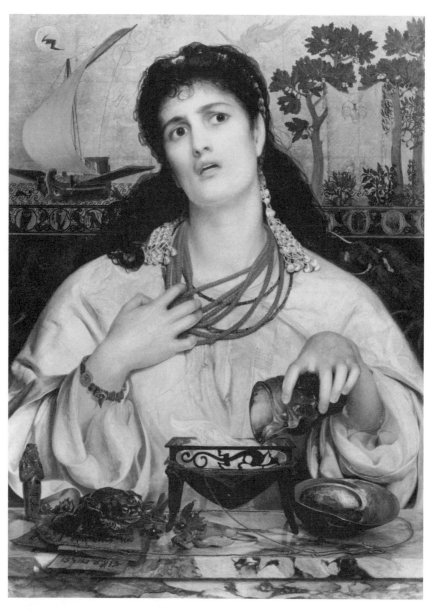

9. Frederick Sandys, *Medea*. Completed 1868. Oil on panel, 24 ¹/₂ × 18 ¹/₄″. Birmingham City Museum and Art Galleries.

aspect of this femme fatale is her horrifying expression, which like Morgan le Fay's, generates various meanings. The wild eyes and the mouth frozen in a scream or chant are a shocking contrast to most Victorian images of femininity. Both Medea and Morgan le Fay behave as if deranged, mentally or sexually or both. The action of Medea's mouth—in the process of changing itself—creates an apotropaic effect, as if Medea is warding off evil with her look. On the other hand, the ugliness of her distorted lips may also suggest the liberation of the woman's senses, her openness to change as well as her susceptibility to evil. To modern eyes the emphasis on this orifice appears quite sexual, as if the viewer is being invited to behold the sorceress's *vagina dentata*.[23]

In the same genre of female alchemy and black magic is John Collier's *White Devil* (ex-Sotheby's), a fin-de-siècle (or later) example that attests to the tenacity of this kind of imagery, derivative of Rossetti and yet part of the necromantic tradition. Collier's problem pictures included subjects like *A Glass of Wine with Caesar Borgia* (Wolsey Art Gallery, Ipswich) of 1893 (*The Laboratory* (ex-Sotheby's) of 1895, and *A Fallen Idol* (current location unknown) of 1913, but *White Devil* (for which the literary source, if any, is unclear) moves beyond prodigal daughters or femmes fatales to the she-devil type, whose worship often resulted in the death or destruction of men. At first glance the sitter's imperious pose, crown, and enthronement suggest her regal status, but these elements mask and upset the viewer's normal expectations when they blend with certain sinister details. Indeed, it is the woman's jewelry which marks her as different; she is crowned with authority, but from infernal sources, not divine ones. Beautiful, composed, and monolithic in appearance, she is nonetheless a dangerous temptress, one whose magnetic and smugly condescending gaze allies her with the petrifying or mesmerizing eyes of Medusa, witches, and enchantresses. Her dress also alludes to necromancy for it is embellished with painted herbs and flowers that are essential for casting spells and enacting forbidden rituals. In her hand is a long chain, with a human skull on one side and a male face on the other; although this "goddess" or Amazonian queen remains unfettered, her male victim has his destiny controlled by her. In some respects this monarchical temptress qualifies as worthy of worship or idolatry, personifying what Nina Auerbach has described in the realm of fiction as "a myth crowning a disobedient woman as heir of the ages and demonic saviour of the race."[24]

The issue of female superiority and sovereignty achieved through witch-craft also manifests itself in the relationship of Merlin with Nimue (as well as with Vivien). Originally Nimue's mentor, Merlin becomes her pawn and prisoner in Tennyson's narration of the Arthurian story. This subject clearly interested Burne-Jones who, besides beginning a watercolor of Morgan le Fay in 1862, treated the figure of Nimue several times, initially in *Merlin and Nimue* (Victoria and Albert Museum) of 1861 and subse-quently in an 1872–1877 oil painting. In the watercolor, Burne-Jones in-scribed the frame itself with text from Malory's *Morte d'Arthur*, hailing Nimue as "the lady of the Lake." Like Sidonia von Bork, Lady Lilith, and numerous others, this enchantress is also blonde, a femme fatale in the Rossettian mold who dominates the composition and is cold and calculat-ing as she practices chants from a book of incantations. The setting charged with silence and bleakness, is an immobile forest, a world outside of Camelot where Nimue unleashes her black magic.[25] As with Medea and other examples, the Arthurian sorceress identifies with the powers of na-ture and the universe, using her abilities to paralyze man and his actions. In the background stands Merlin, who has already paid the price for being beguiled and tricked by Nimue: he clutches one hand to his heart in pain as his former pupil's black magic begins to take effect.

In *The Beguiling of Merlin* of 1870–1874 (Fig. 10; Lady Lever Art Gallery, National Museums and Galleries on Merseyside) the confronta-tion between the two is elevated to almost operatic proportions. Here, the sorceress is clearly a seductress as well; in fact, the artist ironically casts Marie Zambaco, a woman toward whom he felt great passion, in this role (and also in the role of Circe in another picture), perhaps partly portraying himself in the aging person of Merlin.[26] The source here seems to conflate Tennyson's *Idylls of the King* with an English translation of a French ro-mance. The latter includes a scene in which Vivien—wily, malignant, and full of hatred for King Arthur—induces her mentor to take refuge in an old tree during a storm. After extracting secret spells from him, she leaves him there, permanently enchanted.[27] In Tennyson's version Vivien idolizes Merlin but plays him for the fool in order to gain knowledge of the black arts. She is flirtatious and flatters him; a traitress, she "kiss'd his feet" and "writhed toward him, slided up his knee and sat" like a venomous snake, trying to get him to love and trust her.[28] Like Medea and other witches, she has a fiery temper, and her railing approximates the divine madness of

10. Edward Burne-Jones, *The Beguiling of Merlin*. Completed 1874. Oil on canvas, 72 × 43″. Lady Lever Art Gallery, National Museums and Galleries on Merseyside.

Morgan le Fay and other dark sisters. While Merlin sleeps, she takes his
book of charms and begins to usurp his magic and practice her own incantations upon him. Holding the book, she (like Vivien in the 1861 gouache)
looks back over one shoulder at Merlin, who seems unable to move under
the paralysis of her spell and hypnotic gaze. She is a Huntian Lady of
Shalott, too, in this case practicing her black arts in an outside studio, with
the bush as her loom and the book her mirror. As Nimue weaves her spell,
Merlin's image and being become caught in her web of duplicity and black
magic. Like the other sorceresses, Nimue gains her knowledge from forbidden, esoteric books and tongues, in this case reciting spells from Merlin's
ancient tome "writ in a language that has long gone by" (383).

In Tennyson, Nimue/Vivien at one point stands up "stiff as a viper frozen"; the white heat of her anger strikes out and makes a "loathsome
sight." (386). She also lets out a wailing shriek, and a "snake of gold slid
from her hair" (387). Her exquisite beauty, which *The Athenaeum* described as full of "snaky intensity of malice" and shown in Burne-Jones's
painting through "a shimmering light of witches," becomes a weapon used
against "the weak and womanish" Merlin with as much success as black
magic itself.[29] Her head of writhing snakes allies her with the fatal Medusa,
whom Sandys in a drawing circa 1875 (Victoria and Albert Museum) depicted with amazing whip-like strands of snaky hair that suggest her flagel-
lation of her victims and aptly earn her the Swinburnian title of Our Lady
of Pain.[30]

The poses and gender relationships between the two combatants in *The
Beguiling of Merlin* are also powerfully orchestrated. In Tennyson's *Idylls*
Merlin is ultimately "overtalk'd and overworn . . . And in the hollow oak
he lay as dead, And lost to life and use and name and fame" (388).
Whereas Nimue is columnar, upright, and energetic (serpentine only in her
hair), Merlin is enervated, defeated, and sunken in pose as well as expression and emotion. Caught in a web of branches, he is now lifeless and
trapped, and as has been remarked, "the old wizard hangs limply in the
abundant branches . . . His arms droop before him, drained of their
strength, and his legs are crossed in languid uselessness. His face, gaunt
with an ascetic beauty, reveals his terror as he realizes he has been defeated
at his own game."[31] In a stunning reversal of masculine and feminine roles,
Nimue, a former "fallen woman" who previously had grovelled subser-
viently before her mentor, is now erect and fearsome, while he is levelled

and limp (perhaps sexually as well). The spiteful yet sensuous female victor and magician now towers over her victim: "like Tennyson's Vivien, she [has] used her beauty to render Merlin impotent, and then, relishing her new-found power, she [has] destroyed him."[32] In a further heightening of the drama, the convulsive branches of the bush—like the entwined crown of snakes on her head—charge the atmosphere with magic, while the folds of her drapery seem to vibrate sinuously with the power of enchantment.

Besides Sandys and Burne-Jones, another artist who seems obsessed by the theme of female sorcery is John W. Waterhouse. Two years after his *Consulting the Oracle* (Tate Gallery) was exhibited at the Royal Academy in 1884, Waterhouse recycled its idea within the context of a single figure in *The Magic Circle* (Fig. 11; Tate Gallery) which, after its successful reception at the Academy, was bought for the Tate Gallery Collection by the Chantrey Fund. In this celebration of the black arts, a serpent-woman approaches a steaming cauldron. She has a snake coiled around her neck, evoking the primitive and erotic qualities of the snake as a phallus, as well as the more traditional ones of Eve's temptation and sin. With flowing, bewitched hair, she generates an air of sacred or magical madness. Perhaps she has been involved in a ritual with the snake that coils so intimately around her; in contemporary literature such as Flaubert's *Salammbô* of 1862, a woman is sexually intimate with a python and performs rituals with it as the priestess of Baal.[33] Like Medea and other sorceresses, she is affiliated with the power of the natural world; there are herbs, symbolic of both witchcraft and healing power, tucked into her dress which, like Morgan le Fay's, is embroidered with occult, pictographic designs.

Using a magical wand or stick, she draws up force fields from within herself and from the earth. Drawing leylines or invisible tracks of power around her, she marks out a magical, fiery zone, like an artist delineating enchanted ground, or another Lady of Shalott creating magic in her own circular dimension. Perhaps this circle later will be embellished with magical diagrams or apotropaic symbols to ward off evil. The circle was a holy shape to the Druids, and stone circles like Stonehenge were considered megalithic carriers of power. In some folklore tales, witches were turned into stone within circular perimeters because of their abuse of powers.[34] Witches often revelled in midnight ceremonies, building up their powers from the earth and stones. Hidden currents were believed to flow through sticks and stones, making this sorceress's fiery wand even more exotic and

11. John W. Waterhouse, *The Magic Circle*. 1886. Oil on canvas, 72 × 50″. Tate Gallery, London/Art Resource, New York.

terrifying. Some witches used rods from straight branches only, at times inscribing them with magical language or symbols.[35] Other witches used a stick to walk over and then flew away from it like birds. Is the pile of sticks being burned the remains of the victims of Waterhouse's sorceress? Are the black ravens that surround and seem to watch her (one perched atop a human skull) fellow witches or mortals transformed into animal form? Is the frog at the lower right another ingredient of her necromancy or a captive of her charms and spells? In the distance of this painting, "civilization" and a male soldier appear, but the priestess remains a world apart as she claims her own territory. The sacred fire in its tripodic holder further allies her with witchcraft; the fire may also make her a symbolic daughter of Athena's warrior magic. A column of smoke starts to take shape over her cauldron, perhaps materializing into an apparition or vision that she has conjured. In addition, the sickle-shaped tool that she holds may identify her as a daughter of the moon, with its connotations of omens, magic, and prophecies; the instrument also is reminiscent of the one that Perseus wielded to cut off Medusa's head—a "*harpe*, a saw-toothed instrument that Zeus had used to castrate his father Kronos."[36] The castrating potential of this sorceress is thus crystallized in various ways in this and other kindred Victorian paintings.

Waterhouse also painted another cruel, sadistic permutation of the Lady of Shalott in her "artist's studio" in *Circe Offering the Cup to Ulysses* (Fig. 12; Oldham Art Gallery) of 1891. (He painted the Lady herself a number of times.) As with other such pictures, a tripod, incense, a chalice containing consecrated oils or magic potion, and an enchanted wand represent the instruments of witchcraft. In a gesture reminiscent of Morgan le Fay, Circe throws back her head and is shown in the act of casting a spell, holding one hand aloft as her bewitched hair—almost electrically charged—flows around her. Scattered herbs and flowers lie on the ground, and, as with Morgan le Fay, her slipped robe may suggest her fiercely free sexuality. The animistic beasts on the chair seem to come alive, aligning Circe with their darker forces and reminding us of her power to turn men into swine. Interestingly, the mirror in the background, featuring Ulysses, invites comparison with the Lady of Shalott's vision of Lancelot.

Why did this imagery of witchcraft and sorcery appeal to the Victorians? Among other possible explanations, two nineteenth-century trends

12. John W. Waterhouse, *Circe Offering the Cup to Ulysses*. 1891. Oil on canvas, 58 ½ × 36 ¼". Oldham Art Gallery.

seem particularly relevant. Preeminent was the vogue for spiritualism and the occult that began in the 1850s and reached a fever pitch of crystal-gazing, astrology, seances, and mystical philosophy in distinguished circles such as those of William Thackeray, the Brownings, and Sir Arthur Conan Doyle. Another factor was the mounting interest in so-called "degenerate" or "primitive" English prehistory prior to the arrival of the Romans.[37] Worship at prehistoric monuments, archaeological work at holy sites like Stonehenge, and Druid and "pagan" lore mingled with Arthurian legend to pique contemporary curiosity about the female seer and enchantress.

Yet beyond these developments, the cultural construct of the aberrant feminine personality represented by these viragoes must have projected its own fascination.[38] These women in many respects—by dint of what they wear as well as what they do—seem not entirely human, or at least soul-less and often bestial. They are willful exiles and daughters of Lilith: sinis-ter, isolated, romantic outcasts whose roles as anti-heroines are highly seditious in the context of normative Victorian womanhood. Defiant, un-orthodox, and often ferocious as well as sexually active, they combine other unwomanly characteristics such as aggression and the infliction of pain with often beguiling beauty. Confronted with the Victorian version of "black" romanticism in these paintings, male viewers undoubtedly felt a horror of such heinous feminine deeds and potential, but also awe of their powerful allure. The witches and sorceresses might be both admired and abhorred—perceived as coolly beautiful outside yet monstrous inside, morally ugly and unnaturally sadistic. In their hands miracles, wisdom, and healing become tainted and murderous.

Madness or possession by supernatural forces is another common de-nominator shared by many of the women in these paintings. The sor-ceresses have great mental powers and cunning, but they are seized either by uncontrollable rage or a force greater than themselves that propels their evil magic. Often the female body seems possessed, from twisting torso and clothes, to electric hair, riveting gaze, telekinetic powers, and open mouth. The apotropaic power of these women's cruel, destructive faces also suggests their indebtedness to Medusa. Their petrifying or hynpotic gaze is reminiscent as well of the flashing, mesmerizing eyes of Athena.

In all of these examples, the female magicians within their "sanctuaries" of power and evil turn Ruskin's idea of women as "keeper[s] of the hearth" upside down, replacing hallowed domesticity with lethal necro-mancy. A woman's rebellion against her traditional role was often considered pathological, indeed clinically mad, by many Victorians, for whom female hysteria was one symptom of madness.[39] In this respect, sorcery and madness might be considered creative and liberating escapes from everyday reality, a chance for Victorian woman's transformation from passive martyr or "Angel of the House" to actively striving, dynamic controller of herself and of men. In Victorian art the majority of sorceresses are confrontational, not cowering, and they use their sexuality in a forthright, even strident, manner. The enchantress, unlike the femme fatale, rarely suffers punishment or penalty for realizing her sexuality, generating instead an incredible vitality that, while ruinous (or castrating) to men, was in many ways a breath of fresh air after all the stale parlor vignettes of femininity in Victorian painting.

Magic is especially empowering for women because it radically alters and redresses the standard equation of femininity with powerlessness. The figure of the female magician—arrogant, willful, mysterious, and above all imposing her own will on nature and humanity—is also an archetypal image of the artist who, with wand, pen, or brush, summons extraordinary creations through her divination and her imagination.[40] The reinvention of nature as a primary act of power thus becomes accessible through sorcery or witchcraft to women, who are shown to be able to master chaos as well as society. The woman as supreme artificer—energizing, transforming, and subduing man and nature—is at once a triumphant, magnetic creature as well as an unnatural creation who, judged by patriarchal definitions of the feminine norm, is repulsive. Her narcissistic qualities, her deviancy, and her absolute dominion are terrifying; indeed, the freedom she achieves through evil or insanity is a notion that becomes increasingly important in fin-de-siècle art. Excluded from masculine channels of power, these enchantresses nonetheless attain the dark side of wisdom and qualify as both artists and sages. They achieve an iconic supremacy as practitioners of the black arts through inspired language, art, and song. Ultimately these female wizards are more than dissidents; they are women whose gifted temperaments defy the rhetoric of masculine control both in literal and metaphoric terms.

Harriet Martineau
Masculine Discourse, Female Sage

LINDA H. PETERSON

> I believe myself possessed of no uncommon talents, and of not an
> atom of genius; but as various circumstances have led me to think
> more accurately and read more extensively than some women, I be-
> lieve that I may so write on subjects of universal concern as to inform
> some minds and stir up others.
> ——Harriet Martineau, private memorandum, 1829

In both *Household Education* (1849) and her *Autobiography* (1877), Harriet Martineau tells the story of how she learned to write. As a girl of
eleven, she was sent with her sister to a boy's grammar school where
among the traditionally masculine subjects, including Latin and mathematics, she received lessons in composition.

> We were taught the parts of a theme, as our master and many others
> approved and practised them, in sermons and essays: and the nature
> and connexion of these parts were so clearly pointed out, that on the
> instant it appeared to me that a sudden light was cast at once on the
> processes of thought and of composition,—for both of which I had
> before an indistinct and somewhat oppressive reverence. I saw how
> the Proposition, the Reason, the Example, the Confirmation, and the

Conclusion led out the subject into order and clearness, and, in fact, regularly emptied our minds of what we had to say upon it.[1]

That Martineau viewed this knowledge of composition as a "masculine" achievement is evident from her emphasis on a tradition "approved and practised" by her male schoolmaster and from her comment in the *Autobiography* that composition "was a capital way of introducing some order into the chaos of girls' thoughts" (1:64). Learning composition—not only knowing how to organize ideas but also feeling competent in a masculine rhetorical domain—later influenced Martineau's decision to become a writer and to take on subjects like economics, social policy, and Comtean positivism. In 1834, after her spectacular success with the *Illustrations of Political Economy*, she was to praise her schoolmaster for his seminal influence, "probably the cause of my mind being turned so decidedly in that direction" (1:65).

"That direction" was not just political economy but, more generally, the direction of the sage, the writer devoted to dispensing truth, wisdom, and sometimes judgment. Martineau made such dispensing her vocation—from her private resolution in 1829 to "write on subjects of universal concern as to inform some minds and stir up others"; through her groundbreaking tales based on economic theory, intended for readers who could not comprehend learned treatises but wanted to understand "the science in a familiar, practical form"; through her many books on cultural mores, positivistic and necessarian philosophy, education, slavery, sickness, religion, and even mesmerism.[2] Simply to list her major publications is to document the range of her intellectual interests, her commitment to instructive nonfiction, her lifelong career as a sage: *Illustrations of Political Economy* (1832–1833), *Society in America* (1837), *How to Observe Morals and Manners* (1838), *Life in the Sick-Room* (1844), *Eastern Life, Present and Past* (1848), *Household Education* (1849), *A History of England during the Thirty Years' Peace* (1849–1850), *Letters on the Laws of Man's Nature and Development* (1851), *The Positive Philosophy of Auguste Comte* (1853).

The rhetorical practice in these books, like the accounts of learning to write, suggests that Martineau viewed such public discourse as "masculine," and thus her activities in the role of sage as a woman's appropriation of traditionally masculine personae and genres. In the *Autobiography*

Martineau contrasts her production of serious nonfiction with the more "feminine" writing of novelists like Maria Edgeworth. Edgeworth's method —"scribbling first, then submitting her manuscript to her father, and copying and altering many times over"—Martineau dismisses as a waste of time and a loss of "distinctness and precision" (1:121). Her own method— rigorously organizing and outlining first, then writing without revision— she links with a male writer, William Cobbett:

> I was delighted when, long afterwards, I met with Cobbett's advice;—to know first what you want to say, and then say it in the first words that occur to you. The excellence of Cobbett's style, and the manifest falling off of Maria Edgeworth's after her father's death (so frankly avowed by herself) were strong confirmations of my own experience. (1:122)

No doubt this judgment overrates Cobbett and underrates Edgeworth; indeed, modern theorists of composition would validate Edgeworth's process-oriented approach over Cobbett's "think it-say it" method.[3] But underlying Martineau's judgment is a professional need. Might not she link herself to Cobbett in order to dissociate herself from female scribblers and a feminine tradition of the novel, and to align herself with male writers and a masculine tradition of serious nonfictional prose?

This dissociation and (re)alignment become more forceful in a third-person obituary Martineau wrote of herself for posthumous publication. In it she characterizes the first ten years of her professional career as "the days of her success in narrative"; after that period, she observes that she "nearly ceased to write fiction, from simple inability to do it well."[4] Though this "inability" would seem to represent a loss, the implication is actually that, by the late 1830s, she had moved *beyond* a typically feminine phase of fictionalizing to a more abstract, masculine phase of deep thinking and writing. If we compare the self-analyses of the *Autobiography* and the self-composed obituary, we see that the fictional loss coincides with an intellectual gain. The pattern of intellectual development Martineau traces in the *Autobiography* follows Comtean philosophy in positing a progress from a theological, "superstitious" phase to a more advanced "metaphysical" phase of comprehension.[5] The *Autobiography* dates this entry into metaphysical comprehension as the late 1830s, approximately the same period that Martineau lost her fictionalizing capacity.

As Martineau approaches sage discourse, then, she tends to eschew the "feminine" (intuition, emotion, passion, fiction) and to assert the ability of women writers—or at least herself—to produce "masculine" prose (orderly thought, logic, reason, nonfiction). Yet, for all her tendency to valorize masculine writing, both as process and as product, Martineau seems dissociated from the main nineteenth-century tradition of sage writing represented by such male authors as Carlyle, Ruskin, and Arnold. As George P. Landow has delineated that tradition in *Elegant Jeremiahs*, sage writing includes much that is not rational, orderly, or traditionally masculine: it prefers "episodic or discontinuous literary structures" to the logical unfolding of arguments; it frequently concentrates on "grotesque" or "apparently trivial phenomena" as the subject of interpretation; it uses "satiric or idiosyncratic definitions of key terms" and, more broadly, alternates "satire and positive, even visionary statement"; it also uses "a parallel alternation of attacks upon the audience and attempts to reassure"; and it relies upon *ethos* rather than the *logos* of classical rhetoricians (or, one might add, western patriarchy).[6] In this list of features lie the reasons why Martineau avoided the way of her male counterparts. Sage writing in the nineteenth century is the work of the male intellectual, but its rhetorical features are those of an *alienated* intellectual.[7] Its attacks upon the audience, like its preference for satire and parody, suggest a writer who positions himself above—or apart from—the shortcomings and compromises of his culture. Paradoxically, of course, it also suggests a writer who feels he has a significant function in his society: the sage is, as Landow points out, the modern equivalent of the Old Testament prophet.

For Martineau, the role of sage was a difficult one to hold. She liked dispensing judgment: even as a child, she recalls, she was "the absurdist little preacher" that "ever was," quoting maxims to family and strangers alike (1:12). But as a dissenter, a provincial, and especially a woman, Martineau stood apart from the dominant culture—or, more accurately, she had no recognized place in that culture. Her rhetorical dilemmas were how to create a position from which to speak, how to gain credibility and authority, how to make herself heard. Martineau chose, I believe, to align herself not with the sage writing of her Victorian male contemporaries, but with an older tradition of classical rhetoric and, simultaneously, with the modern "scientific" stance of positivism.

The strategies Martineau employed and the difficulties she faced in carrying them out will be the focus of the following sections. In anticipation of my argument, I suggest that Martineau sought to make it possible for women to write as sages by demonstrating their competence in masculine rhetoric, then by breaking down common (mis)assumptions about "masculine" versus "feminine" capacities. Her attempts frequently brought her up short against the problem that feminist theorists today debate about women's writing: whether women (inevitably or essentially) write differently or whether writing is (or can or should be) genderless.

Can a woman's writing be sage writing? Or is sage writing essentially a masculine enterprise? Modern feminists usually take one of three positions on the question of women's writing: (1) like Joyce Carol Oates, some believe that writing is genderless, that "the serious artistic voice is one of individual style"; (2) others, like Ellen Moers, believe that there is something distinctive about the way women write, perhaps most observable in the figurative language women choose; (3) still others, like Mary Ellmann, refer not to "male" or "female" writers but to "masculine" or "feminine" modes of writing, characterizing the "feminine" mode as one that expresses "the disruption of authority" or the "disruption of the rational."[8] Theoretically, a female sage might attempt to write from any of the three positions: she might ignore questions of gender; she might cultivate feminine metaphors or a feminine style; or she might use the "feminine" to challenge the patriarchal status quo. Martineau's practice seems to derive from the first position—in part because she valued her own voice as a writer, in part because she disagreed with the essentialism implicit in the second position, but primarily because, contrary to the third, she sought to establish her authority through the use of reason and through arguments and metaphors with universal applicability.

Martineau's commitment to a genderless ideal for writing is evident in virtually all of her books, in the structure, style, and theoretical models she assumes. Her *Autobiography* takes the (genderless) form of a Comtean progression from theological to metaphysical to positivistic enlightenment. In the version of Comte's *Positive Philosophy* she translated two years before writing the *Autobiography*, she had argued the applicability of Comtean patterns to all human experience: "The progress of the individual mind is not only an illustration, but an indirect evidence of that of the general mind. The point of departure of the individual and of the race being the same, the phases of the mind of a man correspond to the epochs of the mind of the race. Now, each of us is aware, if he looks back upon his own history, that he was a theologian in his childhood, a metaphysician in his youth, and a natural philosopher in his manhood."[9] Martineau adopts this universal structure for her own life story, moving from an early religious phase (1802–1819) through what she calls a "metaphysical fog" (1819–1839) to a final positivistic stage of understanding (1839–1855).[10] With this structure she means to demonstrate that positivism offers a replacement for outmoded biblical patterns of explanation, and that it further provides a genderless model of human development, equally applicable to male and female experience.[11]

Similarly, in *Household Education* Martineau's advice implies a theory of developmental psychology that posits a sexless model of the human mind. This volume, intended to break from the practice of treating female education as a subject separate from male education, argues that the aim of all education should be "to bring out and strengthen and exercise all the powers given to every human being" (19). She acknowledges no differences between the "powers" of the two sexes and attacks older patriarchal schemes in which "women—half the race—were slighted" (19–20). Style reinforces theory. Examples featuring both girls and boys illustrate Martineau's commentary on the development of the powers (will, hope, fear, patience, love, veneration, truthfulness, conscientiousness). Anecdotes using men and women, or girls and boys, make points about intellectual training (of the perceptive, conceptive, reasoning, and imaginative faculties) and about the development of good habits. Throughout the text Martineau uses the now-common feminist technique of alternating masculine and feminine nouns and pronouns: a boy this, a girl that; she this, he that. The very fabric of this work makes differences between male and female, masculine and feminine, difficult to discern.

It is true that in *Household Education* Martineau virtually succumbs to an essentialism in matters of domestic arrangements. The chapter entitled "Family Habits" asserts that girls have a "natural desire and the natural facility for housewifery" (306). It represents boys doing carpentry and lock repairs at their workbench, and girls "making beds, making fires, laying the cloth and washing up crockery, baking bread, preserving fruit, clear-starching and ironing" (305–307). Whether Martineau held such views because she herself enjoyed domestic tasks or because she genuinely believed the female hand was well-suited to the needle, she was nonetheless convinced that the male and female mind alike were suited to the book and the pen. In matters of mental and moral development, *Household Education* asserts the equality of the sexes:

I must declare that on no subject is more nonsense talked, (as it seems to me,) than on that of female education, when restriction is advocated. In works otherwise really good, we find it taken for granted that girls are not to learn the dead languages and mathematics, because they are not to exercise professions where these attainments are wanted; and a little further on we find it said that the chief reason for boys and young men studying these things is to improve the quality of their minds. I suppose none of us will doubt that everything possible should be done to improve the quality of the mind of every human being.—If it is said that the female brain is incapable of studies of an abstract nature,—that is not true: for there are many instances of women who have been good mathematicians, and good classical scholars. The plea is indeed nonsense on the face of it: for the brain which will learn French will learn Greek; the brain which enjoys arithmetic is capable of mathematics (240).

Martineau continues in this vein—offering a series of hypothetical syllogisms, denying or confirming the validity of their premises—until she has countered the common objections to women's education.

As the form of the hypothetical syllogism suggests, *Household Education* is "logocentric": it insists that its form of discourse can reveal untruth and discover truth.[12] The prose depends on logical argument: if x is true, then y is true; if x is not true, then y is not.[13]

If it is said that women are light-minded and superficial, the obvious answer is that their minds should be the more carefully sobered by grave studies, and the acquisition of exact knowledge.

If it is said that such studies unfit women for their proper occupations,—that again is untrue. Men do not attend the less to their professional business, their counting house or their shop, for having their minds enlarged and enriched, and their faculties strengthened by sound and various knowledge; nor do women on that account neglect the work-basket, the market, the dairy and the kitchen. (240–241)

Again, style reinforces argument. In reasoned prose and carefully balanced clauses, Martineau argues for—and simultaneously displays—the powers of the female mind. Her syllogisms cut through the irrationality of her opponents' position and show the superiority of her own logic.

The emphasis on logos, with a parallel deemphasis of pathos, contributes to a peculiarly unfeminine prose style. All is calm, rational, authoritative. In Martineau there are no outbursts, as there are in Charlotte Brontë's *Jane Eyre*, that rebel against the narrow lot of women—no pacing of attic halls in suppressed anger, no impassioned cries that "women feel just as men feel," that "they need exercise for their faculties, and a field for their efforts as much as their brothers do."[14] So, too, in Martineau the depersonalization of examples contributes to a deliberately masculine (or defeminized) style. Many of the cases that illustrate arguments in *Household Education*, like the capacity of girls for abstract studies or their faithfulness to domestic chores, originate in Martineau's own experience as a female learner. Yet the personal knowledge that underlies the examples and syllogisms has been transformed into generalized principles and universal cases—into what might be called genderless rhetorical material.

Martineau's purpose, of course, is to gain access to traditionally masculine domains and to prove that women can master those domains, both in style and content. Her prose seeks to unsex the "masculine" and make it the perogative of both sexes. Thus in *Household Education*, as in many other of her works, she herself becomes a "masculine" female sage—but masculine only because the forms of discourse she uses traditionally have been associated with men, not because men possess any inherent or essential capacity to engage in logical, reasoned argument. That capacity surpasses biological sex or social gender.

Despite her success with logocentric discourse and her dissociation of masculine writing from the male writer, the prose Martineau produces occasionally shows the strains that develop when a female sage appropriates a masculine mode. These strains—which I shall discuss as problems of ethos, theory, and feminine irruptions in the text—are interesting for what they reveal about the limitations of Martineau's rhetoric and what they suggest about alternative, perhaps less limiting strategies that a feminine tradition might have added to her work.

One such strain develops from the depersonalization of example noted above and the difficulties with ethos that ensue. As Landow has argued, the Victorian sage creates ethos—namely, probity and credibility, confidence in himself and his work—through "autobiography": the revelation of intimate experience, the use of personal testimony, the treatment of himself as a sort of *corpus vile*. "The ultimate appeal of the sage, to which all of his other techniques contribute, is that his interpretations . . . can be believed, finally, because he is a morally and intellectually *trustworthy* person."[15] Martineau certainly uses personal testimony in her *Autobiography* obviously, in *Household Education, Life in the Sick-Room, Society in America*, and in her many analyses of social and feminist causes. But she does not expect readers to accept her arguments primarily or ultimately on the basis of personal testimony. Rather, she seeks to establish credibility because of and through her good sense, her rationality, and her lucid arguments. In this she follows the tradition of the wisdom writer, not that of the prophetic sage; she presents "general truths that are not specific to the facts or situation being narrated."[16]

The effect of Martineau's commitment to logos, to general truths and universal principles, is to efface—or at least to minimize—issues of gender as they concern the credibility of the writer herself. This may well have been an effect Martineau intended, given the cultural disinclination of Victorian readers to hear seriously the arguments of "feminine" women. Logos becomes a way of establishing ethos, in other words—although an ethos different from that of the male sage who could risk offering intimate, even extreme or bizarre examples from his personal experience. A secondary effect of Martineau's commitment to masculine discourse, however, may be a more subtle (and unfortunate) effacement of gender where it is actually a crucial issue. When in *Household Education* Martineau alternates examples of girls and boys at "domestic school," she may be asserting the abilities and rights of both sexes to equal education, but she may also be ignoring differences between the ways girls and boys learn. Or, in the same work, when she transforms her personal experience into universal cases, she may be avoiding *ad feminam* arguments, but she may also be lessening the power of lived experience and producing what some readers have dismissed as "a pedantic mode of writing."[17] Does the commitment to general truth and universal example implicate Martineau in just another form of masculine hegemony, a critic might ask?

Martineau might answer—if we can imagine her response to an issue of modern feminist criticism—that one cannot have it both ways; a writer cannot assert the sexlessness of the mind at the same time that she insists on significant differences between male and female learners. Perhaps she would add, too, that the female sage cannot have it both ways. Either women must embrace traditional forms of discourse, call them "public" or "masculine," or women must explore alternate "feminine" approaches and accept the possibility of exclusion from mainstream thought. Martineau's practice consistently prefers the former approach—as more effective rhetoric and more effective feminism.

If the strains that logos introduces to Martineau's writing can be explained (away), it is less easy to explain (away) the effects of her obsession with theory. For Martineau, theory is what authorizes her pronouncements as sage. Theory provides the source for most of her ideas, the grounds for most of her judgments. It was the theory of James Mill's *Elements of Political Economy*—difficult for the average reader but accessible via an intelligent expositor—that justified Martineau's entry into public literary life. It was the inadequate, mistaken theory of female development—propounded in such influential texts as Hannah More's *Strictures on the Modern System of Female Education* (1799)—that spurred Martineau to write her own book on education and revise current views about the female mind. It was her translation of Comte's *Positive Philosophy* that won the public approval of this eminent European philosopher and later motivated her own *Autobiography*, a text which propounds a genderless model for interpreting human experience.

Theory is, however, a two-edged sword. It can liberate and/or subordinate. As modern feminists have learned, theory can provide access to mainstream discourse, impetus to scholarship, even prestige to theoretically astute feminist practitioners; but it can also marginalize women and reinforce the subordination of their work to male theoreticians. If, as some feminists have pointed out, women scholars devote all of their efforts to expounding and refuting male theorists, they implicitly demonstrate the primacy of masculine thought, despite their contrary intentions. Or if, as Elaine Showalter has argued, the "feminine" comes to be identified simply with a "semiotic" or "disruptive" mode of discourse, and if men as well as women can practice the feminine mode, then actual women's work may be marginalized once again.[18] Engaging the work of male theoreticians, even critically, can make a female writer dangerously complicit in—and ultimately subordinate to—masculine values.

Martineau's attempts at masculine discourse might be criticized in similar terms as complicit or subordinate. Her early *Illustrations of Political Economy*, for instance, accepts the subordination of (female) narrative work to (male) theory and theorists: Adam Smith, Jeremy Bentham, Thomas Malthus, James Mill. Her narratives are prefaced by—in some editions followed by—a "summary of principles" from their theoretical texts, which control and master Martineau's imaginative work.[19] Similarly, Martineau's personal history depends upon a (male) theorist as it is remembered and retold in the *Autobiography*; without Comte, her life might have been formless, inchoate, characteristically "feminine." The most striking dependence on a male thinker comes in a work that seems to articulate the most heterodox of Martineau's ideas: the *Letters on the Laws of Man's Nature and Development* (1851). As one example of that dependence, Martineau repeatedly referred to this work as the "Atkinson Letters," despite the fact that Henry George Atkinson was merely her coauthor and probably a man less gifted intellectually than she. As another, Martineau gave up the most challenging theoretical problem of the work in deference to her coauthor. For its composition she had proposed inventing a new language, or at least a vocabulary free from the taint of traditional theology. Atkinson convinced her that philosophers must use familiar language in order to communicate with their readers. Hence Martineau abandoned her scheme for a nontheological, nonpatriarchal vocabulary. The female author succumbed to the wishes of her male collaborator.[20]

It is true that, despite the familiar language, the *Letters on the Laws of Man's Nature and Development* was recognized as a heterodox and disruptive volume. And it is more generally true that Martineau disclaimed originality in most of her thinking and writing. In her self-composed obituary, she estimated her literary production as popularization, not invention: "Her original power was nothing more than was due to earnestness and intellectual clearness within a certain range. With small imaginative and suggestive powers, and therefore nothing approaching to genius, she could see clearly what she did see, and give a clear expression to what she had to say. In short, she could popularize, while she could neither discover nor invent."[21] This modest assessment—or unfortunate denigration—of her own efforts has led some critics, Deirdre David among the most perceptive, to relegate Martineau to the status of "auxiliary usefulness"; while praising her "brave feminism," David concludes that the "conventionally feminine qualities of passivity and acquiescence are both facilitated and reinforced by her writings."[22] Certainly Martineau's modesty looks suspiciously like conventional feminine behavior.

Yet perhaps the problem of Martineau's relation to theory and the apparent self-subordination it involves can be framed in a different way. Personally, Martineau needed theory to fill the intellectual gap left by the loss of religious faith; in this typically Victorian context, her appropriation of Comtean positivism is not different from the appropriation of other secular theories by such male writers as Carlyle, Arnold, and Ruskin. Vocationally, moreover, Martineau faced a problem that many a young journalist still faces: she needed to find writing projects that would gain her an audience and, after her father's bankruptcy, earn her a living; in those projects she needed to fulfill a basic function of the journalist in transmitting ideas from expert theorists to lay audiences. Academic critics, secure in their positions and incomes, often forget that writers like Martineau could not avoid writing for the marketplace—succumbing to "the values of an entrenched land-owning class," as David puts it.[23] What, in fact, is remarkable about Martineau's work is how often she uses her command of masculine discourse and theory *against* the dominant culture and how often she moves from mere journalism to genuine sage writing. She spoke of her *Eastern Life* as "the greatest effort of courage I ever made," greater even than the "bold feats" of "the Population number of my Political Economy, the Women and Marriage and Property chapters in my

American Books, and the Mesmerism affair" (2:345). If she needed theory to back her in these bold efforts, that was its designated function, intellectually and rhetorically. Theory served her vocational commitment and, in this service, it is no more dominant than theory in the works of Thomas Carlyle (German idealism), Thomas Huxley and Herbert Spencer (Darwinism), or Samuel Butler (Lamarckian biology).

What theory cannot do, however, is fully repress certain "feminine" features of discourse that irrupt into Martineau's otherwise "masculine" texts. These irruptions are infrequent, as Martineau was a disciplined writer who composed from strict outlines and kept to firm schedules. Yet feminine discourse leaves its traces in several of Martineau's texts, only one of which I shall analyze: "gossip" in the *Autobiography*.

Gossip is feminine discourse par excellence. As Patricia Meyer Spacks has pointed out, both men and women gossip, but cultural myths identify the practice solely with women: women gossip because they are daughters of Eve, notorious for listening to and repeating false tales; or, women gossip because they are constitutionally feeble, their minds unable "to give serious Attention to anything abstracted"; or, women gossip because, deprived of significant economic function, they lack better things to do.[24] As a female sage committed to serious, abstract thought, Martineau hardly seems a likely candidate for gossip. And yet gossip—not in the form of malicious tale-telling, but in what Spacks identifies as a form of feminine plot-making—interrupts the Comtean pattern of Martineau's *Autobiography*.

In reading the *Autobiography*, one notices that the Comtean progress—from theological superstition to metaphysical fog to positivisitic enlightenment—provides the structure for most of the text. Most but not all. Major sections in volumes 1 and 2 temporarily forget or evade the Comtean pattern and instead recount memories of the literary figures Martineau knew. Such recollections are, admittedly, a generic feature of some Victorian autobiography: the *res gestae* memoir, as distinct from the developmental autobiography, uses recollection and reminiscence as the bases of its form. Martineau's recollections are not nostalgic or random, however; neither can they be accounted for simply by referring to generic conventions. They represent, I believe, an alternate plot, a form of feminine gossip that seeks the truth of experience rather than of abstract analysis.

In the section of the *Autobiography* titled "Literary Lionism,"

Martineau's memories betray a theme that perplexed her throughout her life and that can be understood only by referring to a tradition of feminine discourse. That theme—the vanity of female authorship—originates in Martineau's first production as a public writer, where in a review of More's *Strictures on Female Education*, Martineau confronted the claim that young women who "scribble" do so to gratify their "natural vanity."[25] In the 1823 review, Martineau refuted More by referring to the principles of Christian humility that genuine education inculcates, and by arguing that, if more women were better educated, fewer would have cause for vanity. As Martineau reviewed her own life in 1855 for the *Autobiography*, she seems once again to have recalled More's accusation and desired a fuller, more personal refutation.

A reasoned analysis of the causes of authorial vanity introduces the section on "Literary Lionism," as Martineau explains the market practices that encourage celebrity treatment and the temptations to which authors of both sexes may fall prey. For all its reasonableness, however, there can be no abstract refutation of the claim that women authors are naturally vain—or, if there is, it does not seem to satisfy Martineau. After the analysis, a form of gossip takes over—didactic, moralizing, perhaps even edifying prose, but gossip nonetheless. Anecdote after anecdote recounts the vanity (or humility) of various authors Martineau knew, the overwhelming effect being that male authors show themselves more prone to flattery and literary puffery than female authors. William Taylor, for example, a writer in the town of Norwich where Martineau grew up, succumbs to the vice: "he was completely spoiled by the flatteries of shallow men, pedantic women, and conceited lads" (1:298). The eminent Anna Laetitia Barbauld, in contrast, behaves with decency and normalcy, sitting in the Martineau parlor for "a long morning chat" and "holding skeins of silk for my mother to wind"; "well I remember her gentle lively voice," Martineau notes, "and the stamp of superiority on all she said" (1:302). And as Martineau tells it, many a man more famous than Taylor turns vanity's fool: Lord Brougham lets himself be flattered by silly women, to whom he talks nonsense; Lord Jeffrey "flirt[s] with clever women, in long succession"; Bulwer-Lytton sits "on a sofa, sparkling and languishing among a set of female votaries"; Edwin Landseer enters a room "curled and cravatted, and glancing round in anxiety about his reception" so as to "make a woman wonder where among her own sex she could find more palpable vanity"; Richard Whewell appears "grasping at praise for universal learning" and "liking female adoration"; and so on for fifty anecdotal pages on the vanity of male authors and artists (1:350–352). "I had heard all my life of the vanity of women as a subject of pity to men," Martineau concludes, "but when I went to London, lo! I saw vanity in high places which was never transcended by that of women in their lowlier rank" (1:350). This conclusion to "Literary Lionism" is qualified by a list of four women—Lady Morgan, Lady Davy, Mrs. Austin, and Mrs. Jameson— also subject to "the gross and palpable vanities" of authorship. But the cursory treatment of their sins, followed by compliments to the "true genius" and "moral dignity" of Joanna Baillie, Mrs. Somerville, and Elizabeth Barrett Browning, only underscores the target of Martineau's gossip (1:352). As she tells the stories, it is literary men who are vain and prone to gossip even more than women.

Why should Martineau gossip in this section of her autobiography? I have already suggested that she means to undo the calumny of More's accusations about aspiring young female authors, for if girls followed More's strictures, there would be no female sages. It is also likely that Martineau means to exonerate herself personally from similar accusations and, by including details of her own resistance to being lionized, to show a counterpattern of moral development possible for women writers. She tells, for instance, how she resisted invitations to Lord Lansdowne's soirees because she was "invited there as an authoress": "I went nowhere but where my acquaintance was sought, as a lady, by ladies" (1:333). Such uses of gossip, as Spacks would argue, allow Martineau to imagine an alternate life story, to resist cultural stereotypes and construct another self.

But gossip also fills a rhetorical gap. Unlike the Comtean model that provides a general pattern of intellectual growth, or the abstract analysis of socio-economic conditions that leads to literary lionism, gossip gives access to truth unreachable through traditional masculine forms of discourse. In its tentative, associative, narrative mode, it reveals that male authors—for all their achievement in masculine domains—are as much subject to irrational, erotic motivations as women are said to be. (Why else tell tales of otherwise sensible men getting their erotic kicks out of being lionized by adoring beauties?) Gossip also reveals the limits of masculine rhetoric. (Why else follow a perfectly well-reasoned essay on "Literary Li-onism" with page after page of narrative anecdote?) Martineau's resort to gossip, perhaps even despite herself, turns the masculine/feminine dichot-omy on its head: it shows the irrational that underlies the masculine, the reasonable truth that emerges from the feminine.

An (Almost) Egalitarian Sage
William Morris and Nineteenth-Century Socialist-Feminism

FLORENCE S. BOOS

In the last decade of his life, William Morris developed a sage voice of "fellowship" in works whose most memorable protagonists are outsiders: a working-class revolutionary; a soon-to-be-martyred visionary priest; two "guests" who are displaced from their physical and temporal origins; and two young women who seek to realize new forms of wisdom, independence, and social justice. Throughout his life, Morris had included in his works striking portrayals of women, and a high valuation of characteristics he considered "womanly" remained central to the conceptions of beauty and justice in his late poetry and prose romances. For his period, he was remarkably unpuritanical; his poetic embodiments of sexual relationships are attractively uninhibited, and he was unusual among Victorian poets in his preoccupation with *male* sexual responsibility toward *female* partners, rather than the reverse. In the last years of his life, however, Morris's identification with the socialist movement also led him to create female political heroes who differ markedly from the intensely passionate but dependent heroines of his early works. After his conversion to socialism, moreover, his writings addressed, with characteristic sensitivity and insight, some of the issues raised by nineteenth-century socialist feminists.

Morris's presentations of women have formed the subject of several articles, and the relation of his writings to conceptions of women, gender, sexuality, and feminism are complex and interwoven.[1] I will discuss only three aspects of Morris's writing here: the ways in which his essays on art and socialism foster a prose style which conveys an ethic of egalitarian fellowship, but avoids explicit concern with women's creative work; the extent to which contemporary debates among socialists prompted him to develop a considered defense of women's right to sexual autonomy; and, finally, the confluence of these two achievements in a partial elision of gender stereotypes, which may be found in his more political prose romances.

Morris's essays on art and socialism, written between 1877 and his death in 1896, advocate a radical transformation of art and economy, and are among the most original achievements of his political and literary maturity. Their understated but fervent appeals for the autonomy and the beauty of creative labor are both lyric and conversational. At their best, they achieve a rare convergence of poetic sensibility and political exhortation, and create an unpretentious fellowship of speaker and audience which is seldom present in the work of Carlyle, Arnold, and Ruskin. Morris's appeals for communal ownership of nature and history thus contrast sharply with what George P. Landow has called the "elegant jeremia[d]s" of Victorian exhortatory prose.[2] Like the writings of his predecessors, Morris's secular sermons move from analysis to prophecy; but they exhort to revolution in direct and personal ways, and require no apocalyptic declamations: "When our opponents say, as they sometimes do, How should we be able to procure the luxuries of life in a Socialist society? answer boldly, We could not do so, and we don't care, for we don't want them and won't have them; and indeed, I feel sure that we cannot if we are all free men together. . . . Alas! my friends, these are the fools who are our masters now. The masters of fools then, you say? Yes, so it is; let us cease to be fools then, and they will be our masters no longer."[3] Morris was not considered a charismatic speaker, but the written versions of his speeches to working- and middle-class audiences are remarkably effective. He readily forwent the more erudite critical allusions for which Pater and Ruskin are now remembered, and replaced them with direct references to political controversies and contemporary events, praise of "lesser" art(s) and social action, and direct appeals to personal experience: "A man who notices the external forms of things much nowadays

must suffer in South Lancashire or London, must live in a state of perpetual combat and anger; and he really must try to blunt his sensibility, or he
will go mad, or kill some obnoxious person and be hanged for it."[4]

One ironic consequence of Morris's impassioned but straightforward
tone, fondness for simple words of Saxon origin, and desire to establish a
direct tie with his audience is that he uses the word "man" and its deriva-
tives more often than any other major Victorian essayist:

Art is man's expression of his joy in labour.
. . . works of art, the beauty which man creates when he is most a man,
most aspiring and thoughtful. . . .
. . . a man must have time for serious individual thought, for imagination—for dreaming even—or the race of men will inevitably worsen.[5]

There are depressingly few direct references to women in these essays, and
many of his eloquent pleas for action sound all too much like Wordsworth's "man speaking to men." The same applies to the essays' allusions
to virtually all forms of "useful work":

during all this period the unit of labour was an intelligent man. Time
was when . . . imagination and fancy mingled with all things made by
man, and in those days all handicraftsmen were *artists,* as we should
now call them. But the thought of man became more intricate, more
difficult to express; art grew a heavier thing to deal with, and its
labour was more divided among great men, lesser men, and little
men, till that art, which was once scarce more than a rest of body
and soul, as the hand cast the shuttle or swung the hammer, became
to some men so serious a labour, that their working lives have been
one long tragedy of hope and fear, joy and trouble.[6]

Despite all this, Morris was the only nineteenth-century "sage" who
passionately espoused "the lesser" or decorative arts, usually considered
"feminine." Moreover, his view of the relations of labor and art radically
undermined many of the factitious divisions between sensual and abstract,
natural and "mental," emotional and "rational," which feminists, ecolo-
gists, and others have since identified as sources of oppression. In a shift

which paralleled a growing focus on female autonomy in his socialist literary writings, Morris's later essays on socialism become slightly more inclusive in their language. Allusions to "men" give way more often to alternative abstractions: "the family of blood-relationship would melt into that of the community and of humanity."[7] More importantly, explicit allusions to "women" become somewhat more frequent: "[T]here is an enormous mass of labour which is just merely wasted; many thousands of men and women making *nothing* with terrible and inhuman toil. . . . [Y]ou who are housekeepers know full well (as I myself do, since I have learned the useful art of cooking a dinner) how it would simplify the day's work, if the chief meals could be eaten in common."[8]

It should be kept in mind that most members of the audiences for Morris's earlier speeches were workingmen—male artisans and intellectuals, for the most part. Later Socialist League audiences may well have included several women, among them his two grown daughters. More significantly, the development of Morris's own insights on art and communism in the essays may gradually have deepened his own appreciation of the range of "useful work," and sharpened his perception of the social oppression of women. It is not coincidental, I believe, that the utopian feminist Charlotte Perkins Gilman admired Morris's writings, and that some of the pastoral and artistically pleasing features of *Herland* resembled the environment described in *News From Nowhere*. She visited him in Hammersmith in 1896, shortly before his death, and remarked in her autobiography: "Gray and glorious he was, and most kind." Of his death, she wrote: "That was a great loss to the progress of England, of the world. Fortunately he left large work, long years of giving."[9] Among the better-known nineteenth-century male "sages," only Mill did better by women. Among late-century male novelists only Meredith, Gissing, Moore, and Hardy made comparable efforts to appreciate the demands of feminist "new women," but they often undercut their portraits with anxiety, ambivalence, and suppressed hostility. In the world of Morris's later romances, women are sometimes "heroic," men sometimes practice peaceful and domestic arts, and both value the "feminine" traits of a sense of beauty and kinship with the earth.

The evolution of Morris's responses to "the Woman Question" is sufficiently complex to merit a review of his public and private statements on the issue, a review which must pose several vexed, even painful questions. For example, why were Morris's initial critiques of the oppression of the worker, the corruption of imperialism, and the debasement of the arts of everyday life under capitalism so much bolder than his responses to gender hierarchy? How did a man who understood more than most members of his class the need of workers and artists for self-direction and creativity in labor fail for so long to recognize women's equal drives for creative autonomy in *non*-sexual realms? Why did he collaborate with Ernest Belfort Bax, a rigorous Marxist who was also a notorious antifeminist and antisuffragist? Why, above all, in 1886 did he politely decline to publish criticisms of Bax's public opposition in *Commonweal* to legal redress for battered spouses and children? Finally, can one discern partial resolutions of these apparent contradictions in Morris's later statements on marriage, and the language and plots of the later prose' romances? Did Morris ultimately appropriate aspects of positions he had earlier, for tactical and other reasons, slighted or ignored?

As feminist students of the period are well aware, few of Morris's predecessors and contemporaries among Victorian critics—Arnold in *Culture and Anarchy,* Newman in *The Idea of the University,* Carlyle in *Past and Present,* even Pater in *The Renaissance*—had anything searching, or even anything at all, to say on the nature or role of women, or on the structure of the Victorian family. Ruskin, for example, dealt harshly with the aspirations of actual contemporary women ("Of Queen's Garden's," 1865), despite his nostalgic admiration for mythic goddesses and female medieval saints. The only exceptions to this patriarchal front were John Stuart Mill and Harriet Taylor, whose essay *On The Subjection of Women* (1869) was unique for its advocacy of egalitarian marriage and women's intellectual autonomy. Morris would thus have found no feminist precedents in the two "sages"—Carlyle and Ruskin—whose work otherwise influenced him most, and his evolving views of family structure and women's rights to sexual choice drew on two other sources. The troubles of his own marriage, first, prompted in him a surprising measure of self-awareness and empathy with his wife's dissatisfaction, and by the 1870s inspired reflections on the need to regulate sexual unions entirely by mutual consent. When he later "became a Socialist" in the 1880s, Morris also encountered debates within the movement about the nature of ideal family life under

socialism which confirmed this initial response. Which features of the contemporary Victorian family were the regressive results of capitalist oppression, socialists asked, and which would survive as natural reflections of
liberated human behavior?

In 1884, Friedrich Engels published *Der Ursprung der Familie, des Pri-
vateigenthums und des Staats (The Origin of the Family, Private Property,
and the State)*, the first Marxist-feminist treatise by a member of the Social
Democratic Federation.[10] In April of the following year, *Commonweal* carried Eleanor Marx's review of August Bebel's treatise on *Woman Under
Socialism,* and in April 1886, it published Bax's virulent counterattack on
the campaign for women's suffrage, "woman-lovers," and feminists. Four
years later, after Bax's resignation from the Socialist League, Morris
printed in *Commonweal* (April 1890) his best-known and most eloquent
statements on marriage, which later became chapter 9 of *News From
Nowhere.*

During his time as a founder and sustainer of the Socialist League,
Morris also worked with contemporary activists such as Helen Taylor
(daughter of Harriet Taylor), Annie Besant, Charlotte Wilson, Eleanor
Marx, and other, now-lesser-known figures such as Lena Wardle, and his
own daughter May Morris; he also met the valiant French anarchist
Louise Michel, and entertained the American anarchist Emma Lazarus.[11]
From time to time he was inevitably called on to mediate disputes as editor
of *Commonweal,* state his views on the "woman question," and serve as a
buffer between Bax and other members of the League. Morris also
coauthored public manifestos which expounded his own and Socialist
League views on the bourgeois and socialist family.

Throughout this period, Morris's most conspicuous socialist-feminist
conviction was his firm, even impassioned support for women's right of
sexual choice. The model of the ideal family remained for him that of a
man, a woman, and their offspring—a heterosexual nuclear family—and
he did not foresee any extensive changes in the conventional divisions of
everyday labor, or assume that married women would want or need to
work at most nondomestic tasks, other than weaving (which he held in
high respect and practiced extensively himself). Nor, as an essentially anti-
or nonparliamentary socialist, was he much interested in which sex had
the right to elect members to a "bourgeois" parliament. Personally a very
affectionate father, he largely ignored in his writings issues of childcare

and parental responsibility which might arise when marriages dissolved, and seems to have assumed that most women naturally wished to care for their own and others' children. He apparently believed that the different circumstances of the sexes—above all, the supposed female "dependence" resulting from pregnancy—would persist, and that many existing economic and social distinctions would inevitably persist along with them.

Most damagingly, as I have remarked, he also seems to have muted League debates in the mid-1880's to accommodate the sensibilities of his overwrought collaborator—in part, perhaps, in a misguided appreciation of Bax's usefulness as a rare early "theorist" of English-language Marxism, and in part from a sense that Bax's views were simply exaggerated expressions of opinions still dominant among *Commonweal*'s male socialist readers. Finally, as editor of the League's newspaper and its chief financial supporter, he clearly wished to avoid factional quarrels that would distract members from more bitter and inclusive problems of poverty (not least of women), and class oppression. None of these motives, however, fully exonerates him.

Despite his apparent condonation of Bax's behavior, and despite his relative detachment from an emerging struggle which later engaged the wholehearted efforts of Keir Hardie and Richard Pethick Lawrence, among others, Morris remained notable among the better-known nineteenth-century male "sages" (again, save only Mill) for the complete absence of casual sexism from his speeches, essays, and private writings. Something stoically irenic and basically equable in him, something related to his refusal to blame or stereotype entire classes of people, helped ensure that none of his published statements ever ascribed inferiority to female nature, or relegated women to any of the social roles he condemned.

In view of Morris and Bax's markedly divergent views on sexual and women's issues, as well as the controversies over this issue within the Socialist League, it is not surprising that the assertions about bourgeois marriage and the family in their jointly authored editions of the League's "Manifesto" were carefully qualified. The first edition of the "Manifesto," for example, which appeared in January 1885, simply followed Engels's *Origin of the Family* in blaming capitalism for "venal prostitution" and the property relations of bourgeois marriage. "Our modern bourgeois property-marriage, maintained as it is by its necessary complement, universal venal prostitution, would give place to kindly and human relations between the sexes."[12] The phrase "kindly and human relations" is distinctly Morrisian, but the statement as a whole obviously avoids serious questions of equality and social justice. Should women *not* have equal access to jobs and remuneration? Should *not* new forms of mutual sexual contract or promises of fidelity be advocated in the new society, and if so, how should they be enforced? Should socialists endorse reforms—inevitably partial and piecemeal—of existing marriage laws, and support demands for women's suffrage for elections to the "bourgeois" parliament? Most potentially controversial in its implications then and now: How should childcare duties be apportioned? Most socialists would have agreed with the "Manifesto's" truistic statement as it was first worded, including advocates of "free love"; antifeminists such as Bax, who actively opposed women's suffrage and thought "bourgeois marriage" oppressed *males*; feminists eager to end child prostitution and domestic abuse; communalists who advocated cooperative domestic and childcare arrangements; and even "moderate" social-democrats who chiefly wished for continuation of the nuclear family structure under somewhat liberalized divorce laws.

One critical respondent to this minimal statement seems to have been the twenty-nine year old recent convert to Fabianism, G. B. Shaw, whose essay "The Future of Marriage" Morris politely declined to publish in the April 1885 *Commonweal*.[13] The contents of Shaw's essay are not known, but if consistent with his statements on marriage shortly thereafter, they likely included an attack on female wage slavery, as well as an ironic defense of *both* marriage and prostitution as equally venal forms of socially imposed, female self-barter.[14] Morris's reason for rejecting "the very clever paper which you have kindly sent us" is ambiguously worded: "I should like things altered in your article which I am afraid would take the spirit out of it, and it is too good to spoil."[15] Interpreting Shaw's views as opposed to the basic claims of the "Manifesto," he also notes dryly that "We can hardly attack our own manifesto for instance: also we could not agree that Socialists ought to leave the marriage question alone."[16]

In the rest of his scrupulous response to Shaw (who many years later wrote one of Morris's better-known memorials), Morris also suggested that some vestiges of current marriage law would be needed to protect widows and orphans—a matter on which he felt strongly, as the devoted father of a daughter subject to uncontrolled seizures. That his essentially protectionist views persist can be inferred from the lack of any direct criticism of sex-segregation by occupation, and his tacit acceptance of conventional family structures:

> there are points about the bearing of the present marriage laws, or inheritance laws which to my mind rather damage your point of view. Of course I agree that abolishing wedlock while the present economical slavery lasts would be futile: nor do I consider a man a socialist at all who is not prepared to admit the equality of women *as far as condition goes*. Also that as long as women are compelled to marry for a livelihood real marriage is a rare exception and prostitution or a kind of legalized rape the rule. . . . I think we of the S. L. must before long state our views on wedlock quite plainly and take the consequences, which I admit are likely to be serious: but I think we had better leave the subject alone till we can pluck up heart to explain the ambiguities of our sentence in the manifesto.[17]

Morris's notion of "condition" went "farther" before his death, but its limitations here are obvious.[18]

Others associated with the League may also have found the marriage plank of the "Manifesto" superficial and truistic. For the same issue of *Commonweal* in which Shaw's article did not appear, Morris accepted Eleanor Marx's praiseful review of August Bebel's *Woman Under Socialism*, as an expanded version of which, coauthored with Edward Aveling and retitled *The Woman Question*, became the first Marxist-feminist treatise originally written in English.[19]

The League also published a second, annotated edition of Morris and Bax's "Manifesto" in October of that year, and it included this time a slightly expanded statement about marriage: "Under a Socialistic system contracts between individuals would be voluntary and unenforced by the community. This would apply to the marriage contract as well as others, and it would become a matter of simple inclination. Women also would share in the certainty of livelihood which would be the lot of all; and children would be treated from their birth as members of the community entitled to share in all its advantages; so that economical compulsion could be no more brought to bear on the contract than legal compulsion could be."[20] Future socialists would thus not be bound by marriage laws, and women and children would "share in the certainty of livelihood"; whether this might ever mean *equality* of livelihood, or of access to desirable occupations, remained once again in suspension. Fulfillment of the desire to work and create is one of the deepest human desires, of course, as Morris—one of his century's chief proponents of creativity in labor—knew full well. The statement in the second edition of the "Manifesto" still avoided explicit commitment on most of the deepest issues of the woman question.

Six months later, Bax's vitriolic assault "Some Bourgeois Idols; or, Ideals, Reals and Shams," appeared as the lead article in *Commonweal* for April 1886. Bax's attacks on such "idols" as "Liberty" (defined as laissez-faire market conditions) and the "rights of property" were commonplace enough, at least in *Commonweal*.[21] But his long invective against the "idol" of "equality between the sexes" exhibited a gratuitous truculence (almost) all his own. Most offensively, he expressed his "socialist" dissatisfaction with recent legislative efforts to proscribe marital nonsupport, and wife- and childbattering:[22]

> [T]he cry for "equality between the sexes" has in the course of its realisation become a sham, masking a *de facto* inequality. The inequality in question presses, as usual, heaviest upon the working-man, whose wife to all intents and purposes has him completely in her power. . . . let him but raise a finger in a moment of exasperation, against this precious representative of the sacred principle of "womanhood," and straightway he is consigned to the treadmill for his six months amid the jubilation of the *D[aily] T[imes]*. . . .
>
> Again, we have the same principle illustrated in the truly bestial howl raised every now and again by certain persons for the infliction of the punishment of flogging on men for particular offenses, notably "assaults on women and children." As a matter of fact in the worst cases of cruelty to children, women are the criminals.[23]

Bax, in his own "bestial howl," may have had in mind several changes in British marriage law during the previous two decades; for example, mothers of young children had recently gained the right to marital separation in cases of repeated child assault by fathers.[24] Against a background of widespread proletarian alcoholism and family violence, and then-recent revelations about the existence of child brothels, Bax's opposition to "bourgeois" restraints on domestic violence remains essentially incomprehensible.[25] He concluded his screed with a characterization of women's suffrage as "the handing over of the complete control of the state to *one* sex," and the exaltation of "the female sex into a quasi-privileged class."[26]

Weary historians who have also glanced at Bax's later compilation of his views in *The Fraud of Feminism* (1913) will realize that these outbursts are in fact relatively moderate for him. Absent from the *Commonweal* article are several charges he later made about women's alleged genetic inferiority, mental imbalance, and unfitness for professional or skilled occupations.[27] It is a bitter fact that the most well-read advocate of German Marxism in the English socialist movement of the late 1880s (other than Engels himself) was a vituperative antifeminist bigot. Even Bax's more moderate tone on other issues in most of his articles is so much at variance with that of the coauthored *Socialism: Its Growth and Outcome* as to suggest that Morris may have been even more responsible for the latter's content than has generally been acknowledged.[28]

In any case, what remains most disturbing is Bax's fear that men who committed the ostensibly venial offense of "lifting a finger" "in a moment of exasperation" against wives or children might suffer punishment for their actions. Suffrage for either sex was often dismissed as a reformist goal by the more antiparliamentarian members of the Socialist League. But no one in the League other than Bax ever publicly attempted to vindicate domestic assault or brutality on any grounds. Morris's anxiety to maintain an uneasy peace must be understood in the context of internal Socialist League politics: Bax's loyal support of Morris's departure from the Social Democratic Federation (S.D.F.) in reaction to Henry Hyndman's secretive and authoritarian policies; Engels's personal coolness to Morris; the role of Engels, Marx-Aveling, and Aveling as leaders of the opposition parliamentary faction of the Socialist League; Morris's distaste for the dishonest and philandering Aveling; and the generally acknowledged usefulness of Bax's other contributions to *Commonweal*.

At least two readers of *Commonweal*, however, wrote to protest Bax's views; both apparently criticized his attacks on parents' right to educate their own children, and his bizarre assertions of women's supposed dominance in marriage under British law. One of these respondents was the Reverend William Sharman, who apparently solicited in his letter Morris's personal views on education and the family. In his reply, Morris writes that children "have as much need for the revolution as the proletarians have," but then continues, in an attempt to palliate Bax's outburst: "As to the woman matter, I do not think Bax puts it unreasonably in his article, though I have heard him exaggerate that in talk and have often fallen foul of him."[29] Bruce Glasier, who later married his Glaswegian fellow-lecturer, Katharine Conroy, sent the other, apparently more urgent rebuttal of Bax's views, and Morris deflected Glasier's criticisms of Bax on partly "tactical" grounds:[30]

> I am not quite sure that it would be wise to put it in as it would be cutting the dam of the waters of controversy: since of course Bax must be allowed reply: I will consult with him next Wednesday and do you please consider the matter yourself. . . . Again as to the woman-mattter, it seems to me that there is more to be said on Bax's side than you suppose. For my part being a male-man I naturally think more of the female-man than I do of my own sex: but you must not forget that child-bearing makes women inferior to men, since a certain time of their lives they must be dependent on them. Of course we must claim absolute equality of condition between women and men, as between other groups, but it would be poor economy setting women to do men's work (as unluckily they often do now) or vice versa.[31]

Taken together, these letters represent the nadir of Morris's protectionism, and of his desire to patch together the obvious divisions within the Socialist League. Even as he argues his own more benign views on marriage with Sharman, he tries unsuccessfully to palliate the painful implications of his splenetic friend's opinions on patriarchal dominance. Exactly because he had "often fallen foul" on these matters with Bax, Morris also realized all too well, as Sharman and Glasier probably did not, that the latter's bigoted public views were an expurgated, toned-down version of his private ones, and not amenable to reasoned discussion.

Characteristically, Morris's remark to Glasier about the effects of (multiple) pregnancies also reverses without comment Bax's assertion that women already benefit from *too much* protection. It is undeniable that many Victorian women, middle- and upper- as well as lower-class, bore child after child until they were exhausted, but William Morris and his wife Jane (for example) had only two children, as did his closest friends

Georgiana and Edward Burne-Jones. Bax's remarks had not even addressed the issue of women's appropriate roles and needs; but Morris's attempt to consider them here were misleading and inadequate.

The only other recorded private statement by Morris that bears indirectly on the issue of women's roles may be a casual attempt at conventional role reversal and wry humor. In a September 1888 letter to James Mavor of Glasgow, Morris mentions his correspondence with a bookbinder, Cedric Chivers: "I will see if I can hear of anyone to help in his work; a boy would be easier to find than a girl; women as a rule are very feeble on the artistic side; their line is business and mathematics."[32] Morris's idealized representations of women, of course, often showed them weaving, and several women had already become rather successful as bookbinders and bookcover embroiderers by this period. Some, moreover—such as Catherine Holiday and Kate Faulkner (the sister of the mathematician Charles Faulkner, Morris's lifelong friend)—had executed commissions for Morris and Company for many years.[33] Morris's apparent tongue-in-cheek inversion of gender-stereotypes is his only recorded effort along these lines.[34]

In the summer of 1888, at any rate, Bax rejoined the S.D.F., and ceased thereafter to exert any influence on *Commonweal*.[35] Morris may well have been dissatisfied with the evasive ambiguity of their carefully calculated joint statements on familial and sexual relations, however, and less than proud as well of his uneasy defense of Bax's polemic. When he returned to the task of projecting an ideal society in *News From Nowhere* (1890), in any case, Morris made equity of sexual behavior and flexibility of family ties one of the principal subjects of two of the book's chapters (9 and 24).[36] Significant parts of the river-journey plot turn on two instances of female freedom: Clara's return to her former partner Dick, and Ellen's exploration of new regions with the visiting Guest. Morris also depicts Nowhereian women in a variety of exemplary roles, most traditional, but a few mildly innovative. In his earlier writings, Morris had already presented women of compelling psychological depth—Guenevere, Jehane, Psyche, Gudrun, Philonoë—but *News from Nowhere* is the first major English utopian work by a man which confers the role of wisdom figure or "sage" on a woman. Ellen expresses the book's deepest insights on the meaning and use of history, the distinctive qualities of the new society, and the means by which members of Guest's society will have to strive toward it.

Advocacy of female sexual autonomy as a socialist ideal had already appeared, in fact, in Morris's narrative poem "The Pilgrims of Hope," a tribute to the Paris Commune serialized in *Commonweal* from April 1885 to June 1886 (a series of issues which included the articles of both Eleanor Marx and Bax). The principal narrator of "Pilgrims" accepts his wife's preference for their mutual comrade, Arthur, and all three struggle together on the barricades of the Commune, where the wife dies in an unsuccessful effort to save the stricken Arthur. Recovered from his own wounds, the husband then manages to escape Paris and return to England, where he honors his wife's memory, raises their son, and continues to work for the cause. The wife's estrangement is not condemned, and the husband's communist beliefs are tested not only on the barricades, but also by the more difficult task of accepting his wife's rejection as he preserves their shared ideals. The poem's strength and originality also derive from a long passage in which the wife addresses the infant son who will never know her, as well as the poignancy of the husband's introspective attempts to understand and accept his wife's decision.[37] The socialist marriage plot in "The Pilgrims of Hope" has often been criticized as irrelevant to its political themes; it is not irrelevant, but it *is* virtually unique in the annals of British socialist literature, and remarkable for a male socialist of Morris's period.

In *News from Nowhere,* by contrast, Dick and Clara's marital estrangement eventuates in a mutually gratifying reconciliation, and the entire episode is a subplot of Guest's central journey downstream and his encounters with Dick, Old Hammond, and Ellen. The reunion of Dick and Clara gives Morris a chance to elaborate more fully his views of sexual equity and autonomy, and to contrast pointedly the behavior of Nowhereians with the inequities in the divorce laws of his own time—principally, their heavy penalties for female adultery, dictated by what Eleanor Marx had called "one code of morals for man and one for woman."[38]

In chapter 9 of *News from Nowhere,* "Concerning Love," Guest learns from Old Hammond that his guide Dick hopes to be reunited with his former wife Clara, who had deserted him for another man, and now seeks reconciliation. Guest is somewhat surprised that she has suffered no legal or social penalties, and learns that the couple's children have remained with one of Hammond's daughters, "where, indeed, Clara has mostly been.[39] Patiently, Hammond explains to Guest the need to distinguish

"natural passion" and "friendship," and both from possessiveness: "We
know that we must face the unhappiness that comes of man and woman
confusing the relations between natural passion, and sentiment, and the
friendship which, when things go well, softens the awakening from passing
illusions: but we are not so mad as to pile up degradation on that unhappiness by engaging in sordid squabbles about livelihood and position, and
the power of tyrannising over the children who have been the result of love
or lust" (57). It still remains conspicuous in Nowhere that (most) women
"naturally" gather round to offer hospitality and care for children (as
when Clara and her daughter move in with old Hammond's daughter),
and that women still tend to raise their own offspring. However, Morris's
descriptions of Nowhereian children's education also embody his assumption that childrearing will become an activity of natural interest to all
adults, and he makes it clear that male egotism and impulses toward revenge, not parental irresponsibility, are the principal social evils to be
feared when marriages dissolve: "So it is a point of honour with us not to
be self-centred; not to suppose that the world must cease because one man
is sorry; therefore we should think it foolish, or if you will, criminal, to
exaggerate these matters of sentiment and sensibility: we are no more inclined to eke out our sentimental sorrows than to cherish our bodily pains;
and we recognise that there are other pleasures besides love-making" (58).
In chapter 24, Dick and Walter also recount the story of a man who has
attacked his more successful rival in love and been killed himself in the
ensuing struggle. Both the slayer and the woman involved are deeply depressed after the event, but no legal punishment is imposed on them; Nowhereians have no prisons, and in any case the man had not sought the
quarrel.

It is characteristic of Morris, by the way, that both of these stories
involve a woman who is sought by two men; his writings contain relatively
few instances in which men desert women, or in which two women love
the same man.[40] More generally, the social structure of Nowhere also
exemplifies once again the essentially traditional nature of Morris's
assumptions about (hetero)sexual ties. Nowhere offers no instances
of homosexual unions, adoptive families, group marriages, or even casu-
ally promiscuous men and women. Morris clearly assumes an ethic of
male attachment, and hopes an extended social family will cooperate in

childrearing when disintegration of a family unit becomes inevitable. It remains unclear how he would have interpreted or accommodated widespread paternal desertion of wives and infant children, much less abandonment of the latter by the former, but in fairness to Morris it should be observed that he was hardly alone in this. All contemporary socialists advocated dissolution of ties by mutual consent, but virtually no one—including most of the heroic figures of British and American feminism—envisioned a world in which men shared equally in child care, or in which deserted fathers patiently raised infant children. Eleanor Marx, for example, quoted with approval Bebel's inadvertently revealing description of the independent woman, whose "household and children, if she has any, cannot restrict her freedom, but only increase her pleasure in life. Educators, friends, *young girls,* are all at hand for all cases in which she needs help."[41] Only death seems to confer the responsibility (or privilege) of childrearing on men, as it does on the hero of "Pilgrims of Hope."

Nowhere's reunion of Dick and Clara also recalls the painful emotions of Morris's own marriage; like Clara, Jane Morris had often absented herself from him and their children. Clara is the only figure in the book who responds nostalgically to a Pre-Raphaelite view of women as proper objects of romance. She is described sympathetically, but she clearly has restless impulses which may recall the egocentric pleasures of the hated nineteenth century. When Ellen's grandfather, for example, conjectures that, after all, the society of the nineteenth century may have been preferable to their own, Dick looks uncomfortable and Ellen bursts out in impatient disagreement, but Guest notes that "Clara listened to him with restless eyes, as if she were excited and pleased" (150). When other Nowhereians suggest that art should reflect the strangeness of past history, Clara protests forthrightly, "Well, for my part . . . I wish we were interesting enough to be written or painted about" (103). (Ironically, of course, her wish is granted: they are.)

Other critics have already noted the degree to which Nowhereians continue the role segregation of Morris's own century (and to a depressing extent, ours): the men serve as guides and row the women downstream; at guesthouses women wait on men who sit at tables; sundry novelists and historians, encountered along the way, are all male; men mow hay in the fields during harvest, while the women gather to watch.[42] Among the justifications given for this division of labor is the ambiguous assertion that:

"The women do what they can do best, and what they like best, and the men are neither jealous of it or injured by it" (59). There is one lone but striking exception to these stereotyped roles, however: Philippa, chief carver (sculptor) among "the obstinate refusers" who prefer housebuilding to haymaking, is quite possibly an allusion to Philippa Fawcett, who earlier in the year of *Nowhere*'s publication had placed above the Senior Wrangler in the Cambridge mathematics tripos.[43] The Nowhereian Philippa is a forty-year-old mother of a sixteen-year-old apprentice-carver, and the only female single parent and working mother in the entire book. Since decoration of public buildings would be a primary concern of the new society (according, for example, to "Socialism Triumphant"), Philippa's occupation is highly honorific in Nowhereian terms.[44] In his writings, moreover, Morris often imagines women at work at solitary artistic tasks, and at what he called "administration": "there are many, like the housekeepers I was speaking of, whose delight is in administration and organisation, to use long-tailed words; I mean people who like keeping things together, avoiding waste, seeing that nothing sticks fast uselessly" (84). *Nowhere* is devoid of political rulers and warriors, of course, so an absence of female "political leaders" is tautological. But it should also be observed that the women of the later prose romances, though assertive and geographically mobile, never fill whatever positions of military and political leadership are to be had.

In short, the essential traditionalism of Morris's (widely shared) assumptions about the "natural" division of sexual roles, even in *Nowhere*, undercuts somewhat the appealing implications of his own espousal of "women's" work, but he remained strikingly distinctive among end-of-century socialists in the straightforwardness and sincerity of his insistence that *no* legal or social coercion should constrain a woman's choices of sexual partner and parental role.

There is, moreover, one sturdy token counterexample in *Nowhere* to the prevailing pattern of Morris's portrayals of women, and her contribution is highly valued. Two of the utopia's more astute inhabitants mediate for Guest the nature of the utopian future with special care: one of these "wisdom figures," predictably, is an old man; but the other is Ellen, a young woman. Halfway through the book, the historian Old Hammond recounts to Guest the changes which led to the greater "Change," and sketches the beginnings of the new order which followed. Later, Ellen travels downriver with Guest, and in the course of their conversations comes to represent to him the transformed life in its most self-consciously reflective form. Learned old sages and handsome young women are stock Victorian figures, of course, but it is Ellen's *"sagacity"*—her ability to re-live and interpret history—which becomes most valuable to Guest as he struggles to find a way to express the new society's wisdom to the members of his own.

Other inhabitants of Nowhere have already presented their historical opinions earlier in the book: not only the history-buff Old Hammond, but also Dick, Boffin, Clara, and Ellen's grandfather have all tried in their ways to sort out with Guest the respective merits of the past and the new society. The commonplace criticism that Nowhereians are ahistorical, which takes literally Dick's claim of facile antiintellectualism, is a mistake. Even Dick respects what Morris considered authentic popular history—the commemoration of folk ways and lore, and love of the beautiful artifacts and skills of the past. But it is Ellen (the Helen of the new world) who anticipates Santayana, as she states the narrative's most eloquent endorsement of the power of history: "I think sometimes people are too careless of the history of the past—too apt to leave it in the hands of old learned men like Hammond. Who knows? Happy as we are, times may alter; we may be bitten with some impulse towards change, and many things may seem too wonderful for us to resist, too exciting not to catch at, if we do not know that they are but phases of what has been before; and withal ruinous, deceitful, and sordid" (194).

The most perceptive Nowhereians are also distinguished by their awareness of the miseries that past societies inflicted on their citizens. Ellen, for example, expresses Morris's own view of the narrow class bias of most Victorian fiction.[45] "Some . . . [nineteenth-century books], indeed, do here and there show some feeling for those whom the history-books call 'poor,' and of the misery of whose lives we have some inkling; but presently they give it up, and towards the end of the story we must be contented to see the hero and heroine living happily in an island of bliss on other people's troubles" (151). Ellen also understands very well what her daily life might have been like under capitalism, at its "best" as well as its worst, and her indictment is a set piece of Morris's socialist-feminism: "my beauty and cleverness and brightness . . . would have been sold to rich men, and my life would have been wasted indeed; . . . I should have had no choice, no power of will over my life . . . I should never have bought pleasure from the rich men, and even opportunity of action, whereby I might have won some true excitement. I should have been wrecked and wasted in one way or another, either by penury or by luxury" (204). Here also, for the first time in his writings, Morris identifies explicitly "opportunity of action" as a natural female goal.

Inevitably, of course, Ellen also bears witness to some of the conventional limitations of Morris's ideal. She has little impulse to travel, unlike Guest, and the youthful Morris himself ("I must say that I don't like moving about from one home to another; one gets so pleasantly used to all the detail of the life about one" [190]), and she wants an indefinite number of children ("I shall have children; perhaps before the end a good many—I hope so" [194]).[46] Her desire for children is reflective as well as straightforward, however: she *thinks* through her hopes for these potential children, as does the wife in "Pilgrims of Hope," and yearns to transmit to them her own efforts at empathy and understanding, and those of the people who have gone before them: "[T]hough of course I cannot force any special kind of knowledge upon them, yet, my friend, I cannot help thinking that just as they might be like me in body, so I might impress upon them some part of my ways of thinking; that is, indeed, some of the essential part of myself; that part which was not mere moods, created by the matters and events round about me. What do you think?" (194).

Not since his creation of the Guenevere of *The Defence,* moreover, had Morris taken such care to imagine a woman's consciousness *from within;* by comparison, even Oenone and Gudrun of his middle period are embodiments of passionate intensity externally observed. Above all, none of Morris's female heroes before Ellen can credibly be described as a "sage." She is *News from Nowhere*'s truest wisdom figure, not a distant erotic ideal, but the embodiment of Morris's self-conscious hope for future generations. Not all of Morris's later women are "new women," but his imagination is capable of dwelling with sympathy on a few exemplars, of which Ellen is the most convincing. As the work's most perceptive interpretant of the new society, and an active, unrepressed woman who desires to transmit her physical and cultural identity to future generations, Ellen embodies the limitations as well as the strengths of Morris's socialist-feminism, but she alone in Nowhere fully practices Morris's deepest ideal of popular, living history; and she alone is the spokeswoman of the book's finest insights into the spirit of the new society.

At the end of *News from Nowhere,* a journey to the church at the upper waters of the Thames becomes a kind of secular passage to the new Jerusalem. Ellen is the Christ-figure who leads Guest to the book's final meal, and leaves him tenderly with a final consolation—another great set piece, and one of Morris's most heartfelt declarations of the beauty of earth, "feminine" and universal: "She led me up close to the house, and laid her shapely sun browned hand and arm on the lichened wall as if to embrace it, and cried out, "O me! O me! How I love the earth, and the seasons, and weather, and all things that deal with it, and all that grows out of it—as this has done!" (201). Ellen's brief epiphany has often been quoted for the beauty of its invocation of a socialist ideal. It is that. But it is also Morris's best and most sustained effort to imagine how an egalitarian society might alter the thoughts and inner consciousness of its women.

Victorian Women, Wisdom,
and Southeast Asia

SUSAN MORGAN

I am content to sympathize with common mortals, no matter where they live; in houses or in tents, in the streets under a fog, or in the forests behind the dark line of distant mangroves that fringe the vast solitude of the sea.

——Joseph Conrad, "Preface" to *Almayer's Folly*

Then he asked me in a solemn voice: "You know Stambul, Monsieur?"
"Yes."
"I lived in Stambul a year, and I tell you, Monsieur, it is a hell from which there is no way out."

——Robert Byron, *The Road to Oxiana*

During the last three decades of the nineteenth century a wealth of travel books written by women were published in England. Many of these travel books share distinctive features. They were focussed on countries geographically far removed from England which were non-Western and non-white: in Africa, in the Middle East, in India, in Southeast Asia, and in the Far East. They were often the products of long stays in and substantial familiarity with the countries that were their subjects. The authors did not present themselves, and may not even have thought of themselves, as particularly adventuresome or somehow different from other women. They declared their books to have specific, practical aims which were usually political and economic. Although often implicitly, the books also addressed other, more philosophic questions, about the future of England, the meaning of progress, and the definition of human nature. These books enjoyed a large reading audience in their own era. And, finally, they have all but been forgotten in ours.[1]

Traditional Victorian scholars in the twentieth century focussed on fiction, poetry, and the essays that as a graduate student I was taught to call nonfiction prose. In their critical writings about the period they reconstructed a kind of cultural fantasyland in which every Victorian who was anybody read or was influenced by such wise patriarchs as Carlyle, Newman, Ruskin, and Arnold, the classic Victorian sages. But a great many Victorians were reading, and admiring, the travel writings of Annie Brassey, Anna Forbes, and Margaret Brooke. Yet there is no published study of Victorian women's travel writings about the East, and the potentially major role of these writings in shaping the cultural currents of their age has never been considered. The initial reason, then, why these writings are so significant must simply be that they were so significant.

That significance has an aesthetic as well as a factual dimension. The central charm of these writings, and where both their literary and their historical value should be placed, is in their sensitive acuteness to and complex relations with Eastern cultures. The quality of their prose is inseparable from the moral, emotional, and intellectual sophistication of their insights about what for many readers were, and are, imaginatively remote worlds.[2] That sophistication is based on a particular notion of the value of human sympathy, of the truths of the heart, which spoke to many Victorian readers with powerful eloquence.

There are two distinct but interdependent issues that these travel books raise for a critic today. First, what can their presence as a salient element of Victorian culture tell us about their own time? Second, what can their absence—and, hopefully, their renewed presence—tell us about ours? I want to begin this brief, and necessarily introductory, discussion by turning first to the question of the meaning of these works in their own time.

It may be that the West has always been fascinated with the East—and if not quite always, then certainly long enough. Just as certainly, "to believe that such things happen as a necessity of the imagination, is to be disingenuous."³ In nineteenth-century England the passion for the faraway first appears as a major literary event with Byron's grand tour of the mid-East, and the huge success during the second decade of the century of such poems as *The Turkish Tales* and the Eastern cantos of *Don Juan*.⁴ But the long-term British love affair with the exotic expanded throughout the century and functioned in many ways. Any attempt to understand some of the dimensions of that expansion must begin with Edward Said's brilliant insight that "the Orient was Orientalized not because it was discovered to be 'Oriental' in all those ways considered commonplace by the average nineteenth-century European, but also because it *could be*— that is, submitted to being—*made* Oriental."⁵

If Byron's work was popular due both to the general charm of its eastern topics for the British public and to its author's particular ability to make those topics "Oriental," his poems are still rather different phenomena from the prose accounts of journeys that long have captured the attention of the British public. Byron himself certainly knew other travel accounts, at least in poetry.⁶ He dedicated *The Giaour* to his friend, Samuel Rogers, the author of that forgettable 1810 fragment, *The Voyage of Columbus*. After Byron, the most notable prose account in the first decades of the nineteenth century of a voyage of discovery was Charles Darwin's 1839 *Journal of Researches into the Geology and Natural History of the Various Countries Visited by H.M.S. Beagle*.⁷

The difference between the subject of Rogers's failed poem and of Darwin's popular book highlights the special qualities of the latter. *The Voyage of Columbus* tried to recreate a discovery that was fundamentally a discovery of a place. It was a great physical adventure, a journey into the literal unknown. The larger significance of that journey, its power to change the ways people view the world, had been reverberating for three centuries before Rogers wrote his account. Darwin's *Journal of Researches* was also an account of physical discoveries; of the birds, beetles, and fossil mammals of South America. Yet those discoveries, in themselves minute and cumulative, only carry significance as traces of a meaning that no one, including the author, could know with any confidence at the time the *Journal* was published. This was writing to the moment, and it would take Darwin another twenty years of research to publish the book that limned the significance of that moment. After *The Origin of the Species* was published in 1859 it would take his readers the rest of the nineteenth century, and arguably the twentieth and perhaps the twenty-first century as well, to follow the implications of his insights. Darwin's *Journal,* though written during what often must have been a daring physical adventure, is really an account of the adventures of the scientific mind. Its exciting moments have to do with bone structures and barnacles, with uncovering patterns in the natural world.

There are many accounts of how Darwin spent twenty years tabulating and adding to his findings from the journey of the Beagle in order to write *The Origin of the Species,* only to find his central ideas suddenly and fairly completely anticipated by Alfred Russel Wallace. In May or June of 1858 Wallace, who had conducted his own researches in South America, the Malay Archipelago, and Indonesia, sent Darwin a paper from Southeast Asia with a theory that Wallace said had come to him in "a flash of insight."[8] Wallace was generous in acknowledging that Darwin's years of commitment to the subject took precedence over his "flash." For his part, Darwin was prodded by Wallace's achievement to start writing his own book rapidly enough to have it ready for publication the following year.

What Wallace and Darwin shared, and what made their mutual discoveries and the sorting out of the question of precedence amicable (apart from decency of character), was a commitment to the process of personal observation and fact-collecting that could make a theory stand or fall. That is why Wallace, though publishing the theory first, would concede Darwin's prior claim. It is also why Darwin, absorbed in accumulating and categorizing evidence, took so long to get around to writing out his explanatory conclusions. It is fair to say that Darwin's voyage of discovery lasted from 1831, when Darwin first boarded the Beagle, to 1859, when he directly spelled out the scientific conclusions of that voyage.

Implicit in the unfolding of this publishing event, arguably the most important intellectual event in nineteenth-century history, is the belief that knowledge is a matter of personal involvement, of long, attentive experience. What made Darwin's work truer than Wallace's was not the objective fact, the right answer, the theory of evolution of species through natural selection that both of them had more or less independently arrived at. Darwin's work was seen as truer because of his enormous accumulation of details in five years on the Beagle and twenty more years in England. Thus, Darwin's theory was truer not merely because it was backed by more factual evidence but also substantially because it had evolved from virtually a lifetime of committed involvement. The process gave substance, and value, to the product.

The history of Darwin's researches demonstrates a basic principle of scientific investigation: that what is most essential is not the abstract theory but the concrete evidence that can prove or disprove it. But the publication history of Darwin's discovery demonstrates a great deal more. The value that the various players in that history placed on the research process, far from reflecting just a rule for objective procedure, is part of a familiar and frequent belief among all sorts of writers in nineteenth-century England that what is of value is process. The lived experience matters; out of it come truths that take their quality as truths exactly from the fact of their having emerged from experience. George Eliot, a famous proponent of this organic view, wrote that "we learn *words* by rote, but not their meanings; *that* must be paid for with our life-blood, and printed in the subtler fibres of our nerves."[9] Whether it be a matter of objectivity or emotion, of science or philosophy, of economics or art, wisdom is to be gleaned from the living whole.

The sense that truth comes out of lived experience has long been cited as a defining quality of the intellectual history written by the male Victorian sages. Their most famous critical chronicler, John Holloway, explaining Newman's idea of Real Assent, described it as "directed towards assertions based on the whole trend of our experience."[10] Yet this idea, in tandem with the sages' belief that the purpose of their writing is to modify "the reader's perceptiveness," also constitutes the defining quality of Victorian women's travel writings about Southeast Asia.[11]

The commitment to a wisdom that comes out of lived experience recurs in women's travel writings. Anna Forbes, who travelled with her husband on his naturalist expedition to Java in the early 1880s, wrote her own account. Her direct explanation for the differences in their versions of the journey is that "we shared for the most part the same experiences; but we looked upon them from an entirely different standpoint."[12] Part of the difference in standpoint was not just the matter of their being different people but also of their being a different sex. This was a fact of culture rather than of biology. English women in the East, whatever their number of servants, still attended to such domestic matters as laundry, shopping, cooking, and particularly children, matters that they shared with their foreign counterparts. Their perspectives on Southeast Asia reflect this sense of having a connection to other women that they did not share with English men. And one of the most common ways in which these women writers assert their bonds with women of another country is through motherhood.

The pervasive Victorian belief that truth comes from perceptions felt along the bone, far from providing an exclusive blessing for the oracular writings of Victorian men, also functioned to validate a woman's voice and special experience. Within the genre of travel literature of the period, the organic principle served to distinguish between women's and men's writings about the same country. Finally, it also served to distinguish views between women. One of the most dramatically negative accounts of British station life in Malaya is Emily Innes's *The Chersonese with the Gilding Off* (1885). Innes wrote her exposé explicitly to contrast with Isabella Bird's celebration of the Malay peninsula, *The Golden Chersonese* (1883). Yet, in her conclusion, Innes praises Bird's "delightful" book and goes on to claim that "notwithstanding the brilliancy and attractiveness of her descriptions, and the dullness and gloom of mine, I can honestly say that her account is perfectly and literally true. So is mine. The explanation is that she and I saw the Malayan country under totally different circumstances."[13]

Innes was "a nonentity compared to Isabella Bird."[14] Bird already had a substantial reputation as a travel writer before writing her Malay account and it gave her real power: "Government officers did their best to make themselves agreeable, knowing that she wielded in her right hand a little instrument that might chastise or reward them." One clear measure of the difference between the two women's experiences is that it never occurred to Innes "in those days that I might write an account of it all."[15] Eventually, she realized the power of a public voice. She took up "the little instrument" for the practical power she hoped it would give her as well, in her case to arouse public opinion against the corrupt Colonial Office, which had refused her husband six years of back pay.

Two specific implications of the extensive nineteenth-century commitment to the organic nature of truth are immediately relevant to the question of women and wisdom. First, as Holloway lucidly pointed out over thirty-five years ago, the commitment to finding truth through an observation of and an involvement in concrete life lends itself to novels or, to put it more generally, to the truth-value of ideas embodied in characters and narrative.[16] The distance may not be so great after all between Darwin poring over his barnacles and a literary critic poring over *Middlemarch*.[17] Certainly, there are important similarities between a novel and *The Origin of the Species*. Many readers have noted *The Origin*'s narrative qualities, and have attributed part of its early success, extensive popularity, and impact on a nonscientific audience to its readable personal style.[18]

Second, there is a significant tie in nineteenth-century intellectual history between the influence of Darwinism and the popularity of travel books, and thus between scientific and what I would loosely describe as nonscientific explorations. The journeys of the naturalists in the 1830s, 1840s, and 1850s and the resulting travel accounts—of Darwin in South America, of Wallace in the Malay Archipelago, of Sir Joseph Dalton Hooker in Antarctica, New Zealand and Tasmania—may well form the enabling intellectual context for such travel accounts of the 1870s, 1880s, and 1890s as those by Anna Leonowens about Siam and India, by Brassey about Tahiti and the South Seas, and by Bird, Innes, and Emily Richings about the Malay Archipelago. These women travellers saw their journeys as crucial experiences, most expressing a view similar to Darwin's that the voyage was "by far the most important event in my life."[19] All the writers, male and female, were searching for truth. If the men looked for it in the immediacy of their field experiences, the women hoped to find it in the daily act of living the life that they also observed. Like their naturalist counterparts, the women believed that this truth, once recorded in its organic and concrete form, could cause a public, and important, change in the perspective of their readers.

Apart from the historical accuracy of pointing out critical connections between the accounts of travelling naturalists and the accounts of nonscientific travellers, there is another important advantage. The scientific journey offers a much-needed alternative context to that of the novel through which to approach nineteenth-century travel writings. There are, roughly speaking, three different nineteenth-century genres which need to be distinguished here: scientific writings, often cast in the narrative form of voyage accounts or of journal accounts recording the process of discovery; travel writings, which are usually but not inevitably in narrative form; and novels. All three genres share certain elements. Readers have long been attentive to the connections between science writings and literature, from T. H. Huxley's *Science and Culture* and Edward Dowden's "The Scientific

Movement and Literature" to such present works as Gillian Beer's *Darwin's Plots*, George Levine's *Darwin and The Novelists*, and Peter Morton's *The Vital Science*.[20] The much more limited work on travel writings has attended to their fictional qualities, as in Percy Adams's *Travel Literature and the Origin of the Novel*.[21] Yet the links between scientific and travel writings have been almost completely ignored.[22]

All three kinds of work aim to depict in a concrete form the truths of life. To say this highlights immediately the limitations as well as the advantages of using a fictional model to discuss travel writings. The working fiction about travel writings is that they are about real people and real places, that they are factual as well as true. Quite simply, when the critical models are taken from fiction, what are actual journeys take on the dimensions of generic events, as what Marilyn Butler has called "surrogates for the modern reader's psychic journeys, or symbolic representations of the whole of life."[23] They lose their specific personal and historical status. This is not to say that critics should not read travel accounts in terms of the pattern of fiction, "so intimately are literature and travel implicated with each other."[24] The story (if it is a story) that a traveller tells can be read as either true or false. But it should not lose its dimension as a history.

Working from the example of Victorian scientific journeys immediately suggests distinctions among kinds of nineteenth-century travel writings. One of the most famous versions of the genre is the gentleman's grand tour. There were hundreds of accounts of the grand tour, usually to Europe but sometimes farther, published in the first half of the nineteenth century. Byron's idiosyncratic tours formed the basis for much of his poetry. Alexander Kinglake's 1844 *Eothen*, one of the most popular travel books in Victorian England, is an account to a friend of his grand tour of the Middle East. The charm—and the horror—of *Eothen* lie in its witty style; Kinglake "was one of God's Englishmen, . . . a convinced advocate of the theory that all things English were, on the whole, best."[25] If it weren't for the enormous number of accounts by young English gentlemen with the same attitude, though perhaps with less verbal grace, I could convincingly name Kinglake's book as the direct source for George Meredith's account in his 1879 *The Egoist* of Sir Willoughby Patterne's letters home from his grand tour. As the narrator in *The Egoist* characterizes the hero's travel accounts, a "word, a turn of the pen, or a word unsaid, offered the picture of him in America, Japan, China, Australia, nay, the continent of Europe, holding an English review of his Maker's grotesques."[26]

Meredith's description captures a key element of Kinglake's account, that it contained "a picture of him," with the various places he visited functioning as a sort of backdrop for his virtues and charms. As Kinglake wrote in his "Preface" while arguing for the truth of his little book, "as I have felt, so have I written," thus "refusing to dwell upon matters which failed to interest my own feelings."[27] Darwin, and many other travel writers, could make the same claim. But the important difference is that Kinglake is interested in himself, in part because, as an Englishman, he assumes that he is of superior interest to anything or anyone around him. As Said argues, "Orientalism depends for its strategy on this flexible *positional* superiority, which puts the Westerner in a whole series of possible relationships with the Orient without ever losing him the relative upper hand."[28]

The outrageous point of Kinglake's travels is that in a fundamental sense they are pointless. His travels are not really experiences that can change, affect, or somehow alter his understanding of his life. Instead, they are experiences that do not matter, or that matter precisely because they do not matter, that demonstrate Kinglake's superiority on the very grounds that the rest of the world, even if new, strange, and interesting, can add nothing to what, as an Englishman, he already is. The kind of travel writing exemplified by *Eothen*, ostensibly based on a presumed interest in other places, is finally and essentially about a lack of interest in them. The tremendously flattering and reassuring point for the reader, after having been delightfully entertained, is that by not taking such a journey he has really missed nothing, for there is nothing much out there after all. He already has the essential experience of being English, he already knows all he needs to know by staying at home. And that is the ultimate fact that a record of the grand tour can provide.

The entertainment of this sort of travel writing, what there is for the reader to enjoy, is the narrator himself—the feelings, the wit, the intelligence of a fellow Englishman. If the external world is not of particular interest, the internal world that carries within it all the preestablished criteria of value for Victorian masculine culture is. All the world is a stage, but

the play and the characters are always English, and the lead character is
always an Englishman. In *Eothen* we are to be intrigued not by what Kinglake sees but by how, and to what, he responds. In contrast to the premise
of the scientific voyages of discovery, the premise of this sort of travel
writing is that experience does not matter, and that truth does not emerge
from experience but is already intrinsically felt and known. The result is a
record of encounters with other, radically different cultures that reassures
rather than unsettles its readers, and bolsters rather than challenges their
most basic national and cultural and masculine chauvinism.

Separating out those travel writings that, under the forms of romance or
essay, guidebook or memoir, are really exercises in the superiority of the
travelling Englishmen to whatever wonders he may survey is fairly easy. It
is more difficult to approach those travel writings that seem to be doing
something else. In his fascinating study of twentieth-century British travel
writings between the two World Wars, Paul Fussell is able to suggest patterns of meaning precisely because of his attention to the historical moment, that period following the Great War and continuing until the
ominous rumblings that signalled the beginning of the Second World War.[29]
Fussell's admirable sense of history also reveals, perhaps inadvertently,
that there are limits to what even a properly historical-critical approach
can explain. Thus, Fussell argues that the fondness these travel writings
show for the tropics, for palm trees, and sunny oranges, is a "celebration
of freedom" and a reaction to the freezing barrenness of the trenches.[30] Yet
that explanation hardly will account for the fondness for the tropical exhibited in women's travel writings well before the First World War. One
example among a multitude is Brassey's rhapsodic account of her first visit
to Tahiti: "I look on that voyage now as one long dream of azure seas,
and purple, gold, and crimson sunrises."[31] Fussell's account is startling in
its blithe assumption that the genre is a male phenomenon (perhaps because no women were in the trenches?). Nonetheless, in its commitment to
historical specificity, if not in its apparently unconscious masculine bias,
Fussell's work is an apt reminder that a critical approach to Englishwomen's travel writings in the latter half of the nineteenth century requires
attention to time and place as well as to the conventions of other contemporary modes of writing.

The 1870s, 1880s, and 1890s were a time of increased travel for

Englishwomen, in part because they were a time of increased travel for Englishmen. The long stays in India had always meant that it was commonplace for men to bring their women and children along and for family members from England to visit relatives in India. But during the nineteenth century there were radical changes in the length and safety of the route. The trip around the Cape of Good Hope, even after the end of the Napoleonic wars, took several months and was dangerous enough that many ships did not complete the journey.[32] The overland route across the Suez isthmus was about the same until the opening of the Suez railway in 1858. The Suez Canal opening in 1869 again shortened the trip considerably.[33] From Eliza Fay's *Original Letters From India, 1779-1815* to Harriet Tytler's *An Englishwoman in India: Memoirs, 1828-1858* to Isabel Burton's 1879 *Arabia, Egypt, and India,* the routes to the East were increasingly travelled and written about by Englishwomen.[34]

Not only India but many places in the East became more accessible for Englishwomen in the latter half of the century. First, many originally drawn to India continued on to other parts. Leonowens, who went to live with her mother and stepfather in India as a young girl fresh out of school, married an English officer there who was then transferred to Singapore. Her 1884 memoir of the early 1850s in India subtitled *Recollections of a Journey Before the Days of Railroads* emphasizes the important changes in forms of travel.[35] British commercial interest in the Far East was firmly established with the consolidation of the British areas of Penang, Malacca, and Singapore as the Straits Settlements in 1826 and, after the unease throughout the East that followed the 1857 Indian Mutiny, their transfer in 1867 from the India office to the Colonial Office.[36] By the middle of the century travel between India and the Straits Settlements took a mere eight days. Starting in 1845, steamships replaced sailing ships from England to Singapore, Penang, and Hong Kong, and established a regular biweekly service. A journey that had taken, with luck, four months, now took only four weeks.[37] The result was increased economic growth, particularly in the tin trade, and increased social as well as commercial contact with England.[38]

Two other significant political events need to be mentioned in this overview of the historical context of Victorian women's travel writings. The first was the American Civil War. Regardless of the range of specific English responses, the slavery question generally was elevated to an issue of major public importance that concerned people everywhere. Leonowens's next-door neighbor in Singapore lent her a copy of *Uncle Tom's Cabin* in the early 1860s.[37] Leonowens took her own concern about the evil of slavery to Siam, and much of the private sympathy for the harem women that infuses her writing finds public expression through that concern.[39]

Entwined with the matter of slavery is the matter of women's rights, an increasingly visible and powerful political issue in Victorian England. Travel writings by women continually discuss the situation of women in strange lands, often in comparison with the situation of women in England. While some find the English situation better and some find other situations better, almost all express an admiration for as well as an empathy with the women of Southeast Asia. As Leonowens put it, in a chapter entitled "'Muang Thai,' or the Kingdom of the Free," among the "poor, doomed women" of the royal harem she has known some that accepted their fate with a "sweet resignation that told how dead must be the heart under that still exterior; and it is here, too, that I have witnessed a fortitude under suffering of which history furnishes no parallel."[40]

Frequently, these women's travel writings testify to the validity and the importance of the experience of Southeast Asian women. Again and again, the writers see themselves as witnesses who have the special qualifications to describe the lives of these foreign women, to make their English readers really see. Their accounts commonly emphasize the similarities they notice and the connections they feel with these other women who lead what culturally seem to be deeply different lives. There are such occasional horrors as Florence Caddy's comment on visiting Siam: "how like the 'Arabian Nights' it is to see these three slaves in white garments approach our party with refreshments, and kneel and prostrate themselves in offering the huge silver trays."[41] Caddy is also capable of claiming that "it is another popular fallacy that tropical fruits are delicious; they are not to be compared with ours."[42] Both of these amazing remarks function to mediate, and thereby to denigrate, Caddy's actual experience, one through literature and the other presumably through memory. Clearly, her readers can forget about Siam. They need only read *The Arabian Nights* while eating English pears.

Caddy's commentary directly invokes the chauvinistic authorial posture of *Eothen*. Yet if Caddy and Kinglake are similar in their jingoism and blindness, this is only to say that her work must be classed with his. Such cultural snobbery, so common in the books by male authors about the grand tour, is rare among women's travel books about Southeast Asia. Perhaps because the authors were Englishwomen rather than Englishmen, their books tended to exhibit only occasionally what functioned as a typical convention of the literature of the grand tour: the fundamental assumption that the British traveler was superior to all he surveyed.

There are certainly psychological and cultural explanations for this difference. I want to emphasize here a literary explanation as well. These travel books by women are a different genre, with conventions and perspectives more in keeping with the published accounts of journeys by male scientists than of journeys by gentlemen tourists. Moreover, the mere act of writing about journeys in Southeast Asia appears to have been self-selecting. The women who did not like what they saw, and there must surely have been many, apparently did not bother to write about it. And there are simply many fewer instances of women being ready to view their travels as the occasion to write about themselves.

Their books about Southeast Asia do share a notion of the truth, though not always with the same intensity or clarity. To paraphrase Little Bilham's words in *The Ambassadors,* the truth they wanted their readers really to see is the identity and the value of human nature, of women as well as men, of nonwhite races as well as white, in Borneo as well as in Bournemouth. Thus, Leonowens, at one of her first dinner parties in India, is acutely aware of the "dark restless eyes" of the servants, while the rest of the company discusses British supremacy in India. "I did comprehend, and that very painfully, that no one seemed to mind those dark, silent, stationary figures any more than if they had been hewn out of stone."[43] Within the Victorian debate about human nature, the kindred sense that many British women felt with other peoples, most often with other women, functioned within these travel writings, and thus for their readers, as an argument for the universality of the human condition and the relativity of its cultural manifestations.

Cultural relativity also meant the possibility of comparing British institutions unfavorably with foreign institutions, implying that when the British travel they do have something to learn. One of the features of nineteenth-century European Orientalism was a view of the Orient as primitive, as "ceding its historical preeminence and importance to the world spirit moving westwards away from Asia and towards Europe."[44] Many women's accounts, specifically those that emerged from the experience of living for a time in countries in the East, speak to the real superiority of particular Eastern ways. These views range from Leslie Milne's practical preference for the Burmese Shan's habit of buying shoddy but affordable goods over the English habit of requiring well-made but expensive ones to Leonowens's startlingly impassioned testimonial that in the harem she knew a woman who "helped to enrich my life and to render fairer and more beautiful every lovely woman I have since chanced to meet."[45]

The question of imperial attitudes points to another area in which the specific historical facts of time, place, and person must guide our reading. Nineteenth-century Western travel writings about the East are hardly monolithic. If the gender of the author mattered, so did his or her nationality and activities. A simple example is that the American women (and men) who wrote about Southeast Asia in the 1800s were most often fervent missionaries. Authored by missionaries or not, the genre in its American form typically expresses some version of E. R. Skidmore's horrified and eloquent view of her travel in the East as a matter of "landing in small boats among the screaming heathen."[46] The very zeal that took Americans East allowed them to be particularly sure that the visions they brought with them were superior to the visions they beheld while there.[47]

At least as important as gender and nationality is the actual country the book is about. As Victorian colonialists may have understand better than twentieth-critics, the distinctive qualities of various countries shaped the experience of being there. Those local qualities involved not only the political and economic history of a place but also the history of its relations to Europe, particularly to England. It must have felt notably different to be English in India, even before the 1858 Great Mutiny, than it did to be English in the more peaceable and in many ways less colonially violated areas of Sarawak or Singapore. Southeast Asia was, and is, quite a different region from the Middle East or the Far East. Critical approaches to Victorian travel writings must take into account the countries or regions that are being written about at least as much as the gender and nationality of the author.

Victorian women travelers who wrote about Southeast Asia were looking for truth in their exploration of different cultures in much the same
way as were many of the scientists who explored the organisms and geology of strange lands. Neither kind of exploration can be understood, or its
contributions to human knowledge evaluated, without taking into account
the question of intent, at least to the extent that it appears in the written
record. Is the language of discovery a matter of conquest or a matter of
engagement? Evelyn Fox-Keller has observed that "to see the emphasis on
power and control so prevalent in the rhetoric of Western science as a
projection of a specifically male consciousness requires no great leap of the
imagination.[48] But she goes on to make the central point that "control and
domination are intrinsic neither to selfhood (i.e., autonomy) nor to scientific knowledge."[49] Nor, I would add, are they intrinsic to the literature of
travel, even nineteenth-century Western travel to the East.

Fox-Keller's useful distinction in scientific rhetoric between mastery
over and union with nature can also help to describe and to evaluate accounts of Western explorations in other cultures. Many Victorian travel
writings by women allow for, and even insist on, a sense of identification
with other people as the truth of a travel experience. That sense of identification, made to an extensive reading public back home, carried political
and social implications for Victorian definitions of truth, human nature,
and progress. We cannot begin to chart those implications as long as we
read this genre in relation to that other major narrative genre in Victorian
England, the novel. Relying on the more sophisticated tools we have developed for discussing fiction to guide explanations of this nonfictional mode
of writing, we can too easily term travel literature as the less effective
genre, the little sister of its big brother, the novel. This would have the
political effect of helping to conserve and even to bolster that familiar but
highly dubious truism of cultural history: that Victorian women did not
participate in the public history of their nation.

Travel writings about Southeast Asia indicate that Victorian women
had audible, and often extremely popular, voices outside the novel.
Brassey, who published several travel books during the later decades of the
century, was perhaps the most widely read. Her account of eleven months
of touring the East on her yacht, *A Voyage in the 'Sunbeam,'* went to at
least eleven editions.[50] Whether her works, or books written by other travel

writers, both women and men, had any impact on the changing political, economic, and social conditions in England will have to emerge from a fuller study of the genre than any single article, or even single book, can provide.

It has been a truism of Victorian studies in the twentieth-century that women are more liberated in our century than they were in the nineteenth, and that the dominant ideology of the Victorian period was the notion of the separation of private and public spheres, with women belonging in the private and men in the public. We have been assured almost as often in scholarly journals as in television commercials that "you've come a long way, baby." Connected with this truism is another: that notions of wisdom in the Victorian intellectual context were defined by men, were "masculine," and even when "feminine" were embodied in men (like Pater). Men—and by "men" traditional critics usually mean Carlyle, Ruskin, Arnold, and Eliot in her role as the woman with the masculine mind—were the sages of Victorian culture. These cultural elites decided what wisdom was. They were the prophetic voices, the keepers and feeders of the ethical flame, and were publicly recognized as such.

Can we take Carylye, Ruskin, Arnold, or any of their modern apologists' word for what defined wisdom for a whole culture? At least one reason why we must cease to write about these familiar sages as if they were the representative sages for all Victorians is not so much because we cannot trust these nineteenth-century purveyors of wisdom as because we cannot trust ourselves. After all, academics have been studying Victorian culture for several generations, but until the explosion of feminist studies in the 1970s had smoothly left out an enormous section of Victorian culture. What I would point out here is that this selectivity was possible in part because of the sheer convenience for twentieth-century critics of the notion of separate spheres. It may well have been twentieth-century academics who fulfilled the fantasies of Victorian masculinist writers by inflating a wishful (prescriptive) ideological principle into a full-fledged general truth of actual history. If Victorian women did operate only in the private world, then a responsible scholar could justifiably talk about cultural activities like defining wisdom and behaving as a prophet as occurring in the general, public realm, and not have to consider even published works by women.

There is no doubt that the notion of separate spheres was a significant ideology in Victorian England. There is also no doubt that it has become a most useful ideology about Victorian England in twentieth-century America. But how dominant was it? How many of the lives of real nineteenth-century women fit into it? I would argue that many women put the notion of separate spheres to public use by defining it as incomplete and therefore as an empowering rather than a disabling paradigm. Through the very ideology of truth as organic, they brought the wisdom to which they had special access in the private sphere to bear on philosophic as well as on social issues in the public domain. The question for critics now is how many exceptions we need to gather before the weight of accumulated facts will finally deflate to its proper, and modest, size this long-favored phallic truism.

A substantial number of those ever-accumulating facts are the travel writings of Victorian women. While traditional critics of Victorian culture never mentioned them and almost certainly did not know they existed, the number of editions of such travel books suggests that Victorian readers knew very well that they existed. These works, telling again and again of women living far away from England, well out of the private enclosures of English family life, offer literal proof that Victorian women could, and did, leave home. Further, the kind of detail these books offer about Southeast Asia—ranging from the export price of hemp on a Borneo plantation to the history of the Dyak wars in Sarawak and the diplomatic intrigues between England and France in Siam—makes it impossible for readers to place their female authors in the private sphere, with that sphere somehow transported intact to a distant shore. Moreover, the declared political aims of many of the books, from Brooke's wish to keep Sarawak "from the devastating grasp of money-grabbing syndicates" to Leonowens's ceaseless arguments against slavery, make it clear that the authors saw their words as operating, even powerfully operating, within the sphere of public discourse.[51]

Finally, I suggest that this genre of travel writing by women compels twentieth-century critics to redefine their understanding of the Victorian notion of the sage. The rhetorical strategies of Carlyle, Newman, or Arnold, oracular and prophetic, offer a vision of wisdom that is as assertive in spirit as it is reformist in intent. Nonetheless, regardless of such individual strategies, this vision rests on the firm foundation of the belief in the experiential quality of truth. And that foundation, refusing by its very nature to be exclusive, not only justifies Victorian men's cultural criticism but also justifies Victorian men's scientific accounts and Victorian women's travel writings. All of these kinds of writing lay claim to a wisdom that bases its truth on the extent to which it has emerged as lived experience. That pervasively held Victorian belief, perhaps in connection with the notion of women's emotional powers, may well have provided the cultural context that enabled so many women to write so confidently and sympathetically about their experiences in Southeast Asia.

Her Father's Eyes, Staff, and Support
The Sage Author as Phallic Sister in Nineteenth-Century Fiction

LORI HOPE LEFKOVITZ

A modern edition of Sophocles's *Antigone* begins with Antigone and Ismene emerging together from the great central door of the royal palace,
but any suggestion of women united is quickly dispelled. In this drama of
contrast and conflict, the first conflict occurs between sisters. Antigone
seeks Ismene's cooperation, but Ismene, after an unsuccessful appeal to
their shared femininity ("we must remember that we two are women/so
not to fight with men"), urges at least Antigone's discretion.[1] Her arguments move Antigone only to increasing hostility as she promises that she
will hate Ismene, hate her more if silent, and finally, "I shall hate you first,
and next the dead will hate you in all justice." In spite of Antigone's terrible prediction, Ismene persists in expressing concerned love: "Go, since
you want to. But know this: you go senseless indeed, but loved by those
who love you" (98–99).[2]

Ismene's sentiments, uttered on stage as early as 441 B.C.E., might have
been repeated by Celia Brooke in the opening episodes of George Eliot's
Middlemarch (1872) as Ceila watches her elder, and reputedly wiser, sister
Dorothea reject the affections of the young man whom Celia herself will
later marry and prepare instead to walk alive into a marriage that will be a
kind of tomb. Eliot, who told the famous classicist Richard Jebb that she

was influenced by Sophocles's "delineation of the great primitive emotions," expressly invites the reader to compare Dorothea with Antigone, a comparison that may be responsible for Eliot's repetition of Sophocles's contrast between the sisters as well.[3] In revising the outspoken heroine's tragic fate, however, Eliot recuperates wisdom for femininity and affirms the tie between sisters who initially represent antithetical virtues.

This comparison between an ancient and a Victorian pair of sisters exemplifies a contrast that is part of a larger pattern. Ismene and Antigone are prototypes of other sets of sisters in nineteenth-century narratives in which one sister emerges as heroine because of her powers of mind and speech. A variety of this relationship among sisters occurs in Jane Austen's *Sense and Sensibility* (1811) and *Pride and Prejudice* (1813); George Eliot's *Middlemarch* and *Mill on the Floss* (1860); and Louisa May Alcott's *Little Women* (1869).[4] In the situation of an absent or ineffectual mother, the wise heroine enjoys a special, supplementing relationship with a father who is both powerful as a patriarch and somehow inadequate. Masculinized by the text, she is marginalized in the community of women because of an underlying fear that she is unmarriageable; suspected of usurping male functions, she is threatened with Antigone's fate.[5]

I would suggest that for Austen, Eliot, and Alcott this wise sister is an authorial projection. In the Victorian age, when the prevailing voices of the sage were presumed masculine, and when the assumption by women of male roles was regarded as a mark of degeneracy that threatened culture at large, these writers make feminine and make marriageable the heroine whose outspokenness connotes masculinity. Moreover, Austen, Eliot, and Alcott's close and complex relationships with their fathers, their enduring attachments to their sisters, and the fact that none of the three had a traditional marriage or children suggest that, in changing the fate of Antigone, these authors create heroines who naturalize their own sage discourse for the feminine. Because these explorations of the gender ambiguity associated with sagacity occur in domestic fiction (a genre that promotes gender stereotyping), the generic conventions require a diminishing of the sage author and a domestication of her discourse: she is disguised as a clever girl on the threshold of marriage, and her sphere of influence shrinks from the "family" of readers to the family per se. The weak or weakened figure of the heroine's lover and the compensating renewal of bonds among sisters at the conclusion of these fictions signal unresolved tensions in the work.

In the characters of Antigone and Ismene there is a contrast between what Austen would later call sense and sensibility, but it is unclear which sister is the one with more sense. As Antigone herself remarks to Ismene, anticipating centuries of critical response to the drama: "Some will have thought you wiser, some will not" (557). Antigone's wisdom is ambiguously coded with respect to gender.[6] Oedipus indicates that Antigone's devotion to her father is more appropriate to a son than a daughter. If Antigone's heroism is characterized as unfeminine, *Oedipus at Colonus* (written after *Antigone*) roots that characterization in an early and unnatural father-daughter connection. Oedipus, who derides his sons at length as "homeloving girls," explicitly contrasts them with his daughters, whom he calls "men, in faithfulness."[7] Thus, the daughters' filial position entails a challenge to the sons' masculine identity.

Although they share this transgressive position, Antigone and Ismene are contrasted on the basis of their femininity in a way that implies the incompatibility of wisdom and domesticity. Antigone's capacity to advise Oedipus is linked metaphorically to her status as a physical guide, compensating for her father's deficiencies. She readily assumes the role of advisor to Polyneices.[8] If Oedipus's blindness and crippled limb are symbols of castration, then Antigone herself—as the staff and eyes of Oedipus—incarnates the phallus. Oedipus says of Antigone: "One, since her childhood ended and her body/gained its power, has wandered with me,/ . . . often in the wild/forest going without shoes and hungry,/ beaten by many rains, tired by the sun; yet she rejected the sweet life of home/ so that her father should have sustenance" (344–353). Oedipus's repeated references to Antigone as his eyes, "staff and support" (1108) clarify that the power "gained" by Antigone's body is phallic.

Oedipus praises Ismene for being a "faithful outpost" and wonders, "Why have you left your home to make this journey?" (358–359). Ismene can look forward to Antigone as a wife and mother, but Antigone holds fast to her lost place as a privileged sister-daughter to Oedipus. The *nomos* that Antigone invokes gives precedence to her dead brother over the possibility of a husband and children. Thus, it is Ismene who pleads with Creon not to destroy his own son's bride. Antigone renounces a woman's future specifically: "Not for me was the marriage-hymn, nor will anyone start the song/at a wedding of mine. Acheron is my mate" (813–814); "No marriage-bed, no marriage-song for me,/and since no wedding, so no child to rear" (917–918).[9]

Antigone's strength of character does not seem to compromise her desirability because she is beloved by a prince who dies for her sake. If Ismene has a lover, we do not learn about him. For Creon, however, Antigone threatens his masculinity, *more than his authority as king:* "I am no man and she the man instead/if she can have this conquest without pain" (484–485); "No woman rules me while I live" (527). He commands the incarceration of the sisters on gendered grounds: "They must be women now./ No more free running" (578–579). Creon concludes that Antigone's disobedience is less at issue than the threat of a woman speaking with his authority: "So I must . . . /not let myself be beaten by a woman./Better, if it must happen, that a man/should overset me./ I won't be called weaker than womankind" (677–680). By the same logic, Creon insults his son's manliness: "Your mind is poisoned. Weaker than a woman!" (746). Antigone's speeches, like those of Creon, express her singlemindedness; Ismene, who is internally conflicted, speaks her ambivalence, giving her discourse a complexity that, by contrast with Creon's and Antigone's unyielding positions, sounds like feminine weakness.[10] This apparent weakness saves her life, but Ismene, the lesser character who may after all be richer in both sense and sensibility, is left forlorn, bereft of her sister.

A female embodiment of the phallus, itself an ironic notion, is familiar from traditional psychoanalytic discourse in the figure of the omnipotent "phallic mother."[11] The sharp-tongued heroines of whom I write here differ from the phallic mother precisely because, on the model of Antigone, their phallic identity derives from their status as daughters and sisters.[12] In this scheme, the marriage that would remove these heroines from father and sisters threatens them with the loss of the phallus in the symbolic realm. Thus, the Antigone myth challenges Freud's equation of fetus and penis because Antigone may be said to be subconsciously unwilling to transform her body from phallus into maternal vessel.

George Steiner documents the great extent to which early nineteenth-century Europe was in love with *Antigone*.[13] He speculates that "a pro-

gramme of feminine emancipation associated with the French Revolution"
made this an "emblematic text," but adds that the "exaltation of Sophocles's heroine after 1790 is . . . a surrogate for reality."[14] If Bram Dijkstra
is correct in stating that Victorians feared a degeneracy (an anti-evolution)
that is signalled by a woman's assumption of a man's role, then Antigone's
crime would have been considered an especially serious one in the latter
part of the nineteenth century. Dijkstra, describing Proudhon's exemplary
nineteenth-century views, explains: "women who wanted to usurp part of
men's place in creation were going against nature, becoming mock-men
themselves, caricatures of masculinity, viragoes."[15] Moreover, Victorians
might well have sympathized with Creon's suspicion of Haemon's manliness. As one Victorian physician wrote: "masculine women nearly always
ally themselves with blanched males, weak physically and mentally."[16] Dijkstra implies, however, that the men's weakness was inferred from their
allegiances: "men who consorted with the virago, the feminist, were by
their very nature effeminate."[17] This association helps to account for
readers' perceptions that Elinor Dashwood's Edward, Dorothea Brooke's
Ladislaw, and Jo March's Laurie are disappointing companions for the
strong heroine. Dijkstra describes the transformation of the virago into
"the ideal creature of feminine virtue in the mid-nineteenth century: the
dead woman."[18] Antigone's death may therefore be understood as a gesture that feminizes a masculine heroine, at least for the nineteenth-century
imagination.

The fictional sisters created by Austen, Eliot, and Alcott recombine
qualities of Ismene and Antigone in ways that designedly reassess gendered
traits, unify the sisters, and disarm the perceived threat to male authority
that necessitated Antigone's death. Their fictions depict a wise, young heroine who enjoys a limited power from which marriage might detract; resolution of this conflict between the roles of daughter and wife depends
invariably on the heroine's relationship with her sisters. I hear echoes in
these novels of Antigone's taking action; Creon's insistence that she must
die specifically because she challenges male authority; Creon's accusation
that Antigone's betrothed is effeminate (746); and Antigone's repeated
identification of the tomb and the marital bed (869, 891). Antigone
chooses death. Because marriage is central to the bourgeois novel, however,
the novelist must extricate her heroine from a set of role confusions
that make even her gender ambiguous.[19] Austen, Eliot, and Alcott under-

mine the gender designation that initially marks one woman in each central pair as feminine in comparison with her masculinized, transgressive sister. The heroine's femininity is then validated by a male lover who transfers, or is imagined to have transferred, his love from one sister to another.

Key moments in Austen's *Sense and Sensibility* suggest a subtext about a marriage between sisters, as Marianne learns to appreciate Elinor's wisdom and to deserve Elinor's love.[20] In *Pride and Prejudice,* too, a demystification of marriage and maternity is linked to the potential loss of power for the sister-heroine who, like Antigone, plays a paternal role. Austen's ambivalence with regard to marriage and maternity has been detected in her novels and letters: Mark Schorer describes marriage in Austen's fictions as "a brutal economic fact in an essentially materialistic society"; Lloyd Brown writes that marriage in Austen's fictions has a subordinating effect on women's personality, and he finds in Austen's correspondence what "amounts to the de-romanticizing, or demystification, of marriage and motherhood without the unequivocal rejection of either."[21] I suggest that one problem addressed in Austen's novels is how to place the intelligent daughter into a marriage that does not overly compromise the position she enjoys as a supplemental or surrogate father and a spousal sister.

In *Sense and Sensibility,* the death of the father enables Austen's exploration of sense and sensibility as each quality is essentially embodied in the sisters, Elinor and Marianne. Depicted here is a failure of the father in particular and of patriarchal legislation in general to provide for a widow and her daughters. Like the sons of Oedipus, the son and brother to whom the estate is entailed is deficient in family feeling and is driven by self-interest. This fiction has two motivating enigmas: first, how will this family of women manage (or, in other words, who will fill the paternal role of supporter?), and second, who will the marriageable sisters marry (the key question of domestic fictions)?

Mrs. Dashwood relies on Elinor, who "possessed a strength of understanding, and coolness of judgment, which qualified her, though only nineteen, to be the counsellor of her mother, and enabled her frequently to counteract, to the advantage of them all, that eagerness of mind in Mrs. Dashwood which must generally have led her to imprudence." Elinor is then compared with Marianne, whose cleverness is mitigated by the fact that "the resemblance between Marianne and her mother was strikingly great." The youngest sister, Margaret, is allied with the maternal on the central issue of the novel, as she had "already imbibed a good deal of Marianne's romance."[22] In these descriptions Austen not only establishes the contrasts that are her subject, but she also describes society as a confederation of women whose rampant desire requires masculine control. In *Pride and Prejudice* the checking of feminine excesses (while the women lament the man's failure of sympathy) is a role assigned to the father. Mr. Bennet proves less fit for that role than his daughter Elizabeth. In *Sense and Sensibility,* Elinor assumes this paternal function. Elinor's sense renders her both phallic heroine—a replacement for the missing father—and outsider to the cult of feeling to which her mother and sisters belong.

Elinor and Marianne react in opposing ways to similar disappointments. Marianne's public displays with Willoughby lead everyone to suppose them engaged, and her emotional response when he jilts her results in a nearly fatal illness. Elinor enjoys a deeper, quieter attachment to Edward without ever inviting public speculation. At the center of the novel, when Elinor reveals to Marianne that she has known for months of Edward's engagement to another woman, Marianne is incredulous (246–247). With long, intimate speeches, Elinor persuades Marianne that her composure signified not indifference to Edward but love for Marianne herself. Marianne, transformed, delivers the only love speech in this unsentimental novel about love: "'Oh! Elinor,' she cried, 'How barbarous have I been to you!—You, who have been my only comfort, who have borne with me in all my misery, who have seemed to be only suffering for me!—Is this the only return I can make you?'" (149). Embedded in this marriage plot is a love story between sisters. The narrator comments: "The tenderest caresses followed this confession" (249).

With each sister apparently deprived of her lover, the implicit competition is for the remaining bachelor, Colonel Brandon. In many respects the most eligible man in this society, he is ambiguously located. Initially attracted to Marianne, Brandon suffers her indifference to the man "old enough to be her father" (34); as readers we learn to value him because he shares Elinor's temperament, because Elinor praises him to Marianne, and because we appreciate his paternal qualities and the potential usefulness of his wealth to the Dashwood women. Like their temperaments, Marianne's figure is more striking and Elinor's is more correct. Is Austen hinting, the reader may wonder early on, that Colonel Brandon—who was so struck by Marianne—will transfer his affections to the more "correct" sister? During Marianne's cathartic and transforming illness, Mrs. Jennings (touchstone of social opinion), Elinor's brother, and even Elinor herself entertain the possibility that Brandon has transferred his love to Elinor. For much of the novel, Marianne has two lovers and Elinor none, but at this late stage in the story, we see Elinor as the more marriageable sister.

When Marianne recovers, she recognizes that had she died "it would have been self-destruction" (329). Seeing suicide as a crime against her sister revises *Antigone*'s definition of sisterly duty to include duty to a sister: "Had I died,—in what peculiar misery should I have left you, my nurse, my friend, my sister!" (329). She pursues the fantasy of her own death with passion: "leaving you, for whom I professed unbounded affection, to be miserable for my sake" (330). Mrs. Dashwood entertains comparable regrets for having neglected Elinor's feelings. Once Elinor is admitted into the society of women, the author is free to disentangle Edward and engage Elinor to her first love.[23]

Walton Litz sees this as another novel of "crude antitheses" represented in sisters, and Tony Tanner rightly responds with the observation that Marianne has "plenty of sense" and Elinor "plenty of sensibility."[24] Indeed, Austen creates both a contrast and a mixture in the sisters that ultimately unites them to each other. This union is forged as Marianne, her mother, and the reader come to recognize that the gender ideology that equates masculinity with reason and femininity with emotion is unjust. Elinor's wisdom does not preclude her hopes for marriage. Tanner further observes that Elinor and Marianne use a different vocabulary, and I would add that Elinor uses Austen's vocabulary. Because Elinor and the Austen narrator share a mode of discourse, the reader registers the author's personal investment in establishing Elinor as an insider in the society of women. By novel's end, Marianne has learned to speak more judiciously, in the manner of the sister who is her nearest neighbor and best friend. The plot works to make the feminine sister wise and the wise sister feminine. The ultimate pairings of main characters betray ambivalence, however, as well as the age's prejudice that strong women marry weak men. Edward is constructed as relatively weak. Initially, he is disinherited because he fails to live up to his family's (albeit foolish) expectations of him to *be someone;* he almost loses Elinor because of a youthful mistake in judgment; and generally we know of no reason to love him except that Elinor does. Brandon functions paternally; he becomes Edward's benefactor and Marianne's husband.

Marianne and Elinor marry and move to one estate, and the novel's last sentence comments not so much on the quality of those marriages as on the happily-ever-after of the sisters: "among the merits and the happiness of Elinor and Marianne, let it not be ranked as the least considerable, that though sisters, and living almost within sight of each other, they could live without disagreement between themselves, or producing coolness between their husbands." The husbands are adjuncts to the adult intimacy achieved between the sisters. Elinor retains her strong position in the novel's configuration of women's relationships.

Elizabeth Bennet in *Pride and Prejudice* shares the Austen narrator's characteristic wit. Lively and *physically* active, she willingly risks messing her clothes or getting a suntan, to the dismay of society's women. Alcott's characterization of her autobiographical heroine, Jo March, goes even further in celebrating a heroine's out-of-doors independence. Austen's and Alcott's treatment of their heroines' small liberties as innocent (even loveable) effectively challenges nineteenth-century norms for women. In 1904 Bernard S. Talmey pointed to the masculine qualities of the "sexual hyperaesthesia of the lesbian." He describes her: "She neglects her dress and assumes and affects boyish manners. She is in pursuit of boys' sports. She plays with horses, balls, and arms. She gives manifestations of courage and bravado, is noisy and loves vagabondage."[25] The scandalized reaction to Elizabeth when she appears after a long hike with her petticoat muddied, and Jo's comic indifference to dress as part of her boyish manner are part of the characterizations that link intelligence to the physical freedom associated with men. Insofar as these heroines' intelligence and freedom conspire to connote lesbianism, however, the plots to feminize them work against that effect.

As in *Sense and Sensibility,* in *Pride and Prejudice* the heroine's marriage entails another marriage, one between sisters. Elizabeth is undervalued by her mother and preferred by her father, and her relationship with her more beautiful, gentler sister Jane (whom Darcy initially compares favorably to Elizabeth) is a model relationship in the text. The relationship projected between Elizabeth and her sister-in-law Georgiana (to whom Darcy, like Oedipus, is both brother and father) leads the reader to expect that Elizabeth will not be disempowered by Darcy's paternal qualities. The other pairs of sisters in the novel, the Bingley sisters and Kitty and Lydia Bennet, parody the real friendship between Jane and Elizabeth. Like these examples of false sisterhood, Mary, the middle sister, serves as a negative model of sagacity. Tanner writes, "Mary Bennet sees herself as a sage reflector before she has had any experience."[26] Elizabeth, as a sage reflector with experience and an exemplary sister, corresponds to Austen's self-image; by representing Darcy as unthreatened by either Elizabeth's sagacity or her sisterliness, Austen imagines the man who may marry her favorite heroine.

While Tanner may be right that this novel affirms an individual's ability to hold out against the prescriptions of society—defined in maternal terms as the wishes of Darcy's mother and his maternal aunt—the union of Elizabeth and Darcy brings Elizabeth into her own mother's heart.[27] The novel further compensates Elizabeth for the loss of her place as a supplement to her father by redoubling her function as sister. In the process, Darcy's patriarchal position is weakened because, in marrying Elizabeth, Darcy provides his sister with the model of sage discourse (in Austen, always penetratingly witty) that will free her of his paternal hold. At this novel's end, "Jane and Elizabeth, in addition to every other happiness, were within thirty miles of each other" (349). Moreover: "Georgiana had the highest opinion in the world of Elizabeth; though at first she often listened with an astonishment bordering on alarm, at her lively, sportive, manner of talking to her brother. He, who had always inspired in herself a respect which almost overcame her affection, she now saw the object of open pleasantry. Her mind received knowledge which had never before fallen in her way" (349). By duplicating a strong bond between sisters, Austen asks us to count the ability to form sororal intimacies as a feature of heroism. Georgiana is a student of Elizabeth's discourse. In the duplication of Elizabeth in her new younger sister and in Darcy's pleasure ("the attachment of the sisters was exactly what Darcy hoped to see"), Austen takes another step towards feminizing her own "lively, sportive manner of talking."

Beneath the troubling story of brother and sister, *The Mill on the Floss* is a story that feminizes Maggie's intelligence through a process that entails the doubling and bonding of the cousins, Maggie and Lucy Deane.

Eliot displaces the sister and refuses marriage as a resolution, forcing the masculine heroine to a tragic end. At the same time, these displacements liberate the author from her own position as daughter-sister and celebrate Mary Anne Evans's relationship with her sister Chrissey. Whereas readings of this novel's autobiographical elements focus on the brother-sister relationship, I see in this text Eliot's ritual of mourning for Chrissey and a deep wish to naturalize her own position as a sage (a transgressive position that links author and unwed wife) through an identification with her conventional sister.[28]

The elements of autobiography in the childhood sections of *Mill on the Floss* are familiar: Maggie and Tom are the author and her brother Isaac; Lucy is Chrissey. Mrs. Tulliver's favoring of Tom and Lucy over Maggie and Mr. Tulliver's devotion to Maggie parallel the distribution of affection in the Evanses' home.[29] By making Lucy a cousin to Maggie and Tom, Mrs. Tulliver's preference for her niece is made to seem unnatural in a mother, and Mr. Tulliver's rising to defend Maggie whenever the two girls are compared is justified by Maggie's closer claims of kinship. The latter part of the novel is more fantastic: the ambitious tomboy with a self-cropped mop of hair grows to become a beauty; whereas Mrs. Evans died when Mary Anne was sixteen, Mrs. Tulliver declares feelingly "you've got a mother" when Maggie is abandoned by society.[30] Isaac, "conventional as Tom Tulliver, feared most that his sister's singularity might prevent her from catching a husband."[31] Maggie is also supposed too peculiar to be marriageable; Stephen Guest says to himself: "provided one is not obliged to marry such women, why, they certainly make a variety in social intercourse" (399). Yet Maggie comes to be adored by two men: Philip Wakem, deformed and effeminate ("brought up like a girl" [440]; with "nerves . . . sensitive as a woman's" [447]), yet nurturer of Maggie's intelligence; and later by Stephen himself, the established man of society and Lucy's lover. Maggie's masculine independence and intelligence render her a favorite love object for Mr. Tulliver, Philip, and Stephen.

When critics are surprised that Eliot refers to Maggie's childhood as golden, they exaggerate Mrs. Tulliver's and Tom's failure to appreciate Maggie and miss the compensation of Maggie's relationship with her father. Although "public opinion was . . . always of the feminine gender" (512–513)—mother and maternal aunts representing that gender again—power is of the masculine gender. Maggie is the phallic daughter to the inadequate Mr. Tullliver. He often declares his dependence ("What 'ud father do without his little wench?" [126]), delighting in the cleverness that reflects back on him, always at the expense of his regard for his son. When Maggie cuts her hair, her father praises her spirit; when Maggie runs off to "the gypsies" after pushing Lucy in the mud, he scolds Tom; whenever Tom is moved to justifiable anger because Maggie neglects his interests, Mr. Tulliver ends the matter by checking Tom's severity. With Mr. Tulliver's death, Tom acquires manhood, and Maggie loses her potency as a force in the family.

Fair Lucy and brown Maggie—Maggie unfavored by the society that dotes on Lucy—are also identified together. In her fantasies, Maggie casts Lucy as a queen, but the queen is Maggie "in Lucy's form" (69). Although one might expect rivalry between them, as adults, the cousins cherish an extraordinary intimacy. Lucy's "silliness" (380) is mitigated by her conviction that "there is no girl in the world that I love so well as my cousin Maggie" (380); Maggie confides fully only in Lucy, who "has no secrets from Maggie" (381), and part of the tragedy is that Maggie comes to feel things for Stephen that she could not tell Lucy. Lucy takes Maggie into her home, where Mrs. Tulliver—whom Lucy resembles as Maggie does not—has replaced her own late mother. Although Lucy "feared Maggie too odd and clever" (393) to please Stephen, he comes to prefer Maggie. By mother and lover, the opposite women (one with intellectual, the other with domestic aspirations) are thus exchanged for one another. After Maggie goes off with Stephen, she speaks to Lucy "with an effort like the convulsed clutch of a drowning man" (534), and the women clasp "each other again in a last embrace" (535). This embrace, which prefigures the death embrace of Maggie and Tom, further interchanges the women.[32] Either cousin may be renamed Mrs. Guest. Although "the world's wife" blames Maggie for her betrayal of the cousin who had been a "sister to her" (514), Lucy's response is an empathetic declaration of love. And Maggie's death allows Lucy eventually to become Mrs. Guest.

The fiction unites sisters who were divided by death, and the exchange of Lucy and Maggie means that Maggie rather than Lucy (Mary Anne instead of Chrissey) dies. Haight reports that Eliot's "own sister Chrissey was dearest to her."[33] When Mary Anne entered into her relationship with Lewes—worse for Isaac than Mary Anne's "never catching a husband"— Isaac broke off relations with his sister and urges his siblings to do the same. In 1859 Chrissey wrote to Mary Anne, deeply regretting her lapse in correspondence; Mary Anne responded warmly, but before they could see one another again, Chrissey died of consumption in March 1859. That year Eliot wrote *The Mill on the Floss* (completed March 1860).[34]

In her reading of *The Mill on the Floss* Gillian Beer observes that Eliot is reacting against a literary heritage in which "desire for knowledge . . . had traditionally been enregistered as the man's story."[35] Beer also sees this novel as a version of Antigone's story: "In the story of Antigone, love, duty, kinship, passion and death grumble within one another. . . . Perhaps, too, we should pay attention to the desired act: to give her brother proper burial, to lay him to rest. In the Antigone story, the consequence is that the heroine is buried alive. Maggie Tulliver drowns alongside Tom. But George Eliot survived after Mary Anne Evans' alienation from her brother—was even born out of that alienation."[36] Unlike Antigone's permanent alienation from Ismene, the relationship between Mary Anne and Chrissey, like that between Maggie and Lucy, triumphs over the social forces that would divide the women. Instead, death intervenes. This triumph may have been as enabling for the author as her alienation from her brother.

Lucy's virtue is her unconditional love of Maggie, though Lucy basically shares the Dodsons' commitment to what is "customary and respectable."[37] In *Middlemarch*, Eliot offers a more subtle exploration of the female sage in a society with comparably limited vision as she resigns herself to the idea that a new Antigone no longer has the opportunity to "spend her heroic piety in daring all for the sake of a brother's burial."[38] In *Middlemarch*, Eliot revises the tragic fate of the intelligent daughter by moderating Dorothea's expectations and by giving certain advantages to the sensible sister who is allied to the maternal. The balance shifts as the emphasis is no longer on maternal limitations and excesses but rather on the wise sister's exaggerated piety; here the wish to supplement an inadequate father is decidedly misguided. This novel casts a skeptical eye on the male sage (caricatured in Casaubon) and on the women who naively believe in him. Like Lucy Deane, Celia Brooke (in whom Haight also finds qualities that originate with Eliot's sister Chrissey), recovers her devotion to her sister because of an affection that triumphs over the combined powers of male prerogative and female gossip.[39]

Middlemarch, like *Antigone*, begins with a contrast between sisters. The mundane nature of the conflict—the Victorian sisters are divided over a maternal jewel casket—is a deliberate diminution of the life and death struggle between Ismene and Antigone. Celia is linked to the maternal in her wish to wear her mother's jewels. Dorothea's initial indifference expresses not only criticism of Celia but also an implicit criticism of their late mother, an implication that Celia almost articulates when she says that surely "there are women in heaven now who wore jewels" (14). Dorothea shares Antigone's ardor and pride in her own principled determination. Celia, whose wish to save Dorothea from self-sacrifice seems to be the product of a more feminine reason, faces a dilemma like that of Ismene: how to best express loyalty to a sister who appears to be committed to making a tragic mistake, in this case marriage to a man who said of himself, "I live too much with the dead. My mind is something like the ghost of an ancient" (19). Although the circumstances of the novel divide the sisters, they end united over the birth of their sons. Dorothea is brought into the maternal through Ladislaw (who, as society is quick to point out, is young enough to be her first husband's son) and through her own maternity. There is the overriding regret, however, that she suffered from the "conditions of an imperfect social state" (811), with inadequate education for women.[40] The choice of Antigone as a model proves to Beer that Eliot's heroines are both "specifically female and capable of standing for the full range of human difficulty."[41] Alternatively, I would argue that Antigone represents a heroine whose femininity is at once dubious and affirmed, problematic, open, and an excuse for the tragic end that Eliot wishes, in *Middlemarch,* to rewrite.

Without ever casting doubt on Dorothea's superiority, the sisters are relentlessly compared to Celia's advantage, destabilizing definitions of wisdom. After Dorothea's engagement, "cleverness seemed to [Celia] more pitiable than ever" (82), and the reader is inclined to agree. "The rural opinion of the new young ladies, even among the cottagers, was generally in favour of Celia . . . .Compared with Dorothea, the innocent looking Celia was knowing and worldly wise" (12). Dorothea's naive goodness "made her seem so childlike, and according to some judges, so stupid, with all her reputed cleverness" (51). Like Elizabeth Bennet and Maggie Tulliver (whom Lucy calls "uncanny") and perhaps like Eliot herself, Dorothea's intelligence is associated with a disconcerting independence: men thought Dorothea "bewitching" on horseback. What Dorothea lacks, however, is Celia's sense of female reality: Celia "acquiesced in all her sister's sentiments, only infusing them with . . . common sense" (10); Celia works to make her "negative wisdom tell upon Dorothea" (34), as when she explains to Dorothea, with justice, that "the commonest minds must be rather useful" (49). She adds that it is a pity that "Mr. Casaubon's mother had not a commoner mind. She might have taught him better" (49).

Celia's overriding sisterly affection leads her to fear that Dorothea "is too religious for family comfort" (22). Once more, these fears that the clever heroine is unmarriageable are not justified by the preferences of the men in the novel. Although Mrs. Cadwallader, who stands for the views of society, tells Sir James Chettam that Celia is "worth two of Dorothea," Sir James had earlier concluded to himself that the "second Miss Brooke was certainly very agreeable, as well as pretty, though not, as some people pretended, more sensible and clever than the elder sister. He felt that he had chosen the one who was in all respects the superior" (25). Sir James courts Celia only after Dorothea's firm rejection (as Maggie rejects Stephen and as Jo rejects Laurie, freeing them for Lucy and Amy, respectively). But by initially preferring Dorothea because she is "more sensible and clever," Sir James validates those qualities as feminine and desirable. Because the sisters marry early in the novel, the stratagem of having Sir James transfer his love works to feminize Dorothea's intelligence without sustaining the potential rivalry between the sisters for spouses.[42] In fact, the sisters are consistently generous to one another. Dorothea assumes that Sir James's attentions to her are for Celia's sake, and Celia does what she can to enlighten Dorothea. Celia briefly fears that Dorothea will accept Sir James for the wrong reasons, recognizing that Dorothea, for all of her humility, is ambitious—if not to bury a brother than to hold a pen—and that although Dorothea thinks she wants to be guided, she is looking for a husband whom she can guide.

Society sees Mr. Brooke's inadequacy as a surrogate father when he allows Dorothea to marry Casaubon, who is twenty-seven years her senior. Dorothea wishes to supplement Brooke by doing paternalistic good in his world, but Brooke's misogyny (much like that of Tom Tulliver) thwarts her. She then searches for a husband who will be an inadequate father whom she may supplement; she thinks, "the really delightful marriage must be that where your husband was a sort of father who could

teach you even Hebrew if you wished it" (12–13). But Dorothea wants
not only a father who can teach her the language of the patriarchy
(Hebrew), but also a maimed or blind father so that she might substitute
for the missing part. "She felt sure that she would have accepted the judi-
cious Hooker if she had been born in time to save him from the wretched
mistake he made in matrimony; or John Milton when his blindness had
come on" (12). She is pleased that Casaubon's eyes are weak because it
gives her "more room . . . to help him" (42), and her fantasy is to have
the heroic opportunities of the *daughters* to Milton. Dorothea asks Casaubon if she may read Latin and Greek aloud to him "as Milton's daughters did to their father" (64). In this regard, Dorothea's heroic aspirations
are less like Antigone's insistence on burying her brother, but are like Antigone's having led the great but blinded Oedipus; it is a wish to be the
eyes—the "staff and support"—and a renunciation of the marriage bed
for the tomb.

Dorothea, who rebuffs an "amiable and handsome baronet" with "the
air of a handsome boy," claiming not to conform to "his idea of a lady,"
and whose great "illicit" (12) pleasure is horseback riding, wishes to attain to manhood herself in marriage. The narrator is explicit that Dorothea's wish to supplement her blinded Milton is a naive desire for masculine knowledge: "it was not entirely devotion to her future husband that
she wished to know Latin and Greek. Those provinces of masculine
knowledge seemed to her a standing-ground from which all truth could be
seen more truly . . . .She had not reached the point of renunciation at
which she would have been satisfied with having a wise husband; she
wished, poor child, to be wise herself" (64). Dorothea's wish is Oedipal
but not in the Freudian sense. Dorothea wishes not so much to have sex
with the father as *to be* the father's sex, to be "eyes, staff, and support," to
incarnate the phallus.[43]

That Ladislaw can instruct Dorothea, while respecting her intelligence,
derives from an allegiance to the feminine that has led readers to label him
as effeminate. Frank Kermode matter-of-factly pronounces Ladislaw a
"failure."[44] Henry James called Ladislaw a "woman's man."[45] Ladislaw
contrasts with Sir James, who felt that "he was ready to endure a great
deal of predominance, which, after all, a man could always put down
when he liked," and who delighted in Dorothea's cleverness, knowing that
"a man's mind has always the advantage of being masculine" (23). Beer

writes: "Ladislaw, son of two generations of rebellious women, is shown as lucid about his own feelings and responsive to women. He is not shut up in his own masculinity . . . .He is outside the educational hegemony."[46] Beer observes further that because Ladislaw and Dorothea teach each other, the student-teacher relationship finally promoted abandons the traditional father-daughter model.

Ladislaw is not the only real teacher that Dorothea acquires at the novel's end. In the prelude to *Middlemarch* the narrator describes the bind of a later-born Theresa, whose "ardour alternated between a vague ideal and the common yearning of womanhood" (viii). Antigone abandons the common yearning of womanhood for the sake of a specific ideal; Dorothea finally yields to motherhood. With Dorothea recast from Antigone to the role of a common woman, a mother, Celia finds a sisterly role and need no longer suffer the frustrations of Ismene. Dorothea needs the good effects of Celia's common sense. Celia exclaims, "she will not know what to do with the baby—she will do wrong things with it" (810). The narrator comments: "Such being the bend of Celia's heart, it was inevitable that Sir James should consent to a reconciliation with Dorothea and her husband. Where women love each other, men learn to smother their mutual dislike" (810). The sisters end on a more equal footing, with Dorothea's "cleverness" having been schooled into a sense more appropriate to her common life; her misguided wish to guide a dimsighted father-figure is replaced by a more tangible happiness. But Eliot leaves us with regrets. Dorothea is never fully integrated; neither would we wish her to be. In Dorothea's resignation may be Eliot's celebration of her own decision not to yield to the "common yearning of womanhood."

Because Alcott's *Little Women* is a children's story, an American novel, and a story set in the upside-down time of war, this fiction is most explicit about the heroine's capabilities, masculinity, and the connection between the two. Here, the features of the pattern that I am tracing are bold: the sisters are intimately connected, and they are the novel's subject. Jo works to be a father-replacement, mastering the pen instead of her manners; Meg and Amy worry about Jo's boyishness and both work hard to school her in femininity. Jo's one crowning beauty, her hair, is shorn (like that of the young Maggie), in this case, for cash. In spite of this masculinity that so disturbs her sisters, she is the chosen girl of the only boy in the novel, rendering her independent intelligence a part of her desirability. But Laurie remains the bashful boy to the reader, feminized in a number of ways. Alcott addresses the stereotype of the virago and the "blanched male" by having Amy (who perfects femininity and who, Jo says, will make a better wife to a wealthy man) marry Laurie after Jo rejects him.

The self-declared "man of the family now papa is away," Jo is proud of her boyishness; she whistles in the house, takes poor care of her dresses, "doesn't care for girls or girlish gossip," and shortens her name from Josephine to Jo. Meg, the beautiful eldest sister, is a second mother, playing at parenting by nurturing frail Beth and checking Amy's excesses. In the first volume of *Little Women*, Laurie—who goes by a shortened version of his surname because "Theodore" resulted in the boys' calling him "Dora"—is Jo's special friend. By the end of the second volume, the reader will have imagined the possibility of Laurie with each of the sisters. There are moments in Volume 1 when we fear that he will turn his romantic attention to the beautiful Meg, keeping Jo for his "boy" friend. Laurie's unwavering devotion contributes to our belief that Jo is the most desirable sister, though she is the least feminine, the most clever, the outdoorswoman, and the writer. At the end of the first volume we look forward to their marriage, and Laurie will be able to supply the wants of this family of women because he is both wealthy and generous. The girls are more grown up in the second volume, and Jo takes her vocation more seriously. Her writing earns her the income that compensates for her father's financial setbacks. Laurie is rejected; Beth dies; and Amy marries Laurie. Jo marries the Professor, a father figure who experts a moral influence on her publishing. The compromise seems to be, however, that she puts down her pen and takes up the mothering of sons with a vengeance (to her own sons and the boys at her boys' school), having learned (as her own mother had learned) to master herself.

This compromise was not one that Alcott made in her own life, and the deviations from autobiography are telling. "It is clear" writes Edward Weeks that "*Little Women* is a dramatization of Louisa Alcott's life in Concord before the war." Weeks describes Alcott has having a "do-it-yourself independence and a love of writing," taking on herself "the responsibility of being a substitute parent." Alcott's father, who was her educator, was "so improvident that his family was rarely more than one jump out of debt." Louisa "loved her father" but "saw him more realistically than the other members of the family."[47] Jo is given Alcott's role as a paternal supplement, but the actual portrayal of paternal inadequacy in a children's story would not do. So, while the life of the March family is modelled on the Alcott "family life *before the war*," Alcott sets the story in wartime in order to remove Mr. March. Although he is both too old and too weak to have been drafted, Mr. March volunteers, and thus bravely assumes a patriarchal and patriotic occupation while the women must manage themselves. In fact, Mr. Alcott did not go off to war. His daughter Louisa did. She served as a nurse, a rugged occupation that drew on her experience nursing her sister Lizzie (Beth). Alcott's writing made her famous and enabled her to support her sisters and their daughters. She never married. The fact that Jo is preferred by Laurie to her feminine sisters, and that Jo ultimately secures another man, seems to suggest the compatibility of pen and marriage. But Jo, like Dorothea, becomes a mother, also giving up fantasies of greatness in traditionally masculine spheres. The end of *Little Women* depicts a woman's world, however, as the sisters find strength in their connections to one another, satellites around their own mother, their children surrounding them.

Heroines such as Elinor Dashwood, Elizabeth Bennet, Maggie Tulliver, Dorothea Brooke, and Jo March, distinguished principally by their superiority of mind, typically share other characteristics associated with intelligence. The phallic sister often sports a lesser beauty, or, more pointedly, a less conventionally feminine beauty than her sister(s). This combination of characteristics in the heroine who is less feminine, less attractive, and more intelligent than her sisters finds a suggestive explanation in recent psychological studies which find that people perceive unattractive features to be gender-coded for the "wrong" sex.[48] Power, as Dijkstra demonstrates, is encoded as masculine. Initially the wise sister seems more male and identifies with the paternal rather than the maternal side of the family, enjoying a special relationship with her father. Like Antigone, whose crime against the state threatened male authority, she may speak like a man, or write, or paint, and thereby wield an instrument that was considered phallic in the Victorian imagination or subconscious.[49] While Antigone's outspoken heroism necessitates a sacrifice of marriage and children, the nineteenth-century woman writer challenges this equation by depicting a wise heroine who is rewarded with the conventional fruits of womanhood.

The movement of the wise heroine away from female occupations and lives and towards the paternal is treated with ambivalence: while the wise heroine's maternal insensitivity is regretted, her alliance with the father affords her power and privilege. The economies of character and desire then place the heroine in direct competition with her sisters for a husband. Often in Victorian stories, to an extent that may make us uncomfortable, male characters transfer their affections from one sister to another. This transference ensures the unique feminine appeal of the wise sister, but it is also unsettling because we feel an excess of intimacies: first, these novels invite us to imagine the possibility of the heroine's husband as her brother-in-law or her brother-in-law as her husband; second, we see that in the marriage market of realist fiction women are goods who are placed in competition with their closest female associates—their sisters.

These generalized characteristics of the heroine who is contrasted with her sisters on the basis of a masculine strength of voice invite us to consider the possibility of authorial projection. The wise sister with qualities ambiguously marked with respect to gender embodies anxieties imposed on the sage woman author about her own femininity: Is assuming the pen and the voice of authority compatible with enjoying a conventional woman's life? Like their heroines, Austen, Eliot, and Alcott in their own lives had especially close, complicated relationships with their fathers, and each of these authors maintained an abiding, even overriding, attachment to a sister. Unlike their heroines, they did not marry and have children. Austen's biographers emphasize Austen's lifelong devotion to her sister Cassandra. Alcott used her writing to support her sisters in a way that her father had been unable to do. Mrs. Evans preferred Chrissey, and the less adorable Mary Anne enjoyed her father's preference, a distribution of affection that was both sad and valuable for Mary Anne, as is poignantly expressed in Maggie's history. We see that the pattern within these fictions at once repeats and revises a pattern in the authors' lives: the novels rehearse the risks and pains of appropriating male discourse as the women writers may have experienced those pains, but the heroine triumphs both by the standards of female society and within such society: she marries well and retains the love of her sisters.

After the model of Antigone and Ismene, sisters in literature tend overwhelmingly to be in conflict and to represent antitheses. Antigone neither marries nor has children, nor does she reconcile with Ismene. With the telling exception of Eliot's Maggie, the wise heroine in these fictions finds restored to her not only the possibility of "wedding, marriage bed, and children" that Antigone sacrifices but also her intimate connection with her sister. Reestablishing that intimacy meant straining against conventions of representation. In this context, it is interesting that the Brontë sisters, important as they were to each other, give their heroines no sisters. This lack suggests the Brontë sisters' unwillingness to divide sisters by using them to represent opposites.

Through the efforts of these nineteenth-century women writers, intelligence moves from being gendered as masculine to being recuperated for women; the heroine, typed as "masculine" because she is smart, comes to be regarded as feminine after all. Indeed, her "manliness" becomes part of her sexual appeal. By the end of the century, feminine masculinity is a trait of the so-called New Woman. This androgynous look was regarded as sexy, but as Dijkstra documents, "highminded arguments against the viraginous tendencies of the New Woman" persisted.[50] The authorial valuation of these heroines retains some of the ambiguity so much in evidence in Sophocles's *Antigone* that critics persist in wondering whether Sophocles finally approves or disapproves of his heroine. In nineteenth-century fiction, the ambiguity of gender, power, and truth is no less in evidence and may be attributed to the age's resistance to a heroine's speaking wisely, and to the resultant struggle of the female sage with her own ambivalent self-perception.[51]

Traversing the Feminine in Oscar Wilde's *Salomé*

RICHARD DELLAMORA

In the opening chapter of *The Victorian Sage* (1953), John Holloway has argued that the Victorian sages attempt to communicate knowledge in ways that produce assent without relying on formal logic. Taking John Henry Newman's idea of "Real Assent" as a model of the sort of conviction that the sages aim for, Holloway refers to a "meaning which arises for the individual out of his own history, and exists for him in vivid particular images that bring his belief to life, and naturally lead him in the end to some active and practical step like joining a church."[1] In the following essay on Oscar Wilde, I propose a reading of sexual "history" that includes sexual relations with both intimates and casual acquaintances, with both men and women.

In *Salomé,* which Richard Ellmann has taken to signify a paradigmatic instance of Wilde's enrollment in an Oxonian tradition of sage discourse, I will argue that the "images" of special importance are those of the body, male and female, including fantasies of perverse sexual practices. Although men committed to sexual and emotional ties with other men did in fact gather in particular religious communities and parishes from the late 1860s until the end of the century, the "practical step" to which *Salomé* tends is not, as in the case of Newman, towards the church but towards Wilde's declaration of himself as a lover of men in all senses of the word.[2] The process central to sage writing that David DeLaura has described as

246

"self-exploration and self-manifestation and the manipulation of one's own personal presence for highly personal ends" functions in a new way in *Salomé*.[3] In the play, self-writing convokes and responds to diverse constituencies in a decade in which male homosexual existence became for the first time a significant feature of English middle-class culture. In these novel circumstances, possibilities of meaning occurred that simply had not existed earlier, even in the sexual polemics of Walter Pater, whom Ellmann names as one of the prime precursors of *Salomé*. The very specificity of the audiences for *Salomé*, however, also signals the end of Victorian sage discourse as an attempt to describe a new moral center for contemporary society.[4] *Salomé* takes relish in the eccentricity of its constituencies.

When English censors in 1892 decided to prohibit the staging of Wilde's play, they found it offensive not so much because it expresses desire between men as because Salomé asserts her desire as a woman. Hence, although within Paterian tradition Salomé is a male transvestite, within the field of struggle surrounding the figure of what was referred to at the time as the "New Woman," Salomé is a woman who challenges the ideology of the middle-class woman as an Angel in the House. In the decade in which Havelock Ellis produced case studies of female inversion and in which Wilde went to trial, Salomé also is a lesbian—although problematically so in a text in which lesbian connotation is evoked by a sexually nonconformist male writing for a predominantly male audience of diverse sexualities.[5] Salomé's double significance as a deviant male and a deviant female underscores how closely issues of sexual difference were related to those of gender roles in the 1890s.[6]

Salomé's desire could be used by members of a conservative male homosocial elite in prophylactic mockery of the anxieties that explicit female desire for a male provoked. The censor, Edward Pigott, wrote to a friend that Salomé's "love turns to fury because John will not let her kiss him *in the mouth*—and in the last scene, where she brings in his head—if you please—on a 'charger'—*she does* kiss his mouth, in a paroxysm of sexual despair." Besides defending himself against Salomé's excesses, Pigott's comments reinforce a sense of class superiority over "the average British public" that paradoxically justifies men like Pigott in reserving Wilde's text for themselves.[7] Nonetheless, *Salomé* could also be used by women to assert female power—a fact that Sarah Bernhardt, for instance, perceived immediately. Bernhardt, who intended to use the play as a vehicle with

herself in the leading part, underwrote the expenses of the London production that Pigott subsequently canceled.[8] Moreover, as Sydney Janet Kaplan
has pointed out, to a generation of younger women writers like Katherine
Mansfield, Wilde's assertions of desire were empowering—even if, in *Salomé*, that assertion invites women to a seeming endgame in which the
pursuit of female desire is both repudiated (by John the Baptist) and punished (by Herod).[9] Accordingly, and despite the fact that Ellmann in his
recent biography includes a semi-nude photograph of Wilde dressed as
Salomé and reaching for the decapitated head of John, *Salomé* is a significant document in the history of a specifically female sexuality.

Among the works produced between 1885 and 1895, none is more outspoken, more outrageous, or more bodily than *Salomé* (1891), a play so
sure to enrage English philistines that its conception needed to be translated into—perhaps even to be imagined in—French. Although Wilde developed the script of the play while in Paris, he nonetheless intended an
immediate London production and began a vexed process of arranging its
translation. Likewise, his efforts to bring out an edition in England situate
the text in an artistic milieu that included innovative work by men who
were beginning to be identifiable as "homosexual." Wilde fashions *Salomé*
so as to develop a self-consciously homosexual outlook. By including a
homosexual triangle in the play, he offers a dramatized representation of
explicit male-male desire. He also, however, inscribes these representations
of *l'amour de l'impossible* within relations of power: the page loves his
social superior, the young Syrian captain of the guard, who in turn loves
Salomé, the Tetrarch's niece. The Syrian has been brought to the Tetrarch's court after Herod drove his father, a king, from his throne. Later,
when Herod enters, he jokes that the young man, who has just killed himself, has been "my guest, as it were" (16).[10] The members of the audience
who share Herod's humor at this moment also share his contempt for a
vanquished male—an apt object of aggressive laughter on the part of another male. Yet the identification of the Syrian as captive/captain/prince
carries a subtle suggestion of another kingdom, in which princes would
remain princes and desire between men would not drive one first to emotional isolation and then to suicide.

The fact that the first London production of *Salomé* was to be mounted
for an audience that understood French indicates the elitism of the project.
Moreover, the ability of the audience (and of Wilde) to participate emo

tionally in Herod's assertions of male power indicate the location of the play both inside and outside male homosocial culture. For Wilde, until the time of the 1895 trials, the position of both enjoying the benefits of male privilege and subverting the male gender roles in which these privileges were exercised appears to have been both welcome and necessary. Only when the 1895 trials brought this period to an end, did he fully emerge as homosexual; earlier, he continued to enjoy the benefits of a well-placed man, head of household, husband, and father. Nonetheless, the drive towards undoing this complicit existence is evident in works like *The Picture of Dorian Gray* and even more so in *Salomé*. Both in dramatizing a rebellious woman and in portraying male-male desire, *Salomé* puts normal masculine representation under pressure.

Salomé turns on four spectacles: that of John's delayed entrance; that of Salomé's dance; that of her kissing John's severed head; and that of the final tableau of soldiers who, in the English translation, "rush forward and crush beneath their shields Salomé daughter of Herodias" (36). There is, however, another spectacle not seen in the course of the play but which is its central action: namely, the beheading of John the Baptist. Insofar as this act pertains to Herod, whom Ellmann regards as the protagonist of the play, the execution of John exemplifies the abuse of secular authority by a male agent.[11] The fourth spectacle, that of the execution of Salomé, perpetrates a like abuse. In ordering the execution both of the male as object of desire and of the female as subject of desire, Herod interdicts all sexuality except the conventional kind.[12] In the contemporary political context of the play, the murders resonate outwards to legislation like the Labouchère Amendment and to the office of the Lord Chamberlain, which prevented the performance of Wilde's play in England until 1931.[13]

By way of a number of essays published in the late 1960s, Ellmann has earned a significant place in the emergence of male homosexual desire as a topic of discussion in academic circles. In the Introduction to a collection of Wilde's critical essays (1969), Ellmann argues that Wilde's initiation by Robert Ross into homosexual activities in 1887 prompted the literary creativity of the next few years.[14] Although Ellmann may be mistaken to defer for so long the date of Wilde's entry into sexual activities with other men, his placement of male-male desire at the center of Wilde's work and his argument for the enabling power of that desire have been major contributions to the reconstitution of the sexual politics of the 1890s.[15] In "Overtures to *Salome*" (1968), Ellmann inscribes Wilde anew within the tradition of Victorian sage discourse. Ellmann sees the play as dramatizing the pull between two diverse forces at Oxford in Wilde's undergraduate years: the moralizing aestheticism of John Ruskin and the seductive, critical impressionism of Pater. Ellmann sees *Salomé* as an opportunity for some timely father-slaying on Wilde's part—of Ruskin's "weird chastity" in the figure of Iokanaan and of Pater's "diseased contemplation" in the figure of Salomé: "It is Salome, and not Pater, who dances the dance of the seven veils, but her virginal yet perverse sensuality is related to Paterism."[16] Ellmann misses, however, the side of Ruskin that admires female power as well as the extent to which *Salomé* celebrates in dramatic form the male transvestism already present in Pater's 1869 essay on Leonardo da Vinci. Nevertheless, my main point here is that by identifying Wilde with Herod as protagonist of the play and by a factitious return to order at play's end, Ellmann synthesizes the antagonistic Ruskinian and Paterian elements into a conserving (male) order that recaptures Wilde for a moral tradition of high cultural discourse.

Ellmann contends that "at the play's end the emphasis shifts suddenly to Herod, who is seen to have yielded to Salome's sensuality, and then to the moral revulsion of Iokanaan from that sensuality, and to have survived them both. In Herod Wilde was suggesting that *tertium quid* which he felt to be his own nature, susceptible to contrary impulses but not abandoned for long to either."[17] In view of the fact that immediately before her execution Salomé gives utterance to a long apologia in defense of "l'amour", Ellmann appears to misread the "emphasis" of the play at this moment.[18] Moreover, he takes this view despite the fact that, as Gagnier has pointed out, Wilde "consistently stressed that Salome, rather than Herodias, Herod, or Iokanaan, was to be the focus for the audience."[19]

In effect, Ellmann imposes a Freudian model on *Salomé*, one implicit in the biographical reading of the play that he provides earlier, in which Herod performs the function of regulating ego in relation to the influence of Pater as libido and of Ruskin as superego. Ellmann's desire to conserve the normal structure of male psychology at the end of the play prompts him to identify aesthetic structure as a force that can sublimate the erotic revolts and disturbances of *Salomé* even if this solution means misrepresenting the play. In his reading of the ending, Ellmann fails to see that, as Elliot Gilbert has remarked, when Salomé kisses John's head, "what is, objectively—from the point of view of Herod, for example—the most repellent moment in the drama becomes, when seen from the point of view of Salome, and with a proper sympathy, unaccountably touching."[20] Ellmann's comment overlooks both Salomé's lament and Herod's brutality in ordering the execution with which the play ends.

Ellmann's reading of the ending of *Salomé*, which may be described as the "consciousness-effect" of a conventionally masculine discourse, is motivated.[21] He defends Wilde (and himself, the tradition, and the male reader) against the "feminine" aspect of Pater, safely killed along with Salomé. This critical act murders the part of Pater that is responsive to female experience and, even more tellingly, Pater-as-homosexual, at least in the sense of the sexologists of the 1890s, including those who were themselves homosexual and who argued that the homosexual was a *tertium quid,* a female soul locked in a male body. As Christopher Craft has reminded us, both John Addington Symonds and Ellis share this view, formulated in the 1860s in Germany by Karl Ulrichs, an apologist for male-male desire. Ulrichs "regarded uranism, or homosexual love, as a congenital abnormality by which a female soul had become united with a male body—*anima muliebris in corpore virili inclusa.*"[22] Ellmann metaphorically does away with this corporeal oddity and metaphysical absurdity.

Although Elliot Gilbert also signs Freud's name to his critical reading both of *Salomé* and of Aubrey Beardsley's accompanying drawings, Gilbert's discussion begins a new stage in the consideration of the play, one that I refer to as the first-phase, feminist-identified male response to the emergence of the feminist critique of Victorian literature during the 1970s. Although Sandra M. Gilbert, Susan Gubar, Elaine Showalter, and Nina Auerbach are the best known among this group, their number is legion. Elliot Gilbert corrects Ellmann's reading by emphasizing Salomé's significance as a sign of female power in the face of a male literary culture that was defending itself against self-assertion by women writers, by feminists, and by New Women.[23] Although this response has advanced our understanding of the play, Gilbert's approach requires further revision in order adequately to take into account the interplay between the feminist-identified and the male homosexual politics of Wilde's text.[24] What Gilbert perceives as misogyny pertains less to the play than to his unreflexive use of yet another Freudian paradigm, namely that of the castration complex, which is both misogynistic and homophobic. Similarly, although the play, by remaining complicit to a degree with the male power that it satirizes, is itself also necessarily homophobic, Gilbert exaggerates Wilde's homophobia. Since 1983 when Gilbert wrote his essay, however, gay critics have pointed out the bias of Freud's position, as exemplified, for instance, in "Medusa's Head." In light of these discussions, second-phase, feminist-identified male criticism bears a responsibility, both cognitive and moral, to avoid the deformations of conventional Freudian psychoanalysis.

Craig Owens has pointed out the culpable phrase in Freud's text: "Since the Greeks were in the main strongly homosexual, it was inevitable that we should find among them a representation of woman as a being who frightens and repels because she is castrated."[25] In one sentence, Freud manages to combine a masculinist description of woman (defined in terms of lacking a penis), homophobia (homosexuals are gynephobic), and racism. As for Gilbert's view of woman, he says: "As an artist and *male* homosexual . . . [Wilde] recoils from the full implications of an uncontrolled and murderous female energy. For no generous sharing of the subjectivity of his protagonist can in the end conceal from him the fact that it is *he* who is her proposed victim."[26] Gilbert identifies the Beardsley drawing in which Salomé, suspended in air with her own snaky locks, kisses Johns's severed, Medusan head as *tout court* a representation of the castration complex: "Medusa and her snakey [sic] locks—representing, as Freud suggests, 'the female genitals' and therefore male 'terror of castration/decapitation'—can kill at a glance, and it is this power Beardsley most dramatically portrays in Salomé's hungry peering at Iokanaan's severed head and in the head's blind, reciprocating gaze."[27] *Pace* Gilbert, however, "the head's" eyes are closed. What, moreover, does gender reversal mean in this drawing, in which the Medusa head is male and the subject of the gaze is female? The transposition of genders here suggests a more varied sense of sexuality in Wilde than Gilbert's identification of the drawing with the castration complex permits.

When not looking at Beardsley's drawings and Wilde's text through Freud's spectacles, Gilbert is much more aware of the complexities of *Salomé*. Beardsley was Wilde's most productive collaborator on *Salomé*, and his drawings are especially helpful in emphasizing a host of perverse sexual acts connoted in the script. "It is the *outré* art of Aubrey Beardsley, with its lurid representations of hermaphroditism, masturbation, genetic monstrosities, and full [male] nudity, that most accurately illustrates both the subject matter and the spirit of the play."[28] The drawing discussed above is a case in point.

The earlier version, entitled *J'ai baisé ta bouche Iokanaan* (Fig. 1), was a free drawing that prompted John Lane to commission the illustrations of the 1894 English translation. Wilde, who also was enthusiastic, wrote on the copy that he gave Beardsley: "For Aubrey: for the only artist who, besides myself, knows what the dance of the seven veils is, and can see that invisible dance."[29] The organ that Beardsley's inscription emphasizes is *la bouche,* the mouth. That it may signify both an orifice and an organ is suggested by metaphorical images of the vulva and the erect penis. There are the two upright peacock feathers with their "vulval . . . eyes"; as well, there are the flower and reeds at the bottom right of the drawing.[30] The calamuslike spike under John's head is suggestive of the head of the male member. In that case, a woman (or more likely a crossdressed male) is about to engage in fellatio. If, however, one stays with a Freudian typology in which decapitated head = female *pudenda,* or with a pun on *bouche/* "bush," than Salomé-as-woman may be engaging in lesbian cunnilingus. The proliferation of bodily signs suffused with implications of perverse sexual practices here indicates how Wilde and Beardsley can create representations of sexual difference while playing with a code that, in the register of an orthodox Freudian reading, connotes a masculinist fixation.

In the revision of the drawing for publication (Fig. 2), Salomé's locks undergo a trimming and the title is changed to *The Climax,* a title denoting the forbidden subject of female sexual climax.[31] That Wilde and Beardsley intended this meaning is further borne out by the testimony of Alfred Douglas at the time of the Pemberton-Billing trials in 1918. When the dancer Maud Allan planned with J. T. Grein to mount a production of *Salomé* during World War 1, she was attacked in *The Vigilante.* Allan sued, claiming, in an article entitled "The Cult of the Clitoris," that her portrayal of Salomé had been represented as "an inducement to lesbianism."[32] Douglas, testifying for the defense, answered the following questions put to him by the defendant acting as his own counsel:

"Did Wilde intend that Salome should actually bite the lips of the Prophet?"

1. Aubrey Beardsley, *J'ai baisé ta bouche, Iokanaan*, from Oscar Wilde, *Salome: A Tragedy in One Act*, trans. R. A. Walker (London: William Heinemann Ltd., 1957).

2. Aubrey Beardsley, *The Climax*, from Oscar Wilde, *Salome: A Tragedy in One Act* (New York: Dover Publications, Inc., 1967).

"Yes, certainly."

"Draw blood?"

"Yes."

"Suck them?"

"Yes. That was the idea."

"Was it intended by the writer that she should work herself up into a great state of sexual excitement?"

"Yes."

"Uncontrolled sexual excitement?"

"Yes. A sort or orgasm. It is meant to be the culmination of sexual excitement."[33]

Beardsley's illustrations wittily combine gender confusion and reversal, sexual inversion, and parody. For instance, in the drawing originally entitled *The Man in the Moon* and subsequently retitled *The Woman in the Moon* (Fig. 3), Beardsley caricatures Wilde as the face of the moon.[34] To the right, a nude John shields a similar figure of a fully dressed Salomé. This image draws on the literary tradition of the screen-woman, as in Dante's *La Vita Nuova* where the young poet pretends to address his poetry to one woman so as to screen the identity of another, who is the actual object of his ardor. In the Beardsley drawing, John screens Salomé from the lustful regard of Wilde/the Moon-figure. But John's frontal nudity reveals the actual object of Wilde's gaze, namely, the youthful male body. In this instance, the screen discloses a specifically male-male sexual desire.

Salomé carries the resistance of an earlier generation of polemicists out of sexual-aesthetic literary discourse and into the three-dimensional, collaborative world of the theatre. Wilde chose Charles Ricketts, the spousal companion of Charles Shannon, to design the London production. Likewise, the translation into English, to be written by Douglas, was intended to be a collaboration between the two men committed sexually and affectively to each other. Although Douglas was already polemicizing on behalf of men who loved other men, his linguistic incompetence, arrogance, and jealousy ruled out the possibility of success.[35] Wilde had to rewrite the translation—even though the English text is still headed by the rubric "Translated from the French of Oscar Wilde by Lord Alfred Douglas" in the edition of Wilde edited by his son, Vyvyan Holland.[36] Hence, to borrow a phrase from Jacques Derrida, the English *Salomé* may be regarded

3. Aubrey Beardsley, *The Woman in the Moon,* from Oscar Wilde, *Salome: A Tragedy in One Act* (New York: Dover Publications, Inc., 1967).

as a text "authorized but authorless," ambiguously floating on the waters of what was supposed to be mutual affection but what turned out, in fact, to be acrimony.[37] When the English version eventually appeared, Wilde's name stood on the title page; but the dedication was to Douglas as translator.[38]

Beardsley, who was drawn into the fracas, also unsuccessfully tried his hand at translating the play.[39] Although this sickly young man, only twenty-one in 1893, defined himself against Wilde's sexual deviance, he nonetheless proved to be his most intimate collaborator; the drawings effect a visual synesthesia that succeeds in evoking the somatic and specifically genital processes that Wilde intends his drama to bring vividly to mind. Moreover, while the illustrations evoke Beardsley's satiric view of the exploitative aspects of male-male sexuality, his repeated figurings of Wilde's presence in the play reveal Beardsley to have been one of Wilde's most discerning readers. Besides the figure of Wilde as the man/woman in the moon discussed above, Beardsley also images Wilde as Herod casting a voyeuristic glance at Salomé and, in another drawing, as the costumed master of revels who presents the spectacle that stages his own obsessions.[40] In each of these equivocal images, Beardsley connotes within a sequence of putatively heterosexual representations a drive towards the unmasking of Wilde's fixation on the male body as an object of desire.

The gender of the actor who plays Salomé inflects the sexual politics of any particular production of the play. In *Salomé*, the body is not only an image but also a physical presence. When Stéphane Mallarmé, the hierophant of Symbolism, wrote to Wilde after the publication of *Salomé* in February 1893, Mallarmé located the body in the play between the ideal Symbolist state of consciousness, *le Songe,* and a term that in part signifies preterition, *l'indicible:* "I marvel that, while everything in your *Salome* is expressed in constant dazzling strokes, there also arises, on each page, the unutterable and the Dream."[41] Mallarmé then remarks: "So the innumerable and precise jewels can serve only as an accompaniment to the gown for the supernatural gesture of that young princess whom you definitively evoked."[42] Mallarmé poses *Salomé* between words that are a material, even painterly, veil and actions whose excess indicates a visionary perception. Between language and vision exists the body, the *geste surnaturel* of Salomé's dance and final, rapt kiss. Her body, adorned but withheld by textuality, on the one hand, and transformed into a symbol of the inexpressible, on the other, is dramatically perverse.

In the context of the sexual politics in the male press in England, Salomé's body is most definitely female, and her unleashed sexual appetite queasily conjures the current fears of that self-assertive type known as the New Woman. Linda Dowling has pointed out the connections that contemporary journalists observed between male decadence and the New Woman of the 1890s: "The New Woman . . . was perceived to have ranged herself perversely with the forces of cultural anarchism and decay precisely because she wanted to reinterpret the sexual relationship."[43] Wilde's Salomé, who exists for her own pleasure and not to grace, serve, or reproduce for the benefit of male interests, threatens the stability of normal gender relations. Beardsley accentuates the threat by drawing John as her double in *John and Salomé* (Fig. 4). The fact that Wilde parodies while exploiting the veilings of Symbolist aesthetics should not obscure the existence, on another level, of his parody of the press's satiric representations of modern women, "the Militant Daughters, of Key and Club."[44]

In the opening section, I mentioned the presence of four spectacles in the play. The first of these is the entry of John the Baptist onto the stage, an entry delayed so as to gain maximum advantage from the appearance of a semi-nude, slender male form. The language of Salomé's profane parody of the *Song of Songs* indicates that her attraction to this body is thoroughly phallicized: "Comme il est maigre aussi! il ressemble à une mince image d'ivoire. On dirait une image d'argent. Je suis sûre qu'il est chaste, autant que la lune. Il ressemble à un rayon d'argent. Sa chair doit être très froide comme de l'ivoire" (14).[45] Likewise, her evocation of John's mouth is saturated by an obsession with male hegemonic power:

> Ta bouche est comme une branche de corail que des pêcheurs ont
> trouvée dans le crépuscule da [sic] la mer et qu'ils réservent pour les
> rois . . .! Elle est comme le vermillon que les Moabites trouvent dans
> les mines de Moab et que les rois leur prennent. Elle est comme l'arc
> du roi des Perses qui est peint avec du vermillon et qui a des cornes
> de corail. Il n'y a rien au monde d'aussi rouge que ta bouche. (17).[46]

Salomé projects herself as one of the kings who "take." Similarly, in the second spectacle in the play, or her dance, the bodily power that Herod

4. Aubrey Beardsley, *John and Salome*, from Oscar Wilde, *Salome: A Tragedy in One Act* (New York: Dover Publications, Inc., 1967).

wishes to take from his stepdaughter by staging her performance for the benefit of his visitors is reappropriated by Salomé, who dances for her own pleasure in a series of movements whose genital analogue is the practice of masturbation. The third, unseen spectacle in *Salomé* is the execution of John under the sign of the Tetrarch's authority, *"the ring of death"* (33). The fourth spectacle, a pratfall turned tragic, is the execution of Salomé herself.

The first three staged spectacles turn about the fourth. In terms of conventional sexuality, Salomé's dance represents a force of bodily attraction that is able to subvert the customary superiority of men; in terms that the Victorians would have regarded as perverse, the dance is also masturbatory. The final scene of *Salomé* represents the restoration of patriarchal authority at the price of negating Salomé and Herod as subjects of desire. The scene of the kissing of John's head implies not only a fixation on the cock—as Pigott surmised to his delight—but also a fixation on what a later reader might designate as the phallus.[47] When Salomé takes John's head, she is also taking Herod's power, even though, since she is still playing a game of which Herod is master, taking his power puts her in jeopardy. What makes Salomé's demand insufferable is neither her lust nor her vindictiveness, but the rupture that she forces in the tensions of patriarchal power. Herod attempts to balance the requirements of colonial administration against those of the religion of Jehovah. In his mind, both powers have sway, so that the exercise of his function as King is neither simple nor univocal. By using his oath for herself and against him, Salomé undoes the Tetrarch's uneasy balance of conflicting anxieties. It is for this reason that Salomé must be destroyed—as if the destruction of her body, of her desire, could suture a wound torn in Herod by his desire for (power over) her.

Jonathan Dollimore has recently argued that in the critical apothegms of Oscar Wilde, one may ascertain that dissolution of the individual ego which is perceived as characteristic of our postmodern moment. If Dollimore is correct in suggesting that "for Wilde transgressive desire leads to a relinquishing of the essential self," then Wilde's writing provides one ground for understanding the end of sage tradition as it existed in Victorian England up through Arnold and Pater.[48] Although Wilde begins within this tradition, he produces work in which the body and its practices make their claims at the expense of psychological and social order. Yet if

Salomé is material in the sense of being bodily, it is also material in the way in which it responds to and helps form new constituencies of readers: specifically, women and male homosexuals.[49] The deliberate construction of marginal discourses and their attendant readership occurs at the expense of the writing that characterizes the tradition as Holloway and De-Laura have described it.

By way of a conclusion, I will consider briefly how that tradition begins to be transformed as young women write from novel subject positions. While Virginia Woolf expresses her relation with Wilde by maintaining a complete silence about him in the first two volumes of her letters, other women have left responses that indicate their contradictory relation to the tradition that Wilde both inhabits and subverts.

As an undergraduate journalist, Willa Cather identified herself with Carlylean models of the writer as either "heroic warrior" or "divine creator."[50] Cather's anxiety that being a woman might disqualify her from becoming a serious writer helps explain why, writing late in 1894, she rejects the "driveling effeminacy" of Wilde and his transatlantic epigones.[51] Fear of the male with a female soul likewise signals Cather's concern that she might be accused of being a lesbian, that hybrid creature with the soul of a man in the body of a woman. Earlier in 1894, reviewing a production of *Lady Windermere's Fan,* she had been incensed at Wilde's characterization of Lady Windermere as lacking the natural feelings of a mother.[52] At least in part, her aggressive assertion of the maternal character of female nature functions to ward off allegations that she herself might be unnatural.

This defensive posture is corroborated by the article on Wilde that Cather published in September 1895, after the trials.[53] In this essay, Cather recapitulates the elements of sage writing as characterized by Landow but translated into the terms of one of Wilde's constituencies.[54] After using Wilde's "insanity" as an example of contemporary decadence and remarking that "he has made even his name impossible," Cather nonetheless shows him the respect of specifying his deviance by quoting from an early poem, "Hélas!," where he writes:

> . . . lo! with a little rod
> I did but touch the honey of romance
> And must I lose a soul's inheritance?[55]

And, at the end of the essay, she turns his debacle to prophetic account by wondering aloud "whether Oscar Wilde, and all the rest of us for that matter, will not have another chance . . . where the soul can feel as here the senses do, where there will be a better means of knowing and of feeling than through these five avenues so often faithless, that alike save and lose us, that either starve us or debauch us."[56] This passage looks forward to an utopian time when what was sundered in Wilde will achieve integration. Moreover, by using the pronoun "us," she includes herself among homosexual men and women who face difficulties akin to his.

Cather was able to relinquish the example of Wilde no better than she was able to yield her desire for other women. In "The Novel Démeublé" (1922) she speaks both of love of women—and kinship with Wilde.[57] In this, her best known essay, Cather refers to the female friendship/love that animates her writing: "Whatever is felt upon the page without being specifically named there—that, one might say, is created. It is the inexplicable presence of the thing not named, of the overtone divined by the ear but not heard by it, the verbal mood, the emotional aura of the fact or the thing or the deed, that gives high quality to the novel or the drama, as well as to poetry itself."[58] Sharon O'Brien finds a clue to Cather's allusion to female intimacy in the phrase, "the thing not named," with its conscious echo of "the phrase used as evidence at Oscar Wilde's trial: the 'Love that dared not speak its name.'"[59] In this way, Cather identifies herself with the life of the man whom, in 1895, she had decried.

Katherine Mansfield was also an especially devoted reader of Wilde. After a young woman gave her a copy of *The Picture of Dorian Gray* in the unexpurgated version that had first appeared in *Lippincott's Magazine*, Mansfield copied numerous passages into her journal between 1906 and 1908. She divined a usable moral in Wilde's novel: "To love madly perhaps is not wise, yet should you love madly, it is far wiser than not to love at all."[60] When Mansfield became involved in love affairs with two young women in New Zealand in 1907, she did so directly under the influence of Wilde.[61] And when, two years later, she married George C. Bowden in a moment of panic, Wilde became a sign of all that she now put aside. In an extraordinary letter, written to an unnamed female friend, Mansfield says: "In New Zealand Wilde acted so strongly and terribly upon me that I was constantly subject to exactly the same fits of madness as those which caused his ruin and his mental decay. When I am miserable now—these

recur. Sometimes I forget all about it—then with awful recurrence it bursts
upon me again and I am quite powerless to prevent it—This is my secret
from the world and from you."[62] In this letter, Wilde is portrayed as a
sexual daemon whose unpredictable visitations presage disaster.

While Mansfield was less successful in dealing with lesbian desire and
with the intimidating maleness of literary culture than Cather, Wilde remained a salient point of reference. Years later, shortly before her death,
Mansfield wrote John Middleton Murry, her second husband, to say that
she had had a dream about meeting Wilde after his imprisonment, in a
café, and of deciding to take him home to her parents. Once there, Wilde
tells her of a hallucination that combines fantasies of fellatio, cunnilingus,
and possibly anilingus:

> "You know, Katherine, when I was *in that dreadful place* I was
> haunted by the memory of a *cake*. It used to float in the air before
> me—a little delicate thing *stuffed* with cream and with the cream
> there was something *scarlet*. It was made of pastry and I used to call
> it my little Arabian Nights cake. But I couldn't remember the name.
> Oh, Katherine, it was *torture*. It used to *hang* in the air and *smile* at
> me. And every time I resolved that next time *they let someone* come
> and see me I would ask them to tell me what it was but every time,
> Katherine, I was *ashamed*. Even now. . . ."

When Mansfield in the dream responds by providing the name, "Mille
feuilles à la crême," she obliquely confesses both to the fantasies and to the
carceral state that she shares with Wilde. They are fellow convicts.[63]

Cather's and Mansfield's responses indicate how equivocal the legacy of
Wilde's particular sort of self-expression was for brilliant, unconventional
women. Nonetheless, for women too, Wilde moves forward novel forms of
self-identification; despite the dangers that he signals, he helps women like
Cather and Mansfield claim for themselves both a power of utterance and
a power over their bodies and relationships. Wilde's engagement in sexual
politics marks the contingent character of his writing, contingencies at
odds with the centripetal tendency of earlier sage discourse. In this respect,
he comes at the point of dispersion at the end of a tradition; or, rather, in
a world in which marginalities become crucial, the voice of the sage, as
even in Cather's essay of 1895, prophecies differently.

Notes

Sage Discourse and the Feminine

1. Cynthia Fuchs Epstein, *Deceptive Distinctions: Sex, Gender, and the Social Order* (New Haven: Yale University Press, 1988), 16. For a useful overview of major contributions to feminism across the disciplines, see Coppelia Kahn and Gayle Greene, "Feminist Scholarship and the Social Construction of Woman," in *Making a Difference: Feminist Literary Criticism*, ed. Gayle Greene and Coppelia Kahn (New York: Methuen, 1985), 1–36.

2. Sandra Harding, "Why Has the Sex/Gender System Become Visible Only Now?" in *Discovering Reality: Feminist Perspectives on Epistemology, Metaphysics, and Philosophy of Science*, ed. Sandra Harding and Merrill B. Hintikka (Boston: D. Reidel, 1983), 312.

3. John Holloway, *The Victorian Sage: Studies in Argument* (New York: W. W. Norton, 1953); George P. Landow, *Elegant Jeremiahs: The Sage from Carlyle to Mailer* (Ithaca: Cornell University Press, 1986). See also Landow, *Victorian Types, Victorian Shadows: Biblical Typology in Victorian Literature, Art, and Thought* (Boston: Routledge & Kegan Paul, 1980).

4. Landow, *Elegant Jeremiahs*, 22. According to Landow, "it is the combination of these literary and rhetorical strategies that constitute the genre rather than any particular one of them" (40).

5. Mikhail M. Bakhtin, "Discourse in the Novel," in *The Dialogic Imagination*, trans. Caryl Emerson and Michael Holquist (Austin: University of Texas Press, 1981), 270, emphasis deleted. For an excellent survey of the notion of "discourse" in poststructuralist marxism and the sociology of knowledge, see Diane Macdonell, *Theories of Discourse: An Introduction* (Oxford: Basil Blackwell, 1986).

6. Bakhtin, "Discourse," 259, 263.

7. For reasons internal to his polemics against stylistics, structuralism, and Marxism, Bakhtin promotes the novel as the dialogical genre par excellence, but this

does not preclude the usefulness of his theory of discourse for other kinds of cultural texts.

8. Elaine Showalter, "Looking Forward: American Feminists, Victorian Sages," *The Victorian Newsletter* 65 (1984): 6–9.

9. For a comprehensive treatment of the many issues included under the "Woman Question," see Elizabeth K. Helsinger et al., *The Woman Question: Society and Literature in Britain and America, 1837–1883*, 3 vols. (New York: Garland, 1983).

10. Barbara Taylor, *Eve and the New Jerusalem: Socialism and Feminism in the Nineteenth Century* (New York: Pantheon, 1983).

11. Taylor, *New Jerusalem*, 31.

12. Elaine Showalter, "Feminist Criticism in the Wilderness," *Critical Inquiry* 8 (1981); reprinted in *The New Feminist Criticism: Essays on Women, Literature, and Theory*, ed. Elaine Showalter (New York: Pantheon, 1985), 248, her emphasis.

13. Showalter, "Feminist Criticism," 248.

14. Sandra M. Gilbert and Susan Gubar, *The Madwoman in the Attic: The Woman Writer and the Nineteenth-Century Literary Imagination* (New Haven: Yale University Press, 1979). For the theory of "power/knowledge," see Michel Foucault, "Truth and Power," in *Power/Knowledge: Selected Interviews and Other Writings, 1972–1977*, ed. Colin Gordon (New York: Pantheon, 1980), 109–133. In the field of discourse, "it's not so much a matter of knowing what external power imposes itself . . . as of what effects of power circulate among . . . statements, what constitutes, as it were, their internal regime of power" (112–113).

15. Annette Kolodny, "A Map for Misreading: Or, Gender and the Interpretation of Literary Texts," *New Literary History* (1980); reprinted in *The New Feminist Criticism* as "A Map for Rereading: Gender and the Interpretation of Literary Texts," 47.

16. Elizabeth Barrett Browning, *Aurora Leigh, and Other Poems* (London: The Women's Press, 1978), 9. 929, 932.

17. For background on the Victorian social doctrine of "separate spheres," see Martha Vicinus, ed., *Suffer and Be Still: Women in the Victorian Age* (Bloomington: Indiana University Press, 1972) and *A Widening Sphere: Changing Roles of Victorian Women* (Bloomington: Indiana University Press, 1977).

18. For a discussion of the reception of Elizabeth Barrett Browning's epic poem by Victorian critics, see Cora Kaplan, "*Aurora Leigh*," in *Feminist Criticism and Social Change: Sex, Class and Race in Literature and Culture*, ed. Judith Newton and Deborah Rosenfelt (New York: Methuen, 1985), 138–145.

19. Robin Lakoff, *Language and Woman's Place* (New York: Colophon Books, 1975); Dale Spender, *Man-Made Language*, 2nd ed. (Boston: Routledge & Kegan Paul, 1985). For a critical survey of recent feminist sociolinguistic perspectives on

gender and language, see Alette Olin Hill, *Mother Tongue, Father Time: A Decade of Linguistic Revolt* (Bloomington: Indiana University Press, 1986). An important contribution to this debate is Gilbert and Gubar's study of "feminist and masculinist linguistic fantasy" in "Sexual Linguistics: Women's Sentence, Men's Sentencing," chap. 5 in *The War of the Words*, vol. 1 of *No Man's Land: The Place of the Woman Writer in the Twentieth Century* (New Haven: Yale University Press, 1988), 227–271.

20. Spender, *Language*, 89.

21. Spender, *Language*, 89.

22. Holloway, *Victorian Sage*, 1. On George Eliot's admission into the canon of sages on the condition of her masculinization, see the chapter on Eliot in Deirdre David, *Intellectual Women and Victorian Patriarchy* (London: Macmillan, 1987).

23. Michel Foucault, "The Discourse on Language," in *The Archeology of Knowledge*, trans. A. M. Sheridan Smith (New York: Pantheon, 1972), 225–226, his emphasis.

24. Martha Vicinus, *Independent Women: Work and Community for Single Women, 1850–1920* (Chicago: Chicago University Press, 1985), 9.

25. As Landow explains in *Elegant Jeremiahs*, as an authoritative culture critic, the sage writer must "find a way to be superior" to the audience in order to assign blame and propose solutions for the problems he or she diagnoses; at the same time, the sage cannot afford to alienate the audience entirely (54).

26. Matthew Arnold, *Culture and Anarchy*, in *The Complete Prose Works of Matthew Arnold*, vol. 5, ed. R. H. Super (Ann Arbor: University of Michigan Press, 1960–1977). Chapter 1 is entitled "Sweetness and Light"; this key phrase recurs throughout Arnold's text. For a comparative discussion of sage writing by Arnold, John Henry Cardinal Newman, and Walter Pater, see David J. De Laura, *Hebrew and Hellene in Victorian England: Newman, Arnold, and Pater* (Austin: University of Texas Press, 1969).

27. Nevin K. Laib, "Territoriality in Rhetoric," *College English* 47 (1985): 584.

28. Jane Marcus, "Invincible Mediocrity: The Private Selves of Public Women," in *The Private Self: Theory and Practice of Women's Autobiographical Writings*, ed. Shari Benstock (Chapel Hill: University of North Carolina Press, 1988), 137, her emphasis.

29. Epstein, *Deceptive Distinctions*, 83. Carol Gilligan's fundamental theses appear in "In a Different Voice: Women's Conceptions of Self and Morality," in *The Psychology of Women: Ongoing Debates*, ed. Marty Roth Walsh (New Haven: Yale University Press, 1987), 278–320.

30. Toril Moi, *Sexual/Textual Politics: Feminist Literary Theory* (London: Methuen, 1985), 135.

31. Moi, *Sexual/Textual Politics*, 154.

32. On religious discourse and women's subordination, see, for example, Casey Miller and Kate Swift, "The Language of Religion," in their *Words and Women: New Language in New Times* (Garden City, N.Y.: Anchor/Doubleday, 1976), 64–74.

33. Ellen Messer-Davidow, "The Philosophical Bases of Feminist Literary Criticisms," *New Literary History* 19 (1987): 65, her emphases.

34. Jane Gallop, *The Daughter's Seduction: Feminism and Psychoanalysis* (Ithaca: Cornell University Press, 1982), xii.

35. Marina Warner analyzes Athena as an icon of hegemonic femininity and Medusa as an icon of the feminine revolt against patriarchy in *Monuments and Maidens: The Allegory of the Female Form* (New York: Atheneum, 1985), 104–126.

36. Nina Auerbach, *Woman and the Demon: The Life of a Victorian Myth* (Cambridge, Mass.: Harvard University Press, 1982), 12.

37. See also Bram Dijkstra who surveys the "fundamentally new, massively institutionalized, ritual-symbolic perception of the role of woman" in nineteenth-century art and literature in *Idols of Perversity: Fantasies of Feminine Evil in Fin-desiècle Culture* (Oxford: Oxford University Press, 1986). Dijkstra sees "the nineteenth-century hoisting of woman onto a monumental pedestal" as "a male fantasy of ultimate power, ultimate control" (19), whereas Auerbach in *Woman and the Demon* regards such feminine icons as evidence of women's own rising powers.

38. On homophobia as a crucial issue for Victorian male writers, see Eve Kosofsky Sedgwick, *Between Men: English Literature and Male Homosocial Desire* (New York: Columbia University Press, 1985), *passim*.

39. Messer-Davidow, "Feminist Literary Criticisms," 78.

40. Judith Newton, "Making—and Remaking—History: Another Look at 'Patriarchy'," *Tulsa Studies in Women's Literature* 3 (1984): 130.

41. Newton, "Remaking History," 130.

42. See David's *Intellectual Women* for an especially illuminating discussion of Barrett Browning's desire to preserve certain aspects of the Victorian ideal of femininity and her ambivalence toward George Sand as a 'masculine' woman.

43. David, *Intellectual Women*, 32, her emphasis.

44. Tess Cosslett, *Woman to Woman: Female Friendships in Victorian Fiction* (Brighton, England: Harvester, 1988), 6.

45. Auerbach discusses the crisscrossing of feminine and masculine types in *Villette* in her study of *Communities of Women: An Idea in Fiction* (Cambridge, Mass.: Harvard University Press, 1978), 97–113. "Monstrous" as the masculinized Madame Beck may seem "to some, she presents a less cloying alternative to the fragile hothouse enclosure" of middle-class domesticity represented in Brontë's novel by the Bretton family (103). For their part, Gilbert and Gubar re-

gard the "phallic woman" in modernist literature as a wholly misogynistic construction. See especially their discussion of James Joyce's *Ulysses* in *Sexchanges*, vol. 2 of *No Man's Land*, 332–336.

46. Michel Foucault, *The History of Sexuality: An Introduction*, vol. 1, trans. Robert Hurley (New York: Vintage/Random House, 1980), 18, 48. See also my "Victorian Scandals, Victorian Strategies" in *Victorian Scandals*, ed. Kristine Garrigan (forthcoming).

47. In Ken Russell's 1988 film version of Wilde's play, *The Last Dance of Salomé*, the eponymous heroine lifts the seventh veil to reveal her male genitalia to an astonished but delighted audience consisting of King Herod, Oscar Wilde himself (the honored guest at a performance in a London brothel), and, of course, ourselves.

48. On the negative stereotyping of the masculine woman in Victorian literature and art, see Bridget Elliott, "New and Not So 'New Women' on the London Stage: Aubrey Beardsley's *Yellow Book* Images of Mrs. Patrick Campbell and Réjane," *Victorian Studies* 31 (1987): 33–57.

49. Gilbert and Gubar's generalization that all "modernist men of letters" sought to perpetuate the traditional sex-gender system does not take into account those modernist male writers who revolted against gender stereotypes along with their female contemporaries (*Sexchanges*, 326).

50. Alice Jardine, *Gynesis: Configurations of Woman and Modernity* (Ithaca: Cornell University Press, 1985), 25. Jardine suggests that "gynesis" is an especially characteristic move among postmodern male writers, as exemplified by Derrida and Lacan. On the configuration of modernity and the feminine in the nineteenth-century avant-garde, see Christine Buci-Glucksmann, "Catastrophic Utopia: The Feminine as Allegory of the Modern," *Representations* 14 (1986): 220–229.

51. Elaine Showalter, "Critical Cross-Dressing: Male Feminists and the Woman of the Year," in *Men in Feminism*, ed. Alice Jardine and Paul Smith (New York: Methuen, 1987), 120.

52. Teresa de Lauretis, "Feminist Studies/Critical Studies: Issues, Terms, and Contexts" in *Feminist Studies/Critical Studies*, ed. Teresa de Lauretis (Bloomington: Indiana University Press, 1986), 13.

53. Epstein, *Deceptive Distinctions*, 16.

"The Hero as Man of Letters"

1. *The Works of Thomas Carlyle*, ed. H. D. Traill (New York: Charles Scribner's Sons, (1889–1901), 5: 157. All further page references will be given in parentheses in the text.

2. G. F. Barwick, "The Magazines of the Nineteenth Century," *Transactions of the Bibliographical Society* 9(1912): 237–249.

3. John Gross, *The Rise and Fall of the Man of Letters* (New York: The Macmillan Company, 1969); T. W. Heyck, *The Transformation of Intellectual Life in Victorian England* (New York: St. Martin's Press, 1982).

4. Heyck, *Transformation*, 50.

5. Works published in installments constitute one entry. In "The Sociology of Authorship: The Social Origins, Education, and Occupations of 1,100 British Writers, 1800–1935" (*Bulletin of the New York Public Library* 65 [June 1962]: 389–404), Richard Altick finds that of approximately 20 percent of his sample (authors listed in the *Cambridge Bibliography of British Literature*) three are women. The proportion of women writers, Altick finds, does not change appreciably between 1800 and 1935, although the percent of women who represented themselves as professional writers shows a slow but uninterrupted increase during the period he studies—from 8 percent in 1881 to 16.6 percent in 1931. His figures support my conclusion, drawn from *The Wellesley Index to Victorian Periodicals, 1824–1900*, 4 vols. (Toronto: University of Toronto Press, 1966–87), that very few women in the nineteenth century could be seen as professional "men of letters."

6. See *Literary issues* vol. 3 in Elizabeth K. Helsinger, Robin Lauterbach Sheets, and William Veeder, *The Woman Question: Society and Literature in Britain and America, 1837–1883* (Chicago: University of Chicago Press, 1983), 47–78.

7. Quoted in Helsinger et al., *Literary issues*, 57.

8. Alfred Austin, *The Poetry of the Period* (London: R. Bentley, 1870), 96.

9. Austin, *Poetry*, 79.

10. Robert Buchanan, "The Fleshly School of Poetry," *Contemporary Review* 18 (1871): 338.

11. Gross, *Rise and Fall*, xiii; Heyck, *Transformation*, 24.

12. Heyck, *Transformation*, 121.

13. Margaret Oliphant and F. R. Oliphant, *The Victorian Age of Literature*, 2 vols. (London: Percival and Co., 1892); Clement Shorter, *Victorian Literature: Sixty Years of Books and Bookmen* (London: James Bowden, 1897); Hugh Walker, *The Age of Tennyson* (London: George Bell and Sons, 1904); Hugh Walker, *The Literature of the Victorian Era* (Cambridge: The University Press, 1913); Laurie Magnus, *English Literature in the Nineteenth Century* (New York: G. P. Putnam's Sons, 1909); George Saintsbury, *History of Nineteenth-Century Literature* (London: Macmillan & Co., 1919).

14. There was, in fact, a cult of prose style that emerged in the second half of the century. See Travis R. Merritt, in "Taste, Opinion, and Theory in the Rise of

Victorian Prose Stylism," in *The Art of Victorian Prose*, ed. George Levine and William Madden (London: Oxford University Press, 1968), 4–38.

15. W. C. Brownell, *Victorian Prose Masters* (New York: Charles Scribner's Sons, 1901).

16. Walker, *The Age of Tennyson*, 168.

17. Oliphant and Oliphant, *Victorian Age* 1:146.

18. On the rare occasions when women are represented as sages, it is for their achievements in the novel or poetry. See Anne Thackeray Ritchie, *A Book of Sibyls* (London: Smith, Elder, & Co., 1883), which treats Anna Laetitia Barbauld, Maria Edgeworth, Amelia Opie, and Jane Austen.

19. Walker, *Literature of the Victorian Era*, 708.

20. Frederic Harrison, *Studies in Early Victorian Literature* (London: Edward Arnold, 1895), 40–41.

21. Harrison, *Studies*, 9, 63.

22. "Modern Prose Style," reprinted in *The Collected Essays and Papers of George Saintsbury* (London: J. M. Dent & Sons, 1923), 68.

23. John Middleton Murray, "English Prose in the Nineteenth Century," in his *Discoveries: Essays in Literary Criticism* (London: W. Collins and Co., Ltd., 1924), 215–223.

24. Charles Frederick Harrold and William D. Templeman, eds., *English Prose of the Victorian Era* (New York: Oxford University Press, 1938), iii.

25. Harden Craig and J. M. Thomas eds., *English Prose of the Nineteenth Century* (New York: F. S. Crofts & Co., 1929), 5.

26. Craig and Thomas, *English Prose*, 5.

27. Emile Legouis, *A Short History of English Literature* (Oxford: Clarenden Press, 1934), 311.

28. Harrold and Templeman, *English Prose*, xiv.

29. Harrold and Templeman, *English Prose*, lxxx.

30. G. M. Young, *Victorian England: Portrait of an Age* (Oxford: Oxford University Press, 1960), 187.

31. Bernard Schilling, *Human Dignity and the Great Victorians* (New York: Columbia University Press, 1946), xii.

32. Henry Gifford, review of *The Victorian Sage*, *The Review of English Studies* 5 (1954): 206.

33. S. C. Burchett, review of *The Victorian Sage*, *The Yale Review* 43 (1953): 156.

34. A. Dwight Culler, "Method in the Study of Victorian Prose," *The Victorian Newsletter* 9 (1956): 1–4. See responses to this article in *Victorian Newsletter* 10 (1956): 15–16 and 11 (1956): 1–5.

(Re)interpretations of the Female Sage

1. Robert Gordis, "The Social Background of Wisdom Literature," in his *Poets, Prophets, and Sages: Essays in Biblical Interpretation* (Bloomington: Indiana University Press, 1971), 162.

2. George P. Landow, *Elegant Jeremiahs: The Sage from Carlyle to Mailer* (Ithaca: Cornell University Press, 1986). Since I there make use of abundant quotation from nineteenth- and twentieth-century sages, I shall here generally avoid quoting from authors other than Nightingale for the sake of brevity.

3. Like my emphasis on individual techniques other than imagery, this distinction between sage writing and wisdom literature distinguishes my approach from John Holloway's pioneering work, *The Victorian Sage: Studies in Argument* (London: Macmillan, 1953). For a more detailed discussion of wisdom literature, see my *Elegant Jeremiahs*, 22–24.

4. Florence Nightingale, *Cassandra*, ed. Myra Stark (London: Feminist Press, n.d.), 44. Hereafter cited in text.

5. See my *Elegant Jeremiahs*, 154–188, which compares the use of ethos in fiction and in sage writing and examines a range of techniques sages use to ingratiate themselves with readers. These devices include citing autobiographical experience and admitting the speaker's weakness.

6. William Wilberforce's *Practical View of the Prevailing System of Professed Christians, in the Higher and Middle Classes in This Country, Contrasted with Real Christianity* (1819), commonly known as *Practical Christianity*, which went through dozens of editions, made popular the evangelical distinction between real and nominal faiths.

7. John Ruskin, "Traffic," in *Works*, ed. E. T. Cook and Alexander Wedderburn, 39 vols. (London: George Allen, 1903–1912), 18: 447–448.

8. For the classic statement of this quality of Victorianism, see E. D. H. Johnson, *The Alien Vision of Victorian Poetry: Sources of the Poetic Imagination in Tennyson, Browning, and Arnold* (Princeton: Princeton University Press, 1952).

9. Martha Westwater's *The Wilson Sisters: A Biographical Study of Upper-Class Victorian Life* (Athens: Ohio University Press, 1984), provides examples of women reviewing anonymously for *The Economist*.

10. Linda H. Peterson, *Victorian Autobiography* (New Haven: Yale University Press, 1986).

11. For Rossetti, see George P. Landow, *Victorian Types, Victorian Shadows: Biblical Typology in Victorian Literature, Art, and Thought* (Boston: Routledge & Kegan Paul, 1980), 87–88; for Brontë, see 97–100.

12. Peterson, *Victorian Autobiography*; Mary W. Carpenter, *George Eliot and the Landscape of Time: Narrative Form and Protestant Apocalyptic History* (Chapel

Hill: University of North Carolina Press, 1986); Janet L. Larson, who is working on women writers and the Bible during the last two centuries, promises to create a much-needed overview of this problem in relation to fiction.

13. Frank M. Turner made these observations during the course of an NEH seminar for college teachers at Yale University, Summer 1988.

Tennyson's Gender Politics

1. Aubrey de Vere as quoted in Robert Martin, *Tennyson: The Unquiet Heart* (New York: Oxford University Press, 1980), 288.

2. Lionel Stevenson, "The High-Born Maiden," in *Critical Essays on the Poetry of Tennyson*, ed. John Killham (New York: Barnes and Noble, 1960), 126–136.

3. See Edgar Finley Shannon, Jr., *Tennyson and the Reviewers* (Cambridge, Mass.: Harvard University Press, 1952).

4. John Holloway, *The Victorian Sage* (London: Macmillan Press, 1953).

5. See Leonore Davidoff, "Class and Gender in Victorian England," in *Sex and Class in Women's History*, ed. Judith Lowder Newton, Mary P. Ryan, and Judith R. Walkowitz (London: Routledge, 1983), 16–71. See also Leonore Davidoff and Catherine Hall, *Family Fortunes: Men and Women of the English Middle Class* (Chicago: University of Chicago Press, 1987), and see Alan Sinfield, *Alfred Tennyson* (New York: Blackwell, 1986), 11–56, 127–143.

6. Shannon, *Tennyson and the Reviewers*, 33–46, 92; Hallam Lord Tennyson, *Alfred Lord Tennyson: A Memoir*, 2 vols. (London: Macmillan, 1897), 1: 122.

7. Alfred Austin, "Mr. Tennyson" (1870; reprinted in *Tennyson: The Critical Heritage*, ed. John D. Jump [London: Routledge, 1967]), 294–311; Edward Bulwer as quoted in Martin, *Tennyson*, 169–173; Walter Bagehot, "On Enoch Arden" (1864; reprinted in Jump, *Tennyson: The Critical Heritage*), 282–293, especially 288–290.

8. Arthur Hallam, "Poems Chiefly Lyrical" (1831; reprinted in Jump, *Tennyson: The Critical Heritage*), 34–49. Also see Benjamin Jowett, 30 April 1858, in *The Letters of Alfred Lord Tennyson*, Cecil Y. Lang and Edgar Finley Shannon, Jr., 2 vols. (Cambridge, Mass.: Harvard University Press, 1981), 2: 198.

9. Eve Kosofsky Sedgwick, *Between Men: English Literature and Male Homosocial Desire* (New York: Columbia University Press, 1985), Ch. 7; Sandra M. Gilbert and Susan Gubar, *No Man's Land: The Place of the Woman Writer in the 20th Century, Volume 1: The War of the Words* (New Haven: Yale University Press, 1988), 3–11.

10. Goldwin Smith, "On *Maud*" (1855; reprinted in Jump, *Tennyson: The Critical Heritage*), 186–190.

11. See Sinfield, *Alfred Tennyson*, chapter 2.

12. For an important discussion of Tennyson's vexed relation with an aggressive masculinity, see Carol T. Christ, "Victorian Masculinity and the Angel in the House," in *A Widening Sphere*, ed. Martha Vicinus (Bloomington: Indiana University Press, 1977), 146–162. For distinctions between Victorian constructions of manliness and masculinity, see Marion Shaw, *Tennyson* (Atlantic Highlands, N.J.: Humanities Press International, 1988). On Tennyson and feminization, see Gerhard Joseph, *Weaving Tennyson*, forthcoming. On the state's institution of hegemonic masculinity and its marginalization of many alternative forms of masculinity as well as femininity, see R. W. Connell, *Gender and Power* (Stanford: Stanford University Press, 1987); and Jonathan Rutherford "Who's That Man," in *Male Order: Unwrapping Masculinity*, ed. Rowena Chapman and Jonathan Rutherford (London: Lawrence and Wishart, 1988), 21–67. On hegemonic control, see Robert Bocock, *Hegemony* (London: Tavistock, 1986), and Antonio Gramsci, *Selections from the Prison Notebooks*, ed. and trans. Quinton Hoare and Geoffrey Nowell Smith (New York: International, 1971).

13. See Sedgwick, *Between Men*, 133. Sinfield proposes a similar but more complicated model in *Alfred Tennyson*, with which I have fewer problems. See also Janet Wolff, *The Social Production of Art* (New York: New York University Press, 1981), 48–55. Following Terry Eagleton in his *Criticism and Ideology* (London: New Left Books, 1986), Wolff explicitly delineates a hierarchy of cultural mediations between artist and hegemony, but modifies the unidirectional and uninational appearance of the model.

14. For an explanation of classic realism and the kind of reader and reading it invites, see Catherine Belsey, *Critical Practice* (New York: Methuen, 1980), 67–70.

15. A Dwight Culler, *The Poetry of Tennyson* (New Haven: Yale University Press, 1977), 30–58.

16. Culler, *Poetry of Tennyson*, 38.

17. Christopher Ricks, ed., *The Poems of Tennyson*, 3 vols., 2nd ed. (Berkeley: University of California Press, 1987). All further references are from this edition with page numbers in parentheses.

18. Herbert F. Tucker, Jr., *Tennyson and the Doom of Romanticism* (Cambridge, Mass.: Harvard University Press, 1988), 12–30.

19. U. C. Knoepflmacher, "Tennyson and the Frame of Nonsense" (Paper delivered at the Modern Language Association Convention, San Francisco, December 1987), 3–4.

20. William Wordsworth, "Nutting," *English Romantic Writers*, ed. David Perkins (New York: Harcourt, Brace, and World, 1967), 212, lines 21, 45–48.

21. John Keats, "Sleep and Poetry," *English Romantic Writers*, 1130–1135, lines 107, 105, 108–109.

22. Keats, "Sleep and Poetry," 123, 119.

23. Tennyson, to Mrs. Gatty, 7 Oct. 1868 2: 504–505; Tennyson to Professor Blackie, 6 November, 1868, 2: 505; Tennyson to the Duke of Argyll, 26 March 1862, 2: 301, in *Letters of Tennyson*.

24. Frank Lentricchia, "Patriarchy Against itself—the Young Manhood of Wallace Stevens," *Critical Inquiry*, 13 (Summer 1987): 751.

25. Sinfield, *Alfred Tennyson*, 135.

26. For an analysis of the relationship between *Idylls of the King* and the feminization of culture, see Elliot Gilbert, "The Female King: Tennyson's Arthurian Apocalypse," *PMLA* 98 (October 1983):863–878.

27. See my "*Maud*, Masculinity, and Poetic Identity," *Criticism* 29 (Summer 1987):269–290, for a full working out of gender and "intersexuality" in this monodrama.

28. The ideology of this poem has been intelligently discussed by Sinfield in *Alfred Tennyson*; Sedgwick in *Between Men*; and Terry Eagleton in "Tennyson: Politics and Sexuality in *The Princess* and *In Memoriam*," in *1848: The Sociology of Literature*, ed. Francis Barker et al. (Essex: University of Essex Press, 1978), 97–106; as well as having been touched upon by Tucker, *Tennyson and Doom*. Tucker's emphasis, with which I agree, in contrast to Eagleton's, lies in the multiplicity of positions offered by this poem. He states: "A textbook Victorian compromise, the poem avoids taking a position on a hotly debated issue by taking up any number of positions, letting reciprocally ventilated views cool each other off, and leaving affairs pretty much where they stood" (351). See also Isobel Armstrong, whose exceptionally fine "Re-reading Victorian Poetry" came to my attention only after I had completed this essay (in *Dickens and other Victorians*, ed. Joanne Shattock (London: Macmillan Press, 1988), 123–143. Armstrong argues, rightly, for the reading of Victorian poetry through dialectic and ambiguity.

29. For a more extensive examination of textual excess and narrative codes, see Steven Cohan's and my *Telling Stories: A Theoretical Analysis of Narrative Fiction* (New York: Routledge, 1988), especially chapters 2 and 5.

30. Eagleton, "Tennyson: Politics and Sexuality," 101.

31. Eagleton, "Tennyson: Politics and Sexuality," 103.

32. Tennyson, as quoted in Ricks, *The Poems of Tennyson*, 2: 186.

33. Sinfield, *Alfred Tennyson*, 79–80.

34. Tennyson, Lincoln ms. of *In Memoriam*. The verse from which this heading comes occurs between 117 and 122. Reprinted in *The Poems of Tennyson*, 3:596.

35. Quoted in Christopher Ricks, *Tennyson* (New York: Collier, 1972), 212.

36. Quoted in Ricks, *Tennyson*, 221.

37. Ricks, *Tennyson*, 222.

38. Christopher Craft, "'Descend and Touch and Enter': Tennyson's Strange Manner of Address," *Genders* 1(March 1988):83–101. Craft deftly works out the tracings of homosexual desire in the elegy, arguing ultimately that the poem as a desire machine speaks against its own "submission to its culture's heterosexualizing conventions" (98).

39. Robert Monteith to Tennyson, 14 December 1833, *Letters of Tennyson* 1:103–104.

40. Benjamin Jowett, suppressed by Hallam Tennyson in his *Memoir*, as quoted in Ricks, *Tennyson*, 215. For an extended discussion of the critical and familial anxieties about gender issues in the elegy, see Ricks, *Tennyson*, 215–220.

41. See Julia Kristeva, *Revolution in Poetic Language* (1984); chapters 1–2, 5–10, and 12 are reprinted in *The Kristeva Reader*, ed. Toril Moi (New York: Columbia University Press, 1986), 113–123.

42. The heading is taken from "Merlin and Vivien," *The Poems of Tennyson*, 3:422, line 968.

43. Ricks, *Tennyson*, 276.

Brontë's Voices of Prophecy

Grants from the Rutgers Research Council and from the Graduate School, Rutgers/Newark assisted the work on this essay.

1. Reverend Patrick Brontë, *The Phenomenon or, An Account in Verse, of the Extraordinary Disruption of a Bog . . .* (Bradford: T. Inkersley, and London: F. Westley, 1824); *A Sermon Preached in the Church of Haworth, on Sunday, the 12th day of September, 1824, in Reference to an Earthquake, And Extraordinary Eruption of Mud and Water, That Had Taken Place Ten Days Before, in the Moors of that Chapelry* (Bradford: T. Inkersley, 1824); and *The Signs of the Times; or A Familiar Treatise on Some Political Indications in the Year 1835* (Keighley: R. Aked, 1835): all rpt. in *Brontëana: The Reverend Patrick Brontë, A. B., His Collected Works and Life*, ed. J. Horsfall Turner (Bingley: T. Harrison and Sons, 1898); 201–232. On Martin's influence see Winifred Gerin, *Charlotte Brontë: The Evolution of Genius* (Oxford: Oxford University Press, 1967), 43–49, 592; and Christine Alexander, *The Early Writings of Charlotte Brontë* (Oxford: Basil Blackwell, 1983), 234–236. Alexander notes the importance of Revelation (18).

2. Charlotte Brontë, *A Leaf from an Unopened Volume, or the Manuscript of an Unfortunate Author, edited by Lord Charles Albert Florian Wellesley* (17 January 1834); rpt. ed. Charles Lemon (Haworth: The Brontë Society, 1986).

3. Quoted from an unpublished manuscript, "Well here I am at Roe-Head" (Parsonage Museum Library), in Alexander, *Early Writings of Brontë*, 217, 243. Cf. Fannie Elizabeth Ratchford, *The Brontës' Web of Childhood* (New York: Columbia University Press, 1941), 108.

4. Ruth Y. Jenkins, "Reclaiming Myths of Power: Narrative Strategies of Nightingale, Brontë, Gaskell, and Eliot" (Ph.D. diss., SUNY Stonybrook, 1988), 23.

5. Alexander, *Early Writings of Brontë*, 230.

6. George P. Landow, "Aggressive (Re)interpretations of the Female Sage: Florence Nightingale's *Cassandra*," in *Victorian Sages and Cultural Discourse: Renegotiating Gender and Power*, ed. Thaïs E. Morgan (New Brunswick, N.J.: Rutgers University Press, 1990).

7. Summarizing his career in his final notes, Mikhail Bakhtin writes: "Quests for my own word are in fact quests for a word that is not my own, a word that is more than myself; this is a striving to depart from one's own words, with which nothing essential can be said"; "From Notes Made in 1970–71," *Speech Genres and Other Late Essays*, trans. Vern W. McGee, ed. Caryl Emerson and Michael Holquist (Austin: University of Texas Press, 1986), 149. Sue Lonoff cogently argues that the dialogically composed *devoirs* were crucial in Brontë's development, a missing link between the juvenilia and her adult novels; see "Charlotte Brontë's Belgian Essays: The Discourse of Empowerment," *Victorian Studies* 32 (1989): 387–409.

8. Charlotte Brontë, "Portrait de Pierre l'Hermite" (31 July 1842), rpt. in Elizabeth Cleghorn Gaskell,*The Life of Charlotte Brontë* (1857; rpt. London: Dent, and New York: Dutton, 1946), 155, 157.

9. Gerhard von Rad, *The Message of the Prophets*, trans. D.M.G. Stalker (Munich and Hamburg: Siebenstern Taschenbuch Verlag, 1967, and New York: Harper & Row, 1965), 13.

10. Carolyn De Swarte Gifford, "American Women and the Bible: The Nature of Woman as a Hermeneutical Issue," in *Feminist Perspectives on Biblical Scholarship*, ed. Adela Yarbro Collins (Chico, Calif.: Scholars Press, 1985), 16–19, 24–26.

11. Charlotte Brontë, "The Death of Moses" ("La Mort de Moïse"), rpt. in "More Bronté Devoirs," trans. Phyllis Bentley, *Bronté Society Transactions* 12 (1955): 366. Further citations from this essay are inserted parenthetically into my text. Gaskell's longer title was apparently taken from another manuscript of the Moses essay corrected by Heger that his family showed her (*Charlotte Bronté*, 157).

12. Heger criticized this excursus for pulling up the reins of imagination with reason (Gaskell, *Charlotte Bronté*, 158). But this was precisely what Robert Southey had told Charlotte to do, lest she unfit herself for womanly duties; see the Southey-Bronté letters (March 1837), in *The Brontës: Their Lives, Friendships and*

Correspondence, ed. Thomas James Wise and John Alexander Symington (Oxford: Shakespeare Head Press, 1932), 1:154–159.

13. George P. Landow, *Victorian Types, Victorian Shadows: Biblical Typology in Victorian Literature, Art, and Thought* (Boston: Routledge & Kegan Paul, 1980), 206–207, discusses Melvill.

14. Landow, *Victorian Types*, discusses the use of the Pisgah sight by Milton and a number of Victorian writers, without reference to gender difference (205–231).

15. Charlotte Brontë, "The Death of Napoleon" ("La Mort de Napoléon"), rpt. in "French Essays by Charlotte and Emily," trans. Margaret Lane, *Brontë Society Transactions* 12 (1954): 274–280. Further citations from this essay are inserted parenthetically into my text.

16. Charlotte Brontë, *Villette* (1853; London and Toronto: Dent, and New York: Dutton, 1957), 39. Further citations from this edition are inserted parenthetically into my text. The reader may also wish to consult *Villette*, ed. Herbert Rosengarten and Margaret Smith (Oxford: Clarendon Press, 1984).

17. Gaskell, *Charlotte Brontë*, 154.

18. See the "Canaanite" letter of 8 January 1845, alluding to Matt. 15:21–28, and the English postscript to the letter of 18 November 1845, alluding to Matt. 12:34 (cf. 15:19), in Wise and Symington, *The Brontës*, 2:23–24, 69.

19. Linda S. Kauffman discusses the transformation of Brontë the writer of amorous epistles into the novelist in *Discourses of Desire* (Ithaca: Cornell University Press, 1986), 160–201.

20. Barry V. Qualls discusses Brontë's debts to Carlyle in *The Secular Pilgrims of Victorian Fiction: The Novel as Book of Life* (Cambridge: Cambridge University Press, 1982), 43–84. For Brontë on Carlyle see, e.g., her letter to W. S. Williams (16 April 1849), in Wise and Symington, *The Brontës*, 2:326. In a separate essay I will take up the larger subject of Brontë's gendered revisions of Carylean mythopoesis in *Jane Eyre*. On this novel's fulfillment of "the Carylean project of inventing a new mythos out of the shards of the old," see Sarah Gilead, "Liminality and Antiliminality in Charlotte Brontë's Novels: *Shirley* Reads *Jane Eyre*," *Texas Studies in Literature and Language* 29 (1987): 302–322.

21. Charlotte Brontë, *Shirley, A Tale*, ed. Andrew and Judith Hook (1849; rpt. Harmondsworth: Penguin, 1977), 323. Further citations from this edition are inserted parenthetically into my text. Readers may also wish to consult *Shirley*, ed. Herbert Rosengarten and Margaret Smith (Oxford: Clarendon Press, 1979).

22. With further refinements that I do not observe here, Bakhtin distinguishes between ideologically *authoritative discourse* (privileged language outside us) and *internally persuasive discourse* ("backed up by no authority at all"), noting that they "may be united in a single word" but rarely are. This distinction is introduced by another in the realm of pedagogy, between "reciting by heart" and "retelling in

one's own words," the latter a "mixed" form of discourse that is not repetition but is "able when necessary to reproduce the style and expressions of the transmitted text"; see "Discourse in the Novel," in *The Dialogic Imagination*, trans. Caryl Emerson and Michael Holquist, ed. Michael Holquist (Austin: University of Texas Press, 1981), 341–342. Constantin Heger's educational method for the Brontë sisters was a variation on "retelling" in this sense; see Gaskell, *Charlotte Brontë*, 151–152. Discussing these terms, Caryl Emerson explains that for Bakhtin, recitation accepts "the language of others [as] authoritative . . . there can be no play with the framing context. . . . one cannot enter into dialogue with it" (for example, Sacred Writ); whereas retelling "is the only way we can *originate* anything verbally. . . . The struggle within us between these two modes of discourse, the authoritative and the internally persuasive, is what we recognize as intellectual and moral growth"; see "The Outer World and Inner Speech: Bakhtin, Vygotsky, and the Internalization of Language," *Critical Inquiry* 10 (1983): 255.

23. Discussing the divine call, Jenkins argues that Brontë resolved her adult spiritual crisis over Victorian proscription of women's God-given talents by "reclaiming sacred authority to deny her culture and justify her writing" ("Reclaiming Myths," 121, 114–115). Even when she is praising Ellen Nussey for her unostentatious way of finding "repose" in Scripture—"you can avail yourself of that hallowed communion, the Bible gives us with God"—Brontë uses the (Victorian evangelical) discourse of direct relation with the divine which prophetic women from the biblical Hannah to Sojourner Truth have drawn upon to justify action independent of men's mediations; see Brontë's letter of 5 May 1838 in Wise and Symington, *The Brontës*, 1:66. Irene Tayler treats the gendering of Brontë's muse in *Holy Ghosts: The Male Muses of Emily and Charlotte Brontë* (New York: Columbia University Press, 1990). In this essay I do not take up the problems and powers of Brontë's female muses nor her use of "pagan" muse figures.

24. Elizabeth Cady Stanton and the Revising Committee, *The Woman's Bible*, 2 vols. (1895, 1898; rpt. Seattle: Coalition Task Force on Women and Religion, 1986).

25. In "Answering as Authoring: Mikhail Bakhtin's Trans-Linguistics," Michael Holquist writes that "Bakhtin seems to have had a third ear that permitted him to hear differences where others perceived only sameness, especially in the apparent wholeness of the human voice. The obsessive question at the heart of Bakhtin's thought is always 'Who is talking?'" (*Critical Inquiry* 10 [1983]: 307). In "Who Speaks for Bakhtin?: A Dialogic Introduction" (*Critical Inquiry* 10 [1983]: 232), Gary Saul Morson's "Elle" character explains that Bakhtin and Vygotsky "conceive of thought as dialogues conducted with imagined addressees . . . who are always drawn from voices one has already heard. We *are* the voices that inhabit us. They conduct an unceasing dialogue, in which each of them intones values and

recalls contexts." Morson's "Moi" character says: "For Bakhtin, the creation of a self is the selection of one innerly persuasive voice from among the many voices you have learned, and that voice keeps changing every time it says something."

26. It should be noted that in the New Testament "prophecy" means preaching. In "Discourse in the Novel," Bakhtin discusses many kinds of "double-voiced discourse," or language which manifests its dialogical character, for example, by containing competing definitions of the same thing, or fostering an interplay between an earlier and a later self, or between different ideological views (434, 427), See the glossary in *The Dialogic Imagination* for these and other terms.

27. George P. Landow, "The Female Sage: Florence Nightingale and Cassandra" (Paper delivered at the Modern Language Association Convention, San Francisco, December 1987), 13. See also Landow, *Elegant Jeremiahs: The Sage from Carlyle to Mailer* (Ithaca, New York: Cornell University Press, 1986), 169–172.

28. Charlotte Brontë, *Jane Eyre: An Autobiography*, ed. Q. D. Leavis (1847; Harmondsworth: Penguin, 1987), 35. Page citations from this edition are inserted parenthetically into my text. The reader may also wish to consult the Norton Critical Edition of *Jane Eyre*, ed. Richard J. Dunn (New York: W. W. Norton, 1971).

29. John Holloway, *The Victorian Sage: Studies in Argument* (New York: W. W. Norton, 1953), 16–17; Landow, *Elegant Jeremiahs*, 23.

30. Landow, "Aggressive (Re)interpretations," in this collection.

31. Rebecca Fraser, *The Brontës: Charlotte Brontë and Her Family* (New York: Crown, 1988), 26. Brontë letter to W. S. Williams (21 Sept. 1849), in Wise and Symington, *The Brontës*, 3:24.

32. *Christian Remembrancer* 15 (April 1848): 396–409; rpt. in *The Brontës: The Critical Heritage*, ed. Miriam Allott (London and Boston: Routledge & Kegan Paul, 1974), 90.

33. Brontë letter to George Lewes (18 Jan. 1848), in Wise and Symington, *The Brontës*, 2:181.

34. Neither bloody revenge nor male militancy were precisely what Brontë later said she "did not like" about the *Jane Eyre* preface. She wrote it under the influence of current revolutionary fervor, she confessed somewhat cryptically to her publisher, and felt she had eulogized Thackeray in too "enthusiastic" a "manner" for praise of a living author. See letter to W. S. Williams (11 March 1848), in Wise and Symington, *The Brontës*, 2:198.

35. Michael Cotsell, "Overcoming the Personal, Getting the Girl," *Prose Studies* 10 (1987): 323.

36. *Christian Remembrancer*, in Allott, *Critical Heritage*, 90.

37. Carolyn Williams, "Closing the Book: The Intertextual End of *Jane Eyre*," in *Victorian Connections*, ed. Jerome McGann (Charlottesville: University Press of Virginia, 1989), 75–78.

38. Dayton Haskin, "Damning with Faint Praise: The Uses of Allusion at the Close of *Jane Eyre*" (Paper delivered at conference of the Mid-Hudson Modern Language Association, Poughkeepsie, N.Y., 1981).

39. In "Closing the Book," Williams discusses apostolic succession and notes Jane's contrast between earthly and heavenly marriage (see 83–84).

40. In mid-1836 Brontë wrote to Ellen Nussey that she dreaded "using a single phrase that sounds like religious cant" (Wise and Symington, *The Brontës*, 1:43; cf. Frazer, *Brontë and her Family*, 107). *Jane Eyre*'s valedictory conclusion bears traces of the author's internal debate on her own long respect for missionary heroes; one Belgian "imitation" she may have been rewriting critically here is "Lettre d'un Missionaire, Sierra Leone, Afrique" (apparently unpreserved; mentioned in Gaskell, *Charlotte Brontë*, 159).

41. See Reverend Brontë on young Charlotte's attitude toward the Bible, in Gaskell, *Charlotte Brontë*, 36. Michael Wheeler, whose argument differs from mine but planted some seeds for it, discusses a number of revisionary biblical allusions in *Jane Eyre*, in *The Art of Allusion in Victorian Fiction* (London and Basingstoke: Macmillan, 1979).

42. J. Keighley Snowden, "The Brontës as Artists and as Prophets," *Brontë Society Transactions* 4 (1909): 79.

43. On satire and the grotesque in sage writing, see Landow, *Elegant Jeremiahs*, 29–42, 73–75. The female writer emulating the biblical prophets' use of the grotesque challenges conventional associations of women with the beautiful, the harmonious, and the good. Victorian reviewers of *Jane Eyre* cast Currer Bell as a 'gender grotesque' because for them, as Kauffman puts it, "a woman writing is a contradiction in terms" (see *Discourses of Desire*, 173–175).

44. On these aspects of male sage writing see Holloway, *Victorian Sage*, 4–20; Landow, *Elegant Jeremiahs*, 132–153.

45. Von Rad, *Message*, 19.

46. Qualls, *Secular Pilgrims*, 51–52.

47. Brontë letter to W. S. Williams 28 Oct. 1847, in Wise and Symington, *The Brontës*, 2:151.

48. Qualls, *Secular Pilgrims*, 45. The second quoted phrase is from Frances Bartkowski, *Feminist Utopias* (Lincoln, Neb.: University of Nebraska Press, 1989), 5.

49. Allott, *Critical Heritage*, 25–26. See also reviews reprinted here on pages 88–92, 105–112, 119–121, 122–124. Charles Kingsley reported to Mrs. Gaskell his initial "disgust" with the clerical satire opening *Shirley*, which seemed written by someone "who liked coarseness" (letter of 14 May 1857, in *Charles Kingsley: His Letters and Memories of His Life*, ed. Mrs. Kingsley [Henry S. King, 1877], rpt. in "How Charles Kingsley Changed His Mind," *Brontë Society Transactions* 12 [1952]: 124). See also Mrs. [Sarah] Ellis's review of *Shirley* in *The Morning Call, a*

Table Book of Literature and Art (John Tallis, 1848), extracted by John Mitchell in "The 'Taste' of Charlotte Brontë," *Brontë Society Transactions* 14 (1962): 20–23.

50. Another authorizing text of general service to Victorian women is the parable of the talents in Matt. 25:14–30 (see Gaskell, *Charlotte Brontë*, 329; cf. *Shirley*, 385–386, and *Villette*, 329). For important variants and related sayings of Jesus which complicate the applicability of this parable for women, and to which Brontë alludes, see Matt. 25:1–13 (the foolish virgins), Luke 12:41–48 (the unfaithful servant), Luke 15:1–8 (the dishonest steward), and Luke 16:10–13.

51. Charlotte Brontë, "St. John in the Island of Patmos," in *Selected Brontë Poems*, ed. Edward Chitham and Tom Winnifrith (Oxford: Basil Blackwell, 1985), 6–8. Alexander connects this poem's visionary imagery with Brontë's Chief Genii voice in the juvenilia (*Early Writings of Brontë*, 241–242).

52. Williams, "Closing the Book," 66, 68, 67.

53. Von Rad, *Message*, 165.

54. Ibid., 18.

55. Landow, *Elegant Jeremiahs*, 73–115, expands upon and applies Ruskin's term to Victorian and modern sages.

56. Gary Saul Morson, "Tolstoy's Absolute Language," *Critical Inquiry* 7 (1981): 669. The last phrase is from Landow, "Aggressive (Re)interpretations," in the present volume.

57. Morson, "Tolstoy's Language," 676.

58. Bakhtin, *Dialogic Imagination*, 280. On the "internal dialogism of the word": "every word is directed toward an *answer* and cannot escape the profound influence of the answering word that it anticipates."

59. Jenkins discusses some differences between women's spiritual crisis-writing and men's—notably, the female accent on the polemical ("Reclaiming Myths," 120).

60. Virginia Woolf, "*Jane Eyre* and *Wuthering Heights*," in *The Common Reader* (New York: Harcourt, Brace, and World, 1925), 162.

61. I am endebted to Cora Kaplan for sharing with me her work in progress on *Jane Eyre*'s mobilizing of contemporary discourses on slavery, racial attitudes, missionary work, nation, and empire—the wider reach of Brontë's concerns as a Victorian sage which I have only noted in this essay.

Rossetti and Sage Discourse

1. Quoted by Mary Sandars, *The Life of Christina Rossetti* (London: Hutchinson, 1930), 267. The original of this letter is in the Spenser Collection, University of Kansas Library.

2. Anonymous, "Christina Rossetti's Poems," *Catholic World* 24 (Oct. 1876): 129.

3. Alice Meynell, "Christina Rossetti," *New Review* 12 (Feb. 1895): 206.

4. Anonymous, "The Late Miss Rossetti," [London] *Times* 7 Jan. 1895.

5. Paul Elmer More, "Christina Rossetti," *Atlantic Monthly* 94 (Dec. 1904): 820.

6. R. R. Bowker, "London as a Literary Centre," *Harper's New Monthly Magazine* 76 (1888): 827.

7. William Sharp, *Fortnightly Review* 45 (1 Mar. 1886): 427.

8. Anonymous, "Christina Rossetti," *The Nation* 66 (7 April 1898): 272.

9. Anonymous, *The Dial* 18 (16 Jan. 1895): 37.

10. An archdeacon quoted by Martha Vicinus, *Independent Women: Work and Community for Single Women, 1850–1920* (Chicago: University of Chicago Press, 1985), 74.

11. *The Complete Poems of Christina Rossetti*, ed. R. W. Crump, 3 vols. (Baton Rouge: Louisiana State University Press, 1979–1990), 1:76. Subsequent citations from this standard edition will appear parenthetically.

12. Joan N. Burstyn, *Victorian Education and the Ideal of Womanhood* (New Brunswick, N.J.: Rutgers University Press, 1984), 102.

13. Judith Lowder Newton, *Women, Power, and Subversion: Social Strategies in British Fiction, 1778–1860* (London: Methuen, 1981), 19–20.

14. Christina Rossetti, *Time Flies: A Reading Diary* (London: Society for Promoting Christian Knowledge, 1885), 36. Subsequent citations from this work will appear parenthetically.

15. The sequence of Rossetti's prose religious works is as follows: *Annus Domini: A Prayer for Each Day of the Year, Founded on a Text of Holy Scripture* (1874); *Seek and Find: A Double Series of Short Studies of the Benedicte* (1879); *Called to Be Saints: The Minor Festivals Devotionally Studied* (1881); *Letter and Spirit: Notes on the Commandments* (1883); *Time Flies* (1885); *The Face of the Deep: A Devotional Commentary on the Apocalypse* (1892). For a general discussion of the contents of these works, see P. G. Stanwood, "Christina Rossetti's Devotional Prose," in *The Achievement of Christina Rossetti*, ed. David Kent (Ithaca: Cornell University Press, 1988), 231–247 and Mackenzie Bell, *Christina Rossetti: A Biographical and Critical Study* (London: Thomas Burleigh, 1898), 285–318.

16. Christina Rossetti, *Seek and Find: A Double Series of Short Studies of the Benedicte* (London: Society for Promoting Christian Knowledge, 1879), 30. Subsequent citations from this edition will appear parenthetically.

17. Christina Rossetti, *The Face of the Deep: A Devotional Commentary on the Apocalypse* (London: Society for Promoting Christian Knowledge, 1892), 73. Subsequent citations from this text will appear parenthetically.

18. See Newton, *Women, Power, and Subversion,* 169; and Winston Weathers, "Christina Rossetti: The Sisterhood of Self," *Victorian Poetry* 3 (1965): 81–89.

19. Elaine Showalter, *A Literature of Their Own: British Women Novelists from Brontë to Lessing* (Princeton: Princeton University Press, 1977), 13–14.

20. Nancy Cott cited by Showalter, *Literature of Their Own,* 14.

21. *The Poetical Works of Christina Georgina Rossetti,* ed. W. M. Rossetti (London: Macmillan, 1904), lxiv.

22. Raymond Chapman, *Faith and Revolt: Studies in the Literary Influence of the Oxford Movement* (London: Weidenfield and Nicholson, 1970), 175–196.

23. George B. Tennyson, *Victorian Devotional Poetry* (Cambridge, Mass.: Harvard University Press, 1980).

24. Lona Mosk Packer, *Christina Rossetti* (Berkeley: University of California Press, 1963), 6.

25. Packer, *Rossetti,* 7

26. Georgina Battiscombe, *Christina Rossetti: A Divided Life* (New York: Holt, Rinehart, & Winston, 1981), 31.

27. Packer, *Rossetti,* 7.

28. Packer, *Rossetti,* 55.

29. In an undated, unpublished letter to her close friend Caroline Gemmer, Rossetti responds to a suggestion that she herself might have joined a sisterhood: "So you think I once trembled on 'the Convent Threshold'—Not seriously ever, tho' I went thro' a sort of romantic impression on the subject like many young people. No, I feel no drawing in that direction: really, of the two, I might perhaps have less unadaptedness in some ways to the hermit life. But I suppose the niche really suited to me is the humble family nook I occupy; nor am I hankering after a loftier. Nor, I think I may truly say, did I ever wish to devote myself at any period of my prolonged life. It was my dear sister who had the pious, devotional, absorbed temperament: not I. How enviable she seems now" (Koch Collection, Pierpont Morgan Library, New York, New York).

30. Vicinus, *Independent Women,* 74.

31. Packer, *Rossetti,* 304.

32. Vicinus, *Independent Women,* 48.

33. Vicinus, *Independent Women,* 83.

34. Quoted by Vicinus, *Independent Women,* 81.

35. John Shelton Reed, " 'A Female Movement': The Feminization of Nineteenth-Century Anglo-Catholicism," *Anglican and Episcopal History* 57 (1988), 229.

36. Quoted by Reed, " 'A Female Movement,' " 238.

37. Reed, " 'A female Movement,' " 230–231.

38. Quoted by Reed, " 'A Female Movement,' " 203.

39. Reed, " 'A Female Movement,' " 213.

40. Christina Rossetti, *Letter and Spirit: Notes on the Commandments* (London: Society for Promoting Christian Knowledge, 1883), 43. The subsequent reference to this work will appear parenthetically. Significantly, Rossetti always refers only to mothers when discussing 'filial' relations. She was extraordinarily close to her own mother and dedicated two of her books of religious commentary to her.

41. For a discussion of Rossetti's love poems, see my *Christina Rossetti in Context* (Chapel Hill: University of North Carolina Press, 1988), 89–186.

42. Quoted in Bell, *Christina Rossetti*, 111.

43. Quoted in Bell, *Christina Rossetti*, 111–112, my italics.

44. See, for instance, not only "Goblin Market," but also "The Convent Threshold," " 'No, Thank You, John,' " "Wife to Husband," "Twice," "An Apple-Gathering," "Grown and Flown," and "Love Lives Bleeding."

45. See "Goblin Market," in which the fathers of the apparently female children of the sisters Laura and Lizzie are, at the end of the poem, conspicuously absent; "Noble Sisters," in which a Lizzie-figure tries but seems unable to prevent her sister from pursuing a misguided love; "The Lowest Room," in which one aspiring sister learns humility and patience from her more domestic counterpart and thereby hopes, by being "last" in this life, to become "first" in the next; "Maiden-Song" and "Songs in a Cornfield," in which—as Weathers has noted—sisters "sing" each other home, attaining a kind of spiritual harmony and unity despite the physical separation their respective marriages require; and, of course, "A Triad," in which a kind of sisterhood in unfulfillment is realized.

The Trouble with Romola

1. Mathilde Blind, *George Eliot* (Boston: Little, Brown, and Company, 1904), 206.

2. Anne Fremantle, *George Eliot* (London: Duckworth, 1933), 110–111.

3. Carole Robinson, "*Romola*: A Reading of the Novel," *Victorian Studies* 6 (1962): 41.

4. Sandra M. Gilbert and Susan Gubar, *The Madwoman in the Attic: The Woman Writer and the Nineteenth-Century Literary Imagination* (New Haven: Yale University Press, 1979), 494.

5. Margaret Homans, *Bearing the Word: Language and Female Experience in Nineteenth-Century Women's Writing* (Chicago: The University of Chicago Press, 1986), 190, 196, 197.

6. U.C. Knoepflmacher, *George Eliot's Early Novels: The Limits of Realism* (Berkeley: University of California Press, 1968), 5.

7. George P. Landow, in *Elegant Jeremiahs: The Sage from Carlyle to Mailer*

(Ithaca: Cornell University Press, 1986), provides an illuminating account of the genre of sage- or wisdom-writing as characterized by the writer's self-presentation as "master and true possessor of language" (144).

8. Mary Jacobus, *Reading Woman: Essays in Feminist Criticism* (New York: Columbia University Press, 1986), 27.

9. Jacobus, *Reading Woman*, 29.

10. Felicia Bonaparte, *The Triptych and the Cross: The Central Myths of George Eliot's Poetic Imagination* (New York: New York University Press, 1979); Mary Wilson Carpenter, *George Eliot and the Landscape of Time* (Chapel Hill: University of North Carolina Press, 1986).

11. Carole Robinson notes, for example, that "the motif of choice is essential to *Romola*. Criticism deals with it always where it is dullest, in relation to Tito" ("*Romola*: A Reading," 30). In his useful introduction to the Penguin edition, Andrew Sanders comments that "Tito Melema is the most vivid character in *Romola*," while Romola is "a sober if archetypal George Eliot heroine" (George Eliot, *Romola* [Harmondsworth: Penguin, 1980], 27).

12. Kaja Silverman, *The Acoustic Mirror* (Bloomington: Indiana University Press, 1988), 120–122, 216.

13. Eliot, *Romola*, 85. All further references to the novel will be to the Penguin edition and will be cited parenthetically.

14. Figure 1, *The Blind Scholar and his Daughter*, by Frederick Leighton is for *Romola, Cornhill Magazine*, (July 1862). Leighton not only surrounds Romola's head with a nimbus of light, but also represents her as ascendant over the darkened, bent figure of her father.

15. For the now classic explanation of the function of the female figure as fetishized object in patriarchal narrative, see Laura Mulvey, "Visual Pleasure and Narrative Cinema," *Screen* 17 (1975): 6–18.

16. Silverman, *Acoustic Mirror*, 137; Jacques Lacan, *Feminine Sexuality: Jacques Lacan and the école freudienne*, eds. Juliet Mitchell and Jacqueline Rose (New York: W. W. Norton, 1982), 38, 74–85. See also "Fetishism" in Sigmund Freud, *Sexuality and the Psychology of Love*, ed. Philip Rieff (New York: Collier Books, 1963), 214–219.

17. Jane Gallop, "Reading the Mother Tongue: Psychoanalytic Feminist Criticism" *Critical Inquiry* 13 (Winter, 1987): 328.

18. Naomi Schor, "Female Fetishism: The Case of George Sand," in *The Female Body in Western Culture*, ed. Susan Rubin Suleiman (Cambridge, Mass.: Harvard University Press, 1985, 1986), 368. See also Elizabeth Berg, "The Third Woman," *Diacritics* 12 (1982): 11–20.

19. In the text which "interrupted" the writing of *Romola*, *Silas Marner*, the same

fetishistic golden hair appears, this time transferred to the head of a very Oedipal little girl but also suggesting the mark of a female authorial subject.

20. Heinz Kohut, *The Analysis of the Self* (Madison: International Universities Press, 1971), 37. Kohut does not theorize the psychic apparatus as unitary or coherent, but assumes the subject's construction of a "self" experienced as "coherent" and "firm" to be therapeutic.

21. Although I use the term women readers, I should note that the group to which I refer is probably very homogeneous—predominantly, if not exclusively, white and middle-class.

22. "I know no medium: I never in my life have known any medium in my dealings with positive, hard characters, antagonistic to my own, between absolute submission and determined revolt" (Charlotte Brontë, Jane Eyre, Norton Critical Edition, 2nd ed., ed. Richard J. Dunn [New York: Norton, 1987], 352).

23. Nancy Chodorow, *The Reproduction of Mothering: Psychoanalysis and the Sociology of Gender* (Berkeley: University of California Press, 1978).

24. Figure 2, *The Woman Clothed with the Sun*, from *Pictorial Illustrations of the Old and New Testaments by Westall and Martin* with descriptions by The Rev. Hobart Caunter, B.D. (London: Henry G. Bohn, York Street, Covent Garden, 1838, no. 142. Caunter's commentary on this illustration summarizes Protestant interpretations of this figure in the "continuous historical" school, which understood the Book of Revelation as a "mirror" of all history (see Carpenter, *George Eliot and the Landscape of Time*, Ch. 1). In his *Lectures on the Apocalypse* (Cambridge & London: Macmillan & Co., 1861), the Broad Church minister F. D. Maurice (a good friend of George Eliot and George Henry Lewes) interpreted the "woman clothed with the sun" as a symbol of the Comtean vision of an "old world which was passing away, and the new world which was commencing," referring to the old (male) world of individual heroism, and the new one to be characterized by feminine (social) values (208).

25. Figure 3, Tintoretto, *Michael Fights the Dragon*, in *The Bible in Art: Twenty Centuries of Famous Bible Paintings* ed. Clifton Harby Levy (New York: Covici Friede, circa 1936). In this sixteenth-century representation of Revelation 12, Michael's phallic combat with the dragon occupies the foreground while the "woman clothed with the sun" is positioned both above and behind the action, which she watches serenely but passively. By contrast, in the nineteenth-century British illustration (Fig. 2), she is ascendant over the dragon, whose smaller serpentine curves and circles are dominated and partially contained by the circular structures of her sun and moon.

26. Dianne F. Sadoff reads Romola as a figure for the young Mary Anne Evans in *Monsters of Affection: Dickens, Eliot, and Brontë on Fatherhood* (Baltimore:

Johns Hopkins University Press, 1982), 92, while Homans' in her reading of Romola as a figure for the Virgin Mary treats her as a mother (*Bearing the Word*, Ch. 8).

27. Silverman, *Acoustic Mirror*, 76.

28. Silverman, *Acoustic Mirror*, 74.

29. Elizabeth Barrett Browning, *Aurora Leigh* (London: The Women's Press, 1978); 389.

30. George Eliot, *Westminster Review* 67 (January 1857): 307. See also Gordon S. Haight, *George Eliot* (Oxford: Oxford University Press, 1968), 185, 225.

31. Robinson, "*Romola*: A Reading," 40; Gillian Beer, *George Eliot* (Bloomington: Indiana University Press, 1986), 122.

32. *The George Eliot Letters*, ed. Gordon S. Haight (New Haven: Yale University Press, 1954–1955) 4: 104.

33. Rev. 12. King James (Authorized Version) Bible.

34. The narrative takes care to note that Romola herself has been inspired to "drift away" by a story she has read about another woman who takes that action (588). Had she not read that other woman's story, the narrative suggests, she might not have "written" her own life in that way.

35. Haight, *George Eliot*, 6.

36. See Ruby Redinger, *George Eliot: The Emergent Self* (New York: Alfred A. Knopf, 1975), 37.

37. In one of Kohut's examples of an "idealizing transference," an analysand's narcissistic vulnerability is traced to the instability of his relationship with his mother in early childhood, especially after the birth and almost immediate death of her twin sons when he was three years old (*Analysis of the Self*, 85).

38. Freud, *The Ego and the Id*, trans. Joan Riviere and James Strachey (New York: Norton, 1962), 23.

39. Sadoff, *Monsters of Affection*, 92, 94.

40. Beer, *George Eliot*, 121.

41. George Eliot, *The Mill on the Floss* (Boston: Houghton Mifflin Co., Riverside edition, 1961), 253.

42. Michael S. Roth, "Remembering Forgetting: *Maladies de la Mémoire* in Nineteenth-Century France," *Representations* 26 (1989): 57–60.

43. Barrett Browning, *Aurora Leigh*, 224.

44. Dolores Rosenblum, "Face to Face: Elizabeth Barrett Browning's 'Aurora Leigh' and Nineteenth-Century Poetry," *Victorian Studies* 26 (1983): 321–338.

45. The very excellence of the Penguin edition cited here, which translates all foreign language statements in the notes, may actually defeat the author's purpose.

46. Quoted in Haight, *George Eliot*, 365.

Ruskin and the Matriarchal Logos

1. The most interesting of these attempts is made by George P. Landow in *Elegant Jeremiahs: The Sage from Carlyle to Mailer* (Ithaca: Cornell University Press, 1986). The best way to redefine a patriarchal genre is, of course, to include women in the canon: Landow, for example, treats Joan Didion as a twentieth-century sage. In the present essay I have limited myself to examining patriarchal attitudes in male writers.

2. Quoted in Park Honan, *Matthew Arnold* (New York: McGraw-Hill, 1981), 60.

3. John Ruskin, *The Winnington Letters*, ed. Van Akin Burd (Cambridge: Harvard University Press. 1969), 23. In my remarks about Winnington, I am deeply indebted to Professor Burd's admirable edition and to his introductory essay. For the meaning of Winnington and Rose LaTouche for Ruskin's writing, see John Rosenberg, *The Darkening Glass: A Portrait of Ruskin's Genius* (New York: Columbia University Press, 1961), 160–166.

4. *Letters*, 35–36.

5. Ruskin to John James Ruskin, 11 March 1859, *Letters*, 99–100.

6. Ruskin to John James Ruskin, 13 March 1859, *Letters*, 104.

7. Ruskin to Bell, 22 March 1859, *Letters*, 120–121.

8. John Ruskin, *Works* (Library Edition), ed. E.T. Cooke and Alexander Wedderburn, 39 vols. (London: George Allen, 1903–1912), 18: 346.

9. Ruskin, *Works* 19: 235.

10. For a while the only attempt to defend "Of Queen's Gardens" against Kate Millett's well-known attack was David Sonstroem's "Millet Versus Ruskin: "Of Queen's Gardens,' " *Victorian Studies* 20 (1977), 283–297, which looks convincing until one returns to the text and finds the phrases Sonstroem omits. More recently and more subtly in *The Woman and the Demon: The Life of a Victorian Myth* (Cambridge, Mass.: Harvard University Press, 1982), Nina Auerbach compares the language of "Of Queens' Gardens" and "Of Kings' Treasuries" to show that Ruskin's verbs accord far more activity to the female than to the male governers. She concludes: "Ruskin's essay shows how shallow the roots of patriarchal percepts were in contrast to their rich foundation of mythic perception" (61). Ruskin's male supremacism surely masked a deep fear of female power—as with thousands of his contemporaries. My own reading contains no appeals to the power of the mythic, however.

11. Ruskin, *Works* 17: 123.

12. Nancy Armstrong, *Desire and Domestic Fiction* (Oxford University Press, 1987), 59.

13. Catherine Gallagher, *The Industrial Reformation of English Fiction* (Chicago: University of Chicago Press, 1985), 119–120. Gallagher valuably cites "Of Queens' Gardens" as an example of the merging of Tory paternalism and "domestic ideology" (126), the view that state and home should have parallel hierarchical structures.

14. See my *Ruskin's Poetic Argument: The Design of the Major Works* (Ithaca: Cornell University Press, 1985), Chapter 10.

15. Ruskin, *Works* 18: 144.

16. Terry Eagleton, *The Ideology of the Aesthetic* (Oxford: Basil Blackwell, 1990), 20.

17. Eagleton, *Ideology,* 58–59.

18. Ruskin, *Works* 19: 400.

19. In his well-known essay, Freud interprets the myth of the decapitated Medusa in terms of castration anxiety. According to Freud, a boy sees his mother's genitals and believes her to have been castrated, and this initiates his own fear of castration. See "Medusa's Head" (1922), reprinted in *Sexuality and the Psychology of Love*, ed. Philip Rieff (New York: Macmillan, 1963), 212–213. In my reading of Ruskin's Gorgan-Athena, the castrated being and the agent of castration are combined in a single figure of female aggression. James Eli Adams has treated the figure of the Gorgonian woman in terms of Victorian anxieties about social change in his " 'Red in Tooth and Claw': Nature and the Feminine in Tennyson and Darwin," *Victorian Studies* 33 (1989):7–27. For a recent feminist treatment of a similar figure, see Mary Jacobus, "Judith, Holofernes, and the Phallic Woman," in her *Reading Woman: Essays in Feminist Criticism* (New York: Columbia University Press, 1986), 110–136.

20. Passages like this became common in Ruskin's wasteland writings of the 1870s, particularly in *Fors Clavigera,* his series of letters addressed to the "workmen and labourers of England." Here he divides the female world between the goddess "Fors" or "Fate," who stalks a guilty and polluted latter-day civilization, and the angelic girl-child, whom he here calls St. Ursula and who inhabits garden-spots and other places sacred to a lovelier, more orderly past.

21. Auerbach's reading, once again, differs from mine: "the salvation offered by Ruskin's Athena is not an insipid benediction of the status quo, but the afflatus of a revolutionary new-old force that liberates the sacred from convention while restoring its power of terror" (*Woman and the Demon*, 76).

22. An example of this sort of kinder, gentler nation is of course *Idylls of the King.* (See, for example, Elliot Gilbert, "The Female King: Tennyson's Arthurian Apocalypse," *PMLA* 98 [1982]: 863–878.) But what is "feminine" in Tennyson's Camelot is not "female" power per se but a social order that uses hegemonic persuasion instead of naked force, and runs the usual risk of permissiveness. When

the social order seems to fail, its degeneration can similarly be represented as feminine. See Sandra Siegel, "Literature and Degeneration: The Representation of 'Decadence,' " in *Degeneration: The Dark Side of Progress*, ed. Sander Gilman and J. Edward Chamberlain (New York: Columbia University Press, 1985).

Visions of Female Sages and Sorceresses

1. Recent interpretations include Susan P. Casteras, *Images of Victorian Womanhood in English Art* (London: Associated University Presses, 1987) and also Lynda Nead, *Myths of Sexuality: Representations of Women in Victorian Britain* (Oxford: Basil Blackwell, 1988).

2. There is, for example, only a brief discussion of this strand of imagery in Jan Marsh, *Pre-Raphaelite Women* (London: Weldenfeld & Nicolson, 1987), 109–120. A different aspect is treated in Joseph A. Kestner, *Mythology and Misogyny: The Social Discourse of Nineteenth-Century British Classical-Subject Painting* (Madison: University of Wisconsin Press, 1989).

3. See, for example, Lène Dresen-Coenders, ed., *Saints and She-Devils: Images of Women in the 15th and 16th Centuries* (London: The Rubicon Press Ltd., 1987) and Jane P. Davidson, *The Witch in Northern European Art 1470–1750* (Freren: Luca Verlag, 1987).

4. Dresen-Coenders, *Saints and She-Devils*, 59–82.

5. On the personification of Brittania, see especially Marina Warner, *Monuments and Maidens: The Allegory of the Female Form* (London: Pan Books Ltd., 1987), 38–42, 124–126.

6. Marsh, *Pre-Raphaelite Women*, 110.

7. Dante Gabriel Rossetti, "Body's Beauty," Sonnet 78 from *The House of Life* series in *Ballads and Sonnets* (London: Ellis and White, 1881), 240.

8. F. G. Stephens, *Dante Gabriel Rossetti* (London: Seeley and Co., Ltd., 1894), 69.

9. For a general discussion of the erotic meanings and exoticism of this painting, see Virginia Mae Allen, " 'One Strangling Golden Hair': Dante Gabriel Rossetti's *Lady Lilith*," *The Art Bulletin* 66 (June 1984): 285–294; and letters to the editor on this article in *The Art Bulletin* 67 (June 1985): 317–324.

10. Tate Gallery, *The Pre-Raphaelites* (London: The Tate Gallery, 1985), 291.

11. Tate Gallery, *Pre-Raphaelites*, 290.

12. Tate Gallery, *Pre-Raphaelites*, 290.

13. These lines accompanied the painting in the catalogue when *Medea the Sorceress* was exhibited at the Royal Academy in 1888.

14. On the Lady of Shalott and some of its various permutations of form and

meaning, see Bell Gallery, *Ladies of Shalott: A Victorian Masterpiece and Its Contexts* (Providence, R.I.: Brown University, 1985).

15. Debra Mancoff, "The Arthurian Revival in Victorian Painting" (Ph.D. diss., Northwestern University, 1982), 558. This is the most useful source on Victorian images of Tennyson's "Idylls." For literary contexts especially, see also Christopher Baswell and William Sharpe, eds., *The Passing of Arthur: New Essays in Arthurian Tradition* (New York: Garland Publishing, 1988); Mary Flowers Braswell and John Buggen, eds., *The Arthurian Tradition: Essays in Convergence* (Tuscaloosa: University of Alabama Press, 1988); and Norris J. Lacy, ed., *The Arthurian Encyclopedia* (New York: Peter Bedrick, 1986).

16. On the interrelationship of these Arthurian figures and their ultimate derivation from Celtic mythology and fertility deities, see Myra Mahlow Olstead, "The Role and Evolution of the Arthurian Enchantress" (Ph.D. diss., University of Florida, 1959).

17. Bram Dijkstra, *Idols of Perversity: Fantasies of Feminine Evil in Fin-de-siècle Culture* (Oxford: Oxford University Press, 1986), 305, 325.

18. Dijkstra, *Idols,* 314.

19. The poem and the wood engraving were published in *Once A Week,* 30 Nov. 1861.

20. The daphne flower is identified in Mancoff, "Arthurian Revival," 464.

21. Extract from a 21 January 1875 letter by John Ruskin to F. S. Ellis, in *The Works of John Ruskin,* ed. E. T. Cook and Alexander Wedderburn, (London: George Allen, 1903–1912), 37: 155.

22. On the notion of embowerment and walls restraining femmes fatales, see Susan P. Casteras, "Rossetti's Embowered Females in Art, of Love Enthroned and 'The Lamp's Shrine,' " *Nineteenth Century Studies* 2 (1988): 27–52.

23. On oral fixations and related motifs see Dijkstra, *Idols,* 294, 310.

24. Nina Auerbach, *Woman and the Demon: The Life of a Victorian Myth* (Cambridge: Harvard University Press), 2.

25. This point is also made in Mancoff, "Arthurian Revival," 495.

26. An interesting caricature drawn circa 1870 by Burne-Jones of Maria Zambaco and himself supports this idea and is illustrated in Marsh, *Pre-Raphaelite Women,* 114.

27. Distinctions between the French and English versions of the tale are made in Mancoff, "Arthurian Revival," 515–516. In the French version there is also a moment when Merlin and Nimue pause in their travels through the forest of Broceliane to rest under a white hawthorn tree, as in Burne-Jones's picture, rather than under an oak as in Tennyson's poem.

28. Alfred Lord Tennyson, "Merlin and Vivien," book 8 in "Idylls of the King" in

The Works of Tennyson (New York: The Macmillan Co., 1925), 376. All subsequent citations to this work will be parenthetical in the text.

29. "The Grosvenor Gallery Exhibition," *The Athenaeum* 50 (1877): 584.

30. Marsh, *Pre-Raphaelite Women*, 118.

31. Mancoff, "Arthurian Revival," 517.

32. Mancoff, "Arthurian Revival," 517.

33. Dijkstra, *Idols*, 306–307.

34. Petrification was also a common punishment and a sign of the ability of a sorceress to alter the very landscape with her potent magic. The magical connotations of the stone and circle forms are examined in Janet and Colin Bord, *The Secret Country: An Interpretation of the Folklore of Ancient Sites in the British Isles* (New York: Walker & Co., 1976), 33. Other recent handbooks include John Wilcox, *A Guide to Occult Britain: The Quest for Magic in Pagan Britain* (London: Sidgwick & Jackson, Ltd., 1976).

35. Leslie A. Shepard, ed., *Encyclopedia of Occultism and Parapsychology* (Detroit: Gale Research Co., 1978), 2: 552. This is a useful source for many descriptions of the accessories and meanings of magic and witchcraft.

36. Warner, *Monuments*, 109.

37. Useful discussions of specifically British witchcraft (including some Victorian persecutions of alleged witches) and folklore traditions include Wallace Notestein, *A History of Witchcraft in England from 1558 to 1718* (New York: Russell & Russell, 1911); A.D.J. MacFarlane, *Witchcraft in Tudor and Stuart England* (London: Routledge and Kegan Paul, Ltd., 1970); Keith Thomas, *Religion and the Decline of Magic* (London: Weidenfeld & Nicolson, 1971); and Christina Hole, *Witchcraft in Britain* (London: B.T. Batsford, 1977).

38. Female madness and its cultural connotations are analyzed in Sandra M. Gilbert and Susan Gubar, *The Madwoman in the Attic: The Woman Writer and the Nineteenth-Century Literary Imagination* (New Haven: Yale University Press, 1978); Phyllis Chesler, *Women and Madness* (Garden City, N.Y.: Doubleday Press, 1972); George F. Drinker, *The Birth of Neurosis: Myth, Malady, and the Victorians* (New York: Simon & Schuster, 1984); and also Elaine Showalter, *The Female Malady: Women, Madness, and English Culture, 1830–1980* (New York: Penguin Books, 1987).

39. See especially Showalter, *Female Malady*, 129–134, 147–162.

40. A provocative analysis of the magician as artist metaphor can be found in Anya Taylor, *Magic and English Romanticism* (Athens, Ga.: The University of Georgia Press, 1979).

Harriet Martineau

1. Harriet Martineau, *Household Education* (London: Edward Moxon, 1849), 238; *Autobiography*, 2 vols. (1877; rpt. London: Virago, 1983). Subsequent citations to these works will be parenthetical. In her *Autobiography*, Martineau describes the parts more fully as "the Proposition . . . then the Reason, and the Rule; the Example, ancient and modern; then the Confirmation; and finally, the Conclusion" (1: 63–64). Though I have found no direct source for this particular list, it represents a nineteenth-century variation on the seven-part arrangement of classical rhetoricians, perhaps as filtered through Hugh Blair's *Lectures on Rhetoric* (1783).

2. Martineau, "Preface," *Illustrations of Political Economy*, 9 vols. (London: Charles Fox, 1834), 1: ix.

3. Elsewhere, Martineau expresses admiration for Edgeworth's literary achievement, as well as deep pity for the limitations she endured. In a letter to Fanny Wedgwood dated 23 June 1867, Martineau writes of "the exquisite beauty of M. E's spirit and temper,—the thorough generosity of her whole long domestic life,—the exemption from the worst and most provoking faults of literary women,—and yet—the dreary worldliness and lowness in which she was held down, in spite of all possible capacity for aspiration, and of a temperament made up of enthusiasm! It is one of the most pathetic spectacles that ever came before me,—her life as it was in comparison with what it should have been" *(Harriet Martineau's Letters to Fanny Wedgwood*, ed. Elisabeth Sanders Arbuckle [Stanford: Stanford University Press, 1983], 286).

4. Martineau, "An Autobiographic Memoir," in *Harriet Martineau on Women*, ed. Gayle Graham Yates (New Brunswick, N.J.: Rutgers University Press, 1985), 39.

5. See my discussion of Martineau's self-interpretation in *Victorian Autobiography: The Tradition of Self-Interpretation* (New Haven: Yale University Press, 1986), 135–143.

6. George P. Landow, *Elegant Jeremiahs: The Sage from Carlyle to Mailer* (Ithaca: Cornell University Press, 1986), 28–29.

7. For theories of the intellectual's relation to society, see Deirdre David's *Intellectual Women and Victorian Patriarchy: Harriet Martineau, Elizabeth Barrett Browning, George Eliot* (Ithaca, N.Y.: Cornell University Press. 1987), 1–14. David sees Martineau not as an "alienated" but as an "organic" intellectual—as one who accompanies a social group in its rise to power. Following Julia Kristeva and other modern theorists, we might also associate the rhetorical marks of the sage with the "semiotic" or the "feminine"—that is, with a mode of discourse that opposes hegemonic patriarchy. See Kristeva's *Revolution in Poetic Language*, trans. Margaret Waller (New York: Columbia University Press, 1984), as well as

the discussions of Kristeva, Cixous, and others in *Feminist Literary Theory: A Reader*, ed. Mary Eagleton (Oxford: Basil Blackwell, 1986), 200–237. I take up Martineau's resistance to being "alienated" and "feminized" below.

8. Excerpts from these three theorists are collected in Eagleton, *Feminist Theory*, 208–213.

9. *The Positive Philosophy of Auguste Comte*, trans. Harriet Martineau, in *Auguste Comte and Positivism: The Essential Writings*, ed. Gertrude Lenzer (New York: Harper Torchbooks, 1975), 73.

10. Because Martineau wrote the *Autobiography* in 1855 on what she thought was her deathbed, it does not treat the last twenty years of her life.

11. I discuss Martineau's systematic replacement of Comtean for biblical models in *Victorian Autobiography*, 135–155.

12. The term "logocentric" is used by Terry Eagleton in *Literary Theory: An Introduction* (Oxford: Basil Blackwell, 1983) to describe those discourses that believe in their accessibility to the "full truth and the presence of things" (131–132).

13. On the form of the hypothetical syllogism, see Winifred Bryan Horner, *Rhetoric in the Classical Tradition* (New York: St. Martin's Press, 1988), 142–144.

14. Charlotte Brontë, *Jane Eyre*, ed. Q. D. Leavis (Harmondsworth: Penguin Books, 1966), 141.

15. Landow, *Elegant Jeremiahs*, 164–172.

16. Landow, *Elegant Jeremiahs*, 160.

17. Vera Wheatley gives this estimate in *The Life and Work of Harriet Martineau* (Fair Lawn, N.J.: Essential Books, 1957), 276, but it is implicit in many critics' treatment of *Household Education* as a minor work, a "dress rehearsal for the more systematic personal reminiscences in the *Autobiography*" (Gillian Thomas, *Harriet Martineau* [Boston: Twayne, 1985], 65).

18. Elaine Showalter, "Feminist Criticism in the Wilderness," *Critical Inquiry* 8 (Winter 1981), rpt. in *The New Feminist Criticism: Essays on Women, Literature, and Theory*, ed. Elaine Showalter (New York: Pantheon Books, 1985), 243–270.

19. See the "Summary of Principles illustrated in the first Volume," in *Illustrations of Political Economy* (London: Charles Fox, 1834), 1: xix. This edition moves to the fore what in the original edition had been affixed at the end.

20. See Henry George Atkinson, FGS, and Harriet Martineau, *Letters on the Laws of Man's Nature and Development* (London: John Chapman, 1851), as well as Martineau's extensive discussion of the work in the *Autobiography* 2: 328–370.

21. Martineau, "An Autobiographic Memoir," 48.

22. David, *Intellectual Women*, 32

23. David, *Intellectual Women*, 6.

24. Patricia Meyer Spacks, *Gossip* (New York: Alfred Knopf, 1985), 41. In this

discussion Spacks paraphrases and quotes from late seventeenth and eighteenth century treatises.

25. Martineau, "On Female Education," *Monthly Repository* 18 (1823): 77–81.

Morris and Socialist-Feminism

1. Several other authors have discussed Morris's views of women, among them Norman Talbot, "Women and Goddesses in the Romances of William Morris," *Southern Review* (Adelaide), 3 (1969):339–357; Carole Silver, "Myth and Ritual in the Last Romances of William Morris," in *Studies in the Late Romances of William Morris: Papers Presented at the Annual Meeting of the Modern Language Association, December 1975,* ed. Carole Silver and Joseph R. Dunlap (New York: William Morris Society, 1976) 117–139; Carole Silver, "Socialism Internalized: The Last Romances of William Morris," in *Socialism and the Literary Artistry of William Morris,* ed. Florence S. Boos and Carole Silver (Columbia, Mo.: University of Missouri Press, 1990) 117–126; John Moore "The Vision of the Feminine in William Morris's *Water of the Wondrous Isles,*" *Pre-Raphaelite Review* 3 (1980): 58–85; Norman Kelvin, "The Erotic in *News from Nowhere* and *The Well at the World's End,*" in *Studies in the Late Romances,* 97–114; Florence S. Boos, "Sexual Polarization in William Morris' *The Defence of Guenevere,*" *Browning Institute Studies* 13 (1985): 181–200; and Florence S. Boos, "Justice and Vindication in 'The Defence of Guenevere,'" in *King Arthur Through the Ages,* ed. Valerie M. Lagorio and Mildred L. Day, vol. 2 (Garland: New York and London, 1990), 83–104. See also Charlotte Oberg, "The Female Principle," ch. 3 of *William Morris: The Pagan Prophet* (Charlottesville: University of Virginia Press, 1978), 53–70.

2. George P. Landow, *Elegant Jeremiahs: The Sage from Carlyle to Mailer* (Ithaca N.Y.: Cornell University Press, 1986), 28–29. Of the major Victorian essayists, however, only Carlyle and, to a lesser degree, Ruskin, arguably satisfy most of Landow's seven-part characterization of the Victorian sage. Morris, for example, never attacks his audience (the second of Landow's characteristics); or dilates on "grotesque contemporary phenomena, such as the murder of children" (the fifth). Morris's essays *do* alternate between evocations of present evils and the suggestion of possible alternatives, but their patterns of description, invocation, and personal response are basically congruent with the conversational manner of the essays. They do not concentrate on "apparently trivial phenomena as the subject of interpretation" (characteristic three); and they are not noticeably "episodic or discontinuous" (characteristic four).

3. Morris, "The Society of the Future," in *Artist, Writer, Socialist,* ed. May Morris, 2 vols. (Oxford: Basil Blackwell, 1936), 2:459,468. Henceforth abbreviated as *AWS* in citations.

4. Morris, "The Society of the Future" 2: 469.

5. "Art Under Plutocracy," "Useful Work Versus Useful Toil," "Art and Socialism" in *Collected Works of William Morris*, ed. May Morris, 24 vols. (London: Longmans, 1910–1915), 23: 173, 103, 210. Subsequent citations from the *Collected Works* will be abbreviated as *CW*, followed by volume and page number.

6. Morris, "Art Under Plutocracy," "The Lesser Arts," *CW* 23: 176; 22: 9.

7. Morris, "The Society of the Future," *AWS* 2: 466.

8. Morris, "Art and Socialism," *CW* 23: 195, 199. References to "Ladies" occur in "The Aims of Art" and "Art, Wealth, and Riches," *CW* 23: 93, 154; to "women" in "The Aims of Art," "The Hopes of Civilization," "Art, Wealth, and Riches," "Art and Socialism," and "What Socialists Want," *CW* 23: 92,72,154, 204,218, and in "The Society of the Future," "Thoughts on Education Under Capitalism" and "Under an Elm Tree," *AWS* 2: 466,497,510; and to "female" in "Dawn of a New Epoch," *CW* 23:135 and "Under an Elm Tree," *AWS* 2:509.

9. Charlotte Perkins Gilman, *The Living of Charlotte Perkins Gilman: An Autobiography* (New York: Harper and Row, 1935), 209,212. Of May Morris she notes, "she became a dear and lasting friend" (209).

10. Friedrich Engels, *Der Ursprung* (Hottingen-Zurich: Druck der Schweisenreischen Genossneschaftsbuchdruckerei, 1884); translated into English in 1902, and reprinted as *The Origin of the Family, Private Property, and the State in the Light of the Researches of Lewis S. Morgan* (New York: International Publishers, 1942). Uncompromising in his way, Engels identified the *basic* class oppression as that of "the female sex by the male," found monogamy essentially corrupt, denounced social condemnation of prostitutes, and, most strikingly, asserts that "to emancipate woman and make her the equal of the man is and remains an impossibility so long as the woman is shut out from social productive labor and restricted to private domestic labor" (58,59,148).

11. Morris to Glasier, 21 Dec. 1887, *The Collected Letters of William Morris*, ed. Norman Kelvin, 2 vols. (Princeton: Princeton University Press, 1984, 1987), 2: 728. Emma Lazarus visited Morris in 1883; her 1886 article, "A Day in Surrey," is reprinted in "Leonardo of Retailing," *Gazette of the John Lewis Partnership* 44 (17 March 1962): 158–160.

An excellent examination of Morris's relations with contemporary women appears in Linda Richardson's recent essay, "Daintily Fashioned Engines of War: William Morris and Women of the Socialist Movement: A Lecture Delivered to the William Morris Society, 26th March, 1987." Richardson studies personal influences of socialist women on Morris, and concludes for slightly different reasons that Morris's views evolved during the late 1880s. In "Engines of War" and in "Louise Michel and William Morris," *The Journal of the William Morris Society* 8 (1989): 26–29, Richardson also discusses the military role of Michel and other

Communard women during the siege of 1871, a role not mentioned in *A Short Account of the Commune of Paris*, coauthored by Morris with Bax and Victor Dave (Socialist League, London: 1886). In "The Pilgrims of Hope" (CW 24: 369–408), Morris's heroine appears on the barricades as one who bears "the *brancard* of the ambulance-women" (section 12).

12. Appendix A, "The Manifesto of the Socialist League," *Letters* 2:852.

13. Norman MacKenzie and Jeanne MacKenzie, *The Fabians* (New York: Simon and Shuster, 1977); 42. Shaw enrolled as a Fabian in September 1884.

14. See George Bernard Shaw, *The Quintessence of Ibsenism* (London: Walter Scott, 1891), and the "Preface" to *Mrs. Warren's Profession* (London: Grant Richards, 1902).

15. Morris to Shaw, 18 March 1885, *Letters of Morris* 2: 404.

16. In substance, Shaw's views on marriage during the mid-to-late eighties and early nineties embodied his own idiosyncratic brand of anti-"social purity" arguments, but they also called for wage equality (dismissed by some socialists as a reformist demand of the middle-class "new woman") and a complete abolition of laws governing cohabitation. In an ironic echo of Bax's position, Shaw considered contemporary marriage laws crucial in binding *men* to *women*: as he later wrote to Ellen Terry on 2 July 1897, "Marriage is not the man's hold on the woman, but the woman's on the man ("*The Collected Letters of George Bernard Shaw*, ed. Dan H. Laurence, 2 vols. [London: Reinhardt, 1985–]) 2: 777.

17. Morris to Shaw, *Letters of Morris* 2: 404.

18. A more serious egalitarian may also have observed that Shaw's alternately draconian and reformist position attacked the Socialist League's platform simultaneously from both right and left. He failed to address real legal grievances in the laws governing marriage, sexual violence, and child abuse, for example, and archly ignored the simple fact that distinctions between marriage and "prostitution," however conventional, were crucial to the security and happiness of most English women and their families. He was right, however, that in the absence of the longed-for socialist revolution, crass forms of discrimination in wages, education, and occupation did matter enormously to women. Subsequent Fabian calls for their elimination pointed the way for what grudging progress has since been made.

19. The review of Bebel's *Woman under Socialism* appeared in the *Westminster Review* in 1886, and was reprinted as Eleanor Marx-Aveling and Edward Aveling, *The Woman Question* (London: Swan Sonnenschein, 1887), and in *Thoughts on Women and Society*, ed. Joachim Muller and Edith Schotte (New York: International Publishers, 1987). Marx and Aveling's treatise, unlike many other socialist writings of the period, at least acknowledges contemporary movements on behalf of women, though it condemns them for failing to touch the deeper roots of women's oppression. Another distinction of Marx and Aveling's treatise is its de-

mand for honesty in sexual relations and its recognition—like Morris's, remarkable for its period—of women's needs for sexual expression: "[W]e—and with us . . . most Socialists—contend that chastity is unhealthy and unholy . . . . we call to mind the accumulated medical testimony to the fact that women suffer more than men under these restraints." Marx and Aveling here entered virtually uncharted terrain.

20. Appendix A, "The Manifesto of the Socialist League," *Letters* 2: 857.

21. More controversial might have been his attack on "liberty of conscience," that is, on the right to promulgate religious beliefs.

22. Ray Strachey, *"The Cause": A Short History of the Women's Movement in Great Britain* (1928; rpt. Port Washington, N.Y.: Kennikat, 1969), 222–223. In 1878 a wife was able to secure separation, with custody of her children under ten years of age, if her husband was convicted of "aggravated assault." In 1884 the Matrimonial Causes Act also abolished the penalty of imprisonment for denial of conjugal rights: a wife could no longer be imprisoned for leaving her husband, but she could still be forced to return.

23. Ernest Belfort Bax, "Some Bourgeois Idols; or Ideals, Reals, and Shams," *Commonweal*, April 1886, 25–26.

24. Bax, "Bourgeois Idols," 25–26. Bax may also be referring to debates of the preceding year over the Criminal Amendment Bill of 1885, discussed in April and May before its passage in August of 1885. Aimed at forced prostitution, the bill raised the age of consent for women from 12 to 13 (not 16, as many reformers wished), forbade the renting of premises for prostitution, and punished various forms of procurement and sexual compliance induced by the use of drugs. Women also had made some genuine gains in the previous decade. The Married Women's Property Act of 1882 permitted women to hold property as well as to keep their own earnings, and the Guardianship of Infants' Act of 1886 permitted widows for the first time to be appointed joint-guardians of their own children. Bax probably objected most strenuously to provisions of the sort embodied in the Married Women (Maintenance in Case of Desertion) Act of 1886, which enabled women to sue for maintenance before they went to the workhouse (Parliamentary Act of 25 June 1886); Bax's article appeared in April, and the law was passed later in the year.

25. See Strachey, "The Cause" ch. 10, "The C. D. Acts, 1870, 1871," 187–224; Glen Petrie, *A Singular Iniquity: The Campaigns of Josephine Butler* (London: Macmillan, 1971), 209–259.

26. Bax, "Bourgeois Idols," *Commonweal*, April 1886, 26.

27. Ernest Belfort Bax, *The Fraud of Feminism* (London: Grant Richards, 1913). In ch. 2, "The Main Dogma of Modern Feminism," for example, Bax asserts that "[W]hile man *has* a sex, woman *is* a sex. Let us hear [Otto] Weininger on this

point. 'Woman is *only* sexual, man is *also* sexual' . . . the whole female organism is subservient to the functions of child-bearing and lactation, which explains the inferior development of those organs and faculties which are not specially connected with this supreme end of Woman" (27,32).

28. Rare exceptions are Bax's unexpectedly idealistic essay on "Socialism and Religion," reprinted in *The Religion of Socialism* (London: Swan Sonnenschein, 1886), and some passages from *Reminiscences*, for example, his recollections of Morris's antipuritanism, personal generosity, and solicitude for his friends (*Reminscences and Reflexions of a Mid and Late Victorian*, London: G. Allen & Unwin, 1918, 117–122).

29. Morris to Sharman, 24–30 (?) April 1886, *Letters of Morris* 2: 547.

30. See Laurence Thompson, *The Enthusiasts: A Biography of John and Katharine Bruce Glasier*, London: Victor Gollancz, 1971.

31. Morris to Bruce Glasier, 24 April 1886, *Letters of Morris* 2: 545.

32. Morris to Mavor, Sept. 1888, *Letters of Morris* 2: 824.

33. See Anthea Callen, *Angel in the Studio: Women in the Arts and Crafts Movement* (London: Astragal Books, 1979).

34. Morris's next public statement on the issue of marriage, still coauthored with Bax, was a brief one-paragraph discussion of voluntary "socialist" marriage in the final installment of "Socialism from the Root Up," a *Commonweal* series of articles on socialist history and economic concepts which appeared concurrently with *A Dream of John Ball* from October 1886 to January 1888. Five years later, these essays reappeared in book form, slightly revised, as *Socialism: Its Growth and Outcome* (London: Swan Sonnenschein, 1893).

35. Bax, *Reminiscences*, 82.

36. Morris, *News from Nowhere* in CW 16: 52–63, 159–67.

37. See my "Narrative Design in *The Pilgrims of Hope*," in *Socialism and the Literary Artistry of William Morris*, 147–166.

38. Eleanor Marx, "Supplement," *Commonweal*, April 1885, 63. Not until 1923 did the Matrimonial Causes Act permit divorce to both sexes on the same grounds.

39. Morris, CW 16:57. References to this volume will henceforth be cited in page numbers following the quotation.

40. In the 1889 *Roots of the Mountains*, the Bride and Bow-may, two women-warriors, both love the male protagonist, Gold-mane, but he chooses for his wife Sun-Beam, a woman from another tribe. The plot may represent an attempt by Morris to balance earlier portrayals.

41. Eleanor Marx, "Supplement," 64; italics added.

42. Morris, *News from Nowhere*, CW 16: 47. Also, see Sylvia Strauss, "Women in Utopia," *South Atlantic Quarterly* 75 (1976): 115–131.

43. Strachey, "*The Cause*," 260. In 1890 Phillipa Fawcett's scores at Cambridge

placed her above the Senior Wrangler for that year. This result was announced in June, and Morris's episode appeared in the *Commonweal* for September.

44. Ernest Belfort Bax and William Morris, *Socialism: Its Growth and Outcome* (London: Swan Sonnenschein, 1893), ch. 21, "Socialism Triumphant," 307–308: "Architecture, which is above all an art of association, we believe must necessarily be *the* art of a society of co-operation. . . . Sculpture, as in past times, will be considered almost entirely a part of fine building, the highest expression of the beauty which turns a utilitarian building into a great artistic production."

45. Cf. Morris, "The Society of the Future," *AWS* 2: 465: "You see you will no longer be able to have novels relating the troubles of a middle-class couple in their struggle towards social uselessness, because the material for such literary treasures will have passed away."

46. Socialists were generally cool to calls for birth control prompted by Malthusian fears, believing that population growth would naturally regulate itself in a prosperous and egalitarian society. H.M. Hyndman and Morris's *Summary of the Principles of Socialism* (London: Modern Press, 1884) asserts that: "This foolish Malthusian craze is itself bred of our anarchical competitive system" (43). In chapter 10 of *News from Nowhere*, Old Hammond assures Guest that Nowhereian women have more desire for children than their nineteenth-century foremothers (62), but that "the population is pretty much the same as it was at the end of the nineteenth century" (74). Eleanor Marx and Edward Aveling's *The Woman Question*, by contrast, is conspicuous for a complete absence of favorable references to childbearing, childrearing, and parental roles.

Women, Wisdom, and Southeast Asia

1. See my "An Introduction to Victorian Women's Travel Writings About Southeast Asia," *Genre* 20 (Summer 1987):189–208.

2. See also my "Victorian Women's Travel Writings About Southeast Asia,"

3. Edward W. Said, *Orientalism* (1978; rpt. New York: Vintage Books, 1979), 5.

4. See Wallace Cable Brown, "Byron and English Interest in the Near East," *Studies in Philology* 34 (1937):56–64, and Daniel P. Watkins, *Social Relations in Byron's Eastern Tales* (Cranbury, N.J.: Associated University Presses, Inc., 1987).

5. Said, *Orientalism*, 5–6

6. For a discussion of another romantic poet's indebtedness to travel literature, see Charles Norton Coe, *Wordsworth and the Literature of Travel* (New York: Bookman Associates, 1953).

7. Samuel Rogers, *The Voyage of Columbus* (London: T. Cadell and W. Davies, 1810); Charles Darwin, *Journal of Researches into the Geology and Natural His-*

tory of the Various Countries Visited by H. M. S. Beagle (London: H. Colburn, 1839).

8. Quoted by Ronald W. Clark, *The Survival of Charles Darwin: A Biography of a Man and An Idea* (New York: Random House, 1984), 95.

9. *The Lifted Veil* in *The Works of George Eliot*, vol. 20 (London: William Blackwood and Sons), 326.

10. John Holloway, *The Victorian Sage: Studies in Argument* (1953; rpt. New York: W. W. Norton & Company, 1965), 7.

11. Holloway, *Victorian Sage*, 9.

12. Anna Forbes, *Insulinde: Experiences of a Naturalist's Wife in the Eastern Archipelago* (Edinburgh: William Blackwood and Sons, 1887), vii.

13. Emily Innes, *The Chersonese With the Gilding Off* (London, 1885; rpt. Singapore: Oxford University Press, 1974), 242; cf. Isabella Bird, *The Golden Chersonese And The Way Thither* (1883; rpt. London: Century Publishing Co. Ltd., 1983).

14. Khoo Kay Kim, "Introduction," in *The Chersonese With The Gilding Off*, v.

15. Innes, *The Chersonese With the Gilding Off*, 243.

16. Holloway, *Victorian Sage*, 12–15.

17. Of many studies of the links between Victorian science and literature, see Tess Cosslet's helpful book, *The 'Scientific Movement' and Victorian Literature* (London: Harvester Press, Ltd., 1982).

18. An excellent example is Gillian Beer's *Darwin's Plots: Evolutionary Narrative in Darwin, George Eliot and Nineteenth-Century Fiction* (London: Routledge & Kegan Paul, 1983).

19. Quoted by Nora Barlow, "Preface," *Charles Darwin and the Voyage of the Beagle* (London: Pilot Press, Ltd., 1945), 1.

20. T. H. Huxley, *Science and Culture and Other Essays* (London: Macmillan and Company, 1882); Edward Dowden, "The Scientific Movement and Literature," in *Studies in Literature, 1789–1877* (London: Kegan Paul, 1889); Beer, *Darwin's Plots*; George Levine, *Darwin and the Novelists: Patterns of Science in Victorian Fiction* (Cambridge: Harvard University Press, 1988); and Peter Morton, *The Vital Science: Biology and the Literary Imagination, 1860–1900* (London: George Allen and Unwin, 1984).

21. Percy Adams, *Travel Literature and the Evolution of the Novel* (Lexington: University Press of Kentucky, 1983).

22. An exception is Mary B. Campbell's fine new study of early travel writing, *The Witness and the Other World: Exotic European Travel Writing, 400–1600* (Ithaca: Cornell University Press, 1988).

23. Marilyn Butler, "Voyages in Metaland," a review of *Travel Literature and the Novel* by Adams, *TLS*, 22 June 1984.

24. Paul Fussell, *Abroad: British Literary Traveling Between the Wars* (New York: Oxford University Press, 1980), 212.

25. Jan Gordon, "Introduction," in Alexander Kinglake, *Eothen, or, Traces of Travel Brought Home From the East* (1844; rpt. Oxford: Oxford University Press, 1982), iii, iv.

26. George Meredith, *The Egoist*, ed. Robert Adams (1897; rpt. New York: W. W. Norton & Company, 1979), 23.

27. Kinglake, *Eothen*, 3, 5.

28. Said, *Orientalism*, 7.

29. Fussell, *Abroad*.

30. Fussell, *Abroad*, 203.

31. *Tahiti, A Series of Photographs taken by Colonel Stuart-Wortley with Letterpress by Lady Brassey* (London: Sampson Low, Marston, Searle, and Rivington, 1882), 11.

32. J. K. Stanford, ed., *Ladies in the Sun: The Memsahib's India 1790–1860* (London: Galley Press, 1962), 18–35.

33. C. M. Turnbull, *The Straits Settlements, 1826–67: Indian Presidency to Crown Colony* (London: The Athlone Press, 1972), 28–29.

34. Eliza Fay, *Original Letters From India, 1779–1815*, ed. E. M. Forster (1925; rpt. London: The Hogarth Press, 1986); Harriet Tytler, *An Englishwoman in India: The Memoirs of Harriet Tytler, 1828–1858*, ed. Anthony Sattin (Oxford: Oxford University Press, 1986); Isabel Burton, *Arabia, Egypt, India: A Narrative of Travel* (London: W. Mullan and Son, 1879).

35. Anna Leonowens, *Life and Travel in India: Being Recollections of a Journey Before the Days of Railroads* (Philadelphia: Porter and Coates, 1884).

36. David Joel Steinberg, ed., *In Search of Southeast Asia: A Modern History* (1971; rpt. Honolulu: University of Hawaii Press, 1985).

37. Turnbull, *The Straits Settlements*, 29.

38. C. M. Turnbull, *A Short History of Malaysia, Singapore and Brunei* (1979; rpt. Singapore: Graham Brash Ltd., 1987).

39. Margaret Landon, *Anna and the King of Siam* (Garden City: Garden City Publishing Company, 1944), 19.

40. Anna Leonowens, *Siamese Harem Life* (New York: E. P. Dutton and Company, Ltd., 1953), 9.

41. Florence Caddy, *To Siam and Malaya in the Duke of Sutherland's Yacht 'Sans Peur'* (London: Hurst and Blackett, Ltd., 1889), 196.

42. Caddy, *To Siam and Malaya*, 114.

43. Leonowens, *Life and Travel in India*, 34–36.

44. Edward Said, "Orientalism reconsidered," *Race and Class* 27 (1985):5.

45. Leslie Milne, *Shans at Home*, (1910; rpt. New York: Paragon Book Reprint

Corp., 1970), 138; Leonowens, *Siamese Harem Life*, 202. The rest of the paragraph explicit claims that the woman's great beauty is an expression of her greatness of soul.

46. E. R. Skidmore, *Java, The Garden of the East* (New York: 1899; rpt. Singapore: Oxford University Press, 1984), 2.

47. A good example is Mary Lovina Cort's *Siam: or, The Heart of Farther India* (New York: Anson D. F. Randolph and Company, 1886).

48. Evelyn Fox-Keller, "Feminism and Science," in *The 'Signs' Reader: Women, Gender and Scholarship*, ed. Elizabeth Abel and Emily K. Abel (Chicago: Universtiy of Chicago Press, 1983), 118.

49 Keller, "Feminism and Science," 118.

50. Annie Brassey, *A Voyage In The 'Sunbeam,' Our Home on the Ocean For Eleven Months* (London: Longmans, Green, and Co., 1878).

51. Margaret Brooke, *My Life in Sarawak* (London: Methuen and Co. Ltd, 1913), 313.

The Sage Author as Phallic Sister

1. Sophocles, *Antigone*, trans. Elizabeth Wyckoff, in *Sophocles I*, ed. David Grene and Richmond Lattimore (Chicago: University of Chicago Press, 1954), 61–62. Subsequent citations to lines in the play will be parenthetical in the text.

2. Karl Reinhardt observes that the prologue "opens with a harmony than which nothing could be more heartfelt" and adds that "because of this hope of unity, discord arises all the more violently" (in Karl Reinhardt, *Sophocles*, trans. Hazel Harvey and David Harvey [Oxford: Basil Blackwell, 1979]), 67.

3. The remark to Jebb, made in 1873, is recorded by Gordon Haight in *George Eliot: A Biography* (Oxford: Oxford University Press, 1968), 195; Haight notes *Life and Letters of Sir Richard Claverhouse Jebb* (1907), 155. Eliot read Sophocles in the original; she published "The Antigone and its Moral," a review, in *The Leader*, 29 March 1856. See also George Steiner, *Antigones* (Oxford: Clarendon, 1984), 5. Dorothea is compared to Antigone by the painter Naumann, and again in the finale (*Middlemarch: A Study of Provincial Life*, afterword by Frank Kermode [New York: Signet, 1964]).

4. In *Mill on the Floss*, the autobiographical Maggie Tulliver is contrasted with her cousin Lucy, a character modelled on Eliot's sister Chrissey.

5. In conversation, Elizabeth Freund suggested to me that Shakespeare's comedies, *Twelfth Night* in particular, are a central point in the trajectory that I discover between the Antigone and these nineteenth-century novels. In Shakespeare, mourning a brother's loss and crossdressing (complicated by male actors playing

female roles) mimic Antigone's insistence on retaining phallic power at the cost of marriage. Such gender ambiguity finds unsettled resolution at best in the ultimate heterosexual pairings in Shakespeare's plays.

6. See Steiner, *Antigones*, 241.

7. Sophocles, *Oedipus at Colonus*, in *Sophocles I*, 342–369. Subsequent citations to the play will be parenthetical in the text.

8. It is noteworthy that Polyneices refuses Antigone's advice to withdraw, and that Antigone says to him what Ismene will later say to her, that life will be unbearable without him because his pride is leading him to suicidal behavior. While Antigone retains her loyalty to him, Ismene makes claim to no man, only to her sister.

9. Ismene "loves her sister and mourns . . . tears on her lovely face" (528–530), but of Antigone the chorus remarks: "She is her father's child" (472). Contrasting Ismene and Antigone, G. M. Kirkwood finds Antigone "hard, abrupt, intolerant" and Ismene in possession of "gentleness, affection, and patience"; of Antigone he writes that "Goethe's famous description of her as the 'most sisterly of souls' is right provided that we do not equate sisterliness with gentleness" (*A Study of Sophoclean Drama* [Ithaca: Cornell University Press, 1958], fn.) 119. Kirkwood misses that Goethe's emphasis is on Antigone's sororal relation to her brothers. Steiner documents a steady repression of Ismene in readings of the play until the twentieth century (*Antigones*, 144–151), perhaps because of an exclusionary definition of sorority as sister to brothers. He points out that Antigone "incarnates sisterhood" and thus the play goes to the core of Romanticism and Idealism where brother-sister love is a pervasive expression of the age. Steiner, like Goethe, refers to Antigone's sisterly relation to her brothers (Polyneices and Oedipus both). Kirkwood asks if Antigone suffers by contrast with Ismene: "As a specimen of normal, gentle womanhood, perhaps she does. But it is part of her towering strength to cast aside such normality" (*Sophoclean Drama*, 121).

10. Carol Gilligan documents in *A Different Voice: Psychological Theory and Women's Development* (Cambridge, Mass.: Harvard University Press, 1982) that women's training to see more than a single side to an issue is often interpreted as weakness. Unfortunately, Gilligan herself risks sounding like the Victorians who feared the degeneracy signalled by women's assumption of male roles when she celebrates sexual distinctiveness and regrets women's wishing to have male power.

11. Jane Gallop discusses this concept, elucidating Freudian and Lacanian usages as well as Irigaray and Kristeva's feminist appropriations in "The Phallic Mother: Fraudian Analysis," in *The Daughter's Seduction: Feminism and Psychoanalysis* (Ithaca: Cornell University Press, 1985), 113–131.

12. Freud's equation is made in "Some Psychological Consequences of the Anatomical Distinction Between the Sexes" (1925), trans. James Strachey, in *Sexuality*

and the Psychology of Love, ed. Philip Rieff (New York: Collier Books, 1963), 191. Sandra M. Gilbert makes a point similar to mine. Referring to Eliot's presentation of daughterhood in *Silas Marner*, Gilbert writes: "What she said was what she saw: that it is better to be a daughter than to be a mother and better still to be a father than a daughter" ("Life's Empty Pack: Notes Towards a Literary Daughteronomy," *Critical Inquiry* 11 Spring 1985): 355–384.

13. Steiner, *Antigones*, 4–19.

14. Steiner, *Antigones*, 9–10.

15. Bram Dijkstra, *Idols of Perversity: Fantasies of Feminine Evil in Fin-de-Siècle Culture* (New York: Oxford University Press, 1986), 211.

16. Quoted in Dijkstra, *Idols*, 214–215, from Nicholas Francis Cooke, *Satan in Society* [1870] (by "A Physician").

17. Dijkstra, *Idols*, 394.

18. Dijkstra, *Idols*, 346.

19. In *Adultery in the Novel: Contract and Transgression* (Baltimore: Johns Hopkins University Press, 1979), Tony Tanner rests his argument about the centrality of adultery in the novel on the premise of the heroine's inherent femaleness. The type of heroine who concerns me here challenges that premise. This heroine must be freed from duty to her father, and she must be made feminine, so that she may be the heroine of a comic novel. Tanner writes that "the woman as a biological entity cannot be changed . . . ; her organic determinants are given; the familial identification of daughter and/or sister that are conferred on a female are not inherent qualities, but they are irremoveable categorizations by the irreversible fact of consanguinity (this is Antigone's point about her relation to her brother in Sophocles' play)" (15–16). Tanner continues: "the figure of the wife ideally contains the biological *female*, the obedient *daughter* (and perhaps sister), the faithful *mate*, and the believing *Christian*, and harmonizes all patterns that bestow upon these differing identities" (17). Antigone, as a biological female (and a male in subtext), aggressively a daughter and a sister (to the same man), and a devotee to the gods with a vengeance, exaggerates or perverts these roles in a way that threatens their viability and makes her an implausible wife.

20. See Susan S. Lanser, "No Connections Subsequent: Jane Austen's World of Sisterhood," in *The Sister Bond: A Feminist View of a Timeless Connection*, ed. Toni A. H. McNaron (New York: Pergamon Press, 1985), 53–67.

21. Mark Schorer, "Pride Unprejudiced," *Kenyon Review* 18 (Winter 1956); 83; Lloyd Brown, "The Business of Marrying and Mothering," in *Jane Austen's Achievement*, ed. Juliet McMaster (London: Macmillan, 1976), 31–32.

22. Jane Austen, *Sense and Sensibility*, intro. Lord David Cecil (New York: Oxford University Press 1931), 4. Subsequent citations to the novel will be parenthetical in the text.

23. In David Cecil's argument that Austen's *Sense and Sensibility* attacks the Romantic position of Wordsworth, Coleridge, Shelley, and Byron that referred "opinions to the instinctive movements of the heart," I find the implication that Austen is defending reason against the feminization of culture that came to be regarded by the masculine literary establishment as terribly threatening later in the century. Cecil writes: "on the minute stage of her genteel comedy theatre for the daughters of gentlemen, she presented the struggle that was rending intellectual Europe. Consciously or not, in Elinor is embodied all the philosophy of Dr. Johnson, and in Marianne all the philosophy of Rousseau" (Introduction to *Sense and Sensibility*, xiv).

24. Tony Tanner, *Jane Austen* (Cambridge: Harvard University Press, 1986), 94 and 76–77. Tanner refers to Walton Litz's *Jane Austen: A Study of Her Artistic Development* (1965), and Litz refers to eighteenth-century novels with opposing sisters such as Elizabeth Inchbald's *Nature and Art* and Maria Edgeworth's *Letters of Julia and Caroline*.

25. Bernard S. Talmey, *Woman: A Treatise on the Normal and Pathological Emotions of Feminine Love* (1904), quoted in Dijkstra, *Idols*, 157.

26. Tanner, *Austen*, 123.

27. Tanner, *Austen*, 129.

28. Certainly Maggie and Tom's relationship is central, just as Antigone and Creon's is central in Sophocles's play, but I am comparing Lucy's absence in (even feminist) readings of the novel with the repression of Ismene in readings of Sophocles. See, for example, Mary Jacobus, "The Question of Language: Men of Maxims and *The Mill on the Floss*," 37–52, and Margaret Homans, "Eliot, Wordsworth, and the Scenes of the Sisters' Instruction," 53–72, both in *Writing and Sexual Difference*, ed. Elizabeth Abel (Chicago: University of Chicago Press, 1981).

29. Haight writes in *George Eliot* that "her mother's favourites were Isaac and Chrissey. Chrissey's blond curls were always neat, while Mary Anne's straight light brown hair defied all measures of control. Chrissey's clothes were always tidy, delighting her critical Pearson aunts" (10). After describing Mrs. Evans's death, Haight adds that Mrs. Evans had never been very close to Mary Anne; her father was 'the one deep strong love I have ever known' (*Letters*, I.284), and she resolved to fill the empty place before him as best she could" (21).

30. George Eliot, *The Mill on the Floss* (New York: Signet, 1965), 508. Subsequent citations to the novel will be parenthetical in the text.

31. Haight, *George Eliot*, 40.

32. When Blackwood finished reading the novel's manuscript, he pointed to the embrace between Lucy and Maggie to exemplify how moving the novel's ending is: "I do not envy the man who can read the scene where Lucy falls on Maggie's neck without being affected to tears" (quoted in Haight, *George Eliot*, 320).

33. Haight, *George Eliot*, 26.

34. Word that Chrissey's daughter Katie had died reached Eliot as she was composing Maggie's end (Haight, *George Eliot*, 321).

35. Gillian Beer, *George Eliot* (Sussex: Harvester Press, 1986), 87.

36. Beer, *Eliot*, 75.

37. Eliot was troubled by reviews overly critical of the Dodsons. See Gordon S. Haight, "*The Mill on the Floss*," in *A Century of George Eliot Criticism*, ed. Gordon S. Haight (Boston: Houghton Mifflin, 1965), 340.

38. Eliot, *Middlemarch*, 811.

39. Haight, *George Eliot*, 10.

40. See the ending to the first edition of *Middlemarch*; and also Beer (*Eliot*, 147), where she indicates that the inadequacy of women's education is how the first readers of the novel interpreted its topic.

41. Beer, *Eliot*, 20.

42. The competition is then displaced into a brief and false rivalry between Dorothea and Rosamund, but as Sandra M. Gilbert and Susan Gubar have argued in *Madwoman in the Attic: The Woman Writer and the Nineteenth-Century Literary Imagination* (New Haven: Yale University Press, 1979), these women attain a surprising intimacy.

43. Kermode, in his afterword to *Middlemarch*, writes that this marriage "is so perverse by any standard that we do not miss much the information as to its sexual basis, which Eliot withholds . . . . We may make inferences from the desolation of her wedding trip or from the strange pieta at the end of the fourth book, where Dorothea tends not her child but a failed father figure" (821). When the artist Naumann sees Dorothea he wishes to dress her as a nun, echoing Mrs. Cadwallader's observation that Dorothea's marriage was "as good as going to a nunnery" (59). The reader has the same wish to remove Dorothea from Casaubon's bed, but Ladislaw is kept in the background, enabling us to imagine an aesthetically appealing sexual life for the heroine. Naumann taunts his friend Ladislaw by calling Dorothea his great aunt, and Naumann then imagines her a "Christian Antigone—sensuous force controlled by spiritual passion" (87).

44. Kermode, Afterword to *Middlemarch*, 818.

45. Quoted in Beer, *Eliot*, 17.

46. Beer, *Eliot*, 171–172.

47. Edward Weeks, Introduction to Louisa May Alcott, *Little Women* (New York: Heritage Press, 1967).

48. See Marilyn Safir et al., eds. *Women's World: From the New Scholarship* (New York: Praeger, 1985).

49. See Gilbert and Gubar, *Madwoman*, 3–16.

50. Dijkstra, *Idols*, 215.

51. I wish to thank the Golda Meir Fellowship Foundation that afforded me the opportunity to conduct this research at the Hebrew University of Jerusalem among extraordinarily helpful and responsive colleagues. Particular thanks are due to Elizabeth Freund and Freddie Rokem, both of Hebrew University; to Bruce Heiden (OSU); to Thaïs Morgan, of course; and especially, as ever, to Leonard Gordon (Kenyon College).

Traversing the Feminine in *Salomé*

I would like to thank Gail Finney for providing me with an advance copy of a portion of the chapter on *Salomé* in her book, *Women in Modern Drama: Freud, Feminism, and European Theater at the Turn of the Century.*

1. John Holloway, *The Victorian Sage: Studies in Argument* (New York: Norton, 1965), 7.

2. For the connection between Anglo-Catholicism and emergent male homosexuality, see David Hilliard, "Unenglish and Unmanly: Anglo-Catholicism and Homosexuality," *Victorian Studies* 25 (1982): 181–210.

3. David DeLaura, "The Allegory of Life: The Autobiographical Impulse in Victorian Prose," in *Approaches to Victorian Autobiography*, ed. George P. Landow (Athens: Ohio University Press, 1979), 333. The essay is the most significant further development of Holloway's argument in the opening pages of *The Victorian Sage*.

4. George P. Landow, *Elegant Jeremiahs: The Sage from Carlyle to Mailer* (Ithaca: Cornell University Press, 1986), Introduction.

5. See Sheila Jeffreys, *The Spinster and Her Enemies: Feminism and Sexuality 1880–1930* (London: Pandora, 1985), ch. 6.

6. For the distinction between gender inversion and homosexual desire, see George Chauncey, "From Sexual Inversion to Homosexuality: Medicine and the Changing Conceptualization of Female Deviance," *Salmagundi* 58–59 (Fall 1982–Winter 1983): 116.

7. Quoted in Regina Gagnier, *Idylls of the Marketplace: Oscar Wilde and the Victorian Public* (Stanford: Stanford University Press, 1986), 171.

8. Sara Bernhardt's actions contrast to the role that Dorian Gray projects for "his" actress, Sybil Vane. See Nina Auerbach's reflections on the powers that Victorian women found in acting in *Romantic Imprisonment: Women and Other Glorified Outcasts* (New York: Columbia University Press, 1985), Part 4.

9. See Sydney Janet Kaplan, "Katherine Mansfield and the Problem of Oscar Wilde," ch. 2 of her forthcoming book, *Katherine Mansfield and the Origins of Modernist Fiction*.

10. References to the English version of *Salomé* are to Oscar Wilde, *Salomé: A Tragedy in One Act*, with drawings by Aubrey Beardsley (Boston: Bruce Humphries, n. d.). Unless otherwise noted, references to *Salomé* are to this text.

11. Richard Ellmann, *Oscar Wilde* (New York: Viking, 1987), 326. Unless otherwise noted, references to Ellmann are to this text.

12. I say all because Salomé also connotes lesbian desire. And in the instance of the crossdressed Wilde playing her, s/he denotes male homosexual desire.

13. Gagnier, *Idylls*, 229–230n. The passage of the Labouchère Amendment to the Criminal Law Amendment Act in 1885, a piece of legislation so broad in scope as to make illegal virtually all male homosexual activity or speech whether in public or private, marked a decisive turn for the worse for men in Britain who engaged in sexual activities with other men. The amendment contributed to the social formation of homosexuality by shifting emphasis from sexual acts between men, especially sodomy, the traditional focus of legislation, to sexual sentiment or thought, and in this way to an abstract entity soon to be widely referred to as "homosexuality." In light of Michel Foucault's argument that the shaping of such categories in juridical and medical discourse may help prompt the creation of resistant social groupings (*The History of Sexuality: Volume I: An Introduction*, trans. Robert Hurley [New York: Vintage, 1980], 100–102), the efflorescence of male homosexual culture in England during the ensuing decade should be seen as directed in part towards bringing about the decriminalization of activities and speech expressing male-male desire.

14. The essay is reprinted in Richard Ellmann, *Golden Codgers: Biographical Specualtions* (New York: Oxford University Press, 1973).

15. Ellmann's reading leaves Wilde's engagement with male-male desire in suspension for years after Wilde was trading on sexual ambiguity in the successful pursuit of transatlantic celebrity. Other commentators such as Rupert Croft-Cooke, who dismisses the Ross story as a "myth," have set the date of Wilde's initiation earlier. Croft-Cooke contends that Wilde was active sexually with other men at least from his days at Oxford (*Feasting with Panthers: A New Consideration of Some Late Victorian Writers* [London: W. H. Allen, 1967], 172).

16. Ellmann, "Overtures to *Salome*," in *Codgers*, 50, 57. Pater, however, does not commend virginity.

17. Ellmann, *Codgers*, 58.

18. References to the French text of *Salomé* are to Oscar Wilde, *Salomé*, vol. 4 of *The Plays* (Boston: John W. Luce and Co., 1920).

19. Gagnier, *Idylls*, 165.

20. Elliot Gilbert, " 'Tumult of Images' ": Wilde, Beardsley, and *Salome*, *Victorian Studies* 26 (1983): 144.

21. I adapt the term "consciousness-effect" from Gayatri Chakravorty Spivak,

"Can the Subaltern Speak?" in *Marxism and the Interpretation of Culture* ed., Cary Nelson and Lawrence Grossberg (Urbana: University of Illinois Press, 1988), 287.

22. This is Ulrichs's view as formulated by Havelock Ellis and quoted in Christopher Craft, " 'Kiss Me with Those Red Lips': Gender and Inversion in Bram Stoker's *Dracula*," *Representations* 8 (Fall 1984): 113.

23. Cf. Elaine Showalter, *A Literature of Their Own: British Women Novelists from Brontë to Lessing* (Princeton: Princeton University Press, 1977), ch. 7; "Syphilis, Sexuality, and the Fiction of the Fin de Siècle," in *Sex, Politics, and Science in the Nineteenth-Century Novel*, Selected Papers from the English Institute, 1983–1984, New Series, n. 10, ed. Ruth Bernard Yeazell (Baltimore: Johns Hopkins University Press, 1986); *The Female Malady: Women, Madness, and English Culture: 1830–1980* (New York: Penguin, 1985), 104–106.

24. For Wilde's Ibsenite feminism, see Jane Marcus, "Salomé: The Jewish Princess Was a New Woman," *Bulletin of the New York Public Library* 78 (Autumn 1974): 95–113. See also Gagnier, *Idylls*, 66.

25. Quoted by Craig Owens, "Outlaws: Gay Men in Feminism," in *Men in Feminism*, ed. Alice Jardine and Paul Smith (New York: Methuen, 1987), 229.

26. Gilbert "Tumult of Images," 154.

27. Gilbert, "Tumult of Images," 159.

28. Gilbert, "Tumult of Images," 138.

29. Quoted by Gilbert "Tumult of Images," 135.

30. Gilbert, "Tumult of Images," 153.

31. Gilbert, "Tumult of Images," 158.

32. Gagnier, *Idylls*, 199.

33. Quoted in H. Montgomery Hyde, *Lord Alfred Douglas: A Biography* (London: Methuen, 1984), 225.

34. Gilbert, "Tumult of Images," 153.

35. For Douglas's efforts to have sexual activities between men decriminalized, see Hyde, *Douglas*, ch. 2.

36. Oscar Wilde, *Complete Works*, intro. Vyvyan Holland (London: Collins, 1967), 552.

37. Jacques Derrida, "Women in the Beehive: A Seminar," in *Men in Feminism*, ed. Alice Jardine and Paul Smith (New York: Methuen, 1987), 189.

38. Ellmann, *Wilde*, 380–381.

39. Hyde, *Douglas*, 46.

40. See the illustrations facing pp. 24 and 18.

41. "J'admire que tout étant exprimé par de perpétuels traits eblouissants, en votre *Salomé*, il se dégage, aussi, à chaque page, de l'indicible et le Songe" (quoted in Ellmann, *Wilde*, 354).

42. "Ainsi les gemmes innombrables et exactes ne peuvent servir que d'accompagnement sur sâ robe au geste surnaturel de cette jeune princesse, que définitivement vous évoquâtes" (quoted in Ellmann, *Wilde*, 354).

43. Linda Dowling, "The Decadent and the New Woman in the 1890's," *Nineteenth-Century Fiction* 33 (1978): 440–441.

44. Quoted from *Punch* (1894) in Dowling, "Decadent and New Woman," 440.

45. "How wasted he is! He is like a thin ivory statue. He is like an image of silver. I am sure he is chaste as the moon is. He is like a moonbeam, like a shaft of silver" (10). The final sentence in French is not translated.

46. "Thy mouth is like a branch of coral that fishers have found in the twilight of the sea, the coral that they keep for the kings! . . . It is like the vermilion that the Moabites find in the mines of Moab, the vermilion that the kings take from them. It is like the bow of the King of the Persians, that is painted with vermilion, and is tipped with coral. There is nothing in the world so red as thy mouth" (12).

47. According to Ellmann, Wilde, who did not practice anal copulation, favored the practices of "oral and intracrural intercourse" (*Wilde*, 433, 259).

48. Jonathan Dollimore, "Different Desires: Subjectivity and Transgression in Wilde and Gide," *Genders* 2 (July 1988): 31.

49. Elaine Scarry has discussed the relation between the body and textuality in her Introduction to *Literature and the Body: Essays on Populations and Persons* (Baltimore: Johns Hopkins University Press, 1988), xx-xxi.

50. Sharon O'Brien, *Willa Cather: The Emerging Voice* (New York: Oxford University Press, 1987), 147.

51. Willa Cather, *The Kingdom of Art: Willa Cather's First Principles and Critical Statements 1893–1896* (Lincoln: University of Nebraska Press, 1966), 135. O'Brien, who cites the passage in *Willa Cather* (151), has an excellent discussion of the masculinist bias of Cather's aesthetic at the time (ch. 7).

52. Cather, *Kingdom*, 389.

53. Eve Kosofsky Sedgwick has commented on the homophobia of the essay in "Across Gender" (Paper delivered at the Program Session "Men Reading Lesbian Literature and Women Reading Gay Literature," Modern Language Association Convention, San Francisco, 29 December 1987).

54. "The Victorian sage adopts not only the general tone and stance of the Old Testament prophet but also the quadripartite pattern with which the prophet usually presents his message . . . . The prophets of the Old Testament first called attention to their audience's present grievous condition and often listed individual instances of suffering. Second, they pointed out that such suffering resulted directly from their listeners' neglecting . . . God's law. Third, they promised further, indeed deepened, miseries if their listeners failed to return to the fold; and fourth, they

completed the prophetic pattern by offering visions of bliss that their listeners would realize if they returned to the ways of God" (Landow, *Elegant Jeremiahs*, 26).

55. Cather, *Kingdom*, 389, 391.

56. Cather, *Kingdom*, 393.

57. O'Brien, *Cather*, 125–126.

58. Willa Cather, *On Writing: Critical Studies on Writing as an Art* (New York: Knopf, 1949), 41–42. Next to this passage in the copy that I use from Robarts Library at the University of Toronto, are pencilled glosses: "not named" and "grt. line."

59. O'Brien, *Cather*, 126–127.

60. Quoted in Jeffrey Meyers, *Katharine Mansfield: A Biography* (London: Hamish Hamilton, 1978), 25.

61. Antony Alpers, *The Life of Katherine Mansfield* (New York: Viking Press, 1980), 46.

62. Quoted in Alpers, *Mansfield*, 91.

63. Katherine Mansfield, *Letters to John Middleton Murry: 1913–1922*, ed. John Middleton Murry (London: Constable, 1951), 582–583; italics are Mansfield's.

Contributors

FLORENCE S. BOOS is a Professor of English at the University of Iowa, where she teaches Victorian poetry, women's writing, and nineteenth-century culture. She is the former chairperson of the Governing Committee of the William Morris Society in the United States. She has edited Morris's *Juvenilia* (1982) and *Socialist Diary* (1981; reprinted in 1985); coedited (with Carole Silver) *Socialism and the Literary Artistry of William Morris* (1990); assembled and edited *The Bibliography of Women and Literature* (1989); written *The Poetry of Dante G. Rossetti* (1976) and *The Design of 'The Earthly Paradise'* (1990); and published articles on Catherine Macaulay, Mary Wollstonecraft, Pre-Raphaelitism, and a variety of topics in Victorian poetry.

MARY WILSON CARPENTER is an Associate Professor of English and a Queen's National Scholar at Queen's University in Kingston, Ontario. She is the author of *George Eliot and the Landscape of Time* (1986) and has published an article on George Eliot in *Genders*, "'A Bit of Her Flesh': Circumcision and 'The Signification of the Phallus' in *Daniel Deronda*" (1988). She has also published articles in *Literature and History*, *PMLA*, and *Milton Studies* and is currently working on a book on the Bible, the body, and British women's writing in the nineteenth century.

SUSAN P. CASTERAS has written numerous articles, essays, and exhibition catalogues on Victorian art, and since 1977 has been a curator at the Yale Center for British Art and a member of the History of Art Faculty at Yale. Among her recent publications are such books as *Victorian Childhood*, *Images of Victorian Womanhood in English Art*, and *English Pre-Raphaelitism and Its Reception in America in the Nineteenth Century*.

CAROL T. CHRIST is a Professor of English at the University of California, Berkeley. She has published numerous articles and two books, *Victorian and Modern Poetics* and *The Finer Optic: The Aesthetic of Particularity in Victorian Poetry*. Currently, she is working on the subject of death and representation in Victorian literature.

RICHARD DELLAMORA teaches in the Department of English and in the Programs of Cultural and Women's Studies at Trent University in Peterborough, Ontario. He is the author of *Masculine Desire: The Sexual Politics of Victorian Aestheticism* (University of North Carolina Press, 1990).

ANTONY H. HARRISON is a Professor of English at North Carolina State University. He is author of *Swinburne's Medievalism: A Study in Victorian Love Poetry* (1988), *Christina Rossetti in Context* (1988), and *Victorian Poets and Romantic Poems: Intertextuality and Ideology* (1990). He has also published numerous articles on Victorian and Romantic writers and edited a special issue of the *John Donne Journal* on "The Metaphysical Poets in the Nineteenth Century." Currently, he is editing the collected letters of Christina Rossetti, and coediting *Gender, Voice, and Image in Victorian Literature and Art* (with Beverly Taylor), and *Rewriting English Literary History from Feminist Perspectives* (with Ellen Messer-Davidow). He has been awarded fellowships by the National Endowment for the Humanities, the Folger Library, and the National Humanities Center.

GEORGE P. LANDOW is a Professor of English and Art at Brown University. He has written on nineteenth-century literature, art, and religion as well as on educational computing. He has been a Fulbright Scholar, a Guggenheim Fellow, a Fellow of the Society for the Humanities at Cornell University, and has received numerous grants and awards from the National Endowment for the Humanities and the National Endowment for the Arts. He has helped organize several international loan exhibitions including *Fantastic Art and Design in Britain, 1850 to 1930*, and his books include *The Aesthetic and Critical Theories of John Ruskin* (1971), *Victorian Types, Victorian Shadows: Biblical Typology and Victorian Literature, Art, and Thought* (1980), *Approaches to Victorian Autobiography* (1979), *Images of Crisis: Literary Iconology, 1750 to the Present* (1982), *Ruskin* (1985), and *Elegant Jeremiahs: The Sage from Carlyle to Mailer* (1986). He is currently editing a gathering of essays on hypermedia and literature with Paul Delany and completing a volume entitled *Hypertext: The Convergence of Technology and Contemporary Critical Theory*.

JANET L. LARSON, is an Associate Professor of English at Rutgers University, Newark, where she teaches Victorian literature and the Bible as/and literature. She is the author of *Dickens and the Broken Scripture* (1985). Her articles on nineteenth-century and twentieth-century subjects have appeared in *The Dickens Studies Annual, Nineteenth-Century Fiction, Modern Drama, Religion and Literature, Cross Currents,* and *The Christian Century.* At present she is working on a book about women's biblical interpretation in nineteenth-century England and America which includes Charlotte Brontë.

LORI HOPE LEFKOVITZ, an Associate Professor of English at Kenyon College, is author of *The Character of Beauty in the Victorian Novel* (1987), and essays on literary theory, pedagogy, and nineteenth-century literature. She is now writing a book about the representation of blood sisters and editing a collection, *Textual Bodies.*

SUSAN MORGAN is a Professor at Vassar College. Her major critical interests have been romantic poetry and the novel. Her books include *In The Meantime: Character and Perception in Jane Austen's Fiction* and *Sisters in Time: Imagining Gender in Nineteenth-Century British Fiction.* She is presently preparing an edition of *The Romance of Siamese Harem Life* and researching a book on Victorian women's travel writings, which requires travel to Southeast Asia.

THAÏS E. MORGAN, an Assistant Professor of English at Arizona State University, teaches literary theory and nineteenth-century studies. She has published articles on intertextuality, semiotics, feminist theory, and Victorian poetry and criticism. Translator of Gérard Genette's *Mimologics: A Voyage into Cratylusland* (forthcoming from University of Nebraska Press), she has coedited the collection *Reorientations: Critical Theories and Pedagogies* (University of Illinois Press, 1990). Currently, she is working on a book concerning the construction of masculinity and the politics of the literary canon.

LINDA H. PETERSON is an Associate Professor of English and Director of the Bass Writing Program at Yale University. She is the author of *Victorian Autobiography: The Tradition of Self-Interpretation* (1986), and numerous articles on Victorian poets, novelists, and prose writers.

PAUL SAWYER is an Associate Professor of English at Cornell University. He has published several articles and a book, *Ruskin's Poetic Argument.* Currently, he is working on a general study concerning the intersection of political hegemony, the female body, and the aestheticization of culture in Victorian literature.

LINDA M. SHIRES, an Associate Professor of English at Syracuse University, is the author of *British Poetry of the Second World War* (1985), coauthor of *Telling Stories: A Theoretical Analysis of Narrative Fiction* (1988), and editor of the forthcoming *Theory, History, and the Politics of Gender: Re-writing the Victorians*. Her current projects concern the transplantation and gendering of rituals and rhetoric from one geopolitical sphere to another, as well as a longer study of Tennyson.

Index

Aestheticism, 47, 53, 250

Alcott, Louisa May, 3, 13, 14, 15, 226, 229, 233, 243–245; *Little Women*, 226, 241–243

Alma-Tadema, Lawrence, 144–145; *A Priestess of Apollo*, 144–145

Anglicanism, 67, 77; and Oxford Movement, 95, 98; Victorian feminist, 8, 18, 87–104 *passim. See also* Newman, John Henry Cardinal; sisterhood, Anglican

Anglo-Catholicism. *See* Anglicanism

Arnold, Matthew, 4, 7, 19, 22, 24, 27, 28, 29, 30, 35, 44, 88, 130, 140, 174, 182, 188, 191, 208, 222, 223, 261; *Culture and Anarchy*, 7, 191

Auerbach, Nina, 12, 161, 251, 268nn37, 45, 289n10

Austen, Jane, 3, 13, 14, 15, 226, 227, 229, 230–234, 243–245; *Pride and Prejudice*, 226, 230–234, 238; *Sense and Sensibility*, 226, 230–233, 307n23

authorship, anxiety of, for female Victorian sage writers, 5, 68, 70, 79, 85. *See also* feminization; power

autobiography: in relation to sage writing, 171–173, 179, 183–186, 235, 242–243, 247, 272n5, 288n34; women's, 40–41, 44, 76, 78–81, 171–173, 183–186, 235, 242–244, 304n4

Avelung, Edward, 195, 197, 298–299n19, 301n46

Bakhtin, Mikhail M., 3, 5, 72–73, 265–266n7, 277n7, 278–279n22, 279–280n25, 280n26; dialogism, 3, 5, 73, 78, 84, 277n7, 280n26; hybridization, 78–79; verbal-ideological world, 3–4, 13. *See also* discourse; voice

Bax, Ernest Belfort, 191–200, 298n16, 299n24, 300nn28, 34. *See also* Morris, William

Beardsley, Aubrey, 16, 251–260; *The Climax*, 253–254, 255; *"J'ai baisé ta bouche, Iokanaan,"* 253, 254; *John and Salomé*, 259, 260; *The Woman in the Moon*, 256, 257

Bebel, August, 192, 195, 202